CAMBRIDGE STUDIES IN AMERICAN LITERATURE AND CULTURE

Frederick Douglass: New Literary and Historical Essays

Selected books in the series

Charles Altieri, *Painterly Abstraction in Modernist American Poetry: The Contemporaneity of Modernism*

Douglas Anderson, *A House Undivided: Domesticity and Community in American Literature*

Sacvan Bercovitch and Myra Jehlen (eds.), *Ideology and Classic American Literature*★

Ronald Bush (ed.), *T. S. Eliot: The Modernist in History*

Michael Davidson, *The San Francisco Renaissance: Poetics and Community at Mid-Century*

George Dekker, *The American Historical Romance*★

Stephen Fredman, *Poets' Prose: The Crisis in American Verse, 2nd Edition*

Susan Stanford Friedman, *Penelope's Web: Gender, Modernity, H. D.'s Fiction*

Albert Gelpi (ed.), *Wallace Stevens: The Poetics of Modernism*★

Richard Godden, *Fictions of Capital: Essays on the American Novel from James to Mailer*

Russell Goodman, *American Philosophy and the Romantic Tradition*

Richard Gray, *Writing the South: Ideas of an American Region*★

Ezra Greenspan, *Walt Whitman and the American Reader*

Alfred Habegger, *Henry James and the "Woman Business"*

David Halliburton, *The Color of the Sky: A Study of Stephen Crane*

Susan K. Harris, *19th Century American Women's Novels: Interpretive Strategies*

John Limon, *The Place of Fiction in the Time of Science: A Disciplinary History of American Writing*

Susan Manning, *The Puritan-Provincial Vision: Scottish and American Literature in the Nineteenth Century*

John McWilliams, *The American Epic: Transformation of a Genre, 1770–1860*

David Miller, *Dark Eden: The Swamp in Nineteenth-Century American Culture*

Michael Oriard, *Sporting with the Gods: The Rhetoric of Play and Game in American Literature*

Tim Redman, *Ezra Pound and Italian Fascism*

Eric Sigg, *The American T. S. Eliot: A Study of the Early Writings*

David Wyatt, *The Fall into Eden: Landscape and Imagination in California*★

For a complete listing of books available in the series, see the pages following the Index.

★ Now available in hardcover and paperback

FREDERICK DOUGLASS

NEW LITERARY AND HISTORICAL ESSAYS

Edited by

ERIC J. SUNDQUIST

University of California, Los Angeles

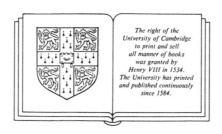

The right of the
University of Cambridge
to print and sell
all manner of books
was granted by
Henry VIII in 1534.
The University has printed
and published continuously
since 1584.

CAMBRIDGE UNIVERSITY PRESS

Cambridge

New York   Port Chester   Melbourne   Sydney

Published by the Press Syndicate of the University of Cambridge
The Pitt Building, Trumpington Street, Cambridge CB2 1RP
40 West 20th Street, New York, NY 10011, USA
10 Stamford Road, Oakleigh, Melbourne 3166, Australia

First published 1990

Printed in the United States of America

Library of Congress Cataloging-in-Publication Data
Frederick Douglass : new literary and historical essays / edited by
Eric J. Sundquist.
p.   cm. – (Cambridge studies in American literature and
culture)
Includes bibliographical references.
ISBN 0-521-38040-5
1. Douglass, Frederick, 1817?–1895 – Literary art.   I. Sundquist,
Eric J.   II. Series.
E449.D75F74   1990
973.8'092 – dc20   90–1705
CIP

British Library Cataloguing in Publication Data
Frederick Douglass : new literary and historical essays. –
(Cambridge studies in American literature and culture).
1. United States. Slavery. Abolition. Douglass, Frederick
1817–1895
I. Sundquist, Eric J.
306.362092

ISBN 0-521-38040-5 hardback

Contents

Introduction   *page* 1
ERIC J. SUNDQUIST

"Ironic Tenacity": Frederick Douglass's Seizure of the Dialectic   23
STERLING STUCKEY

From Wheatley to Douglass: The Politics of Displacement   47
HENRY LOUIS GATES, JR.

Writing Freely? Frederick Douglass and the Constraints
of Racialized Writing   66
WILSON J. MOSES

Faith, Doubt, and Apostasy: Evidence of Things Unseen
in Frederick Douglass's *Narrative*   84
DONALD B. GIBSON

Franklinian Douglass: The Afro-American as Representative
Man   99
RAFIA ZAFAR

Reading Slavery: The Anxiety of Ethnicity in Douglass's
Narrative   118
DAVID VAN LEER

The Punishment of Esther: Frederick Douglass and the
Construction of the Feminine   141
JENNY FRANCHOT

v

Race, Violence, and Manhood: The Masculine Ideal in
Frederick Douglass's "The Heroic Slave" 166
RICHARD YARBOROUGH

"We Hold These Truths to Be Self-Evident": The Rhetoric of
Frederick Douglass's Journalism 189
SHELLEY FISHER FISHKIN AND CARLA L. PETERSON

The Frederick Douglass–Gerrit Smith Friendship and Political
Abolitionism in the 1850s 205
JOHN R. MCKIVIGAN

The Shadow of Slavery: Frederick Douglass, the Savage South,
and the Next Generation 233
WAYNE MIXON

Frederick Douglass's *Life and Times*: Progressive Rhetoric and
the Problem of Constituency 253
KENNETH W. WARREN

Images of Frederick Douglass in the Afro-American Mind:
The Recent Black Freedom Struggle 271
WALDO E. MARTIN, JR.

Selected Bibliography 287
Notes on Contributors 289
Index 293

Introduction

ERIC J. SUNDQUIST

"It is an American book, for Americans, in the fullest sense of the idea," wrote the black abolitionist James McCune Smith in his preface to *My Bondage and My Freedom* (1855), the second version of Frederick Douglass's autobiography (*MB*, 23).[1] The revised version of Douglass's life story, with its forceful invocation of republican principles and the rights of revolution, is marked by the versatile rhetoric of the escaped slave turned public orator. Whereas the power of the *Narrative of the Life of Frederick Douglass, An American Slave* (1845) lay in part in its spare style and candid dramatization of the main facts of Douglass's life as a slave, *My Bondage and My Freedom* pointed ahead to the iconographic black American success story Douglass would tell of himself in the third version of his autobiography, the *Life and Times of Frederick Douglass* (1881; amended in 1892). But James McCune Smith's characterization of *My Bondage and My Freedom* as a particularly "American" book could be applied to any of the three autobiographies. Against the crushing historical weight of slavery and racism Douglass's story exemplified his individual achievement of greatness as an orator and writer, as well as his public recognition, according to the eminent nineteenth-century black historian George Washington Williams, as "the first man of his race in North America." What was perhaps most American about his life as a slave, an abolitionist, and a post–Civil War public servant and leader in the struggle for black civil rights was just that doubleness of being that he constantly fought to overcome, the "double consciousness" of "American" and "Negro" set forth in W. E. B. Du Bois's later well-known formulation in *The Souls of Black Folk* (1903): "two souls, two thoughts, two unreconciled strivings; two warring ideals in one dark body, whose dogged strength alone keeps it from being torn asunder."[2]

Compared to Du Bois or to Martin Delany, his initial coeditor on the *North Star*, the abolitionist newspaper he founded in 1847, Douglass was far less a black nationalist than a man who fervently believed that the ideals of American democracy were capable, in principle, of encompassing all races. Indeed, in the more self-congratulatory prose of the *Life and Times*, Douglass's story would appear to be the classic account of a model African-American life, one that, in the words of Rayford Logan's 1962 introduction to the volume, "has inspired Negroes and other disadvantaged Americans to believe that, despite the imperfections of American democracy, a self-made man may aspire to greatness." Like Abraham Lincoln, however, Douglass in all his work was a symbolic incarnation of freedom that remained open to conflicting interpretations. For example, Booker T. Washington's 1906 biography of Douglass praised his model democratic life and his fight for black industrial education; but claiming that Douglass accepted postwar southern white supremacy, Washington appropriated Douglass's later career to his own accommodationist vision of "construction and reconciliation." Against this, Du Bois argued in a chapter of *The Souls of Black Folk* contesting Washington's philosophy that Douglass throughout his life "bravely stood for the ideals of his early manhood, – ultimate assimilation *through* self-assertion, and on no other terms." Washington's spirt of compromise in the three crucial arenas of suffrage, civil rights, and higher education, Du Bois went on to imply, was an utter betrayal of Douglass. The argument between Washington and Du Bois over Douglass, like the more extreme arguments that found Lincoln alternatively to be a white supremacist and a martyred champion of immediate black rights, presaged later arguments over the significance of the rival careers of Washington and Du Bois themselves. Such conflicts indicate both the protean character of Douglass's life and writings – his willingness to adapt his strategies to exploit most effectively the ideological cross-currents of a given era – and his commanding presence in the history of African-American thought.[3]

The "doubleness" of Frederick Douglass's life and soul, his uneasy reconciliation of American and African-American traditions, came from several sources: his preservation of the materials and memories of black folk life within a narrative devoted to public action in predominantly white intellectual and political circles; his own notable ambivalence about his unknown but almost certainly white father and his subsequent fascination with the theme of genealogy; and his acute understanding that, whether in the South or the North, he was still a black man in nineteenth-century America and liable everywhere to discrimination and violent treatment. Douglass belonged to an age in which economic mobility and increasing confusion over the fluidity of social roles gave rise in both literature and political culture to a self-consciousness about roles and fragmented or doubled identities. Perhaps no one better exemplified this mobility and fragmentation than the escaped slave, who inevitably brought with him out of slavery a complicated social persona. Because the African-

American slave, as John Blassingame has argued, was continually subject
to daily pressures that required the adoption of subtle strategies of masquerade, the slave narrative (or the slave orator) bore evidence of that
behavior and often illustrated the complex construction of a new self in
a new world.[4] In the context of America's race crisis and the flourishing
national literature of the antebellum decades, marked as it was by the
exploration of social masquerade in the writings of Melville, Hawthorne,
Whitman, and Poe, Douglass's own doubleness can be read as a virtual
symbol of the identity crisis that tore apart the entire nation, leaving it,
in Lincoln's famous phrase, a "house divided."

Douglass's career as a speaker, editor, and autobiographer reflected
this array of pressures, and an estimate of his importance must rely not
on a single activity or narrative but on the whole range of his life and
work. Recent scholars have sifted fact from myth and provided a rich
contextual portrait of Douglass's life, but the starting point for any interpretation of Douglass must be his early autobiographies, which have
remained the central source of biographical information about his life,
particularly before the 1850s.[5] The publication of the Narrative in 1845
exposed Douglass as a fugitive slave, subject to capture and return to
the South. Having begun his career as an abolitionist speaker within two
years of his escape in 1838, Douglass had found his rise to prominence
marred by continual reminders that, as a black man, he was subject to
northern segregation laws, to mob violence, and to condescension at the
hands of his white coworkers. Appearing at a moment when antislavery
activity was strong but also factionalized over such issues as the utility
of nonviolence, women's participation in public protest, the role of the
churches, and northern prejudice against free blacks, the 125-page Narrative,
offered for fifty cents, was enormously popular, selling some 30,000
copies in the United States and Europe within five years, and soon
translated into French and German. Its gripping story, along with Douglass's commandingly original voice, immediately distinguished it from
most slave narratives that had appeared by the 1840s. A significant number
of the most popular narratives, including those of Moses Grandy, Charles
Ball, Lunsford Lane, and Moses Roper, concentrated on the traumatic
family separations and physical violence of slavery. In this respect they
resembled Theodore Weld's influential American Slavery as It Is: Testimony
of a Thousand Witnesses (1839), which depicted the degrading treatment
of southern slaves by a mass of evidence culled from 20,000 newspapers.
Douglass, as readers quickly realized, did more than reveal the sins of
the South and the suffering of black slaves. Like Harriet Jacobs in Incidents
in the Life of a Slave Girl (1860), he made the facts of his life a dramatic
representation of the great interplay of cultural and political forces that
constituted the nation's crisis over slavery. He offered a virtually mythic

embodiment of the acts of speech and self-making largely denied to slaves, and his *Narrative* summed up the purpose of testimony by former slaves, namely, to illustrate the spiritual survival of the black family and community within the cauldron of plantation life, and to explore the means by which dehumanization could be overcome and power gained over the political acts and cultural signs that lend full dignity to life.[6]

The *Narrative* is the most widely read of Douglass's writings, but there are definite limitations to it as a revelation of Douglass's identity and thought. The preference that a number of recent literary critics have shown for the 1845 *Narrative*, over *My Bondage and My Freedom* and especially the more self-indulgent *Life and Times*, indicates not just a distrust of the patriotic rhetoric, the gothic and sentimental literary conventions, and the myth of self-made success that are more characteristic of the later volumes. It also suggests a problematic historiographical choice to be made between the Douglass closest to, and thus presumably best able to articulate, the experience of slavery and the Douglass who purposely constructed for himself a linguistically more sophisticated "American" identity, with figures such as the framers of the Constitution or Benjamin Franklin as his models. In making himself an orator capable of combating both slavery in the South and racism in the North, Douglass faced an important paradox: The less like a slave he acted or sounded, the less likely audiences were to believe his spoken story. The *Narrative* was set down primarily so that Douglass might guarantee its authenticity (although it too was considered to be fraudulent by some readers), but also that he might take personal possession of it, declare it his own property, thereby capping the quest for literacy that had been so crucial to his resistance to and escape from slavery.

At the same time, however, the *Narrative* does not suggest the full significance of Douglass's possession of his own story. What Douglass's speeches of the 1850s and *My Bondage and My Freedom* report in greater detail is that his initial quarrel with northern white abolitionists came precisely over the question of whether or not he was qualified to interpret the meaning of his own life. To be taken as another speaker's "text" was Douglass's primary role in his early career: "I was generally introduced as a '*chattel*' – a '*thing*' – a piece of southern '*property*' – the chairman assuring the audience that *it* could speak." Or "I was a 'graduate from the peculiar institution . . . *with my diploma on my back!*' " The condescending instructions Douglass received from William Lloyd Garrison and other abolitionists required that he stick to the "facts" and leave the "philosophy" to others. As Douglass noted, however, he was by then "reading and thinking," and it "did not entirely satisfy me to *narrate* wrongs; I felt like denouncing them" (*MB*, 220).

The differences between the equally effective life stories recorded in the *Narrative* and *My Bondage and My Freedom* must be judged in this context, just as the autobiographies themselves, built in part from the astonishingly rich record of Douglass's speeches, essays, and editorials, must be read as carefully drawn portraits of himself by Douglass the public figure. Douglass's blending of his campaign for black freedom and black rights with a telling of his own representative story constitutes the key to his own rise to self-possession and historical greatness. When he transfigured the text of his scarred slave's body into the *Narrative*, Douglass changed "property in man" into property in himself, as it were, and created a public "American" self that was the first step in a lifelong series of reinterpretations of his life.

Born in 1818 on a Tuckahoe, Maryland, plantation to the slave Harriet Bailey and an unidentified white father, Frederick Augustus Washington Bailey (the name given him by his mother) had an experience of slavery that was in many ways atypical. For one thing, the size of the plantation on which he lived in childhood was unique and gave him a quite diverse picture of slaveholding in the antebellum years. Owned by Colonel Edward Lloyd V, Maryland's three-time governor and two-time senator, the plantation comprised numerous farms and used the labor of more than 500 slaves on Lloyd's home plantation and his other holdings. Although his narratives could not record the facts that were unavailable to him, Douglass would have been able to trace his African-American roots on Maryland's eastern shore back five generations, to at least 1701. His grandmother, Betsey Bailey, was a strong, self-reliant woman who, although a slave, lived a comparatively independent life and was considered a community leader; and his mother, Harriet Bailey, was one of twelve children born to Betsey and Isaac Bailey (Douglass's apparent grandfather, a slave manumitted in the late eighteenth century), most of whom, like her, were raised to be field hands on Lloyd's farms. Harriet bore six children besides Frederick, but little else is known of her apart from the fragmentary memories recorded in Douglass's autobiographies, the most important, perhaps, being the unusual fact that she had learned to read.

Douglass's purported father, his master Aaron Anthony, employed by Colonel Lloyd, was known to be a harsh and capricious man who raised himself from poverty to middling success as the owner of Holme Hill Farm before declining into ill health and mental instability. He died in 1826, within a year of Harriet Bailey; the two of them were buried in unmarked graves near one another on Anthony's land. In addition to the physical cruelties Douglass himself recorded, such as the whipping of his Aunt Esther (Hester) when she preferred the affections of a black man over those of Anthony, he once sold the two children of Douglass's Aunt Jenny and Uncle Noah, which prompted them to escape, events Douglass would later set down only in his *Life and Times*, when it was safer to do so. In his early writings Douglass offered contradictory opinions about whether or not Anthony actually was his father, and in the *Life and Times*, in fact, Anthony is not mentioned at all as his possible father. No surviving records are conclusive. As Douglass's master, Anthony appears to have treated him fairly well and to have been indirectly responsible (perhaps because he *was* Douglass's father) for setting Douglass on the path to escape and success. The historical evidence suggests that Douglas was not so physically deprived in childhood as his narratives would indicate; and when his gifted intelligence was recognized, Douglass was afforded opportunities not given other slaves, including being sent at age eight to the Baltimore home of Hugh Auld, where he acquired literacy and had his first glimpse of the conjoined worlds of intellectual achievement and freedom.

Douglass's narratives mention the kindness of his first mistress, Lucretia Auld, Anthony's daughter (and thus possibly Douglass's half-sister), and of Sophia Auld, her Baltimore sister-in-law. It did not, however, serve his rhetorical purposes to reveal that he ever received special treatment. Later in his career he would take note of such facts; but the life as he records it partakes rather of the strategy he admitted in a well-known public letter to his one-time owner, Thomas Auld (Lucretia's husband), published in Garrison's antislavery newspaper the *Liberator* in 1848 and later appended to *My Bondage and My Freedom*. There his charges of brutality against Thomas Auld were deliberately inaccurate, an act for which he later apologized in an 1859 letter. But he revealed his hand in saying that, although "I entertain no malice towards you personally," "I intend to make use of you as a weapon with which to assail the system of slavery – as a means of concentrating public attention on the system, and deepening their horror of trafficking in the souls and bodies of men" (*MB*, 270–1). Thomas Auld became the symbol of the peculiar institution, just as Frederick Douglass, author and orator, was its refutation.

The letter "To My Old Master" can in some respects stand as an emblem of Douglass's intention to use both his life and those who figured in it as "weapons" in his fight for freedom and equality. There is no question that the narratives in the main offer accurate and reliable portraits of his experience, even of the blurred, partial memories of his childhood. Nonetheless, the rhetorical shaping of his experience that Douglass perfected as an abolitionist speaker is everywhere evident in the written texts, and the interest of the stories lies equally in the dramatic persona that he constructs and revises over the course of his career. This means, in particular, that Douglass chooses deliberately the elements of his life that he will illuminate and does so in a carefully crafted manner. For example, his account of his relations with his mother and grandmother – those elements of his life presumably closest to the authenticity of the African-American slave experience – are augmented in the changes from the *Narrative* to *My Bondage and My Freedom*, not just in order to tell us more about Douglass's childhood but also to accentuate Douglass's overarching examination of slaveholding paternalism and its consequent corruption of the family. The account of Douglass's life with his grandmother, her symbolic carrying of him into slavery at Aaron Anthony's farm at age six, and the scant recollections he has of his mother's visits are all fleshed out and given new emphasis in *My Bondage and My Freedom* in order to underline Douglass's argument that a central purpose of slavery is to obliterate "from the mind and heart of the slave, all just ideas of the sacredness of *the family*, as an institution" (*MB*, 29).

Like the symbolic figure of the father, the sacred image of the family, claimed by North and South alike in the debates over slavery, had become part of an ideological conflict that Douglass the public figure could, by 1855, more accurately judge and use to advantage as fact, memory, and rhetorical strategy merged into the multidimensional phenomenon that Douglass made his life story. Accordingly, the extended description of his mother's death in *My Bondage and My Freedom*, about which he had a slight recollection, must be seen to reflect Douglass's reading of *Uncle Tom's Cabin*,[1] whose very popular sentimental melodrama now provided an ironic counterpoint to his own scant memories: "Scenes of sacred tenderness, around the deathbed, never forgotten, and which often arrest the vicious and confirm the virtuous during life, must be looked for among the free, though they may sometimes occur among the slaves." Having "no striking words of hers treasured up," Douglass has to "learn the value of my mother long after her death, and by witnessing the devotion of other mothers to their children." Because he later discovers that his mother could read, Douglass attributes his "love of letters" to her "native genius," and this mythic ascription further validates the fact that Douglass's maternity, especially as it is portrayed in *My Bondage and My Freedom*, participates as much in the literary construction of an ideological family as does the portrait he draws of his anonymous father. The expanded view of Douglass's relation to his family in the second autobiography can thus be seen to have a double purpose that is relevant to other revisions as well. Whereas the *Narrative* does capture Douglass's experience of slavery more directly, the latter narrative, in fact, provides more detail about slave life – for instance, in Douglass's amplified discussion of slave songs or the significance of holidays on the plantation – while at the same time transfiguring such details into part of his own counterattack against slavery.

It may be for this reason that Douglass, in his autobiographical writings, does not do for his own wife and children what he does symbolically for his mother's and grandmother's families. One of the disappointments of the autobiographies is their virtual deletion of his relation with his first wife, Anna Murray. The daughter of Bambarra and Mary Murray, Anna was a free black woman who worked as a housekeeper when Douglass met her at a meeting of the East Baltimore Mental Improvement Society after he had been returned to the city a second time, at age eighteen, to live with the Aulds while laboring in a shipyard. Immediately after his escape from slavery in 1838, Anna followed him north to become his wife and eventually the mother of his five children. Even so, his children and his wife (in her case perhaps because she was illiterate and stood outside the antislavery circles of Douglass's fame) are barely mentioned in his autobiographies. The relatively greater importance accorded white women in Douglass's story – beginning with Lucretia and Sophia Auld, but including the British abolitionist Julia Griffiths (reputed by some, especially Douglass's detractors, to have become his lover for a time) and his second wife, Helen Pitts, a white former secretary whom he married in 1884, two years after the death of Anna – painfully obscures the important personal role played by Anna. The subordination of his own wife and children, and the relatively minor role played by women, especially black women, in Douglass's autobiographies, cannot be overlooked. But such facts are evidence as well that Douglass's narratives corresponded to the model of most nineteenth-century autobiographies and were public political acts with a single goal foremost in view – the establishment of racial equality by the swiftest means.

Douglass's tracing of the source of his own literacy to his mother establishes a motive in his self-creation that is not coincidental in his autobiographical portrait, for his true "beginning in the world" (*MB*, 43) came at the moment he discovered the means to gain mastery of himself and seize control of his most powerful weapon – language. The famous episodes that deal with his learning to read and write in Baltimore are tied forthrightly to the issue of democracy. Antiliteracy slave laws, made more restrictive in the wake of Nat Turner's 1831 uprising in Southampton, Virginia, were often justified philosophically on the grounds that slaves, because they were not fit for the exercise of democratic rights, would misunderstand the power given them by literacy or be misled by "fanatical" abolitionist propaganda. In his proslavery tract *Liberty and Slavery: Or, Slavery in the Light of Moral and Political Philosophy* (1860), for example, the Virginian Albert Taylor Bledsoe argued that laws directed against slave learning and abolitionist writings were based on the fact that African Americans could "neither comprehend the nature, nor enjoy the blessings, of the freedom which is officially thrust upon them. [For] if the Negro race should be moved by their appeals, it would only be to rend and tear in pieces the fair fabric of American liberty . . . by far the most beautiful ever yet conceived or constructed by the genius of man."[8] When he ties his lessons in reading and writing to an initial attempt to learn the meaning of the talismanic word *abolition*, which he has heard in connection with acts of slave resistance (*Narrative*, 56), Douglass thus subverts a central tenet of the ideology of slavery and forecasts his own career, which he knew from his experience of slavery would not have the utmost power as an act of resistance until it was allowed to take written form. In doing so, Douglass placed himself within an already developed tradition of black writing that was inherently an act of political assertion, joining those before him who had challenged Europe's "fundamental sign of domination, the commodity of writing, the text and technology of reason."[9]

Although his autobiographies are of greater literary interest, Douglass's journalism and his oratory provide the fullest record of his achievements as an abolitionist and black political leader. In his speeches Douglass did not hesitate to attack the North, and when the publication of his *Narrative* forced him to flee temporarily to England, he had a further opportunity to study European reform movements and to judge objectively the failure of the United States to realize its democratic ideals. In a letter to Garrison published in the *Liberator* in 1846 and later reprinted in *My Bondage and My Freedom*, Douglass contrasted his unbiased treatment in England with his remembrance of being told repeatedly on his lecture tours in northern America, "*We don't allow niggers in here!*" The people of England and Ireland, Douglass argued, "know nothing of the republican negro hate prevalent in our glorious land" (*MB*, 226–7). Throughout his tour, during which he was lionized by the British press, Douglass no doubt exaggerated the differences between Europe and the United States to suit his polemical purposes. But his warm reception on so many occasions spurred his desire to be a leader, not just a follower, in the antislavery movement. Thus, when British sympathizers arranged to purchase his freedom from the Auld family (an event that caused great controversy among American abolitionists, who thought that such a move amounted to an admission of property rights in humans),[10] Douglass returned to the United States determined to publish his own newspaper.

Although his autobiographies had a significant readership throughout his lifetime, Douglass's newspaper career was arguably more important in shaping and disseminating his views. "But for the responsibility of conducting a public journal, and the necessity of meeting opposite views from abolitionists in this state," Douglass wrote of his break with Garrison, "I should in all probability have remained as firm in my disunion views as any other disciple of William Lloyd Garrison" (*MB*, 243). Douglass's treatment of the break – which dated to his founding of the *North Star*, perhaps even to the writing of the *Narrative*, but which increased to the point of no return with Douglass's adherence to the Liberty Party, his endorsement of the Constitution, and his critique of the limits of Christian radicalism – is very brief and restrained. It is absurdly out of proportion to Garrison's own attacks on Douglass, which at their peak led him to print Douglass's articles in the "Refuge of Oppression" column of the *Liberator*, a space normally devoted to proslavery opinion. Yet Douglass's linking of the break to the founding of the *North Star* and his writing and publishing career substantiates the editorial opinion of a contemporary black journal, *The Rising Sun*: "Frederick Douglass' ability as an editor and publisher has done more for the freedom and elevation of his race than all his platform appearances" (Foner, I, 93). By itself, the lecture platform, one might guess, was too much like the auction block; the newspaper, like the autobiography or his one short story, "The Heroic Slave," offered Douglass the opportunity to "edit" and create his public self as a newly revised and more vitally marketed "thing" – a man with property in himself.

Launched in Rochester in 1847 over the objections of Garrison and others, the *North Star* (its name was later changed to *Frederick Douglass' Paper*) quickly became the most important black abolitionist newspaper in the country. Although it exacerbated his differences with Garrison, Douglass's editorial role gained him a wider audience (even though most of it, Douglass sometimes lamented, was white) and crystallized his personal campaign to make his literacy the most potent weapon in the battle against slavery. The *North Star*, whose motto was "Right is of no sex – Truth is of no color," made Douglass more independent of white abolitionists and gave him the opportunity to speak out on a variety of issues, further defining his campaign as one for human rights, not just African-American rights. Douglass, in fact, was a constant supporter of women's rights and other reform causes. He attended the Seneca Falls convention in 1848 as an advocate of women's suffrage and frequently spoke in favor of women's political rights both within and beyond the antislavery movement. By the same token, however, he did not hesitate, both before the Civil War and more openly after it, during the debate over the Fifteenth Amendment, to argue that suffrage for blackmen was more important than – and separable from – suffrage for white (and black) women.[11] Here as elsewhere, his willingness to break ranks was a function not just of his strong personality but of the independence fostered by his career.

Douglass's rapidly evolving public role in the years after his return from England changed his own notion of himself as it had first been presented in the 1845 *Narrative*. In the retrospective view of the *Life and*

Times, Douglass's longer account of his newspaper career demonstrates that he conceived of it as a signal instance of American self-reliance. "I have come to think," he writes in 1881, "that, under the circumstances, it was the best school possible for me," making it "necessary for me to lean upon myself, and not upon the heads of our antislavery church. . . . There is nothing like the lash and sting of necessity to make a man work, and my paper furnished the motive power" (*LT,* 264). This striking conversion of slavery's whip into the self-wielded work ethic of American success is emblematic of Douglass's postwar role as a black leader, and it underlines the function of the weekly newspaper in clarifying the "doubleness" that his whole career as a writer entailed. "Shut up in the prison-house of bondage," said Douglass in his highly influential 1848 "Address to the Colored People of the United States" at the National Negro Convention in Cleveland, "we are blotted from the page of human existence, and placed beyond the limits of human regard" (Foner, I, 332). Not simply the voice, but also the pen, was the key to liberty, no less for black Americans than it had been for the pamphleteers of the Revolutionary period.

When Douglass issued *My Bondage and My Freedom* in 1855, the persona that he adopted was shaped by the intervening activities and therefore recast his interpretation of his discovery of freedom. In particular, Douglass's treatment of literacy in *My Bondage and My Freedom* is embedded in his arguments about the slave's right of revolution; and much of the prose becomes oratorial, as in Douglass's reflection on the impact of his reading of the speeches in the *Columbian Orator*: "Knowledge had come; light had penetrated the moral dungeon where I dwelt; and, behold! there lay the bloody whip, for my back, and here was the iron chain; and my good, *kind master,* he was the author of my situation" (*MB,* 101). It is exactly such language that some modern readers have found regrettable in *My Bondage and My Freedom.* Yet the text reminds us often that the language of revolutionary liberation and the language of sentiment are virtually synonymous, not just in the best antislavery writing but in the whole era's grappling with the problem of bondage.[12] The literature of American slavery transplants the language of oppression and liberation from the romantic and gothic traditions, where it had been a particular spur to Britain's successful antislavery movement, into a new national setting where it is bound together with the language of American Revolutionary sentiment. In this and many other passages devoted to his acquisition of the tools of language, Douglass demonstrates that literacy is linked to the power to enslave and, alternatively, to the power to create one's own subjectivity and redeem one's community.

A further index of Douglass's changed conception of himself as a black leader during the early 1850s, a time of growing sectional tension over the passage of the Compromise of 1850, may be found in his only work of fiction. "The Heroic Slave," a short story appearing in an 1853 gift book entitled *Autographs for Freedom* (a collection of antislavery statements edited by Julia Griffiths to raise money for the financially troubled *North Star*), also has resonant autobiographical overtones. As a fictive version of the 1841 slave revolt aboard the *Creole*, led by Madison Washington, "The Heroic Slave" may be read as Douglass's own "autograph for freedom," the signature of his declaration of liberty through escalating acts of literacy and rebellion. Madison Washington appeared in Douglass's speeches as early as the 1847 lectures in Britain, and he was featured in a resounding 1849 address at a New York Anti-Colonization meeting as a model of black achievement. It was, Douglass announced in his tirade against the official posture of the government (which sought the return of the escaped rebels when they landed in the Bahamas), "a black man, with woolly head, high cheek bones, protruding lip, disended nostril, and retreating forehead, [who] had mastery of that ship" (Foner, V, 117). In "The Heroic Slave," Douglass cannily exploits the domestic cult of George Washington but subverts its inherent conservatism by making Madison Washington, the black Virginian rebel, an archetypal slave patriot, able to articulate his ideal of liberty: "We have done that which you applaud your fathers for doing, and if we are murderers, so were they" (Foner, V, 503). As Robert Stepto has argued, the loosely parallel facts of Washington's and Douglass's lives support the implication that "The Heroic Slave" belongs to the series of "acts of literacy" through which Douglass defined his increasing independence and public stature at the same time that he explored a narrative that was itself rich in the "doubleness" of the African-American experience.[13]

In defining for himself a role of public leadership analogous to that of Madison Washington, Douglass signifies the intricate symbolism of "fathers" that could be said to preoccupy him in much of his autobiographical work. In a typically American gesture, he makes himself his own father – a mask or fictive self composed at once of the absent father who so absorbs his attention in the opening chapters of *My Bondage and My Freedom*, the black rebel slave who leads others to freedom *and* converts a white audience to antislavery, and the founding fathers whose rhetoric of democratic liberty punctuates Douglass's writing after 1848 and begins fully to flower in the break with Garrison. The doctrine of self-reliance that would become conspicuous in Douglass's later speeches and the *Life and Times* is at the center of his creative process insofar as it partakes of the impulse to liberate the ego from inherited constraints, to seize and aggrandize the power of domineering ancestors or their surrogates in order to fashion one's own ancestry.

The act of self-fathering, that is to say, had become an important weapon in Douglass's arsenal by the 1850s, a weapon of charged doubleness empowered by the fact that Douglass's own paternity was lost, absorbed into the causal reproduction of property in humans. The contradictory laws of the southern slaveholding fathers and the northern democratic fathers – agonizingly fused in the Fugitive Slave Law – required of Douglass a complex psychological response, one that is evident in his subtle treatment of the issues of paternity and slaveholding paternalism. Increasingly throughout the 1850s and beyond, Douglass depicted slaveholders to be just as much the victims of slavery as their slaves. Indeed, when he met with the eighty-year-old Thomas Auld in 1877, they both shed tears, and Douglass remarked, "I did not run away from *you*, but from *slavery*" (*LT*, 443). Even in an 1859 letter to Hugh Auld, Douglass had written, "I love you, but hate slavery" – this to the man whose suppression of his wife's reading instruction of the young slave had apparently led her to become even more of a tyrant than he.[14] Douglass's divergence from the standard antislavery strategy of constant attack upon the slaveholders themselves, along with his increased concentration on the *ideology* of brutality rather than on specific instances of abuse, suggests Douglass's comprehension of the all-encompassing destructive character of such power.

The symbol of that power, the whip, could be coveted by whites and blacks alike, Douglass asserted. "everybody, in the South, wants the privilege of whipping somebody else" (*MB*, 50). One need not consent to the much debated thesis that, in its brutal dehumanization of slaves and inducement in them of an imitative pattern of behavioral bondage, the plantation resembled the concentration camp, the prison, or other total institutions, in order to be struck by this aspect of Douglass's revision of his life portrait in *My Bondage and My Freedom*, especially his new account of Lloyd's immense plantation.[15] He not only gives a fuller picture of slave life, but the greater detail and the gothic emphasis on the plantation's self-sufficient, dark seclusion, maintained by diverse labor and transbay trade on Lloyd's own vessels, create of this deceptively abundant, "Eden-like" (*MB*, 47) garden world a veritable heart of darkness. Both the size of Lloyd's estate and his prominent public roles allow Douglass to expand his own unusual experience into a national archetype of the slave institution. In this era of reform movements and utopian communal projects, the plantation posed as a pastoral asylum in which state control and paternal coercion alike imprisoned slaves in a corrupt "family" – one they might belong to by blood but not by law – and fused the theory of property in humans with the sexuality of power. The apotheosis of the total institution of slavery lay for Douglass in this "double relation of master and father" (*N*, 49), as he called it in the *Narrative* before making it the defining figure of *My Bondage and My Freedom*.

When Douglass, like David Walker before him or William Wells Brown in his own day, called for an uprising of black slaves on the ground that the American Revolution authorized it, he entered the era's great debate over the meaning of the legacy of the Founding Fathers and its distinct but converging paternal ideologies. The passage on the ethics of stealing is revised in his second autobiography by the assertion that if the slave steals, "he takes his own; if he kills his master, he imitates only the heroes of the revolution" (*MB*, 119). In the most remarkable event of Douglass's life story, the fight with the slavebreaker Covey, the tone of the expanded exclamation of freedom underlines its appeal to international democratic ideals and highlights its alternative to the then widely popular capitulation of Uncle Tom to the murderous whip of Simon Legree.[16] Most strikingly, Douglass accuses the slaveholder of violating "the just and inalienable rights of man" and thereby "silently whetting the knife of vengeance for his own throat. He never lisps a syllable in commendation of the fathers of this republic, nor denounces any attempted oppression of himself, without inviting the knife to his own throat, and asserting the rights of rebellion for his own slaves" (*MB*, 165). For Douglass, the Revolutionary fathers, like Thomas Auld, had become weapons in the battle against slavery. Whereas proslavery ideologues such as Thomas Dew and James Henry Hammond warned that abolitionist propaganda would tear down the slave "family" and its white paternal structure of protection, making slaves "*parricides* instead of *patriots*," Douglass said it could make them both.[17]

During the 1850s Douglass's oratory, which was said by some to rival that of Daniel Webster or Abraham Lincoln, focused on these themes. In one of his greatest addresses, the July 5, 1852, address on the significance of the Fourth of July to blacks (also appended in abbreviated form to *My Bondage and My Freedom*), Douglass placed himself *outside* the American dream but *within* the circle of the post-Revolutionary generation's principal rhetoric: "You have no right to enjoy a child's share in the labor of your fathers, unless your children are to be blessed by your labors. . . . Washington could not die until he had broken the chains of his slaves. Yet his monument is built up by the price of human blood, and the traders in the bodies and souls of men shout – " 'We have Washington [as] *our father*' " (Foner, II, 188). The entrapments of perpetual union and perpetual youth inflicted upon the post-Revolutionary generation a paralysis on the issue of slavery that was not broken until Lincoln, a figure equal to the Founding Fathers' heroic stature, embraced and overcame them at the same time, saving the Union *and* abolishing slavery.[18] Lincoln's speeches appropriated the Founding Fathers' power in order to return it to the true course of democratic liberty. When Douglass made his Fourth of July address, however, Lincoln was still following the moderate proslavery course that would rule American politics until the cataclysm of war finally forced him to act against the peculiar institution. Likewise, although

Lincoln rejected the infamous Supreme Court decision in the case of Dred Scott (which denied that the Constitution gave blacks any rights as citizens of the United States) as an unwarranted extension of the powers of slavery beyond its authorized territory, Douglass found that the decision involved something more fundamental: "It is an open rebellion against God's government. It is an attempt to undo what God has done, to blot out the broad distinction instituted by the *Allwise* between men and things, and to change the image and superscription of the everliving God into a speechless piece of merchandise" (Foner, II, 411). In the decade preceding the Civil War, Douglass was the truer "son," the truer inheritor of the flawed yet redeemable ideals of the Revolutionary generation.

Even though Douglass more openly endorsed violent resistance to slavery by the 1850s, he wisely refused an opportunity to join John Brown's ill-fated attack on Harper's Ferry in 1859. Fearful of arrest for his apparent association with Brown's conspiracy, however, Douglass fled to Canada and then to England during the early months of 1860. By the time he returned, the ultimate conflict over sectionalism was upon the nation. During the Civil War, Douglass worked to recruit black Union troops (two of his own sons served with the Fifty-Fourth Massachusetts Regiment); continued his work as an editor until 1863, when his paper, by then a monthly, was disbanded; lectured widely, including his first visit to the Maryland scenes of his childhood since his escape from slavery; and consulted on several occasions with Lincoln about black troops, emancipation, and civil rights for freed African Americans.[19] Although he had come to be an active supporter of the new Republican Party by 1860 (first switching, for pragmatic reasons, from the abolitionist Liberty Party to the Free Soil Party), Douglass, like other black and white abolitionists, was disappointed by Lincoln's hesitancy about immediate emancipation, his apparent endorsement of colonization, and his reluctance to act more quickly on issues of interest to black Americans. What Douglass recognized was that the cause of the Union and the cause of black freedom remained far from synonymous. In the wake of the 1859 rejection by New York voters of a state amendment granting blacks nondiscriminatory voting rights even as they cast ballots in favor of Lincoln's presidency, Douglass wrote: "We were overshadowed and smothered by the presidential struggle. . . . The black baby of Negro Suffrage was thought too ugly to exhibit on so grand an occasion. The Negro was stowed away like some people put out of sight their deformed children when company comes" (Foner, II, 532).

Throughout the nineteenth and early twentieth centuries, Douglass and other black leaders remained ironically in Lincoln's shadow. Douglass's own ambivalence about Lincoln and what he represented can be judged best by the terms he employed to celebrate Lincoln on the public occasion of the dedication in Washington, D.C., of the Freedman's Memorial Monument to Lincoln in 1876. Douglass no doubt identified with Lincoln the self-made man who studied his "English Grammar by the uncertain flare and glare of the light made by a pine-knot," the "son of toil himself [who] was linked in brotherly sympathy with the sons of toil in every part of the Republic." But he stood apart from Lincoln just the same: "It must be admitted, truth compels me to admit, even here in the presence of the monument we have erected to his memory, [that] Abraham Lincoln was not, in the fullest sense of the word, either our man or our model. In his interests, in his associations, in his habits of thought, and in his prejudices, he was a white man." "You are the children of Abraham Lincoln," said Douglass, returning to the divisive rhetoric he had employed in such powerful forms as the Fourth of July address. "We are at best only his step-children; children by adoption, children by forces of cir-cumstance and necessity" (Foner, IV, 312–17). Despite this subversive undercurrent to a speech full of praise, Douglass's oration, one of the most famous and personally memorable of his career, was not without consequences. The next year, taking a minor place in the post-Lincoln generation, Douglass was appointed by President Rutherford B. Hayes as United States Marshal for the District of Columbia; James Garfield would make him Recorder of Deeds; and Benjamin Harrison Minister to Haiti – not the appointments he would have valued most, but still significant achievements of recognition.

Douglass later confessed that he did not like Thomas Ball's design for the monument, which may itself have inspired his metaphor of the stepchild. The statue, in Benjamin Quarles's words, "revealed Lincoln in a standing position, holding in his right hand the Emancipation Proclamation, while his left hand was poised above a slave whom he gazed upon. The slave was represented in a rising position with one knee still on the ground. The shackles on his wrists were broken. At the base of the monument the word 'EMANCIPATION' was carved."[20] It is especially significant, then, that Douglass appended his speech to his third autobiography, the *Life and Times*, for in comparison to the appendixes to his earlier narratives it reveals an interesting pattern. In his early oratorical mode, the famous appendix to the *Narrative* attacks the relation of American churches and American slavery with vicious irony; the appendixes of *My Bondage and My Freedom* consist of extracts from Douglass's public letter to Thomas Auld, the Fourth of July Address, and other documents whose message and tone belong to the phase of Revolutionary fervor that informs his thought from 1848 through the Civil War; and the Lincoln Monument speech shows Douglass at his most formal and public, ambiguously embracing American's martyred hero while struggling with him at the same time, just as Lincoln himself had embraced and overthrown the Founding Fathers. Lincoln, one might say, became for Douglass the last "father" – including his own anonymous father, the paternalistic abolitionists, and the mythic figures of the Founding Fathers – with whom he would have to struggle in the arena of double consciousness that continued to define and constrain him.

Not surprisingly, his political appointments frequently made Douglass more guarded in his public statements than he had been before the Civil War. While serving as Recorder of Deeds in 1883, for example, Douglass delivered an address that carefully responded to the Supreme Court's landmark reversal of the Civil Rights Act of 1875 (an address also reprinted in the *Life and Times*). On the one hand, Douglass condemned the Court's "moral weakness" and longed for a Court "which shall be as true to the claims of humanity as the Supreme Court formerly was to the demands of slavery"; but on the other, he defied the press or any man "to point out one sentence or one syllable of any speech of mine in denunciation of that Court" (*Life and Times*, 541–53). The spirit of "self-reliance, self-respect, industry, perseverance, and economy" that Douglass urged on his audience at the end of the *Life and Times* (*LT*, 480), a spirit that dominates the volume and its later revision as thoroughly as the rhetoric of the Revolution dominates *My Bondage and My Freedom*, has led commentators to dub him a "black Franklin" or a "black Horatio Alger."[21] Because Douglass's vision was decidedly integrationist, Booker T. Washington could easily, if somewhat disingenuously, consider himself Douglass's heir. In the year of Douglass's death, 1895, Washington delivered his famous Atlanta Exposition address (which became a watchword, in the view of many, for capitulation to white supremacy), a coincidence to which he called special attention in his own autobiography, *Up From Slavery* (1901). It would be foolish, however, to accept the charge later leveled by the black Marxist Eugene Gordon that Douglass and Washington alike were beguiled by "the miasma of opportunism" and that "Douglass, turned petty Republican politician, vegetated like a contented cabbage on the outskirts of Washington, D.C., while millions of blacks all around him wallowed in ignorance and neglect."[22] Such an indictment demeans both men and ignores the significant work of Douglass's late career. Like virtually all black intellectuals and writers of the late nineteenth century, Douglass was strongly governed by middle-class conceptions of political progress and cultural life borrowed from the Euro-American world, and he therefore struck a fine balance between protest and assimilationist values. He was critical of the ideology of race pride or black separatism (which he feared would foster segregation), but he never lost the capacity to define freedom in demanding terms and to promote recognition of a dignified, separate African–American cultural tradition.[23]

Although the 1892 *Life and Times* concluded by declaring that the consulship in Haiti, and Douglass's subsequent appointment to represent Haiti at the World's Columbian Exposition of 1893 in Chicago, were "the crowning honors to my long career and a fitting and happy close to my whole public life" (*LT*, 620), the true lesson of Douglass's appearance at the Exposition must be found elsewhere. Except for exhibits devoted to African (not African–American) life, blacks were initially excluded from any official role in the Exposition. As Douglass wrote in his introduction to a pamphlet by black Americans protesting this cultural ignorance and injustice, "when it is asked why we are excluded from the World's Columbian Exposition, the answer is Slavery" (Foner, IV, 473). Whereas Lincoln himself and his generation overcame the burden of the Founding Fathers and the political problem of slavery, Douglass and his generation continued to face the legacy of enslavement that emancipation had not destroyed. Even here, however, Douglass's posture displayed a characteristic mixture of idealism and pragmatism. When Douglass was finally approached to help organize a "Negro Day" at the fair, some black leaders resented the belated and feeble gesture, but Douglass accepted the offer. As the black activist Ida B. Wells–Barnett would write, Douglass

> persevered with his plans without any aid whatever from us hotheads and produced a program which was reported from one end of the country to the other. The American nation had given him his opportunity for scoring its unfairness toward Negro citizens and he did not fail to take advantage of it in the most fitting way. . . . I was so swelled with pride over his masterly presentation of our case that I went straight out to the fair and begged his pardon for presuming in my youth and inexperience to criticize him for an effort which had done more to bring our cause to the attention of the American people than anything else which had happened during the fair.[24]

By the end of Douglass's career, when the mantle of leadership had passed to Washington, Du Bois, Wells–Barnett, and others, black literature and art were on the verge of the "New Negro Renaissance," a thirty-year period of unprecedented creative achievement that took place in spite of the decline in the quality of freedom afforded African Americans during the increased segregation and racial violence of those same years.[25] By the turn of the century, the voices of other black leaders had replaced that of Douglass, but none failed to pay tribute to the man whose life and career, no less than his vision itself, had embraced the history of his race from slavery through freedom.

The present volume comprises original essays that cover the range of Douglass's achievements as an orator and politician, as an editor, and as a writer of journalism, fiction, and autobiography. Our aim has been to demonstrate the complexity of Frederick Douglass as a man, as well as to study in its historical context his long record of leadership in the struggle for black rights that would last far beyond his own life. This collection appears nearly a century after Douglass's death and more than thirty years after the advent of the modern civil rights era. Few will dispute the fact that Douglass is only today receiving the wide attention from literary scholars and historians that he has long deserved. Nor will many dispute the continuing relevance of Kelly Miller's remarks about the significance of Douglass's life for all Americans in the early years of the twentieth century. Observing that Douglass (unlike Washington) "built no institutions and laid no material foundations . . . no showy tabernacles of clay," Miller argued that "the greatest things of this world are not made with hands, but reside in truth and righteousness and love." The true lesson of Douglass's life lay in his love of liberty, his courage, and what Miller rightly judged to be the transcendent dimension of his life: "Douglass was the moral leader and spiritual prophet of his race. Unless all signs of the times are misleading, the time approaches, and is even now at hand, which demands a moral renaissance."[26]

NOTES

Parts of this introduction originally appeared in Eric J. Sundquist, "Frederick Douglass: Literacy and Paternalism," *Raritan: A Quarterly Review*, Vol. VI, No. 2 (Fall 1986).

1 References to Douglass's works, cited parenthetically, employ the following editions: *Narrative of the Life of Frederick Douglass, An American Slave*, ed. Houston A. Baker, Jr. (New York: Penguin, 1982); *My Bondage and My Freedom*, ed. William L. Andrews (Urbana: University of Illinois Press, 1987); *Life and Times of Frederick Douglass*, ed. Rayford W. Logan (New York: Collier, 1962); *Life and Writings of Frederick Douglass*, 5 vols., ed. Philip S. Foner (New York: International Publishers, 1950–75).

2 George Washington Williams, *History of the Negro Race in America, From 1619 to 1880*, 2 vols. in 1 (1883; rpt. New York: Arno Press, 1968), II, 438; W. E. B. DuBois, *The Souls of Black Folk* (1903; rpt. New York: Signet, 1969), p. 45.

3 Rayford Logan, "Introduction," *Life and Times*, p. 15; Booker T. Washington, *Frederick Douglass* (Philadelphia: George W. Jacobs, 1906), p. 349; DuBois, *The Souls of Black Folk*, p. 86. As Harold Cruise argues in *The Crisis of the Negro Intellectual* (1967; rpt. New York: Quill, 1984), "it was Du Bois who

upheld Douglass and carried his abolitionist-protest-civil rights trend into the twentieth century" (p. 558).

4   Blassingame, *The Slave Community: Plantation Life in the Antebellum South* (1972; rev. New York: Oxford University Press, 1979), pp. 223–322. See also Bertram Wyatt-Brown, "The Mask of Obedience: Male Slave Psychology in the Old South," *American Historical Review* 93 (December 1988), 1228–52.

5   The standard modern biography, William F. McFeely's *Frederick Douglass* (New York: W. W. Norton, 1990), appeared too recently to be consulted by the editor or the contributors to this volume. Biographical information that follows is taken from the following sources: Dickson J. Preston, *Young Frederick Douglass: The Maryland Years* (Baltimore: Johns Hopkins University Press, 1980); Foner, *Life and Writings*; Waldo E. Martin, Jr., *The Mind of Frederick Douglass* (Chapel Hill: University of North Carolina Press, 1984); Nathan Irvin Huggins, *Slave and Citizen: The Life of Frederick Douglass* (Boston: Little, Brown, 1980); and Benjamin Quarles, *Frederick Douglass* (1948; rpt. New York: Atheneum, 1968). The most important psychological interpretation of Douglass's presentation of his biographical self is Peter F. Walker, *Moral Choices: Memory, Desire, and Imagination in Nineteenth-Century American Abolition* (Baton Rouge: Louisiana State University Press, 1978), pp. 209–61. See also Henry Louis Gates, Jr., *Figures in Black: Words, Signs, and the "Racial" Self* (New York: Oxford University Press, 1987), pp. 98–124; Houston A. Baker, Jr., *Blues, Ideology, and Afro-American Literature: A Vernacular Theory* (Chicago: University of Chicago Press, 1984), pp. 39–50; and Valerie Smith, *Self-Discovery and Authority in Afro-American Narrative* (Cambridge: Harvard University Press, 1987), pp. 20–8. Other essays on Douglass are collected in Harold Bloom, ed., *Critical Essays on Frederick Douglass' Narrative* (New York: Chelsea House, 1988), and William L. Andrews, ed., *Critical Essays on Frederick Douglass* (Boston: G. K. Hall, 1991).

6   On abolition, see Louis Filler, *The Crusade Against Slavery, 1830–1860* (New York: Harper & Row, 1960); James Brewer Stewart, *Holy Warriors: The Abolitionists and American Slavery* (New York: Hill and Wang, 1976); Jane H. Pease and William H. Pease, *They Who Would Be Free: Blacks' Search for Freedom* (New York: Atheneum, 1974); Ronald G. Walters, *The Antislavery Appeal: American Abolitionism After 1830* (Baltimore: Johns Hopkins University Press, 1976); and Lawrence J. Friedman, *Gregarious Saints: Self and Community in American Abolitionism, 1830–1870* (Cambridge: Cambridge University Press, 1982). On slave narratives, see Charles H. Nichols, *Many Thousands Gone: The Ex-Slaves' Account of Their Bondage and Freedom* (Bloomington: Indiana University Press, 1963); *Art of the Slave Narrative: Original Essays in Criticism and Theory*, ed. John Sekora and Darwin T. Turner (Macomb: Western Illinois University Press, 1982); and William L. Andrews, *To Tell a Free Story: The First Century of Afro-American Autobiography, 1760–1865* (Urbana: University of Illinois Press, 1986).

7   On the impact of *Uncle Tom's Cabin*, see Eric J. Sundquist, ed., *New Essays on Uncle Tom's Cabin* (New York: Cambridge University Press, 1986); J. C. Furnas, *Goodbye to Uncle Tom* (New York: William Sloane, 1956); and Jane

Tompkins, *Sensational Designs: The Cultural Work of American Fiction, 1790–1860* (New York: Oxford University Press, 1985), pp. 122–46.

8   Eugene D. Genovese, *Roll, Jordan, Roll: The World the Slaves Made* (New York: Random House, 1974), pp. 561–6; E. N. Elliott, ed., *Cotton Is King, and Pro-Slavery Arguments* (Augusta, Ga: Pritchard, Abbott, and Loomis, 1860), p. 289.

9   Henry Louis Gates, Jr., "Writing 'Race' and the Difference It Makes," in *"Race," Writing, and Difference* (Chicago: University of Chicago Press, 1986), p. 12.

10 See Aileen S. Kraditor, *Means and Ends in American Abolitionism: Garrison and His Critics on Strategy and Tactics, 1834–1850* (1967; rpt. New York: Vintage, 1970), pp. 220–2.

11 See Martin, *The Mind of Frederick Douglass*, pp. 136–64, and Paula Giddings, *When and Where I Enter: The Impact of Black Women on Race and Sex in America* (New York: Bantam, 1984), pp. 57–74.

12 See David Brion Davis, *The Problem of Slavery in Western Culture* (Ithaca, N.Y.: Cornell University Press, 1966), pp. 333–90, and Philip Fisher, *Hard Facts: Setting and Form in the American Novel* (New York: Oxford University Press, 1985), pp. 87–127.

13 Robert B. Stepto, "Storytelling in Early Afro-American Fiction: Frederick Douglass' "The Heroic Slave," *Georgia Review* 36 (Summer 1982), 356; see also Ronald Takaki, *Violence in the Black Imagination: Essays and Documents* (New York: Putnam's, 1972); Howard Jones, "The Peculiar Institution and National Honor: The Case of the *Creole* Slave Revolt," *Civil War History* 21 (March 1975), 28–50; and William L. Andrews, "The Novelization of Voice in Early African American Narrative," *PMLA* 105 (January 1990), 23–34. On Douglass and "heroism," see also Martin, *The Mind of Frederick Douglass*, pp. 253–78.

14 Preston, *Young Frederick Douglass*, p. 168.

15 On slavery and total institutions, see Stanley M. Elkins, *Slavery: A Problem in American Institutional and Intellectual Life*, rev. ed. (Chicago: University of Chicago Press, 1976); Blassingame, *The Slave Community*, pp. 223–331; and Ann J. Lane, ed., *The Debate Over Slavery: Stanley Elkins and His Critics* (Urbana: University of Illinois Press, 1971).

16 Among the many readings of this episode in Douglass's autobiographies, see especially Andrews, *To Tell a Free Story*, pp. 280–91; David Leverenz, "Frederick Douglass's Self-Refashioning," *Criticism* 29 (Summer 1987), 341–70; and Donald B. Gibson, "Reconciling Public and Private in Frederick Douglass' *Narrative*," *American Literature* 57 (December 1985), 549–69.

17 Thomas R. Dew. "Abolition of Negro Slavery," in Drew Gilpin Faust, ed., *The Ideology of Proslavery: Proslavery Thought in the Antebellum South, 1830–1860* (Baton Rouge: Louisiana State University Press, 1981), p. 59. On slaveholding paternalism, see also James Oakes, *The Ruling Race: A History of the American Slaveholders* (New York: Random House, 1982), pp. 192–224.

18 See George B. Forgie, *Patricide in the House Divided: A Psychological Interpretation of Lincoln and His Age* (New York: Norton, 1979); Kenneth M. Stampp, *The*

Imperiled Union: Essays on the Background of the Civil War (New York: Oxford University Press, 1980), pp. 3–36; and Eric J. Sundquist, "Slavery, Revolution, and the American Renaissance," in *The American Renaissance Reconsidered*, ed. Walter Benn Michaels and Donald Pease (Baltimore: Johns Hopkins University Press, 1985), pp. 1–33.

19   See especially David W. Blight, *Frederick Douglass' Civil War* (Baton Rouge: Louisiana State University Press, 1989).

20   Quarles, *Frederick Douglass*, p. 277. A photograph of the Ball statue may be found in Hugh Honour, *The Image of the Black in Western Art: From the American Revolution to World War I* (Cambridge, Mass.: Harvard University Press, 1988), Vol. 4, Part 1, p. 265. On Douglass and the legacy of the Civil War, see also Blight, *Frederick Douglass' Civil War*, pp. 120ff.

21   Alain Locke, "Introduction," *Life and Times of Frederick Douglass* (New York: Pathway Press, 1941), p. xix; James McPherson, preface to Quarles, *Frederick Douglass*, p. v.

22   Eugene Gordon, "Blacks Turn Red," in *Negro: An Anthology*, orig. ed. Nancy Cunard (1933); abridged ed. Hugh Ford (New York: Frederick Ungar, 1970), p. 139. On Douglass and Washington, see also James Olney, "The Founding Fathers – Frederick Douglass and Booker T. Washington," in *Slavery and the Literary Imagination*, ed. Deborah E. McDowell and Arnold Rampersad (Baltimore: Johns Hopkins University Press, 1989), pp. 1–24.

23   See August Meier, *Negro Thought in America, 1880–1915: Racial Ideologies in the Age of Booker T. Washington* (Ann Arbor: University of Michigan Press, 1963), pp. 75–8; Sterling Stuckey, *Slave Culture: Nationalist Theory and the Foundations of Black America* (New York: Oxford University Press, 1987), pp. 222–6; and Dickson D. Bruce, Jr., *Black American Writing and the Nadir: The Evolution of a Literary Tradition, 1877–1915* (Baton Rouge: Louisiana State University Press, 1989), pp. 11–55.

24   Ida B. Wells-Barnett, *Crusade for Justice: The Autobiography of Ida B. Wells*, ed. Alfreda M. Duster (Chicago: University of Chicago Press, 1970), pp. 118–19.

25   The New Negro Renaissance may be said to have begun in the 1890s, thus embracing the careers, for example, of Charles Chesnutt, W. E. B. Du Bois, Pauline Hopkins, and Paul Laurence Dunbar, as well as the significant flourishing of black music and theater that preceded the more widely studied Harlem Renaissance of the 1920s. See Wilson J. Moses, "The Lost World of the New Negro, 1895–1919: Black Literary and Intellectual Life Before the 'Renaissance,' " *Black American Literature Forum* 21 (Spring–Summer 1987), pp. 61–82; and Henry Louis Gates, Jr., "The Trope of a New Negro and the Reconstruction of the Image of the Black," *Representations* 24 (Fall 1988), pp. 129–55.

26   Kelly Miller, *Radicals and Conservatives, and Other Essays on the Negro in America* (originally published under the title *Race Adjustment* in 1908; rpt. New York: Schocken Books, 1968), pp. 233–4.

"Ironic Tenacity"

Frederick Douglass's Seizure of the Dialectic

STERLING STUCKEY

> *Everywhere in Africa, I have noticed that no greater affront can be*
> *offered a Negro than insulting his mother. "Strike me," cries a*
> *Mandingo to his enemy, "but revile not my mother!"*
> Mungo Park,
> *Travels in the Interior Districts of Africa*

Of all the travelers to Africa in the years of the Atlantic slave trade, none
better captured the place of the African woman in the life of her people
than Mungo Park. Weary and dejected, in dire need of food, Park was
approached by a slave woman who offered him a "seasonable satisfaction"
of nuts and departed before he could thank her. Sometime thereafter, he
encountered another woman, one returning "from the labors of the field."
This time offered "a supper of very fine fish . . . broiled upon some
embers," he described the scene that followed:

> The rites of hospitality being thus performed towards a stranger
> in distress; my worthy benefactress . . . called to the female part
> of her family, who had stood gazing on me the while in fixed
> astonishment, to resume the task of spinning cotton; in which they
> continued to employ themselves [the] great part of the night. They
> lightened their labour by songs, one of which was completely ex-
> tempore; for I was myself the subject of it. It was sung by one of
> the young women, the rest joining in a sort of chorus. The air was
> sweet and plantive . . . I was oppressed by such unexpected kindness;
> and sleep fled from my eyes.

The women sang:

> The loud wind roar'd, the rain fell fast;
> The white man yielded to the blast;
> He sat him down, beneath our tree;

23

For weary, sad, and faint was he;
And oh, no wife or mother's care,
For him, the milk or corn prepare.   Chorus

The White Man, shall our pity share;
Alas, no wife or mother's care,
For him, the milk or corn prepare.

The storm is o'er; the tempest past;
And Mercy's voice has hushe'd the blast.
The wind is heard in whispers low,
The white Man, far away must go; –
But ever in his heart will bear
Remembrance of the Negro's care.   Chorus

Go, White Man, go; – but with thee bear
The Negro's wish, the Negro's prayer;
Remembrance of the Negro's care.[1]

Captives of the slave trade to North America and elsewhere in the
New World, such women knew oppression that denied their humanity.
To an impressive extent, Betsey Bailey, Frederick Douglass's grandmother,
embodied their skill and spirit. Product of a tradition of work that has
not been fully acknowledged, her role in slavery casts new light on the
cultural environment of the young Douglass and calls for consideration
of the nature of slave skills and the spiritual context in which they found
expression.

At the center of slave culture in Maryland was Douglass's grandmother,
whose little slave cabin had for him "the attractions of a palace" and
"whose kindness and love stood in place of [his] mother's," from whom
he was separated at a very early age.[2] So vivid were the impressions
made on him by his grandmother, who resided in Tuckahoe County,
Maryland, on one of Colonel Edward Lloyd's plantations, that his descriptions of her activities and attitudes in his autobiographies reveal an
accuracy of detail that meets several tests for comparative analysis and
enable us to search beneath appearances for the substance of reality so
that we can understand the deeper influences on her and others in the
slave community.

Douglass's description of her physical appearance prepares the ground
for important revelations, his use of language serving that end with great
precision. She is described as advanced in years, "as was evident from
the more than one gray hair which peeped from beneath the ample and
graceful folds of her newly and smoothly-ironed bandanna turban . . .
a woman of power and spirit." Muscular and elastic in movement, on
one long journey to a neighboring plantation, he tells us, using a Kimbundu

term, the statuesque slave "toted" him, who "hardly seemed to be a burden to her."[3]

The prolonged and enforced absences of his mother and his exposure of but a few years to his grandparents – he says little of his grandfather – mirror the disruptive impact of slavery on the young Douglass, but he was fortunate to have had such a grandmother. His confidence in himself and his self-respect, despite the fierceness of opposing forces, owed much to her extraordinary example. In an important passage, he reveals something of her intelligence. Known to be a good nurse and "withal somewhat famous as a fisherwoman," she possessed still more skills:

> I have known her to be in the water waist deep, for hours, seine-handling. She was a gardener as well as a fisherwoman, and remarkable for her success in keeping her seedling sweet potatoes through the months of winter, and easily got the reputation of being born to "good luck." In planting time, Grandmother Betsey was sent for in all directions, simply to place the seedling potatoes in the hills . . . for superstition had it that her touch was needed to make them grow.[4]

According to Talbot, fishing is the main occupation of African coastal peoples and many kinds of nets are employed, some "the self-acting sort either put right across a current so that the fish become entangled in the meshes, or, more ordinarily, so that this forms a chamber into which they can find their way, but from which escape is impossible." In particular:

> Seine nets are fairly common in the estuaries or on the seashore. . . . [A]mong the Ekoi [fishing] is looked upon as most exclusively women's work. . . . Each is supposed to give her husband one big fish from her hand and some to her father and mother. Before starting she usually rubs "lucky leaves" over her hand-net.[5]

It is likely that Betsey Bailey's ancestors were southern Nigerians, a coastal people steeped in fishing lore and tradition, quite possibly Ekoi. Her demonstrated ability at fishing is alone sufficient reason for studying slave women in relation to fishing and the making of nets. Moreover, the reference to her having been born to "good luck" appears to establish a mystical connection between agriculture and fishing, since the touch of the hand was associated with a favorable outcome in each skill. Her brilliance in agriculture could hardly have been more impressive, considering that she worked sandy, worn-out, desertlike soil that was notorious for its infertility. Douglass recalled that ruin and decay were everywhere visible "in this dull, flat, and unthrifty district, or neighborhood, surrounded by a white population of the lowest order, indolent and drunken to a proverb." Slaves of that district "seemed to ask, 'Oh! what's the use?'

every time they lifted a hoe." But "exceeding care" was taken by Betsey Bailey in "preventing the succulent root [of the sweet potato] from getting bruised in the digging, and by placing it beyond the reach of frost by actually burying it under the hearth of her cabin during the winter months." That superstition might be a factor in performing well seems a real possibility, especially when working in a tradition of excellence at a particular skill. Apparently Douglass did not give serious consideration to that possibility.[6]

Douglass's grandmother was an invaluable source of African influences, but he was too young to have discussed such matters with her when in her care. In a rare reference to slave trade activity and to the peopling of the Lloyd plantation, he does write that "there were slaves on Mr. Lloyd's place who remembered being brought from Africa."[7] Douglass was aware of this by the late 1820s, approximately two decades after the suppression of the African slave trade. Though most slaves were brought to Maryland through Virginia, where the trade had ended in 1778, as late as the 1850s there was an African spiritual and artistic presence in Virginia, so more than being brought directly from Africa was a factor in that presence.[8]

Well into the nineteenth century, African traditions of spinning and weaving were alive in Virginia, as they were with Betsey Bailey and other slaves in Maryland. Since Maryland slaves were usually brought from Virginia, it is likely that their attitudes toward spinning were similar to those of Virginia slaves. In this regard, a former Virginia slave remarked: "Mother said dey would always spin in pairs – one would treadle whilst de other would wind de ball. You got to wind fast, too, an' take de thread right off de spindle, else it git tangled up. An' mamma tole me dey would all pat dey feet an' sing":

> Wind de ball, wind de ball
> Wind de ball, lady, wind de ball
> Don't care how you wind de ball
> Wind de ball, lady, wind de ball
> Ding, ding, ding, – wind de ball
> Wind de ball, lady, wind de ball.[9]

Like the women encountered by Mungo Park in the interior of Africa, they lightened their labor with song.

Douglass makes no mention of his grandmother weaving, but he states that she made nets that were highly prized, which means that she did indeed weave, and extremely well, probably weaving nets from cotton, as was done in certain parts of Africa. And he informs us that slaves did the weaving at the home plantation of Colonel Lloyd. Since we know that slave women dominated weaving across the South, and since it is becoming increasingly clear that the slave trade extended into areas of

Africa where weaving was common, we can conclude that many slaves were influenced by African traditions of weaving. There should be, on balance, a serious question as to who taught whom and no reason to question that the pattern as a whole was for slave girls to learn from slave women. There is much irony here, for in Africa weaving was mainly done by men, whereas in America it was overwhelmingly done by slave women. In any event, Douglass writes that on Colonel Lloyd's estate, "blacksmiths, wheelwrights, shoemakers, weavers, and coopers, were slaves."[10]

Significant numbers of slaves, on entering America, were taught certain skills by whites; others, sizable numbers again, were "taught" some skills they had mastered before; and still others, especially those who were to work as field hands, arrived in colonial America to perform some kinds of farming skills without being trained by whites. Certainly by the time of the American Revolution, the clear pattern had emerged of slaves teaching slaves almost all the plantation skills. Although Africans may have felt free to teach whites certain handicraft and farming skills in the seventeenth century, as the institution of slavery matured and racism deepened, few slaves were likely to assert knowledge of a particular skill rather than allow whites to think that they were teaching them that skill. Under the circumstances, it was probably difficult for whites to admit that an African had taught them anything, for the slave's Africanness was a crucial element, so the rationale went, of his or her enslavement as an inferior.[11]

The more assimilated the African, the easier it would have been for whites to acknowledge his or her skills, for they could be, and were, attributed to the influence of whites. But whites on numerous plantations were confronted by skilled Africans who spoke a language with strong African influences in grammar and syntax. On this point there is a passage from Douglass that has been ignored by students of slave culture, one that relates to that culture in the particular and universal sense, with implications for a number of disciplines, not the least of them linguistics:

> There is not, probably, in the whole south, a plantation where the English language is more imperfectly spoken than on Col. Lloyd's. It is a mixture of Guinea and everything else you please. At the time of which I am now writing, there were slaves there who had been brought from the coast of Africa. They never used "s" in indication of the possessive case. . . . "Oo you dem long to?", means, "Whom do you belong to?" "Oo dem got any peachy?" means, "Have you got any peaches?" I could scarcely understand them when I first went among them, so broken was their speech.[12]

This was the language of field hand and artisan, of practically all of the slaves on the plantation, its force so influential that some whites were affected by it as well. Douglass's most profound insight into slave culture was developed among slaves speaking the "jargon" that he described. In fact, it is when referring to slave artisans that he identifies the spiritual anchor of the slave community. Nowhere are his powers of observation, and his ability to understand, greater than in this passage:

> The reader has already been informed of the handicrafts carried on here by slaves; "Uncle" Toney was the blacksmith, "Uncle" Harry the cartwright, and "Uncle" Able was the shoemaker and these had assistants in their various departments. These mechanics were called "Uncles" by all the younger slaves, not because they really sustained that relationship to any, but according to plantation etiquette, as a mark of respect, due from the younger to the older slaves.[13]

Douglass builds on this reference to African etiquette on the plantation:

> Strange and even ridiculous as it may seem, among a people so uncultivated and with many stern trials to look in the face, there is not to be found among any people a more rigid enforcement of the law of respect to elders than is maintained among them. I set this down as partly constitutional with the colored race and partly conventional. There is no better material in the world for making a gentleman than is furnished by the African.[14]

Douglass's thesis that slaves enforced the law of respect for elders affirmed that self-generative quality in them that preserved the central tenet of their faith. In a remarkable statement, he argues that an elder "shows to others, and exacts for himself, all the tokens of respect which he is compelled to manifest toward his master." "Others," in this context, is a clear reference to other slaves: "So uniformly are good manners enforced among slaves, I can easily detect a 'bogus' fugitive by his manners."[15]

From the age of seven or eight, on Colonel Lloyd's plantation, he observed slaves "direct from Guinea . . . and many who could say their fathers and mothers were stolen from Africa. . . . Such . . . was the community, and such the place, in which my earliest and most lasting impressions of slavery, and of slave-life, were conceived." In that community and place, a younger slave approached an elder artisan "with hat in hand," and "woe betide him if he failed to acknowledge a favor of any sort, with the accustomed 'tank'ee.'"[16]

Little did Douglass know that the workshop was at the center of the compound of some traditional African societies, that in Africa there were artisans greatly respected for their skill. He was not aware, for example, that the heritage of the slave blacksmith was more complex than that of his European counterpart, whose tradition of work was undoubtedly a source of influence on the plantations. Not only did blacksmithing extend into the distant African past, it rose to such heights in some African cultures that it was thought a divine gift: "A figure wrought in iron is not a simple abstraction," writes Lester Wunderman, "if the smith who forged it is believed to have descended from his remote predecessor who brought the secret of iron making from heaven itself."[17] Often the black-smith was also a goldsmith, as in Guinea, or a mediator between the living and the dead, as in Mali, both areas being among those affected by the slave trade. Moreover, his role in Africa as supplier of the instruments of agriculture – repeated on the plantations of the South, but under circumstances of forced labor – made the blacksmith a pivotal figure in the eyes of his people.[18]

Martin Delany, a contemporary of Douglass, had a more complex reality in mind than Douglass when thinking of slave artisans. Though some persons even now regard his views as extremely provocative, there is growing evidence, drawn from the African background, that Delany's position, on balance, is worthy of the most serious consideration. Alluding to indigenous African cultures, he asserts that Africans "Though pagans for the most part in their own country [were] required not to be taught to work, and how to do it; but it was only necessary to bid them work, and they at once knew what to do, and how it should be done." Despite evidence that at times slaveholders called in white mechanics to train slaves, Delany's argument that "[t]he greater number of the mechanics of the South are also black men" is not disputed by historians.[19]

His overall position is one that Douglass would have had the greatest difficulty accepting at the time he got to know slave artisans in his youth, for he was convinced that he "could not have been dropped anywhere on the globe, where I would reap less, in the way of knowledge from my immediate associates, than on this plantation."

> Even "Mas' Daniel," by his association with his father's slaves, had measurably adopted their dialect and their ideas, so far as they had ideas to be adopted. . . . Mas' Daniel could not associate with ignorance without sharing its shade; and he could not give his black playmates his company, without giving them his intelligence, as well. Without knowing this, or caring about it at the time, I, for some cause or other, spent much of my time with Mas' Daniel, in preference to spending it with most of the other boys.[20]

Perhaps at this time, when Douglass had been exposed to an array of slave work skills, he thought it "natural" that they somehow performed such skills. It appears that he never made the leap that Delany made in thinking, for example, that slaves taught whites how to cultivate rice, which is, on the basis of present evidence, the most logical explanation for its successful cultivation as early as the 1690s in South Carolina. It was Delany's view that

> from their knowledge of cultivation – an art acquired in their native Africa – the farming interests in the North and planting in the South were commenced with a prospect never dreamed of before the introduction on the continent of this most interesting, unexampled, hardy race of men. . . . Hemp, cotton, tobacco, corn, rice, sugar, and many other important staple products, are all the result of African skill and labor in the southern states of this country. . . .[21]

Douglass was no more prepared to accept African origins for skills in agriculture than to acknowledge such origins for handicraft skills. Yet time and again he leads us in the direction of Africa for deeper understanding.

We know from Lewis C. Gray that cotton was cultivated by slaves in Maryland, as elsewhere in the South, but, blinded by racism, Gray never suspects that cotton was widely cultivated in sections of Africa from which Africans were forcibly taken to North America. In Nigeria, it was so abundant that it grew wild in certain regions, it is repeatedly referred to by anthropologists and travelers as being spun and woven into fabrics in various African traditional societies.[22] Even had Africans not taught whites how to cultivate rice or cotton, evidence is abundant that scores of thousands of them did not need to be taught either of those skills, since they possessed them from childhood.

Of all the skilled slaves discussed by Douglass, except for his grandmother, nowhere does he write as revealingly as when discussing Barney, a white-haired old man "of a brownish complexion, and a respectful and dignified bearing." Referred to as "Old Barney," he carried all sorts of skills behind his title of coachman:

> He was much devoted to his profession, and held his office as an honorable one. He was a farrier as well as an ostler, and could bleed horses, remove lampers from their mouths, and administer medicine to them. No one on the farm knew so well as Old Barney what to do with a sick horse. . . .[23]

Barney's son worked with him, and there were other apprentices under his guidance as well.

Art historian Robert F. Thompson recalls the response of "a priest near Whydah in Dahomey" to a photograph "of an equestrian figure in wood": "That rider sits with force. The force of the horse is seen. He has the speed and the power of the horse in his body." Thompson considers it "especially African" to believe that "a rider acquires the very force of his mount," and he draws our attention to the annual Damba ceremony in "the divisional capitols of Gonja, in what is now Ghana, where members

of the ruling state perform . . . motions of horseback riding as both
horse and rider. In other words, horse and rider can be, at least in some
African civilizations, conceived of as one."[24] In areas of Africa as diverse
as those of the Sonninke, Mossi, and Chadic regions, one finds examples,
in metal, of the rider on his mount that date back a thousand years, six
centuries before the Atlantic slave trade was launched. It is not surprising,
therefore, that Delany observed of slaves:

> Nor were their skills as herdsmen inferior to their other proficiencies,
> they being among the most accomplished trainers of horses in the
> world. Indeed, to this class of men may be indebted the entire
> country for the improvement in the South in the breed of horses.
> And those who have travelled in the southern states could not have
> failed to observe that the principal trainers, jockeys, riders, and
> judges of horses were men of African descent.[25]

It is interesting to note, in this connection, that Douglass could not have
been unaware of Delany's views on Africans and horses, handicrafts, and
agriculture, for at the time Delany drafted his statement on slave skills,
they were locked in a heated dispute over emigration, which is the issue
raised by Delany in his important essay on slave skills and emigration.
Why Douglass didn't consider Delany's explanation for the brilliance of
slave skills, at least in some form, is a matter that merits consideration.

But to argue that slaves retained certain African work skills is to
confront the reality that they practiced them under radically different
circumstances in America. Gone was the rite of puberty as a means of
introducing skills in an environment in which pride is taken in the flowering
of youth. Under slavery in America, severe restrictions were placed on
slave activities, and the idea of the slave family was little more than that.
Disappearing also were those differences in African spiritual outlook that
were tied to ethnicity as the process of Pan-Africanization – Du Bois
called it a "mingling of heathen rites" – ran its course.[26]

As ethnic differences were increasingly subordinated by force of circumstances, a new form of Africanness centering on the primacy of unity
in slavery came to prevail. In this atmosphere, many Africans, perhaps
most, discovered that they had shared similar work habits in agriculture
and handicrafts – across ethnic lines – in the ancestral home. Work skills,
then, were an important grounding for a sense of Africanness that was
achieved in slavery in ways not achieved in Africa. Under such circumstances, work songs were created out of a deeper sense of Africanity than
has heretofore been acknowledged. Moreover, when it is borne in mind
that Africans, in addition to sharing certain work skills, entered America
with roughly similar spiritual and artistic attitudes, the depths of Africanity
on which they drew are better understood.

Douglass had no illusions that the environment in which slave skills flourished was Christian. In fact, no one argued more powerfully than he that the great majority of slaves were denied access to Christianity. With slaves in mind, and following in the tradition of Richard Allen, David Walker, and Henry H. Garnet, he says of Christians, North and South, in the Appendix of his *Narrative*: "They love the heathen on the other side of the globe. They can pray for him, pay money to have the Bible put into his hand, and missionaries to instruct him; while they despise and totally neglect the heathen at their own doors."[27]

African work skills were not despised. They were the foundation of slavery and found expression in much the same way as African spiritual and artistic values – as necessary to one's continuing sense of humanity, as a means of ordering one's world to prevent chaos from welling up from despair. Since labor was required to feed, clothe, and shelter the slave as well as the master, an intense irony obtained wherever the African was enslaved, and the text of much slave cultural life was writ large by that condition. It was a matter, in Douglass's case, of relating music as well as work skills to that text.

Since Douglass's treatment of slave music is his most direct contribution to our understanding of black culture, it is peculiar that it remains largely unexamined. His reflections on slave songs led W. E. B. Du Bois to entitle the last chapter of *The Souls of Black Folk* "Of the Sorrow Songs,"[28] but even Du Bois did not go much further in his treatment of Douglass on slave songs. In any case, the complex inner core of black music that consists of joy and sorrow received masterly attention from Douglass, who anticipated by more than a century many of the essentials of James Baldwin's wonderful treatment of the subject in *The Fire Next Time*. But it was sometime after slavery that Douglass began more fully to understand the music of his youth. Six years after his escape, he states: "I did not, when a slave, fully understand the deep meaning of these rude and apparently incoherent songs. I was, myself, within the circle, so that I could then neither hear nor see as those without might see and hear."[29]

In his reflections on slave handicrafts, Douglas was never to match his judgments on black music, possibly because he was "within the circle" of song and not intimately involved with slave artisans in the plantation setting. There is also the fact that music reaches the mind and emotions, and so much in slave settings worked to confirm in Douglass the sentiments of a given song. But the depth of understanding that he was later to express undoubtedly owed much to his own agony as a slave and to what he knew other slaves experienced. "Slaves were expected to sing as well as to work," he tells us, adding: "A silent slave was not liked, either by master or overseer. 'Make a noise there! Make a noise there!,' and 'bear a hand,' were words usually addressed to slaves when they were silent." Under such circumstances, seldom did they not sing.[30]

We can, therefore, scarcely imagine the degree and variety of singing that Douglass heard. His description of some of the music – or is he referring to most? – is similar to Baldwin's treatment of black music, especially this passage that begins his discussion of a number of musical genres under a single, nameless heading:

> The slaves selected to go to the Great House Farm, for the monthly allowance for themselves and their fellow-slaves, were peculiarly enthusiastic. While on their way, they would make the dense old woods, for miles around, reverberate with their wild songs, revealing at once the highest joy and deepest sadness. They would compose and sing as they went along, consulting neither time nor tune. The thought that came up, came out – if not in the word, in the sound; – and as frequently in the one as in the other. They would sometimes sing the most pathetic sentiment in the most rapturous tone, and the most rapturous sentiment in the most pathetic tone.[31]

In that passage, Douglass captures the essence of black music, from the spirituals to jazz. Baldwin's comment on black music could very well have been influenced by Douglass:

> White Americans seem to feel that happy songs are *happy* and sad songs are *sad*. . . . Only people who have been down the line, as the song puts it, know what this music is about. I think it was Big Bill Broonzy who used to sing "I Feel So Good," a really joyful song about a man who is on his way to the railroad station to meet his girl. She's coming home. It is the singer's incredibly moving exuberance that makes one realize how leaden the time must have been while she was gone. . . . This is the freedom that one hears in some gospel songs, for example, and in jazz. In all jazz, and especially in the Blues, there is something tart and ironic, authoritative and doubled-edged. . . . White Americans do not understand the depths out of which such an ironic tenacity comes. . . .[32]

Douglass probed the depths of such "ironic tenacity," to use Baldwin's phrase, and what he has to tell us is relevant, once more, for the music of his people since as during slavery: "Such is the constitution of the human mind, that, when pressed to extremes, it often avails itself of the most opposite methods. Extremes meet in mind as in matter. . . . Slaves sing more to *make* themselves happy, than to express their happiness."[33] With that he offers the best explanation yet of the source of that genius in black art that allows the music of sadness to contain its seeming

opposite in the sound of joy. What connects that sadness and joy is the
courage to live, the capacity to confront tragedy without wincing and
thereby allow the human spirit to assert itself undiminished.

As described by Douglass, the emotional tones of the sacred and
secular, as well as their contexts of expression, were often the same.
Because slave institutions, owing to the challenge of slavery, were often
fluid and formless, taking shape in one place then disappearing, only to
reappear as slaves assembled elsewhere, that which was sacred coursed
throughout much of the slave community. Only with the lapse of time
has context more clearly and separably defined the sacred and secular in
black musical life. No one has done as much as Douglass to help us
understand this reality.

Douglass blurred the line between the sacred and the secular, in the
process noting the principles that inform slave music as a whole. One is
not sure whether the sacred or the secular predominated among the slaves
he heard singing, though there is reason to think that the former was
sovereign. In any case, a lot of singing was being done to work rhythms
also, and songs were created in that context that were no less spiritual.
And we know that spirituals were sung in work contexts, pushing them,
with the threat of the lash as punishment, closer than ever to the blues.
Douglass describes songs created during work that have all the power
of religious appeal, that stretch irony to such tautness that suddenly the
singer is overcome with sadness as tension snaps within. In all such songs
of allowance day and the great house farm, he writes, "there was ever
some expression in praise of the great house farm; something which
would flatter the pride of the owner, and, possibly draw a forcible glance
from him:

> I am going away to the great house farm,
> Yea! O yea! O yea!
> My old master is a good old master,
> O Yea! O Yea! O Yea!"

The irony is rich, the illusion of respect for the master a shield thrown
up almost as a means of softening the blow that the song delivered:

> This they would sing, with other words of their own improvis-
> ing – *jargon to others but full of meaning to themselves*. . . . In the most
> boisterous outbursts of rapturous sentiment, there was ever a tinge
> of deep melancholy . . . I have sometimes thought, that the mere
> hearing of these songs would do more to impress truly spiritual-
> minded men and women with the soul-crushing and death-dealing
> character of slavery, than the reading of whole volumes of its mere

physical cruelties. They spoke to the heart and to the soul of the thoughful.[34]

Thus, Douglass was astonished to find people in the North who thought the singing of slaves "evidence of their contentment and happiness. It is impossible to make a greater mistake. Slaves sing most when they are most unhappy."[35]

Nothing more clearly revealed the spiritual wasteland inhabited by slaveholders than their hearing slaves sing, indeed forcing them to sing, without being reformed by what they heard. Douglass's assertion that the singing of slaves was constant is a powerful indictment of the slaveholder's deafness to the humanity of the slave. "Every tone was a testimony against slavery and a prayer to God for deliverance from chains." He found that, on hearing those "wild notes," his spirit was depressed and he was filled with "ineffable sadness." For Douglass, slave music was the means by which he traced his "first glimmering conception of the dehumanizing character of slavery. I can never get rid of that conception. Those songs still follow me, to deepen my hatred of slavery, and quicken my sympathy for my brethren in bonds."[36]

An "elastic spirit" was the irreducible source of slave creativity, and it was not to the credit of those who bade slaves sing and dance. "We are told . . . that their masters frequently give them wherewith to make merry," Douglass writes, and admits that sometimes the slave does dance, sing, and "appear to be merry." He thought it proved "that though slavery is armed with a thousand stings, it is not able entirely to kill the . . . spirit of the bondman." It was no thanks to the slaveholder that that spirit rose and walked abroad, extracting "from the cup of nature occasional drops of joy and gladness. No thanks to the slaveholder, nor to slavery, that the vivacious captive may sometimes dance in his chains; his very mirth in such circumstances stands before God as an accusing angel against his enslaver."[37]

Douglass did not know that slaves were under African religious influences that were the source of their manners. His view was that the slave, cut off from Christianity, was nevertheless "endowed with those mysterious powers by which man soars above the things of time and sense, and grasps, with undying tenacity, the elevating and sublimely glorious idea of God."[38] Though Douglass had no apparent knowledge of how the slave's conception of God provided the primary context for slave art, his treatment of sacred and secular music implies such knowledge. His achievement is the more impressive because he stepped across a cultural threshold a world away to call slave art proper to the slave without fully understanding why.

Trying to extract some joy and gladness from desolation was the engine of slave creativity that seldom ceased. What the slaveholder sought to use for his own purposes slaves generally used for their own. Out of the necessity to confront the injustice of their lives, they created art that addressed and responded to the nature of their experience. Douglass thought, in this context, that the songs of the slave represented "the sorrows of his heart; and he is relieved by them, only as an aching heart is relieved by its tears."[39] He thought artistic expression the chief means by which slaves responded to the horror of their condition. Where the work of slaves was most decisive – in the fields – slavery was most brutal. The overseer strutted, walked, or rode about, "dealing blows, and leaving gashes on broken-spirited men and helpless women," a business so disgraceful "that, rather than engage in it, a decent man would blow his brains out." The overseer's cruelty and coarseness, "rank as weeds in the tropics," punctuated the rhythms of work, and out of that hell much of slave art was created.[40] The slave woman and man, in such an environment, could well appreciate a song such as "Sometimes I Feel Like a Motherless Child":

> Sometimes I feel like a motherless child,
> Sometimes I feel like a motherless child,
> Sometimes I feel like a motherless child,
> A long ways from home;
> A long ways from home;
> True believer
> A long ways from home
> A long ways from home

The refrain – "A long ways from home" – flows like an undercurrent through the song, deepening the pain of experience, reminding one, at one's lowest point, of origins:

> Sometimes I feel like I'm almost gone,
> Sometimes I feel like I'm almost gone,
> Sometimes I feel like I'm almost gone,
> A long ways from home;
> A long ways from home;
> True believer
> A long ways from home
> A long ways from home.[41]

Douglass has given us our best sense of how much work influenced the slave's creative process. His emphasis on the degree to which it conditioned a great deal of music and established its context, when coupled with what we know of the relationship between art and work in Africa, where art has been so deeply functional, gives us a new perspective on the process of slave creativity. And thanks to him, we have a better awareness of the politics of slave artistic expression, of the degree to which consciousness of oppression was inevitable for the slave, especially for the field hand. Wherever song was heard between sunup and sundown, one was likely to find some level of work and awareness, by white and black, that the plantation economy was dependent on slave brawn and skill: "there was generally more or less singing among the teamsters, at all times. It was a means of telling the overseer, in the distance, where they were and what they were about."[42]

It is small wonder, with such a tradition of work and art behind them, that after slavery blacks could voice, in a new but related form of oppression, an unusual blend of pride:

> Dis ole hammer
> Ring lak silver
> Shine lak gold, baby,
> Shine lak gold.
>
> Take dis hammer
> Throw it in de river,
> It'll ring right on, baby,
> Ring right on.

and disaffection

> Captain, did you hear
> All yo' men gonna leave you,
> Next pay day, baby,
> Next pay day?[43]

Slave art was used for general indictments of slavery, subtly expressed, and for explicit attacks on slavery, at times during holidays, through song with percussive accompaniment – "Jubilee beating." At such times, improvisation was a hallmark of performance. Douglass's description of "Juba" beating is superb, with its emphasis on the correspondence between word and hand, the one confirming the rhythm of the other: The Jubilee beater "sings his merry songs, so ordering the words as to have them fall pat with the movement of his hands. . . . Among a mass of nonsense and wild frolic, once in a while a sharp hit is given to the meanness of slaveholders." Douglass chose this example of song, with accents beat against the body in rhythmic and ironic accompaniment:

> We raise de wheat,
> Dey gib us de corn;
> We bake de bread,
> Dey gib us de crust;
> We sif de meal,

Dey gib us de huss;
We peel de meat,
Dey gib us de skin,
And that's de way
Dey take us in.
We skim de pot,
Dey gib us the liquor,
And say dat's good enough for niggers.[44]

Douglass thought it "not a bad summary of the palpable injustice and fraud of slavery, giving – as it does – to the lazy and idle, the comforts which God designed should be given solely to the honest laborer."[45]

The relaxed atmosphere on the plantation during holidays – slaves were encouraged *not* to work on such occasions – led to an extraordinary number of slaves coming forth with fiddles: The fiddling and dancing and the beating of Jubilee were "going on in all directions." That Juba beating often took the place of the fiddle suggests the rhythmic uses to which the fiddle was put in slave hands. But slave culture, on the occasion of holidays, was very much under the influence of the master class and was used as part of a larger plan, for "keeping the minds of slaves occupied with prospective pleasure, within the limits of slavery."[46] At such times, the married slave could visit his wife; the mother and father could see their offspring; the young slave could go courting; the drunken slave could secure plenty of alcohol; and the man of religion could pray, preach, and exhort:[47]

These holidays are conductors or safety valves to carry off the explosive elements inseparable from the human mind, when reduced to the condition of slavery. But for these, the rigors of bondage would become too severe for endurance, and the slave would be forced up to dangerous desperation. Woe to the slaveholder when he undertakes to hinder or to prevent the operation of these electric conductors. A succession of earthquakes would be less destructive, than the insurrectionary fires which would be sure to burst forth in different parts of the south, from such interference.[48]

Holidays were part of "the gross fraud, wrongs and inhumanity of slavery." The fraud reached its pervasive high (or low) point when large numbers of slaves were encouraged to get drunk as a means "to disgust [them] with their temporary freedom, and to make them as glad to return to their work, as they were to leave it. By plunging them into exhausting depths of drunkenness and dissipation, this effect is almost certain to follow." Thus, scenes of debauchery often reached scandalous extremes in which "multitudes might be found stretched out in brutal drunkenness, at once helpless and disgusting."[49]

Douglass was exposed to the best and the worst of the character of his people, seeing it develop, or fail to, under the least advantageous conditions. Such influences within the slave community were important in his early development, those of his mother and grandmother foremost among them, though he spent virtually no time with his mother and relatively little with his grandmother. That both his mother, who could read, and his grandmother, who possessed numerous skills, were field hands suggests the need for reconsideration of the nature of the relationship between that group of slaves and others, especially when considering the knowledge of agriculture that large numbers of Africans brought to the plantations of the South. There is, in short, reason to believe that field hands, who have not received proper credit for their artistic achievements, were far more enlightened than scholars have led us to believe.

Reflecting on the life of his grandmother, Douglass sang a tragic song. Her history was one of great gifts, yet her towering figure stands assault-ed – and immortalized – as the ultimate emblem of the inhumanity of slavery. Her vast contribution to the wealth of slaveholders is as difficult to measure as the suffering slavery brought to her over a period of generations. During much of her life she represented, unbroken from Africa, certain traditions of work that were shared by significant numbers of slaves. Her character, under the oppression of slavery, could well have been the source of Douglass's elegance of spirit, her acuity of mind a likely and important source of his genius.

More than anything else that fueled his hatred of slaveholders was their treatment of her. She had served "old master" from youth to old age, rocking him in infancy, caring for him in childhood. She "was the source of all his wealth . . . had become a great-grandmother in his service." At his death, she had "wiped from his icy brow the cold death-sweat, and closed his eyes forever."

> She was nevertheless left as a slave – a slave for life – a slave in the hands of strangers; and in their hands she saw her children, her grandchildren, and her great-grandchildren, divided, like so many sheep, without being gratified with the small privilege of a single word, as to their or her own destiny. . . . The hearth is desolate. The children, the unconscious children, who once sang and danced in her presence, are gone. She gropes her way, in the darkness of age, for a drink of water. . . . The grave is at the door. And now, when weighed down by the pains and aches of old age, when the head inclines to the feet, when the beginning and ending of human existence meet, and helpless infancy and painful old age combine together – at this time, this most needed time for the exercise of that tenderness and affection which children only can exercise toward

a declining parent – my poor old grandmother, the devoted mother
of twelve children, is left all alone, in yonder little hut, before a
few dim embers.[50]

The prevailing historical wisdom about the state of African skills in
the era of the slave trade must be reconsidered in light of growing evidence
that Africans were perhaps second to none in cotton and rice cultivation,
in fishing and animal husbandry, in weaving and blacksmithing – areas
of importance in the workshop and field of the plantation South. When
we add what has been discovered of African music, dance, and sculpture
in the era of the trade, the force of African historical reality will surely
assert itself in new and profound ways.

From what we know of Douglass's observations regarding slave
skills, we can be assured that in coming years more will be discovered
of African influences on slave labor. Simply to know more of such
influences in Maryland is to know more of such matters in Virginia
and in other regions of the South, for slaves in Maryland and Virginia
were, via the domestic slave trade, sold farther south and to the South-
west. Not only has Douglass provided us with a new agenda – and,
implicitly, an approach – for scholarship on slave skills, he has put his
finger on the crux of spirituality for his people by identifying respect
for the elders as a cardinal tenet of their faith. With the exception of
Herman Melville, no other American intellectual of the slave era was
as perceptive on this point as he.[51]

Yet Douglass chose not to draw on the insights of Delany in his
discussion of slave skills. It is hard to avoid the conclusion that he
sought to avoid complicating a strategy of liberation already difficult
enough to carry to a successful conclusion, fearing perhaps that he
might compound the problem by contending that slaves, and therefore
the overwhelming majority of blacks in America, were in numerous
ways African. Still, for him it was primarily a matter of emphasis,
not one of exclusion, a matter of failing to suggest possible African
origins in those areas that were indispensable to the economy of the
nation in his day. Even though he knew little of the evolution of the
African qualities identified, in areas of spiritual and artistic importance
he did not avoid calling them African.

Even with his silence on those matters raised by Delany, Douglass is
emerging as a truly important theorist of black culture, especially through
his thought on slave music, which he sees rooted in economic and political
oppression, under continuing African influence while taking on a life of
its own, continually renewing itself at the fount of improvisation. Moreover, in realizing that a great deal of slave music exuded spirituality, he
makes an abolitionist case for the force of moral suasion in the midst of
slaveholders, and an aesthetic case for the sovereign influence of the sacred

in slave music at work and at play, on sacred *and* secular occasions. Just as there is for him no clear line between sadness and joy in slave music, there is for him little division between sacred and secular music under conditions of oppression.

Perhaps Douglass's most lasting theoretical contribution, his reflections on music, contains language that comes as close to suggesting an African *approach* to music as one might find. He speaks of "the natural disposition of the Negro to make a noise in the world" as a factor in the quality and degree of singing heard in slavery. His pioneering comments on slave speech help us appreciate seeming peculiarities of sound associated with slave singing that, though universal in spiritual appeal, sounded "wild."[52] As important as the question of origins is to understanding slave music, Douglass's writings are more important for what they tell us of the artistic *response* of Africans to the tragedy of slavery in North America. He does that with such accuracy of ear, sympathy of feeling, and depth of understanding that he appears to have command of that which is timeless in slave musical art.

NOTES

1 Mungo Park, *Travels in the Interior Districts of Africa* (New York, 1971), pp. 103–4; 295–6. Originally published in 1799. Describing what he saw at the frontier town of Joag in the kingdom of Bambara, from which many Africans were forcibly brought to North America, Park writes, most interestingly, that "to the westward of the town is a small river, on the banks of which the natives raise great plenty of tobacco" (p. 97).

2 Frederick Douglass, *Life and Times of Frederick Douglass* (1881; rpt. New York: Collier Books, 1967), p. 30.

3 Ibid., *Life and Times*, pp. 31–2. There is some controversy about the etymology of "tote." Whereas linguist Morris Goodman thinks that it is a Kimbundu term, the *Oxford English Dictionary* does not assign that etymology to the word. Yet it does not, in fact, offer an alternative explanation. Conversation with Morris Goodman, March 27, 1990.

4 Ibid., *Life and Times*, p. 28.

5 P. Amaury Talbot, *The Peoples of Southern Nigeria* (London: Oxford University Press, 1926), pp. 917–19. In pathfinding research on the colonial period, Peter Wood, in *Black Majority* (New York: W. W. Norton, 1974), Chapter IV, shows how African skill in fishing led slaves to dominate in that area in South Carolina.

6 Douglass writes, in regard to his grandmother's cultivation of sweet potatoes, that "superstition had it if Grandmomma Betty but touches them at planting, they will be sure to grow and flourish. This high reputation was full of advantage to her, and to the children around her. . . . She remembered the hungry little ones around her." Frederick Douglass, *My Bondage and My Freedom* (1855; rpt. Chicago: Johnson Publishing Company, 1970), pp. 27–

8. Of course, it is entirely possible that Betsey Bailey learned fishing or farming, or possibly both skills, from slaves who were not Nigerians, which would militate against the view that she was of Nigerian descent.

7   Douglass, *Life and Times*, p. 50.

8   For a discussion of African values in Virginia as late as the 1850s, see Sterling Stuckey, *Slave Culture: Nationalist Theory and the Foundations of Black America* (New York: Oxford University Press, 1987), pp. 31–6, 39–40.

9   Roscoe Lewis, *The Negro in Virginia* (New York: Arno Press, 1969), p. 90.

10 Park comments, regarding the making of nets: "the small fish were taken in great numbers in hand nets, which the natives weave of cotton, and use with great dexterity." Park, *Travels*, p. 74. Equiano notes an exception to the general rule, writing: "When our women are not employed with the men in tillage, their usual occupation is spinning and weaving cotton, which they afterwards dye, and make into garments." Olaudah Equiano, *The Life of Olaudah Equiano, or Gustavas Vassa, The African, Written by Himself* in Arna Bontemps, *Great Slave Narratives* (1789; rpt. Boston: Beacon Press, 1969), p. 78. For a discussion of the overall dominance of male weavers, see Talbot, *The Peoples of Southern Nigeria*, p. 939, and R. S. Rattray, *Religion and Art in Ashanti* (London: Oxford University Press, 1927), pp. 233–4. For a discussion of white and black mechanics in slavery, see Douglass, *Life and Times*, p. 38.

11 An indication of how difficult it would have been for a white person to acknowledge a slave's ability at agriculture or handicrafts is found in an overseer's attitude toward slaves. William Howard Russell writes of his visit to a Louisiana plantation a few years before emancipation: "The first-place I visited with the overseer was a new sugar-house, which negro carpenters and masons were engaged in erecting. It would have been amusing had not the subject been so grave, to hear the overseer's praises of the intelligence and skill of these workmen, and his boast that they did all the work of skilled labourers on the estate, and then to listen to him, in a few minutes, expatiating on the utter helplessness and ignorance of the black race, their incapacity to do any good, or even to take care of themselves." William Howard Russell, *My Diary North and South* (New York: Harper and Brothers, 1863), p. 104.

12 Douglass, *My Bondage*, p. 59. Although Colonel Lloyd's plantation was in the Maryland interior, there were numerous plantations across the South, similarly situated, that contained large numbers of slaves who spoke English as broken as that heard by Douglass. One such North Carolina plantation, containing hundreds of slaves, was visited by Edward Warren before slavery came to an end. Warren writes that "these antiquated darkeys spoke a sort of gibberish, which was a medley of their original dialect and the English language, and to me was perfectly unintelligible." Edward Warren, *A Doctor's Experiences on Three Continents* (Baltimore: Cushings and Baily, 1885), p. 200. I have no doubt that rich rewards await scholarship in this area. Such scholarship, incidentally, should take into account the language of blacks in the North as well, especially that of runaway slaves. As late as the 1850s, Douglass reports, some spoke a language similar to what he had heard

decades earlier in Maryland. Of Shields Green, a runaway who later joined John Brown at Harper's Ferry, Douglass writes: "He was a man of few words, *and his speech was singularly broken*, but his courage and self-respect made him quite a dignified character." Douglass, *Life and Times*, p. 317 (italics added).

13 Douglass, *Life and Times*, p. 42.

14 Ibid., p. 42.

15 Douglass, *My Bondage*, p. 54. William Channing Gannett wrote of Sea Island blacks: "Orphans are at once adopted by connections, and the sick are well nursed by their friends. The old are treated with great reverence, and often exercise a kind of patriarchal authority. Children are carefully taught 'manners,' and the common address to each other, as well as to the 'buckra people,' is marked by extreme courtesy." William Channing Gannett "The Freedmen at Port Royal," *North American Review*, CI (July 1865), p. 7.

16 Douglass, *My Bondage*, pp. 70, 67, and 54.

17 Quoted in Jean Laude, *African Art of the Dogon* (New York: Viking Press, 1973), p. 13.

18 Laude, *Dogon*, p. 42. Speaking of iron, Park comments regarding the debt of the Moors to West Africans: "They are likewise sufficiently skillful to convert the native iron, which they procure from the Negroes." He states, further, that "Negro slave merchants . . . are called Slatees; who, besides slaves, and the merchandize which they bring for sale to the whites, supply the inhabitants of the maritime districts with native iron." Finally, he makes this crucial statement: "In their early intercourse with Europeans, the article that attracted most notice was iron. Its utility, in forming the instruments of war and husbandry, made it preferable to all others; and iron soon became the measure by which the value of all other commodities was ascertained." Park, *Travels*, pp. 37, 39, 225. Also, see Camara Laye, *The African Child* (1954; rpt. London: Fontana Books, 1959), p. 22.

19 Quoted from "The Political Destiny of the Colored Race" in Sterling Stuckey, ed., *The Ideological Origins of Black Nationalism* (Boston: Beacon Press, 1972), p. 266. Delany's contention that Africans did not have to be trained to work finds striking confirmation in one source. Edward L. Pierce reports that "a tax-commissioner, now at Port Royal, and formerly a resident of South Carolina, told me that a native African belonging to his father, though a faithful man, would perpetually insist on doing his work in his own way, and being asked the threatening question, 'A'n't you going to mind?' would answer, with spirit, 'No, a'n't gwine to!' and the master desisted." Edward L. Pierce, "The Freedmen at Port Royal," *Atlantic Monthly*, XII (September 1863), 301.

20 Douglass, *My Bondage*, pp. 59–60.

21 Delany, "Political Destiny," p. 216. See Peter Woods's discussion of Africans and rice in *Black Majority*, chapter 2.

22 Lewis C. Gray, *History of Agriculture in the Southern United States* (Washington, D.C.: Carnegie Institute, 1933), pp. 183, 232, 888, 893. See Melville and Frances Herskovits, *Dahomey* (New York: Augustin, 1938), pp. 45–6; Talbot, *Southern Nigeria*, p. 939; and Rattray, *Ashanti*, 232–4. Park writes, especially

of the West African town of Pisania: "I observed, likewise, near the towns
. . . cotton and indigo. The former of these articles supplies them with
clothing, and with the latter they dye their cloth of an excellent blue colour."
Of the Jaloffs, he notes that their superstitions, manners, and government
resemble those of the Mandigoes "but excell them in the manufacture of
cotton cloth; spinning the wool to a finer thread, weaving it in a broader
loom, and dying it a better colour." And: "As the Moors purchase all their
clothing from the Negroes, the women are forced to be very economical in
the items of dress. In general, they content themselves with a broad piece
of cotton cloth, which . . . hangs down like a petticoat. . . . The King is
distinguished by the fineness of his dress: which is composed of blue cloth,
brought from Tombuctoo." Park, *Travels*, pp. 14, 24, 233.

23   Douglass, *Life and Times*, p. 61.
24   From Robert F. Thompson's commentary on *A Spiritual Ordering: The Metal
     Arts of Africa*, a documentary film produced by the Sewall Art Gallery, Rice
     University, Houston, Texas, and the African American Institute of New
     York City, 1983.
25   Delany, "Political Destiny," p. 217.
26   W. E. B. Du Bois, *The Souls of Black Folk* (1903; rpt. New York: Kraus-
     Thompson, 1973), pp. 250–64.
27   Frederick Douglass, *Narrative of the Life of Frederick Douglass* (1845; rpt.
     Cambridge: Harvard University Press, 1960), p. 159. Richard Allen was a
     bishop of the African Methodist Episcopal Church, which had branches in
     the South; David Walker, the son of a free mother and a slave father and
     eminent among the abolitionists, lived for approximately forty years in
     Wilmington, North Carolina; and Henry Highland Garnet was a former
     slave in Maryland and a Presbyterian divine. All thought that slaves were
     overwhelmingly heathen. Now we can add the name of Frederick Douglass.
     Those scholars who insist that the slave population was mainly Christian
     face the fact that almost no one in antebellum America thought so – certainly
     not slaves and slaveholders; certainly not prominent black and white religious
     leaders. This is not to deny that a creative minority of slaves gave transcendent
     expression to Christianity, profoundly affecting the faith. Black religious
     leaders, including Douglass, were aware of this. In fact, as we see from the
     following, Douglass's emphasis was about right: "I was not more than
     thirteen years old when I felt the need of God, as a father and protector.
     My religious nature was awakened by the preaching of a white Methodist
     minister, named Hanson. . . . I cannot say that I had a very distinct notion
     of what was required of me; but one thing I knew very well – I was wretched,
     and had no means of making myself otherwise. . . . I consulted a good
     colored man, named Charles Johnson and, in tones of holy affection, he
     told me to pray, and what to pray for. I was, for weeks, a poor, broken-
     hearted mourner, traveling through the darkness and misery of doubts and
     fears. I finally found that change of heart which comes by 'casting all one's
     cares' upon God, and by having faith in Jesus Christ, as the Redeemer,
     Friend, and Savior of those who diligently seek Him. . . . The desire for

knowledge increased, and especially did I want a thorough acquaintance with the contents of the Bible. I have gathered scattered pages from this holy book, from the filthy steet gutters of Baltimore, and washed and dried them, that in the moments of my leisure, I might get a word or two of wisdom from them." Douglass, *My Bondage*, pp. 129–31.

28   Du Bois, *Souls*, pp. 250–64.

29   Douglass, *Narrative*, p. 37.

30   Douglass, *Life and Times*, p. 54.

31   Douglass, *Narrative*, p. 36.

32   James Baldwin, *The Fire Next Time* (New York: Dell, 1962), pp. 60–1.

33   This view, taken from *My Bondage and My Freedom*, does not appear in the *Narrative*. It is obviously the result of Douglass's having pondered the "deeper meaning" of slave music for some time. See *My Bondage*, p. 77. On hearing this section of Douglass read, Melville critic and mathematician Joshua Leslie remarked: "He has seized the dialectic." Conversation with Leslie, November 1989.

34   Italics mine. The reference to jargon in the italicized portion of the sentence is all-important in light of Douglass's earlier remarks, discussed previously, regarding speech so African influenced that he at first could not understand it. His treatment of the subject, in *My Bondage and My Freedom*, is under a heading entitled "Jargon of the Plantation." *My Bondage*, pp. 59, 76.

35   Douglass, *Narrative*, p. 38.

36   Ibid., p. 37. The melancholy feeling experienced on hearing slaves sing was felt by Douglass on hearing, "during the famine of 1845–6," the "wailing notes" of Irish song that "much affected" him. Douglass, *My Bondage*, p. 76.

37   Douglass, *My Bondage*, pp. 340–1.

38   Douglass, ibid., p. 339.

39   Douglass, *Narrative*, p. 38.

40   Douglass, *My Bondage*, p. 81.

41   The lyrics are taken from Paul Robeson's *Songs of My People*, RCA Victor (recorded on Jan. 7, 1926), LM-3292.

42   Douglass, *Life and Times*, p. 54.

43   Sterling A. Brown, Arthur P. David, and Ulysses Lee, eds., *The Negro Caravan* (New York: Dryden Press, 1941), p. 466.

44   Douglass, *Life and Times*, p. 146.

45   Ibid., p. 147.

46   Ibid., p. 147.

47   Ibid., p. 147.

48   Douglass, *My Bondage*, p. 196.

49   Ibid., pp. 196, 197.

50   Douglass, *Life and Times*, pp. 99–100.

51   Eugene Genovese, in *Roll, Jordan, Roll* (New York: Pantheon, 1974), pp. 388–98, and Charles Joyner, in *Down By the Riverside* (Urbana and Chicago: University of Illinois Press, 1984), pp. 70–80, provide important statements on African influences on slave handicrafts. They are among the few historians

to do so to date. See Joshua Leslie and Sterling Stuckey, "The Death of Benito Cereno: A Reading of Herman Melville on Slavery," *The Journal of Negro History* 67 (Winter, 1982), 287–301. For a detailed discussion of the role of elders in slave culture, and of African antecedents to that role, see Chapter I of Stuckey, *Slave Culture.*

52   Douglass, *Life and Times*, p. 54.

From Wheatley to Douglass

The Politics of Displacement

HENRY LOUIS GATES, JR.

===========

*I have never heard, that an ourang-outang has composed an ode.
Among the defenders of slavery, we do not find one half of the
literary merit of Phillis Wheatley or Francis Williams.*
Robert Boucher Nickolls, 1788

*This evening read "Poems of Phillis Wheatly" [sic], an African
slave, who lived at the time of the Revolution. She was a
wonderfully gifted woman, and many of her poems are very
beautiful. Her character and genius afford a striking proof of the
falseness of the assertion made by some that hers is an inferior race*
Charlotte L. Forten, July 28, 1854

*I have thus far seen no book of importance written by a negro
woman and I know of no one among us who can appropriately be
called famous.*
Frederick Douglass, August 27, 1892

Deborah McDowell, in an essay that traces the canonization of Frederick Douglass and his 1845 *Narrative* among contemporary male critics of African-American literature, has persuasively argued that Douglass's election as the "father" of the tradition is central to the construction of an image of the black canon as both male engendered and male dominated.[1] McDowell's analysis raises questions about the nature of the process of canonization and the issue of gender in contemporary literary politics. But it also forces us to wonder about these issues as they relate to Douglass's literary reputation in the nineteenth century among his own contemporaries and about the fate of the eighteenth-century poet Phillis Wheatley among those who would seek to chart a line of formal descent in the African-American literary tradition. For the election of Frederick Douglass as the "representative colored man" of the tradition, an election effected by

47

both black and white abolitionists in the middle of the nineteenth century, led to what we might think of as the cultural erasure of a female progenitor.

The "recovery" of Frederick Douglass by contemporary literary theorists who have analyzed his 1845 *Narrative* extensively, and with satisfying formal results, is one of the most important signs of the shift of African-American Studies away from the dominance of historians, whose work held sway from the beginning of the field in the late 1960s until the late 1970s, when Robert Stepto and Dexter Fisher published *Afro-American Literature: The Reconstruction of Instruction* (1979), a book that included three important readings of Douglass's text. Douglass had long been a favorite of historians because he wrote so much, and with such eloquence, about the sensibilities of the slave. Drawing upon his autobiographies as unproblematic and untroubled sources for their re-creations of the slave's historical past, these historians failed to notice, in their enthusiasm, that he often revised his opinions from text to text, including his representations of his mother and father, among other crucial matters.[2] But historians seized upon Douglass's life and works as subjects and as primary sources for another reason as well: None could conceive a more fitting candidate than Douglass for resurrection from the dark nineteenth-century past as the tradition's very own Representative Man, a title that he enjoyed for much of his professional life.

And so he does today. Over the past decade, Douglass's *Narrative* has received a considerable amount of critical attention, in part because it lends itself so readily to contemporary modes of analysis. In the process, as McDowell shows so well, such readings as those by Robert Stepto, William Andrews, Robert O'Meally, Houston Baker, Peter Walker, and James Olney, among others, have given Douglass's *Narrative* pride of place in the canon.

At whose expense, we must wonder? But my concern in this essay is not with the contemporary dynamics of canon formation but with a specific movement in the nineteenth-century deployment of exemplary black figures, specifically within the abolitionist movement. The phenomenon I wish to examine – largely through the pages of the abolitionist press, white and black – is that the rise of Frederick Douglass as a standard bearer of Negro creativity and cultivation was marked by the simultaneous eclipse of the previously favored exemplar, Phillis Wheatley.

In 1866, in an essay entitled "What's to Be Done with the Negroes," George Fitzhugh makes a remark *en passant* that helps us understand the sheer presence that Douglass had, by that time, come to have in American letters as the metaphorical sign of the intellectual potential of the African-American. "We are not perfectionists, like the northern people," Fitzhugh writes, "and should not expect or *try* to make Solomons or even Frederick Douglasses of the negroes."[3] Douglass's displacement of Phillis Wheatley as the icon of African genius – the role that Wheatley had played in virtually every discourse on the African's "innate intellect" and "perfectibility" from the publication of her *Poems* in 1773 until the middle of the next century – would be reflected in the literary criticism of the century to come.

Between 1773 and the middle of the nineteenth century, Phillis Wheatley virtually *was* the canon of black American letters. What's more, virtually all commentators thought so, and were proud of that fact. Her poems and letters, her book and books about her life, were reprinted widely, reviewed prominently, and praised roundly as the work of the founding "genius" of African-American letters. Nowhere was she held in higher esteem than within abolitionist circles, as a survey of the abolitionist press between 1827 and 1860 would suggest.[4]

In 1827, *Freedom's Journal*, the first black periodical, published a biographical account and excerpts from two of her poems, later listing her as one of the world's truly outstanding persons of African descent; on November 2, a letter to Samuel Cornish, one of the *Journal's* editors, described Wheatley as "our poetess" and as the "African genius." A year later, Abigail Mott's *Sketches and Interesting Anecdotes of Persons of Colour* provided a biographical account of Wheatley and reprinted part of one of her poems. Samuel Kettell, in his pioneering anthology, *Specimens of American Poetry with Critical and Biographical Notices* (three volumes, 1829), listed three of Wheatley's poems, and William Allen, in *An American Biographical and Historical Dictionary Containing an Account of the Lives, Characters, and Writings of the Most Eminent Persons in North America* (1832), pointed to her poem "On Imagination" as a work about which "Africa may boast."

William Lloyd Garrison's *Liberator* was perhaps most effective in establishing Wheatley's preeminence. Between February 4 and December 22, 1832, Garrison reprinted no fewer than thirty-seven of Wheatley's poems, including the entire text of her 1773 volume. That same year, Lydia Maria Child referred quite favorably to her place among eighteenth-century poets in *An Appeal in Favour of That Class of Americans Called Africans*, and Elizabeth Haskins, in *The Literary Remains of Joseph Ladd*, called her poems "ingenious." *Freedom's Journal*, on February 11 and 18, reprinted two more of her poems.

A year later, in 1833, Jared Sparks, writing in *The Writings of George Washington*, declared that Wheatley's poems "exhibit the most favorable evidence on record of the capacity of the African's intellect for improvement." In 1834 two *Memoirs* about Wheatley, by Margaretta Matilda Odell and by Benjamin Bussye Thatcher, appeared, the latter with a new edition of her 1773 *Poems*. These memoirs, both published in Boston, attracted a great deal of critical attention, including notices and essays on Wheatley in *New England Magazine*, the *Christian Examiner and General Review* (a five-page critical essay by William J. Snelling), and a ten-page essay entitled "African Anecdotes" published in *Knickerbocker Magazine or New York Monthly Magazine*. Between August 23 and December 13, *The Liberator* printed advertisements for Wheatley's book twelve times, offering the book for sale "at the New England Anti-Slavery Society, No. 46 Washington Street, Boston," for fifty cents.

In 1835, two more editions of Wheatley's poems were published, one including Thatcher's *Memoir*, the other including Odell's. Between January 10 and June 20, *The Liberator* again reprinted ads for her book eleven more times. In October of that year, the *Athenaeum* printed an essay about the "singular taste for poetry" displayed by this "sable devotee of the muses."

In 1836, the *Anti-Slavery Record* printed a two-page essay on Phillis Wheatley, and Garrison's *Liberator* printed nine advertisements for her book, now priced at twenty-five cents, between July 4 and September 24. On October 27, 1837, the *Liberator* listed the poems and both *Memoirs* for sale, urging that it "will be well to have [the poems] always at hand, that we may have some conception of the amount of genius which slavery is murdering" (Robinson, 56). In 1838, Issac Knapp of Boston published the third edition of the Wheatley–Odell *Memoir and Poems*. By the time Frederick Douglass published his *Narrative* in 1845, Wheatley occupied a place in African–American letters that would have appeared to be unassailable and permanent, even to the most casual observer. And yet, after its publication, Wheatley disappeared almost entirely from the abolitionist press.

We must not exaggerate the eclipse. Black writers were still quick to point to Wheatley's achievements or draw upon her work as an influence, as Ann Plato did in one of the poems printed in her *Essays* (1844), in which she "appropriated a half dozen lines from one of Wheatley's poems," according to William Robinson. R. S. Lewis's *Light and Truth* (1844) judged Wheatley favorably and reprinted long excerpts from two of her works. Armistead Wilson, in *A Tribute for the Negro* (1848), cited the opinion of the *Edinburgh Journal* in arguing that Wheatley's work "shows a very considerable reach of thought, and no mean power of expression." He also reprinted ten excerpts of her poems. William Allen, in *Wheatley, Banneker, and Horton* (1849), devoted a third of this book to Wheatley's place in the canon, and Martin R. Delany, in *The Condition, Elevation, Emigration, and Destiny of the Colored People of the United States, Politically Considered* (1854), devoted twelve pages to Wheatley and praised her as "one of the brightest ornaments among the American literati." William Wells Brown, writing in *The Black Man, His Antecedents, His Genius, and*

His Achievements (1865), also praised Wheatley, repeating his opinions in *The Rising Son, The Antecedents and Achievements of the Colored Race*, published in 1874. Finally, an anonymous essay published in *The Anglo-African Magazine* in 1859, "Afro-American Picture Gallery," argued strongly for Wheatley's special place in the literary tradition.

In addition to these scattered references to Wheatley by black chroniclers and commentators, there were allusions to her in Caroline May's *The American Female Poets* (1848), Rufus W. Griswold's *The Female Poets of America* (1849), and Evert and George Duyckinck's *Cyclopedia of American Literature* (two volumes, 1856), the last declaring that Wheatley's translation from Ovid's *Metamorphoses* "exceeded her Roman model."

Nevertheless, the downturn in Wheatley's fortunes in abolitionist circles was dramatic. Between 1845 and 1860, for example, only the *Anglo-African*, among all of the abolitionist and black periodical publications, discussed Wheatley and her place in the history of black letters. By the end of the nineteenth century, her displacement was nearly complete. When the editor of an anthology of biographies entitled *Notable Negro Women* wrote to Douglass asking for the names of famous black women authors, Douglass wrote back, scornfully, to say that he could think of none, and he could think of none because there were none! He also chastised his correspondent for claiming too much for black women writers and thereby engendering the contempt of white Americans who knew better:

Mr. M. A. Major

Cedar Hill, D.C., August 26, 1892

Dear Sir:

We have many estimable women of our variety but not many famous ones. It is not well to claim too much for ourselves before the public. Such extravagance invites contempt rather than approval. I have thus far seen no book of importance written by a negro woman and I know of no one among us who can appropriately be called famous.

This is in no way a disparagement of the women of our race. We stand too near a former condition to have any famous work in science, art, or literature, expected of us. It is not well to ship the paddle wheels before we have steam to move them. You will therefore pardon me if I do not find it consistent to enlarge the list of famous negro women. Many of the names you have are those of admirable persons, cultivated, refined and ladylike. But it does not follow that they are famous. Let us be true and use language truthfully.

Respectfully yours

Frederick Douglass[5]

Douglass apparently had forgotten a letter he had written to Harriet Tubman, in which he said that "the midnight sky and the silent stars have been the witnesses of your devotion to freedom" (August 29, 1868).

What had happened in the second half of the nineteenth century, of course, was Douglass's ascent as "representative man of the negro race," whose works were widely thought to be pinnacles of African-American intellection. Douglass's prestige supplanted Wheatley's, and the critical establishment, even to this day, has followed suit. But what were the politics of this displacement?

The American abolitionists had searched desperately for an exemplary African with whom to refute the claims of racists and proponents of slavery that the African was "by nature" fit to be nothing but a slave. Wheatley had served this purpose admirably, as evidenced by her pervasive presence in the *Liberator* in the 1830s. (For a brief period, as we shall see, George Moses Horton was prominent as well.) It is clear enough, I think, why a black author was needed in the discourse of abolition. Since the Enlightenment, the index of any race's "humanity" was its possession of reason, which was to be known through its representation in writing, particularly writing in its more exalted or "literary" forms. Writing of this sort was the visible sign of reason. Within abolitionist and antislavery discourses between 1750 and 1825, the citation of black written arts was fundamental to attempts to refute claims of the African's "innate inferiority." And Phillis Wheatley, more than anyone else, was called upon as evidence that the African's "place in nature," in the "great chain of being," was with human beings rather than with apes.

By 1831, when the weekly abolitionist press was launched with the publication of *The Liberator*, the relation of poetry to the abolitionist movement had become a profoundly different matter than it had been in the previous century. What this relation between the arts and politics became in such a clear form after 1831 can perhaps be suggested by an early essay in *The African Repository* and the curious case of George Moses Horton's campaign for freedom.

In its first issue, which appeared in 1825, a featured essay in *The African Repository* attacked those who thought the African to be "a distinct order of beings; the connecting link between men and monkies." The accounts of the splendid "Ethiopian" and "Cushite" civilizations of the ancient black world refuted this notion: "at a time when the rest of the world was in a state of barbarism, the Ethiopian family [was] exhibiting prodigies of human genius." Even the Egyptians, who had "originated the arts and sciences," were said to be black. A second essay suggested that contemporary Africans bore similar capacities, especially the "Soosoo" tribe. Finally, a third essay, called "Specimens of African Genius," reprinted

a vivid account of the court of "King Yaradee, a West African monarch."[6]
What is odd about these essays is that *The African Repository* was an organ
of the American Colonization Society, which meant to repatriate blacks
to Africa *en masse*.[7] As Alexander Hill Everett, in an address before the
Massachusetts Colonization Society, would remark in 1833, the black
Egyptians cited by Herodotus alone disproved "a miserable heresy": that
the African slave was "incapable of improvement and civilization, and
condemned by the vice of his physical conformation to vegetate forever
in a state of hopeless barbarism." "So much," Everett concluded, "for
the supposed inferiority of the colored race, and their incapacity to make
any progress in civilization and improvement."[8] As George M. Fredrickson
concluded, this tendency of the colonizationists to portray "African genius"
not only attested to the success of the early antislavery writers' use of
Wheatley and her fellows but also stemmed from the implicit acceptance
of a radical environmentalist posture.[9] Nevertheless, its use was an anomaly:
"This tendency of colonizationists to celebrate basic Negro character
seemed to their critics to be hopelessly at odds with their image of the
miserable, degraded state of the American free blacks and their desire
for a total separation of the races."[10]

Nevertheless, by 1828, *The African Repository* was publishing statements
on innate African inferiority that are more in line with the idea of re-
colonization:

> In every part of the United States, there is a broad and impassible
> [sic] line of demarcation between every man who has one drop of
> African blood in his veins and every other class in the community.
> The habits, feelings, all the prejudices of society – prejudices which
> neither refinement, nor argument, nor education, nor religion itself
> can subdue – mark the people of colour, whether bond or free, as
> the subjects of a degradation inevitable and incurable. The African
> in this country belongs by birth to the lowest station in society;
> and from that station he can never rise, be his talent, his enterprise,
> his virtues what they may.[11]

This statement that "a degradation inevitable and incurable," beyond
individual literary or scientific talent, fit the African to be a slave sounds
perilously similar to Thomas Jefferson's related remarks sent in his letter
to the Abbe Gregoire after reading his *Enquiry*. It is almost as if the
eighteenth century's campaign to pass antislavery laws with legal briefs
built around Wheatley and Ignatius Sancho had forced proslavery writers
to reformulate their rationale for the African's enslavement.

Undaunted, however, the movement that, after William Lloyd Garrison
founded *The Liberator* in 1831, became the abolition movement continued
to draw upon the sublimity of the black mind by reprinting and reviewing

Wheatley's work and by encouraging, editing, and sometimes writing that autobiographical genre called "slave narratives." But these direct usages of the slave's literacy were first employed in a futile attempt to secure the freedom of the "slave poet" George Moses Horton.

Founded in 1827, *Freedom's Journal*, an antislavery weekly, was the first American periodical published by blacks. Its editorial purpose, as outlined by its senior editor, Samuel E. Cornish, was to secure for the slaves the freedom and rights granted to all American citizens: "We are Americans. Many would rob us of the endeared name of 'Americans,' a description more emphatically belonging to us, than to five-sixths of this nation, and one that we will never yield."[12] From its earliest issues, *Freedom's Journal* devoted front-page columns to literary criticism, consisting largely of long biographical summaries of eighteenth-century black poets followed by short extracts of their published works. Frequently "reviewed" authors include Phillis Wheatley,[13] Ignatius Sancho,[14] Olaudah Equiano,[15] Ottobah Cuagono,[16] Cesar,[17] and especially George Moses Horton.[18] A typical review is that of Phillis Wheatley, published in the issue for November 12, 1827. Acknowledging that from the "want of education has also arisen the idea of 'African inferiority' among many, who will not take the trouble to inquire into the cause," the editor then printed a two-column account of Phillis Wheatley, citing her as a hero of the race:

> Boston is the place where that sweet poetess of nature, Phillis Wheat-ley, first tuned her lyre under the inspiration of the Muses, putting to shame the illiberal expressions of the advocates of slavery in all parts of the globe. So incredible were the public concerning the genuineness of poems, that they are ushered into the world with the signature of the Governor, Lieutenant-Governor, and other distinguished men of Massachusetts affixed to them. O Liberality, thou art not certainly a being of this lower sphere! for why should the natural powers of man be rated by the fairness of his complexion?[19]

Horton[20] was discussed so frequently in *Freedom's Journal* because that newspaper led a campaign to have the "slave poet" freed. A front-page story was printed in the August 8, 1828, edition. It described him as "an extraordinary young slave . . . who has astonished all who have witnessed his poetic talent." Three weeks later, on August 29, a story announced that "it is with pleasure we inform our readers that measures are about to be taken to effect the emancipation of this interesting young man." This notice introduced a letter from "a North Carolina correspondent" who wrote that "a philanthropic gentleman of this country being on a visit to Chapel Hill as one of the members of the Board for an annual visitation at the college" encountered Horton's poetical genius and "since that time has undertaken the unpopular task of casting about to see if George's liberation can be effected." The correspondent had written to Horton's master, who "has replied that he is not in circumstances to do without the manual labor of the young man, as he is no less a farmer than a poet, but towards the close of the year he might be induced to take a fair price for him." The correspondent then concluded with an appeal for $400 or $500:

> Situated as you are, at a distance from our scenes of action you might suppose in such an extent of territory as is embraced in N. Carolina, a sum like 4 or $500 might soon be gathered – and so it might, but for any other purpose sooner than the emancipation of a fellow human being – it is contrary to the policy of this country, and the few philanthropists whose hands act with their hearts, must despair of effecting this desirable object, without such auxiliaries as we fancy your caste to be.[21]

The September 5 edition printed a poem called "Gratitude" by Horton, "dictated to the Gentleman who takes so kind an interest in his behalf." Two stanzas read:

> Philanthropy, thou feeling dove,
> Whose voice can sound the vassal free,
> Upon thy wings of humane love
> I'll fly to liberty.

> Thus may the feeling heart rejoice,
> And cause me to rejoice with thee,
> And triumph with a cheerful voice,
> The voice of liberty.[22]

On September 12, the appeal took a more urgent tack: "*Something must be done – George M. Horton must be liberated from the state of bondage.* Were each person of colour in this city [New York] to give but one penny, there would be no danger about obtaining his liberty." On October 3, an article announced:

> We feel proud in announcing the name of David C. Walker of Boston, Mass., as a subscriber to the fund to be raised for the purchase of George M. Horton, of North Carolina . . . appeals to the humane and charitable have become, we are well aware, so frequent of late, that many persons whose means are small, are at a stand to know which are the most deserving of their charity. As the time is drawing near when efforts will be made by the gentleman who has benevolently come forward to purchase him, we hope all who feel disposed to assist in this case of Christian Philanthropy,

will send us their names, in order that the expectations which have
been raised by our correspondent of North Carolina, may not be
disappointed.[23]

Nothing came of the *Journal*'s campaign. Twenty years later, Horton
addressed a college audience at Chapel Hill and completed the story:

> [Governor] John Owen of North Carolina made an extraordinary
> proposition [to his master, James Horton, of Chatham County,
> North Carolina] which was refused with a frown of disdain. The
> proposition was to pay $100 more than any person of sound judgment
> should say I was worth. To this my master would not accede. Such
> was the miscarriage of the proposition from the feeling Governor
> of a man who had no regard for liberty, science or genius. Not
> even a spark of generosity then pervaded his iron heart.[24]

Undaunted, Horton, with the assistance of Joseph Gales, editor of the
Raleigh *Register* and regional secretary of the American Colonization
Society, which promoted repatriation of blacks to Liberia, decided to
publish a volume of poetry, the proceeds of which would secure his
freedom. In 1829, with twenty-two poems and twenty-one pages, the
appropriately entitled *The Hope of Liberty* was published.[25] It was the first
volume of poetry published in English by a black person in fifty-six
years, since Phillis Wheatley's *Poems* appeared in 1773.

What is of interest here is the "Explanation" that prefaces the volume.
In part, it explains the circumstances surrounding the publication of *The
Hope of Liberty*:

> Many persons have now become much interested in the promotion
> [of Horton's] prospects, some of whom are elevated in office and
> literary attainments. They are solicitous that efforts at length be
> made to obtain by subscription, a sum sufficient for his emancipation,
> upon the condition of his going in the vessel which shall first af-
> terwards sail for Liberia. It is his earnest and only wish to become
> a member of that Colony, to enjoy its privileges, and apply his
> industry and mental abilities to the promotion of its prospects and
> his own. It is upon these terms alone, that the efforts of those who
> befriend his views are intended to have a final effect.[26]

Noting that "to put to trial the plan here urged in his behalf, the paper
now exhibited is published," the publishers add that the size of the volume
has been kept small, so that "expense will thus be avoided, and the money
better employed in enlarging the sum applicable for his emancipation."[27]
After printing his master's name and address, the "Explanation" concludes:

> Come, melting Pity, from afar,
> And break this vast enormous bar,
>   Between a wretch and thee;
> Purchase a few short days of time,
> And bid a Vassal soar sublime,
>   On wings of Liberty.[28]

With *The Hope of Liberty*, the poetry of the black slave has indeed become a *commodity*, to be purchased to secure the "freedom" of material "property." Even more ironically, the idea that "the arts" could secure for the African an elevated place on the great chain of being has come to be reified. After 1831, Horton, and especially the authors of the slave narratives, would use literacy to attempt to secure their literal freedom. Only as the crassest material echoes do the uses to which Beattie, Blumenbach, and the Abbe Gregoire put the African's arts – to posit for the African a place in the human family – survive. For, from 1831 at least to 1925, progressively more urgent and compelling formulations would put the matter of the Afro-American's freedom in ever more markedly reified terms. Perhaps because of his poetry, the African could no longer be mistaken for an ape; but despite his poetry, he or she was not yet free.

After Horton's usefulness abated, the abolitionists were able, if only briefly, to erect the figure of James Williams as their resplendent instance of African intellection.

Let us consider the strange case of James Williams, a black ex-slave who, but for an accident of history, might very well occupy the place in African-American letters that Douglass has occupied since the middle of the nineteenth century. Williams was an American slave, as the subtitle of his narrative tells us, "who was for several years a driver on a cotton plantation in Alabama." He supposedly escaped to the North, sought out members of the Anti-Slavery Society, and told an incredibly well-structured story of the brutal treatment of the slaves in the South and of his own miraculous escape, forging documents using the literary training that he had "stolen," as Frederick Douglass would write just seven years later. So compelling, so gripping, so *useful* was his tale that the abolitionists decided to publish it and distribute it widely, sending copies to every state and to every congressman. Williams's impact upon the abolitionists was amazing. He arrived in New York on New Year's Day in 1838. By January 24, he had dictated his complete narrative to John Greenleaf Whittier. By February 15, it was in print and was being serialized in the *Anti-Slavery Examiner*. Even before the book appeared, rumors had spread in New York that slave catchers were on his heels, so his new friends shipped him off to Liverpool, England, where he apparently was never heard from again.

In the meantime, back in the States, all hell was about to break loose.
Here is one account of it:

> In an informing article prepared for the New York *Nation* and
> published in the issue of April 29, 1897, Mr. P. K. Foley has recounted
> the controversy as to the trustworthiness of the narrative, which
> followed soon after the publication of the book. The trial so clearly
> blazed by Mr. Foley has been followed here and supplemented by
> information derived from sources to which he did not have ready
> access at the time.
> The issue of the *Emancipator* for January 25, 1838, contained the
> first announcement of the proposed publication of "James Williams,"
> and that of February 15 listed it as "recently published." In the
> *Emancipator* for April 19 appeared an extract from the *Alabama
> Beacon* of March 29, denouncing the narrative as a "foul fester of
> falsehood," and appended to this was an editorial rejoinder, containing
> the reference to Whittier quoted above. In the issue of August 16
> it was announced that the sale of the book had been discontinued
> pending the examination of certain data furnished by the *Beacon*.
> The sale seems to have been resumed later, as evidenced by references
> in the *Emancipator* of September 20 and elsewhere. The *Emancipator*
> for August 30 devoted ten columns to the controversy under the
> heading "*Alabama Beacon* versus James Williams"; the article was
> prepared by James G. Birney and Lewis Tappan and came to no
> final conclusion. A further rejoinder appeared in the *Emancipator* of
> September 20, followed by this brief note, the statement therein
> quoted being from the *Pennsylvania Freeman* of September 13, of
> which Whittier was then the editor:
>> Credibility of James Williams. Friend Whittier, who is not over
>> credulous, and is certainly honest, gives his present judgment of
>> the matter in these terms: "We have examined the Southern
>> testimony; and while we candidly admit that it has created doubt
>> in our mind of the accuracy in some minute particulars, of a
>> statement made by the fugitive to several gentlemen in this state
>> and in New York (and which was written down from his lips
>> by ourself) we are still disposed to give credit in the main to his
>> narrative. . . . Our cause needs no support of a doubtful character."
> The final word appeared in the *Emancipator* of October 25, headed
> "Statement authorized by the Executive Committee," and concluded
> "that the statements in the Narrative, so far as they are cited above,
> and contradicted by the writers of the letters, are wholly false, and
> therefore they [the members of the committee] cannot with propriety
> ask for the confidence of the community in any of the statements

contained in the Narrative." This "statement" ends with the resolution, "That . . . the Publishing Agent be directed to discontinue
the sale of the work." (Whittier Bibliography, 33–4)

Williams's *Narrative*, it seems, was not a slave narrative; it was a fiction, a product, one commentator put it, "purely of the Negro imagination,"
as probably were the slave catchers who were supposedly in hot pursuit,
and whose purported existence earned for Williams a free trip to England,
and a new life.*

Williams's text bears an uncanny direct relation, formally, to Douglass's.
In ways too numerous to detail here, Williams's text (widely distributed)
established what our generation of readers thinks of as the repeated structure
of the slave narrative. Had his narrative been true, Williams would most
likely have been used by the abolitionists to supplant Phillis Wheatley as
the founder of the tradition. At the very least, Douglass would have
found it necessary to share the great platform of fame with Williams,
rather than appearing to come out of nowhere onto the stage of African-
American letters.

Williams had sorely embarrassed the American abolitionist movement.
He was widely touted as prima facie proof of the horrors of slavery, one
who was both object and subject, or one who had traversed that terrible
discursive terrain from object to subject and could be a witness to that
journey with his own lips or, better yet, with his own pen. As *The
Emancipator* put the matter in its August 30, 1838, number, Williams's
Narrative "has excited a great deal of interest everywhere – not so much
because it revealed atrocities unparalleled by others which were already
known of the system of slavery, but because it brought many such
together, and connected them in the form of a regular narrative, in which
the narrator himself was the principal actor, and to most of the particulars
of which he could himself testify." Here we can see the rationale for the
valorization of *narrative* over poetry, which Wheatley's work had represented. This linear, straightforward, "plain and unvarnished tale" (frequently cited in references to Douglass's *Narrative* a few years later)
achieved greater primacy during the 1830s than it had ever had before,

---

* And what, ultimately, are we to do with Williams and his text? What can we
do with a work that purports to be fact, or history, or autobiography, but that –
alas – is merely a work "purely of the Negro imagination"? I submit that we
reclaim this wonderful lost text from abolitionist authentication, shift it from
the bibliographical category of fraudulent or dubious slave narratives, and give
it its rightful place as the first *novel* in the African-American tradition. For what
else can a fictionalized slave narrative be?

in part because of the enhanced role of newsprint and its linear nature. What's more, "an authentic narrative of this slave – now a *freeman* – self-emancipated," as an *Emancipator* ad for James Williams's *Narrative* put it (January 25, 1838), was thought to be of vastly more worth than the elegiac poems of an eighteenth-century black woman. "We venture to say," the *Emancipator* ad continued, that "no work more interesting has been published, since the beginning of the Anti-Slavery discussion. It will be a narrative of facts," the ad concluded, "illustrating the cruelties and blasphemies connected with slavery." Embarrassed by Williams's fiction, the abolitionists urgently needed a black male replacement, one as persuasive and articulate as Williams had been, but one whose story could stand and whose authenticity was unquestionable, and one who could *write*. Into the void left by James Williams stepped Frederick Douglass, whose "representative" tale would render Phillis Wheatley's voice mute and redundant, a pale female shadow in the face of the representative "manliness" of Frederick Douglass.

The embarrassment that Williams's novel had caused the abolitionist movement led, as we might expect, to even more demands for verisimilitude among the slave narrators, and, of course, to the need for a suitable replacement figure – someone who had been there, who was both trustworthy and eloquent, someone who was "presentable" in the most public way. As John W. Blassingame's first volume of *The Frederick Douglass Papers* reveals, Frederick Douglass soon emerged as the most eligible substitute for Williams.[29] Beginning with a speech in October 1841 ("I Have Come to Tell You Something About Slavery," delivered in Lynn, Massachusetts), Douglass became a regular speaker on the abolition circuit, delivering over 150 major speeches between 1839 and the publication in May 1845 of his *Narrative*. (Between 1841 and 1845, he was a paid lecturer for the Massachusetts Anti-Slavery Society.) Douglass was able, through his speeches, to hone his oratorical skills and to recall and shape the facts of his enslavement into a compelling narrative of his slave life. Public deliveries of this story also gave the defenders of slavery an opportunity to emerge early on, since their views were widely reported, summarized, and reprinted in the press. As Blassingame reports, Douglass was one of the very few slaves who turned to the printed word to authenticate his own *oral* testimony about his slave experience:

> By 1844, Douglass's oratorical skills and thoughtful analyses caused many observers to doubt him; some claimed he had never been inside the peculiar institution. Skepticism increased as Douglass refused to divulge his slave name or verifiable facts about his slave past for fear he would be kidnapped and returned to bondage. Since

Douglass was unwilling to compromise his usefulness as a reform lecturer, he chose to tell the story of his bondage in autobiography, *Narrative of the Life of Frederick Douglass*. Published in 1845, *Narrative* effectively stilled the debate over Douglass's authenticity, but it increased fears that he would be recaptured and returned to the Eastern Shore of Maryland. This anxiety sent Douglass to Great Britain and initiated another phase of his speaking career.[30]

But his oral testimony also authenticated his *Narrative*. At least one reviewer admitted as much. He wrote, "We should have doubted the practicability of such a book being produced by a poor runaway slave, had it not been that we are assured that his efforts as a public speaker are quite equal to what he has here shown himself to be and a writer," both exemplary of "the highest intellectual culture" (*Anti-Slavery Bugle*, August 22, 1834, 4).

Douglass was the perfect substitute for Williams as the object-become-subject. As Wendell Phillips put the matter in a letter, he was "the most remarkable and by far the ablest colored *man* we have ever had here. Language, taste, fancy eloquence, vigor of thought, good sound common sense – *manliness* are all his."[31]

The *Narrative* was widely reviewed and just as widely praised. Reviewers pointed to its capacity to "partake of the sublime and the pathetic" and to "thrill," as *The Liberator* did on May 30, 1845 (1). Other reviews, such as those printed in *The Liberty Press* (June 28, 1845, 136), *Chambers Edinburgh Journal* (January 24, 1846, 56–9), and *Littels's Living Age* (April 4, 1846, 47–50), either reprint long extracts from the *Narrative* itself or else give the reader close summaries. Just as it had done for Phillis Wheatley, *The Liberator* printed notices of the publication of new editions, complete with prices and sales totals.[32] But *The Liberator* did much more.

A review in the May 30, 1845, number of *The Liberator* (reprinted from the *Lynn Pioneer*) declared that Douglass's book was "the most thrilling work which the American press ever issued – *and the most important*." While possessing "burning eloquence," the *Narrative* was "yet simple and unimpassioned. Its eloquence is the eloquence of truth, and so is as simple and touching as the impulses of childhood." As for its status as what we think of as "canonical" literature, the reviewer claimed that "there are passages in it that would brighten the reputation of any living author, – while the book, as a whole, judged as a mere work of art would widen the fame of Bunyan or DeFoe" (86). The *Boston Transcript* similarly called the *Narrative* "an extraordinary performance" (reprinted in *The Liberator*, June 6, 1845, 90). Douglass's elevation, as an author equal to the greatest authors of his time and before, was immediate.

"The feelings and the adventures that have been so affecting through the living voice," one commentator said of Douglass, "are [no] less so from the printed page" (*Liberator*, June 20, 1845, 97, reprinted from the

New York Tribune). Douglass's apprenticeship as a speaker had enabled him to shape an eloquent narrative, to write and find a voice.

It was this spoken and written "voice" that the abolitionists wanted to exploit, as the audible and visible signs of *reason*, to connect the members of the slave community to the whole of the human family. Douglass's *Narrative* at once became tied to the larger discourse on race that the works of his black literary antecedents had been linked to as well, at least since Phillis Wheatley. "It is an excellent piece of writing," the *Tribune* review declared, "and on that score to be prized as a specimen of the powers of the black race, which prejudice persists in disputing." Relating Douglass's book to the writings of Alexander Dumas and a "quadroon" author from New Orleans named Soulie, the reviewer argued for the potential of the African "element" to merge with the European "element" and produce "genius":

> Two wise and candid thinkers, – the Scotchman, Kinmet, prematurely lost to this country, of which he was so faithful and generous a student, and the late Dr. Channing, – both thought that the African race had in them a peculiar element, which, if it could be assimilated with those imported among us from Europe, would give to genius a development, and to the energies of character a balance and harmony beyond what has been seen heretofore in the history of the world. Such an element is indicated in their lowest estate by a talent for melody, a ready skill at imitation and adaptation, an almost indestructible elasticity of nature. It is to be remarked in the writings both of Soulie and Dumas, full of faults but glowing with plastic life, and fertile in invention. The same torrid energy and saccharine fulness may be felt in the writings of this Douglass, though his life being one of action or resistance, was less favorable to such powers than one of a more joyous flow might have been.[33]

Whereas France had Soulie and Dumas, and Russia had Pushkin, America now would have Douglass, and no longer Wheatley, a Douglass who, as William Lloyd Garrison put it in the very first review of the *Narrative* (May 9, 1845, 75), "in physical proportion and stature commanding and exact – in intellect richly endowed – in natural eloquence a prodigy – in soul manifestly 'created but a little lower than the angels' – yet a slave, ay, a fugitive slave," a Douglass who "excels in pathos, wit, comparison, imitation, strength of reasoning, and fluency of language. There is in him that union of head and heart, which is indispensable to an enlightenment of the heads and a winning of the hearts of others." A Douglass whose apostrophe to the sails on Chesapeake Bay inspired Garrison to say, "Who can read that passage, and be insensible to its pathos and humanity? Compressed into it is a whole Alexandrian library of thought, feeling and sentiment – all that can, all that need be urged, in the form of expostulation, entreaty, rebuke, against that crime of crimes – making man the property of his fellow man! O, how accursed is that system, which entombs the godlike mind of man, defaces the divine image, reduces those who by creation were crowned with glory and honor to a level with four-footed beasts, and exalts the dealer in human flesh above all that is called God!" It is Douglass who possessed, among all of the slaves, "true manliness of character," and whose book would prove to be "a lifting of the veil," as Garrison put it just two weeks later (*The Liberator*, May 23, 1845, 82). The lifting of the veil from the eyes of a blind female Justice, exposing the storehouse of African knowledge figured in a lost Alexandrian library, would be achieved by the manly narrative text of Frederick Douglass rather than the elegiac verse of Phillis Wheatley.

NOTES

1   Deborah McDowell, "In the First Place: Making Frederick Douglass and the Afro-American Tradition," in William Andrews, ed., *Critical Essays on Frederick Douglass* (Boston: G. K. Hall, 1991).

2   See my "Frederick Douglass and the Language of the Self," in *Figures in Black: Words, Signs, and the "Racial" Self* (New York: Oxford University Press, 1987), pp. 98–125.

3   Fitzhigh's essay appeared in *DeBow's Magazine* in 1866.

4   The listings of references to Wheatley that follow are taken from William H. Robinson, *Phillis Wheatley: A Bio-Bibliography* (Boston: G. K. Hall, 1981). See especially pp. 36, 57, and 62. References listed in the black press can be found in *Black Periodical Literature*, edited by Henry Louis Gates, Jr. (Alexandria, Va.: Chadwyck-Healey Press, 1989).

5   Douglass's letter is reprinted in Dorothy Sterling, *We Are Your Sisters: Black Women in the Nineteenth Century* (New York: W. W. Norton, 1984), p. 436. Deborah McDowell directed me to this reference.

6   *African Repository* I (March 1825), 7–12, 19–21, 30–2.

7   See P. J. Staudenraus, *The African Colonization Movement, 1816–1865* (New York: Columbia University Press, 1961), passim. See also George M. Fredrickson, *The Black Image in the White Mind: The Debate on Afro-American Character and Destiny, 1817–1914* (New York: Harper & Row, 1972), pp. 1–43.

8   Quoted in Samuel J. May, *The Right of the Colored People to Education Vindicated* (Brooklyn: 1833), pp. 19–20.

9   See Fredrickson, *Black Image*, pp. 13–17.

10 Ibid., p. 15.

11 *African Repository* IV (June 1828), 118.

12 Samuel E. Cornish, cited in Bella Gross, *Clarion Call: The History and Development of the Negro People's Convention Movement in the United States from*

1817 to 1840 (New York: Privately printed, 1947), p. 8. Cf. "Our Own Concerns," *Freedom's Journal*, December 21, 1827.

13   *Freedom's Journal*, May 18, 1827, p. 38, col. 1; November 2, 1827, p. 135, col. 2.

14   Ibid., May 18, 1827, p. 38, cols. 1–2.

15   Ibid., May 18, 1827, p. 38, col. 1.

16   Ibid., May 18, 1827, p. 38, col. 1; November 21, 1828, p. 276, cols. 2–3.

17   Ibid., May 18, 1827, p. 38, col. 1.

18   Ibid., August 8, 1828, p. 153, cols. 2–3; August 29, 1828, p. 179, cols. 2–3; September 12, 1828, p. 194, col. 3; p. 195, col. 4; and October 3, 1828, p. 218, col. 3.

19   Ibid., November 12, 1827.

20   Horton has attracted wide critical attention. Often he is compared with Burns. See Caroline Lee Hentz, *Lovell's Folly* (New York: Hubbard & Edwards, 1833), pp. 259–60. For a perceptive discussion of these critical sources, see Merle A. Richmond, *Bid the Vassal Soar: Interpretive Essays on the Life and Poetry of Phillis Wheatley and George Moses Horton* (Washington, D.C.: Howard University Press, 1974), pp. 81–199.

21   *Freedom's Journal*, August 28, 1828.

22   George Moses Horton, "Gratitude," ibid., September 5, 1828.

23   Ibid., October 3, 1828.

24   George Moses Horton (the Black Bard), "Address to Collegiates of North Carolina: The Stream of Liberty and Conscience," unpublished. North Carolina Collection, University of North Carolina. See also "Sketch of the Author," *Naked Genius* (Raleigh: Wm. B. Smith, 1865); Richard Walser, *The Black Poet: The Story of George Moses Horton, A North Carolina Slave* (New York: Philosophical Library, 1966), pp. 38–9; and Richmond, *Bid the Vassal Soar*, pp. 105–15, 152–6.

25   George Moses Horton, *The Hope of Liberty* (Raleigh: J. Gales & Son, 1829). The second edition, entitled *Hope of Liberty – Poems by a Slave*, was published at Philadelphia in 1837. A third edition was published with Odell's *Memoirs and Poems of Phillis Wheatley* (Boston: Issac Knapp, 1838). His second volume, *The Poetical Works of George M. Horton*, was published in 1845.

26   "Explanation," *Poems by a Slave*, ibid. (1838 edition), p. 119.

27   Ibid., pp. 119–20.

28   Ibid., p. 121.

29   See "Partial Speaking Itinerary, 1839–46," in John W. Blassingame, ed., *The Frederick Douglass Papers*, Vol. 1: 1841–46 (New Haven: Yale University Press, 1979), pp. lxxxvii–cii.

30   Ibid., p. lii. Blassingame contrasts Douglass's oratorical skills with those of other slave orators:

> Many fugitives, of course, could tell stories as interesting as those recounted by Douglass. Douglass was unusual because he did not use the halting, stammering dialect and malapropisms commonly associated with fugitives. Upon attending a lecture by Lewis Clarke, a more typical fugitive, a reporter found that "the uncouth awkwardness of his language had a sort of charm, like the circuitous expression, and stammering

utterance, of a foreign tongue, striving to speak our most familiar phrases. His mind was evidently full of ideas, which he was eager to express; but the medium was wanting." Another fugitive, when introduced to a meeting in 1847, "could not get the 'hang of the school-house' and sat down after a few remarks." In contrast, the eloquence and "intellectual greatness" Douglass demonstrated only four years after his escape from slavery was "cause of absolute astonishment," an observer wrote from Northbridge, Massachusetts, in 1842. The "astonishment" of whites was a direct out-growth of their limited contacts with articulate blacks. A Wisconsin journalist felt, for instance, that Douglass's oratorical skills were "a matter of wonder," because "we are so accustomed to mental stupidity and moral dulness in the blacks that an exception surprises and startles us." (p. xlvii)

31   Emphasis added. Wendell Phillips to Elizabeth Pease, February 24, 1845, cited in Blassingame, *Frederick Douglass Papers*, Vol. 1, p. liii.

32   See *The Liberator*, January 2, 1846, p. 3.

33   *The Liberator*, June 20, 1845, p. 97.

Writing Freely?

Frederick Douglass and the Constraints of Racialized Writing

WILSON J. MOSES

"Luckily for the World, Dumas was born in France and not in America, where he would have been circumscribed and might have used his genius in the struggle for elementary liberty like his notable Negro contemporary, Frederick Douglass."[1] This observation by the great Afro-American historian J. A. Rogers outlines the fundamental struggle of Douglass's literary career. His development as an artist and intellectual was circumscribed by the time and place in which he was born. Almost everything he wrote was focused on slavery, racial discrimination, or the indelible imprint they left on his life.

Douglass's major work was an autobiography that was dominated by the themes of his personal struggle against slavery, humiliation, stereotyping, and sexual repression. He was apologetic about the autobiographical nature of his writing. "I write freely of myself, not from choice, but because I have, by my cause, been morally forced into thus writing," said Douglass in the fourth and final version of his autobiography.[2] Writing freely, and yet lacking choice; writing freely, and yet feeling forced. These contradictions did not result from a careless formulation of ideas, but from the dilemma of Douglass's life and literary career.

Douglass's early development as a writer had been assisted but also hemmed in by white friends, who had strong ideas about what roles black Americans ought to play in American literary and intellectual life, as well as in their own emancipation. Early in his lecturing career, Douglass found himself in conflict with well-meaning patrons who suggested that he confine himself to the narration of his experiences as a slave. "Give us the facts, we will take care of the philosophy," said John A. Collins, general agent of the Massachusetts Anti-Slavery Society. Some of them even suggested that he cultivate the plantation dialect when speaking in public.[3] But Douglass soon got tired of restricting himself to the theatrical display of his stripes and the dramatic mimicking of his erstwhile masters and overseers. He wanted to express himself on a variety of subjects, including but not restricted to slavery and the race problem in the United States. In his early years, Douglass struggled against confining himself to the narrative tradition on the podium. In his later years he attempted, with partial success, to free himself from the literary confinement of the slave narrative.

A metaphor for the literary confinement of Douglass can be found in the adventure of Henry "Box" Brown, who escaped from slavery by allowing himself to be nailed inside a large wooden crate and shipped off to the free states.[4] Douglass found that he had to confine himself within a literary box. The slave narrative was a means to freedom, but it also represented a tactical confinement and imposed what might be called a genre slavery that deprived its author of literary and intellectual elbow room. "I was growing, and I needed room," he said when reflecting on his rupture with the Garrisonians.[5] Throughout his career, Douglass gave evidence that he thought of liberal expectations as confining. The role of escaped slave and the literary convention of the slave narrative exposed him to a reading public and provided him with work that he loved. It gave him an opportunity to say things that he wanted to say and that very much needed to be said. But although Douglass rejoiced in the opportunity to make these statements, he sometimes disliked the way in which he was expected to make them. Douglass came to resent the restriction of his public speaking career to the recitation of his narrative. He resented being asked to speak in the plantation vernacular. He resented the advice of his white liberal friends that there was no need for him to found his own press.[6]

Although Douglass never completely abandoned the slave narrative formula in any version of his autobiography, it is clear that he struggled increasingly to escape its confines. The later versions of the autobiography asserted a much stronger sense of individuality than did the earliest one. The very title *Narrative of Frederick Douglass, an American Slave* reveals the dominance of the slave narrative formulas by which the author was bound. It reveals something of the expectations of Douglass's audience and his sponsors, against whom he increasingly rebelled. Originally, his autobiography had been a generically typical work of abolitionist propaganda, a slave narrative of pamphlet length. Forty-seven years later, however, the work had grown to become a weighty 700-page tome and a very different sort of autobiography. In the final version, Douglass asserted that he was addressing questions "which range over the whole field of science, learning and philosophy . . . some of which might be difficult even for a Humboldt, Cuvier or Darwin." He was clearly struggling, in his old age, to fashion a work that would go beyond the genre of a slave narrative, and this was indicated by the magisterial title he gave it: *The Life and Times of Frederick Douglass.*[7]

Douglass expended many words asserting that his authorial motives were altruistic, saying that he wrote so freely of himself in order to give voice to the aspirations of "a people long dumb," who had been "much misunderstood and deeply wronged" but had not been able to speak for themselves.[8] Although Douglass's reasons for writing derived from moral conviction, it seems likely that he had additional motivations, and that beneath the assumed modesty of his introduction to the 1892 edition there was a thinly veiled self-concern:

> I know and feel that it is something to have lived at all in this Republic during the latter part of this eventful century, but I know it is more to have had some small share in the great events which have distinguished it from the experience of all other centuries. No man liveth unto himself, or ought to live unto himself. My life has conformed to this Bible saying, for, more than most men, I have been the thin edge of the wedge to open for my people a way in many directions and places never before occupied by them.[9]

His superficial act of self-effacement was skillfully transformed into a shrewd act of self-presentation. Beginning with the artful device of a humble apology, he rapidly progressed to presenting himself as the embodiment of an age, but with seeming modesty and candor. Douglass admitted to a desire to "tell my story as favorably towards myself as it can be," professing at the same time to "a due regard to truth."[10] The reader must assume, as one would when reading any autobiography, that Douglass might have had good reasons for not always revealing the inner workings of his mind. Furthermore, it is clear that although altruistic moral compulsions undoubtedly contributed to his becoming a writer, Douglass's frankness was certainly controlled by the fact that words were his livelihood.

If writing freely means writing not only abundantly, but with absolute or impolitic candor, Douglass did not write freely of himself. Douglass's literary act of self-presentation was skillfully engineered to produce desired effects on certain sets of white liberals. He thus made certain to display his proletarian credentials as a "voice of the negro," a representative and advocate of the ostensibly "voiceless" black American. On the other hand, he aspired to the position of a world historical figure, asserting that his credentials were "the singularity of my career, and . . . the peculiar relation I sustain to the history of my time and country".[11]

Douglass, like his contemporaries Ralph Waldo Emerson, Abraham Lincoln, and Phineas T. Barnum – all cunning manipulators of their public images – was both a product and a casualty of his own self-promotion. Like them, he was so successful a creator of himself as a public symbol that he frustrated the attempts of succeeding generations to know the man behind the image. The ability to manufacture a public personality was Douglass's bread and butter, and although he did not become rich directly from the sales of his autobiography, he did become wealthy as a result of the literary creation of his life. It was a creation of self for economic, as well as for moral and ideological, ends. Like Emerson, Lincoln, and Barnum, he interpreted his life as a moral precept, inviting his contemporaries to learn from his experiences and to weave them into the developing web of American values. His life symbolized the myth of American individualism, but it also symbolized the ideals of American communalism, altruism, and self-sacrifice. The successful man in America was expected to share the secret of his success and to enrich himself by doing so. Poor Richard, like Horatio Alger's Ragged Dick and the legendary Dick Whittington, was a prototype of the American success manual. Frederick Douglass's rags-to-riches success story was typically American in that it was told not only for the benefit of the teller but for that of the listener as well. But Douglass became a stereotype, limited by the constraints of the myths to which he so successfully contributed. These were the conventions shared by the myth of rags to riches and the myth of the heroic slave.

One need not question Douglass's sincerity to make the observation that his life as a literary creation was a market commodity. Nor is it necessary to doubt his honesty in order to observe that he was concerned with depicting himself in ways that would appeal to liberal Christian readers and valorize bourgeois social conventions. The same qualities that make for effective propaganda often lead to financial success; the message must be simply and passionately stated in order to catch the attention of a broad audience. The author may find it advisable to avoid ambivalence and ambiguity in propaganda writing, since the material must deal in absolutes if the author is to catch up his audience successfully in the swell of his moral convictions. In a slave narrative, the purpose of telling one's life story was "to make slavery odious and thus to hasten the day of emancipation."[12] The early versions of the autobiography were intended to indict slavery, and Douglass insisted that it was only for this reason that he had originally written his life story. The later versions of the narrative he justified in much the same terms, arguing that his people, though free, were still oppressed and "as much in need of an advocate as before they were set free."[13] In all versions, however, the author insisted that his personality was of less importance than the moral message that the narrative was supposed to symbolize. When W. E. B. Du Bois titled the 1940 edition of his own narrative *The Autobiography of a Race Concept*, he revealed an important truth about black autobiographical writing: It often reduces the individual to an abstraction and converts the author into a mere representation of racial oppression.[14]

Douglass, like Du Bois, realized that he had converted his life into an expression of a "race concept," but in Douglass's autobiographical writings, subordination of self-consciousness to race consciousness is far more complete than in Du Bois's. Douglass lacks the confessional, self-critical quality that is present in Du Bois. The black American writer Carl Senna, in contrasting the slave narrative genre with works such as *The Auto-biography of Benjamin Franklin*, notes that Franklin's confessions of youthful sexual improprieties give a quality of personality and sincerity to the work, convincing us of the reality of its author. The spirit of self-questioning and revaluation, the repentance of past attitudes that exists in the auto-biographies of Franklin and Du Bois, the admission of mistakes and the readjustment of fundamental conceptions of life, are not evident in Doug-lass. The lack of the confessional in Douglass, especially in the area of his sexual life and moral values, demonstrates the extent to which Yankee, liberal, feminized abolitionist culture determined the shape of his literary mask. Unlike his rival William Wells Brown, Douglass does not invite the reader to participate vicariously in his amoral adventures, nor does he, like Josiah Henson, share with the reader his midnight anguish over remembered sins.[15] The autobiographical writings of Douglass, like those of Booker T. Washington, unveil no instances of personal malfeasance, sexual or otherwise.[16] Nonetheless, one is well aware that slave com-munities, with their peculiar moral codes, provided ample opportunity for sexual adventure.

Douglass admits to having been a mischievous child and a headstrong youth, but, as I have previously intimated, his autobiographical writings are devoid of any hint of the sexual precocity that is usually attributed to black boys and men in the United States. We must, perhaps, be willing to entertain the possibility that Douglass remained virginal throughout twenty years of slavery, since none of his autobiographies makes any mention of sexual awakening or interest. Although certain aspects of the slave narrative are, as other scholars have observed, determined by the gender of their authors, almost to a stereotypical degree, all versions of Douglass's autobiography avoid mentioning the author's attitudes toward sexuality or romantic love.[17] Sexuality has an ethnic dimension, but we are left to speculate on the putatively characteristic elements of black male sexuality that have been purged from Douglass's public statement of experience in order to meet the tastes of its audience. Personal experience is subordinated to political ends. The narrative is a sort of prison house in which the narrator describes himself both as actor and as object, but always in terms of the social situation to which his identity is subordinated. Unlike the continental mulattoes, Dumas and Pushkin, who created al-ternative imaginative worlds that practically reeked with sex, Douglass, in order to meet the needs of racial propaganda, created a literary self-image in which his own sexuality was brought into conformity with Puritan demands.[18]

Douglass's unwillingness to discuss his sexuality derives partially from his own conception of the slave narrative genre, which he admittedly viewed as less concerned with the freeing of ego than with the embodiment of the struggle for certain democratic and egalitarian ideals. These ideals were supposedly universal, transcending even the Christian moralism from which the abolitionist movement had derived. The slave narrative is propaganda, and propaganda often reduces its subjects to stereotypes, depriving them of the opportunity to express their personal singularities, idiosyncrasies, and quirks. Black males who wrote slave narratives were fully aware that their audience was made up of evangelical Christians. The ultimate foundation of abolitionist morality was based on the idea that slavery was an assault on the nuclear family and the sacred place of woman within the home. Abolitionist audiences wanted to be told that slavery destroyed households and corrupted sexual morality; they were not prepared to hear black males question the very sexual values that abolitionism was crusading to protect.[19]

As Mary Helen Washington has observed, Harriet Jacobs, author of *Incidents in the Life of a Slave Girl*, felt compelled to discuss her sexual life, and indeed it is this aspect of her narrative that has attracted the greatest amount of attention from recent critics.[20] Black men avoided the topic of their own sexuality, and when they alluded to sexuality at all, it was to condemn the sexual abuse of black women. Both in the antebellum and in the postbellum slave narratives, female sexuality is a constant theme. In contrast, it is remarkable how little we know about the sexual lives of black males under slavery. Jacobs's sexuality is the source of much of her torment, and much of the attention that has recently been given to her narrative focuses on her reaction to sexual oppression as a component of the American social order. Black masculine sexuality could be mentioned only in oblique terms, and that is why the narrative of Douglass spoke more openly of the sexual oppression of black females than of the sexual humiliation of black males. Nonetheless, although Douglass revealed little of the cultural aspects of black male sexuality that derived from the plantation experience, he made numerous oblique references to sexual aspects of the struggle. Furthermore, his narrative became an assertion of traditional masculine values, as recent feminist critics have observed.[21]

Professor Washington is correct; black females were indeed compelled to discuss their sexuality. They were compelled to do so by an audience of prurient white feminists who forced black women into hypersexual roles, thereby closing them off from any access to the cherished Victorian middle-class value system that they denounced, but nonetheless valued and protected. This same audience conspired with white males to deprive black males of their sexuality. Douglass capitulated to the demands of white men and women who insisted that black males become superior to sexuality, and that they deprive themselves of plantation sexuality, while at the same time demanding that they maintain plantation language, ignorance, and dependence. Douglass accommodated, in a sense, but maintained a rebellious stance in his relationships with white women, which represented at once rebellion and accommodation. Yet there is no question that he publicly abandoned the plantation-derived, black male sexual standard and that he repressed all discussion of it in his narrative.

Not all black male narrators avoided the subject of masculine sexuality. The various narratives of William Wells Brown are not characterized by the altruism or the puritanism that we find in the narratives of Douglass.[22] Brown, who was the personification of the Afro-American trickster, boasted of his ability to sweet-talk the wife of a local Ku Klux Klan leader.[23] Like Douglass, he underwent his childhood and puberty on a plantation, where he witnessed and experienced the daily humiliation of black males by white males and females. Brown describes an occurrence in his childhood when all the young male slaves on his plantation were called by the old mistress and ordered "to run, jump, wrestle, turn somersets, walk on our hands, and go through the various gymnastic exercises that the imagination of our brains could invent." All of these exercises were performed while wearing the one-piece "unmentionable garment" that was the sole article of clothing for slave children. Brown and his comrades exerted themselves without stint, however, since they realized that the winner of the contest would be selected as a house servant and the companion of the young master of the house, who was in need of a playmate and guardian:

> Every one of us joined heartily in the contest, while old mistress sat on the piazza, watching our every movement – some fifteen of us, each dressed in his one garment, sometimes standing on our heads with feet in the air – still the lady looked on.[24]

Whether or not, or to what degree, this incident might have been degrading to a prepubescent slave boy, Brown later reflected, when recalling the incident as an adult, that some indignity was involved on the part of the watchful mistress as well as on the part of the performers. In retrospect, the occurrence revealed to Brown his sexual vulnerability and the willing participation of white women in his sexual humiliation.

Douglass's avoidance of the subject of sexuality is perhaps no more prudish than that of other black writers among his contemporaries, but he does give us some clues as to why he cannot write freely about his sexual and romantic concerns. He describes his dawning awareness of sexual vulnerability by recalling his perceptions of the behavior of adult men and women, both black and white. He describes himself as a small boy, hiding in a closet while his lascivious old master stripped his Aunt Hester (Ester) to the waist and administered a beating because of his jealousy of a young black man on another plantation.[25] This experience introduced him not only to the ability of white masters to abuse black women, but to make use of their sexual *Herrenrecht* to humiliate and terrorize black men and boys. Black men became agents in the humiliation of black women, as Douglass recalled in telling of how one woman was locked up in a cabin with a black man until she became pregnant.[26] Black women, by their liaisons with white men, whether voluntary or involuntary, became instruments for the humiliation of black men.

In the first edition of the *Narrative*, Douglass recounted the rumor that his master, Captain Aaron Anthony, was also his father, and in *My Bondage and My Freedom*, he supplemented this revelation with descriptions of a complex and ambivalent relationship with Anthony, who sometimes led him by the hand, "patting me on the head, speaking to me in soft caressing tones, and calling me his little Indian boy."[27] In the earlier versions of the autobiography, Douglass had mentioned the rumor that his master was his father but made no mention of the affectionate fatherly relationship. In the final version of the autobiography, *Life and Times*, he alluded to a fatherly relationship but did not repeat the rumor of his paternity. A reading of the middle and later versions is necessary in order to see the contradictions and complexities of Douglass's familial relations. In the 1845 version he tells us, "I was seldom whipped by my old master, and suffered little from anything else than hunger and cold." In the 1855 version he says that he received "a regular whipping from my old master, such as any heedless and mischievous boy might get from his father."[28]

Allison Davis recalls the rumor that Anthony Auld was Douglass's father and speculates on the possibility that Douglass's early life was significantly removed from the typical experience of slavery. He is particularly interested in the relationship between Douglass and Lucretia Auld, who would have been his half-sister, assuming that Captain Anthony was his father. Davis argues convincingly, based on Douglass's own recollections, that Douglass enjoyed a status quite different from that of other slaves because Miss Lucretia pitied him and perhaps even loved him. In addition to her tender words and looks, she would sometimes bestow on him an extra ration of bread and butter, "solely out of the tender regard and friendship she had for me." Once after a scrap that he had gotten into with Ike, another slave boy, she had bound up a rather severe wound on his forehead "with her own soft hand." On the occasion of his leaving the plantation to live in Baltimore, it was Miss Lucretia who prepared him for the journey. She instructed him to scrub himself clean and promised him a set of trousers, "which I should not put on unless I got all the dirt off me." Davis identifies an important element in Douglass's life when she argues that Douglass "enjoyed a special status apart from other slave boys."[29]

"Enjoyed" may be too strong a term, but, as Douglass says, the experience of being transferred to a relatively benevolent situation at the age of seven or eight years, and going to live in Baltimore with Thomas and Sophia Auld, provided him with special advantages beyond the experiences of rural slaves in the cotton belt. It should not be forgotten, however, that Douglass traveled with the blessings of members of his extended white family. Both at Captain Anthony's plantation and at the big house of Colonel Lloyd, he experienced the solicitude and affection of young white adults. He learned to speak a form of English that reflected "little of the slave accent." This resulted from his having been the companion of Daniel Lloyd, whom he accompanied on hunting trips and who protected him from the bullying and coarser influences of other slaves.[30]

Thus, although this family did not openly acknowledge him, they certainly did not ignore him. Its female members were particularly solicitous of his welfare, perhaps even affectionate and indulgent. In the 1845 *Narrative*, Douglass described the initial kindness of Sophia Auld as a new and strange experience, claiming that he had never before seen "a white face beaming with the most kindly emotions." With the 1855 publication of *My Bondage and My Freedom*, Douglass revealed that such benevolence was not altogether novel. He had been indulged by Lucretia from early childhood, and even "Master Hugh" tended for the most part to overlook his transgressions of the slave code, allowing him to meet with Father Lawson to pray and read the scriptures. In later versions of the auto-biography, having freed himself to some extent from the confines of the propagandistic slave narrative, he was able to express somewhat more of the complexity of his experience. He demonstrated that his life had not been the simple parable that he had presented in the first version of the *Narrative*.[31]

He was a clever and mettlesome lad, probably very "cute." One wonders if his white relatives would have been so quick to look after him if he had been dull or deformed. There was clearly a gender dynamic in Doug-lass's early attempts at literacy. He was taught to read by Sophia Auld, who was torn between her maternal affection for the attractive, precocious youngster and her connubial loyalty to a husband who forbade her to instruct the young slave. But neither of the Aulds seemed inclined to break completely the boy's will. The family had already decreed that he was to be afforded special treatment, hence the decision to send him away from the plantation and make him into a house servant. And, as he later observed, "a city slave is almost a free citizen in Baltimore."[32]

By the time he had reached adolescence, Douglass's independent spirit, and the unfortunate fact of his being removed from the household of Hugh Auld and falling under the power of Hugh's vindictive brother Thomas, led to his removal from Baltimore and his assignment to the slavebreaker Edward Covey. The often-recounted story of his fight with Covey celebrates an initiation into manhood – nineteenth-century ritual of regeneration through violence. One does not doubt either the brutality of the conditions to which Douglass was subjected or his version of how he triumphed over Covey by resisting his brutality, but one must nonetheless question the exact nature of Douglass's experience on Covey's farm. How, indeed, was Douglass able to resist Covey successfully, even though all the members of Douglass's immediate white family were now dead and there was no one left to protect him? The answer is that although the work was exhausting and the beatings were severe, the ordeal imposed by "Master Hugh" was never intended to break Douglass completely. It was rather to teach a favored, privileged urban slave his place in society and to reinforce his awareness of his vulnerability.

In each version of the *Narrative*, Douglass speaks of the many beatings visited on him by Covey and tells us that, as a result, his "natural elasticity was crushed" and his "intellect languished," that the dark night of slavery closed in upon him and that he was virtually "transformed into a brute."[33] Strangely, however, he illustrated this brutalization by recalling the high-spirited emotions with which he often apostrophized the ships of the Chesapeake Bay:

> You are loosed from your moorings, and are free; I am fast in my chains and am a slave! You move merrily before the gentle gale, and I sadly before the bloody whip! You are freedom's swift-winged angels, that fly round the world; I am confined in bands of iron! O that I were free! O, that I were on one of your gallant decks and under your protecting wing! Alas! betwixt me and you, the turbid waters roll. Go on, go on. O that I could also go![34]

From what we know of Douglass, it is easy enough to envision his Byronic figure poised "upon the lofty banks of that noble bay," addressing the ships with flashing eyes and floating hair. This does not, however, sound as if his "elasticity was crushed" or as if his "intellect languished," and these are not the thoughts of a brute or an automaton. Douglass's knowledge of standard American English dated back to his experiences on the Lloyd plantation. His fascination with purple prose had begun in Baltimore when he had practiced his reading skills on the *Columbian Orator*. In fact, it is easy to believe that the early exposure to literacy, combined with an innate literary talent, must have led the youth to a heightened realization, especially during this wrenchingly unfamiliar experience, that his tragic life held great potential for literary exploitation.

Douglass's later oratory and writing celebrated not only a struggle against the reactionaries of the slave power but also a victory over the abolitionists who encouraged him to speak substandard English (slave vernacular) and discouraged him from starting his own newspaper. No version of the narrative dwells in detail on Douglass's philosophical objections to Garrisonian tactics. Perhaps he felt compelled to pull his punches when it came to public criticism of white liberals. The issues in the clash were not limited to Garrison's interpretations of the Constitution, nor did they have to do solely with the headstrong and irascible character of Garrison. They had to do with attitudes among white liberals about the roles that blacks were expected to play in American intellectual movements.

Douglass symbolically established his personal independence by rejecting the name he had borne as a slave. He established his literary independence by rejecting the urging of certain white supporters that he revert to the black vernacular. Abandoning not only the slave language but also his slave name, he took his new one from the world of letters – Sir Walter Scott's novel *The Lady of the Lake*. He showed no interest in becoming a plantation variety of Robert Burns, preferring to cultivate an American bourgeois English that was literary rather than vernacular, more comparable to that of Daniel Webster than to that of his erstwhile peers on the Maryland plantation. His high-flown style of oratory, like that of Webster, had vernacular roots in the traditions of American evangelicalism, and to this extent was proletarian, but it was not derived from the speech habits of the slaves.

The opposition that Douglass encountered from Garrison as he developed his skills with words recapitulated the problems he had encountered in the Auld household while learning to read. Hugh Auld did not approve of the affectionate familial relationship that grew up between Douglass and and Mrs. Auld, who taught Douglass to read. Garrison did not approve of the literary friendship that grew up between Julia Griffiths and Douglass when years later, in order to accomplish his goals as a writer and editor, he worked closely with the white English woman, even moving her into his family household for a time. Garrison responded with sexual innuendo, which Douglass felt it necessary publicly to refute. Although Douglass felt compelled to deny that the presence of Miss Griffiths had led to conflict between himself and his wife, he demonstrated in one of his own editorials his awareness that the relationship, despite its chasteness, constituted a violation of sexual mores.

Douglass knowingly displayed aggressive and competitive masculine sexuality and defined himself in terms of sexual confrontation with white males throughout his life. Whether or not he was actually seen emerging from a house of ill repute in Manchester – a charge that he not only denied but was prepared to challenge with a lawsuit – there was always a hint of sexual transgression in his public image. He enjoyed being intentionally provocative, both in the opinions he expressed and in his personal conduct. It was hardly innocence or ignorance that led him to the "glaring outrage upon *pure American* tastes" that he once described in his newspaper, *The North Star*:

> There had arrived in New York, a few days previous, two *English* Ladies, from London – friends of Frederick Douglass – and had taken apartments at the Franklin House, Broadway; and were not only called upon at that Hotel by Mr. Douglass, but really allowed themselves to take his arm, and to walk many times up and down Broadway in broad day light, when the great thoroughfare was crowded with pure American ladies and gentlemen.[35]

Aside from these lines, Douglass never wrote freely of his relationship with Julia Griffiths, certainly not in any version of the narrative. The relationship was of dynamic importance for him both emotionally and intellectually, for it symbolized a symbolic eruption from the box of sexual confinement. The relationship with the Griffiths sisters facilitated his escape from the confinement of the slave narrative. Founding *The North Star* with the assistance of Griffiths came to represent both literary and sexual liberation. The relationship with Julia Griffiths recapitulated the relationship with Sophia Auld and presaged Douglass's second marriage to Helen Pitts after the death of his first wife, Anna. Douglass's relationships with women were of fundamental importance in his struggle for freedom, not only his freedom from slavery but also from the constraints of the American liberalism represented by Garrison. If Anna Douglass's assistance was fundamental in gaining his physical freedom, Julia Griffiths's was equally useful in gaining his literary freedom.

Douglass's freedom of spirit and his attractiveness to women clearly had much to do with his development as an abolitionist and man of letters, but Douglass tells us little of his relationships with women, either black or white. He reveals almost nothing of his relationship with Anna Murray Douglass, tells us nothing of how he met her, reveals nothing of the forces that compelled her to throw in her lot with him, to risk her financial resources and her freedom for him, and to assist him in his escape. In fact, neither of his wives plays much of a part in his narratives.

Douglass's decision, at the age of sixty-six, to marry Helen Pitts, a forty-six-year-old white woman, illustrates the ways in which his personal values often brought him into conflict with the expectations of American liberalism.[36] The biography of Douglass, ghost-written by S. Laing Williams for Booker T. Washington, stated that Douglass lost status in the black community after his second marriage, and Douglass wrote bitterly of the "false friends of both colors" who had loaded him with reproaches.[37]

His response to his detractors was that they had never complained of his marriage to his former wife, "though the contrast of color was more decided and pronounced than in the present instance."[38] In a letter to Elizabeth Cady Stanton, he maintained that his second marriage had been a purely personal matter:

> I could never have been at peace with my own soul or held up my head among men had I allowed the fear of popular clamor to deter me from following my convictions as to this marriage. I should have gone to my grave a self-accused and a self-convicted moral coward. Much as I respect the good opinion of my fellow men, I do not wish it at [the] expense of my own self-respect. Circumstances have during the last forty years thrown me much more into white society than in that of colored people. While true to the rights of the colored race my nearest personal friends owing to association and common sympathy and aims have been white people and as men choose wives from friends and associates, it is not strange that I have so chosen my wife and that she has chosen me.[39]

Douglass's second marriage was symbolic of his long-held view that black and white America must eventually amalgamate. It represented his refusal to be confined to roles, values, or modes of thought that predominated in a society where all thinking was racialized. He denied the existence of a significant black culture, arguing that the "religion and civilization of [the Negro] were in harmony with those of the people with whom he lives," and that permanent territorial or even ethnic separation of the races was impossible. Black Americans were not destined to remain a distinct class:

> Ignorant, degraded, and repulsive as he [the Negro] was during his two hundred years of slavery, he was sufficiently attractive to make possible an intermediate race of a million, more or less. If this has taken place in the face of those odious barriers, what is likely to occur when the colored man puts away his ignorance and degradation and becomes educated and prosperous? The tendency of the age is unification, not isolation; not to clans and classes, but to human brotherhood.[40]

Waldo Martin has suggested that Douglass's marriage to Helen Pitts was the cause of his increasing opposition to racial separatism during his later years.[41] This is certainly a reasonable position. I think it more likely, however, that a long-standing distaste for racial chauvinism was probably the source of his ability to develop the relationship with his second wife. Douglass, who had been an opponent of territorial separatism and back-to-Africa movements since midcentury, began to state an unequivocal position against all forms of racial exclusiveness or constraint. A literary career that had begun as a protest against slavery, segregation, and what he referred to as "caste" had evolved into a protest against all varieties of racial consciousness and voluntary separatism. In a 1891 interview with Irvine Garland Penn, Douglass demonstrated a continuing ambivalence about the role of the black press and, by implication, the idea of a racial literature:

Q: In your judgement, what achievements have been the result of the work of the Afro-American editor?

A: It has demonstrated, in a large measure, the mental and literary possibilities of the colored race.

Q: Do you think the Press has the proper support on the part of the Afro-American? If not, to what do you contribute [sic] this cause?

A: I do not think that the Press has been properly supported, and I find the cause in the fact that the reading public, among the colored people, as among all other people, will spend its money for what seems to them best and cheapest. Colored papers, from their antecedents and surroundings, cost more and give their readers less than papers and publications by white men.

Q: What future course do you think the Press might take in promoting good among our people?

A: I think that the course to be pursued by the colored Press is to say less about race and claims to race recognition, and more about the principles of justice, liberty, and patriotism.[42]

Douglass's statement on "The Negro Press" did not offer a definitive opinion on black writing. In fact, his statements contradicted one another at several points. He disparaged the quality of black journalistic writing and yet claimed that it demonstrated the literary "possibilities" of the black race. He felt that the black press should "say less about race and claims to race recognition," yet he called on it to "say more of what we do for ourselves." Douglass's prescription for black writers reflected the contradictions that he had demonstrated by his own career as a writer. He had protested mightily against racialization while making his living as a racial spokesman, writing almost invariably on racial themes. A desire to depart from the strictures of race led to a total immersion in racial themes. One might attempt to deracialize one's writing, but this was impossible while engaged in the fight for racial freedom. This dilemma was one that he could not satisfactorily resolve, hence the garbled and contradictory nature of his statement.

Long after his escape from slavery, Douglass felt that he was prevented from writing or speaking freely. I refer not only to the obvious point of his reluctance in the first version of the narrative to disclose the details of his escape or the names of persons who had helped him. Equally significant was the fact that he felt the necessity of abandoning the characteristic language and behavior of black males that predominated both on the plantation and in nineteenth-century urban America. It is a matter of some significance that Douglass made every effort to separate himself from the speech patterns typical of the slave community. As he developed as a speaker, he departed from the simple recitation of the wrongs that he had experienced as a slave. By the end of his career, his most popular lecture was on the subject "Self-Made Men," a standard speech that, according to Waldo Martin, owed more to the American success myth than to the slave narrative tradition.[43] What was true of his oratory was true of his writing, and with each successive version of the narrative, he moved further away from the slave narrative formula.

It was, of course, necessary that he depart from the slave narrative formula in his later speeches and writings, not only because he had wider and more varied experiences to report but because, as an intellectual, he was growing and needed space. He was increasingly discontent with writing protest literature and found himself straining toward a vaguely conceived goal outside the realm of racial apologetics. Douglass achieved a measure of escape from the role assigned to him by the white abolitionists of the 1840s by founding his newspaper and taking control of his own literary destiny, but he never realized the goal of deracialized writing that he preached in the interview with Penn.

Perhaps one of the reasons for the rambling and confused quality of Douglass's statement to Penn arose from his ambivalence about having made his life into an industry, his recognition that in order to market himself as a product, he had to confine himself within a package. He wanted to deracialize his life but found that he could not divest himself of the racial issue. Not only was race his livelihood, the struggle against slavery had been his entré into American letters. There was a contradiction here, for although he resented the idea that race should be perceived as his only reason for being, he never became fully comfortable with the daemonic egocentrism of the nineteenth-century artistic temperament. Flashing eyes and floating hair notwithstanding, he betrayed an apologetic attitude toward writing freely about himself and justified his doing so in terms of racial loyalty and altruism.

Here another contradiction arose, for it became increasingly evident with the passage of years that Douglass resented being classified as a black man. He protested against the prejudice that referred to "a man of mixed blood" as a Negro. The source of this attitude, he stated, "is not a desire to elevate the Negro, but to humiliate and degrade those of mixed blood."[44] By 1889 he was openly speaking against "the cultivation of race pride," saying, "I see in it a positive evil." Although he sympathized strongly with the struggles of the black masses, he viewed himself as a man between the races. "I have no more reason to be proud of one race than another," he said, and although he claimed to take pride in "any great achievement, mental or mechanical, of which a black man or woman was the author," he insisted that this was "not because I am a colored man, but because I am a man."[45] Although he advised a rising generation of black writers to abandon the concepts of race pride and racial unity, he never even came close to escaping the constraints of racialized writing. His struggle against the literary confinement imposed by his audiences, whether white and liberal or black and conservative, was only partially achieved by the expansion of his autobiography beyond the confines of the slave narrative. Douglass was able to achieve only a partial literary emancipation, and he was fated never to attain any public image beyond that of a racial writer and spokesman.

NOTES

1 Joel Augustus Rogers, *World's Great Men of Color* (New York: Collier, 1972), p. 117.

2 Frederick Douglass, *Life and Times of Frederick Douglass, Written by Himself: His Early Life as a Slave, His Escape From Bondage, and His Complete History.* With a New Introduction by Rayford W. Logan. Reprinted from the revised edition of 1892 (London: Collier Books, 1962), p. 511.

3 Douglass, *Life and Times*, p. 218.

4 Henry Box Brown, *Narrative of Henry Box Brown* (Manchester, England: Lee and Glynn, 1851).

5 Douglass, *Life and Times*, pp. 217–18.

6 Robert B. Stepto, "Narration, Authentication, and Authorial Control in Frederick Douglass' Narrative of 1845," in Dexter Fisher and Robert B. Stepto, eds., *Afro-American Literature: The Reconstruction of Instruction* (New York: Modern Language Association, 1979), discusses the presentation of the author by white abolitionists. Douglass's struggle to found his own press, and the attendant bitterness, are described in *Life and Times*, p. 259.

7 I have made no attempt here either at an analytic bibliography or a complete publication history of Douglass's autobiography. The earliest form of the autobiography was *Narrative of the life of Frederick Douglass, an American slave. Written by himself* (Boston: American Anti-slavery Society, 1845). Douglass expanded the narrative and described his early experiences in the abolition movement in *My Bondage and My Freedom* (New York and Auburn: Miller, Orton and Mulligan, 1855). *Life and Times of Frederick Douglass* was originally published in 1882, and a revised edition appeared in 1892.

8 Douglass, *Life and Times*, p. 511.

9 Ibid., p. 514.

10 Ibid.

11   Ibid.

12   Ibid., p. 511.

13   Ibid., p. 512.

14   W. E. Burghardt DuBois, *Dusk of Dawn: An Essay Toward an Autobiography of a Race Concept*, With a Tribute to Dr. DuBois by Martin Luther King, Jr. (New York: Schocken, 1968).

15   The sometimes cruel and often tricksterish qualities of William Wells Brown are discussed by William Andrews in *To Tell a Free Story: The First Century of Afro-American Autobiography* (Urbana: University of Chicago, 1986), pp. 146–7. Josiah Henson, in *The Life of Josiah Henson* (Boston: A. D. Phelps, 1849), tells of his undying sense of guilt at having once betrayed a group of fellow slaves.

16   One may, of course, define Douglass's confessed theft of food as malfeasance, but I am inclined to accept Douglass's reasoning that it makes no sense to speak of a slave's "stealing" food from his master, since the slave produces the food and the food consumed merely increases the value of the master's possession. See *Life and Times*, pp. 105–6.

17   Mary Helen Washington, *Invented Lives* (New York: Doubleday, 1987), p. xxii, notes that black women, by contrast, were compelled to discuss their sexuality.

18   Rogers, *World's Great Men of Color*, pp. 79–88, 109–22.

19   James A. McPherson, *Battle Cry of Freedom: The Civil War Era* (New York: Oxford University Press, 1988), relates abolitionism to domestic feminist values (pp. 35–9).

20   Washington, *Invented Lives*, pp. xxii–xxiii. See also Jean F. Yellin's introduction to Harriet A. Jacobs, *Incidents in the Life of a Slave Girl Written by Herself* (Cambridge: Harvard University Press, 1987).

21   Mary Helen Washington cites Valerie Smith, *Self-Discovery and Authority in Afro-American Narrative* (Cambridge: Harvard University Press, 1987).

22   See Andrews, *To Tell a Free Story*, p. 146.

23   William J. Simmons tells the story in his *Men of Mark, Eminent, Progressive, and Rising* (Cleveland: George M. Rewell and Co., 1887), pp. 448–9.

24   William Wells Brown, "Memoir of the Author" in his *The Black Man, His Antecedents, His Genius, and His Achievements* (Boston: R. F. Wallcut, 1863).

25   Douglass, *Narrative*, pp. 6–7.

26   Douglass, *Life and Times*, pp. 123–4.

27   Douglass, *My Bondage and My Freedom*, p. 80.

28   Allison Davis has observed these discrepancies. Davis also suggests that Captain Anthony, Douglass's putative father, was guilty of incest, and that incest is one of the "outrages dark and nameless," mentioned in *Bondage and Freedom*, p. 79. See Allison Davis, *Leadership, Love and Aggression* (New York: Harcourt Brace Jovanovich, 1983), p. 22. He may have sexually exploited his slave Betsy, who was Douglass's grandmother. According to Douglass he had also imposed sexual relationships on Betsy's daughters, Harriet and Hester, who were Douglass's mother and aunt (pp. 2, 6). Douglass, *Narrative*, p. 29; Douglass, *My Bondage and My Freedom*, p. 129.

29   Davis, *Leadership, Love and Aggression*, pp. 24–5.

30   In *My Bondage and My Freedom*, the author devoted a subsection to "Jargon of the Plantation." This discussion is replaced in *Life and Times* by Douglass's explanation for his own lack of a slave accent (p. 44).

31   Douglass, *Narrative*, p. 32. Hugh Auld threatened to punish Douglass for meeting with Father Lawson in *Life and Times* (p. 91), but although aware of the continued meetings, "he never executed his threat" (p. 94).

32   Douglass, *My Bondage and My Freedom*, p. 147.

33   Douglass, *Narrative*, p. 66; *Life and Times*, p. 124.

34   Douglass, *Narrative*, pp. 66–7; compare to *Life and Times*, 125–6.

35   *The North Star*, May 25, 1849.

36   Waldo E. Martin, Jr., *The Mind of Frederick Douglass* (Chapel Hill: University of North Carolina Press, 1984), pp. 98–100.

37   Douglass, *Life and Times*, p. 534.

38   Philip S. Foner, ed., *The Life and Writings of Frederick Douglass*, Vol. 4 (New York: International, 1950–5), p. 427.

39   Foner, ed., *Life and Writings*, Vol. 4, p. 410.

40   Ibid., p. 412.

41   Martin, *Mind of Frederick Douglass*, p. 100.

42   "The Negro Press: Answers of Frederick Douglass to questions submitted by Irvine Garland Penn," in Foner, ed., *Life and Writings* Vol. 4, p. 469.

43   Martin, *Mind of Frederick Douglass*, pp. 256–7.

44   Douglass, "The Future of the Colored Race," *The North American Review* (May 1886), pp. 437–40, reprinted in Howard Brotz, *Negro Social and Political Thought, 1850–1925* (New York: Basic Books, 1966), p. 310.

45   Douglass, "The Nation's Problem," a speech delivered before the Bethel Literary and Historical Society in Washington, D.C., April 16, 1889, published as a pamphlet (Washington, D.C., 1889) reprinted in Brotz, *Negro . . . Thought*, p. 317.

Faith, Doubt, and Apostasy

Evidence of Things Unseen in Frederick Douglass's Narrative

DONALD B. GIBSON

=====

*Strange order of things! Oh, Nature, where art thou. Are not
these blacks thy children as well as we?*
J. Hector St. John de Crèvecoeur[1]

*My Lord and Master, help me! My load is more than I can bear.
God has hid himself from me and I am left in darkness and
misery.*
An Anonymous Slave Mother[2]

Jesus is dead and God has gone away.
The Souls of Black Folk[3]

Henry Bibb recounts in his *Narrative* of 1849 how he tried, time and
time again, to rescue himself from slavery's bondage, and finally he
succeeded.[4] So frequently did he run away that he was often sold, and
each owner concealed the fact from each successive owner. During one
of many unsuccessful attempts, he underwent an extraordinarily harrowing
experience – not at the hands of his pursuers but at nature's – an experience
so profoundly unsettling as to shake him to his roots.

At the time, he was owned by Francis Whitfield, a deacon in the
Baptist church but, in Bibb's eyes, more like a demon from below. Bibb
was encouraged by his former owner, who was anxious to rid himself
of the constant runagate, to seek his next owner. Bibb chose Whitfield
because "he was represented to be a very pious soul, being a deacon of
a Baptist church" (117). Bibb's good opinion soon changed: "I afterwards
found him to be one of the basest hypocrites that I ever saw. He looked
like a saint – talked like the best of the slave-holding Christians, and
acted at home like the devil" (118). Recaptured after an earlier attempt
to escape from Whitfield, he meets Whitfield as he is being returned to
the deacon's plantation: "I had almost as soon come in contact with Satan

himself" (135). On the occasion of which I speak he was again fleeing
Whitfield, this time with his wife and infant child, in order to avoid a
severe beating of 500 lashes that Whitfield promised him for going to a
prayer meeting without his permission.

Bibb and his "little family" arrive at the banks of the Red River in
Louisiana. Unable to cross directly, they find a tree that grows out over
a large island dividing the waters of the river. Though imperiled, they
succeed in getting on the island, where they find no immediate way to
cross over to the opposite bank. Making a bed of fallen leaves, the hungry
and wearied fugitives at once fall asleep:

> About the dead hour of the night I was aroused by the awful
> howling of a gang of blood-thirsty wolves, which had found us
> out and had surrounded us as their prey, there in the dark wilderness
> many miles from any house or settlement.
>
> My dear little child was so dreadfully alarmed that she screamed
> loudly with fear – my wife trembling like a leaf on a tree, at the
> thought of being devoured there in the wilderness by ferocious
> wolves.
>
> The wolves kept howling and were near enough for us to see
> their glaring eyes, and hear their chattering teeth. I then thought
> that the hour of death for us was at hand; that we should not live
> to see the light of another day; for there was no way for our escape.
> My little family were looking up to me for protection, but I could
> afford them none. And while I was offering up my prayers to that
> God who never forsakes those in the hour of danger who trust in
> him, I thought of Deacon Whitfield; I thought of his profession,
> and doubted his piety. I thought of his handcuffs, of his whips, of
> his chains, of his stocks, of his thumbscrews, of his slave driver
> and overseer, and of his religion. . . . I thought of God, I thought
> of the devil, I thought of hell; and I thought of heaven, and wondered
> whether I should ever see the Deacon there. And I calculated that
> if heaven was made up of such Deacons, or such persons, it could
> not be filled with love to all mankind, and with glory and eternal
> happiness, as we know it is from the truth of the Bible. (126–7)

The wolves are thrown into confusion, scatter, and retreat when Bibb
runs at them, waving a bowie knife and screaming at the top of his voice.
He and his family survive this night and the next day make their way
to the opposite shore, though they are later captured.

During this episode the strength of Bibb's faith is severely tested, and
one might wonder whether this version as reported in the narrative is
an account of the experience as Bibb actually recalls it, or whether a
conscious revision has been made for the sake of evading the questions

of faith, doubt, and apostasy, which would arise more sharply than they do had he not put in assurances of the steadfastness of his faith. It seems hardly likely that Bibb, in the heat of the moment of fear and panic, would have thought about such fine points of doctrine as he claims. He reports in such a way as to suggest revision. His poetizing at the end of this passage has little to do with the feelings he was undergoing at the time: "I was so much excited by the fierce howling of the savage wolves, and the frightful screams of my little family, that I thought of the future; I thought of the past; I thought the time of my departure had come at last" (127).

The juxtaposition of ideas during the description of Bibb's reactions at the time of the attack lends the account a tone of veracity. At the point at which he decides that he is unable to protect his family, doubts arise. He attempts to quell the suspicion of doubt in the reader's mind: "I was offering up my prayers to that God who never forsakes those in the hour of danger who trust in him," and at this very moment "I thought of Deacon Whitfield." The implication is that he is indeed in the process of doubting, and the source of his doubt is his situation in relation to Whitfield. "If God has not protected me from that monster in the past," the logic runs, "how can I expect him to protect me from these monsters who presently beset me?" "I thought of God, I thought of the devil." The truth of God (faith) and the truth of experience (Whitfield, Satan, the devil) are in contention in Bibb's mind. Bibb wonders whether Whitfield would be found in heaven. Perfect faith would have ruled out the question, for "the truth of the Bible" would have given the answer had not Bibb doubted. Bibb's logic is not as reported. What he says is that if the likes of Whitfield are admitted to heaven, then "it could not be filled with love to all mankind." The implicit logic of his utterance would have it that if Whitfield is going to be in heaven, then I am lost right now. These wolves will devour me and my family, for faith, God, and religion are meaningless. "Jesus is dead and God has gone away."

Such submerged expressions of apostasy and doubt among slaves and black freemen in the antebellum South are virtually the only ones we are likely to be able to identify, for they belong to no organized or systematized facet of the social structure, not even traditionally to academic history, since it, until rather recently, has tended to discount testimony rendered by blacks in whatever form. Whereas black faith and belief have the institution of the church to record their constancy, apostasy and doubt have no sponsored vehicle, and their recording is likely to be random and happenstance. Frederick Douglas certainly knew that there existed the possibility – even the likelihood – that his narrative could be read as an expression of doubt and apostasy. For that reason he added an Appendix, a contrary one; ordinarily, appendixes are taken out for reasons of health – not put in. Frederick Douglass puts his in for the sake of sanitizing the implications of the *Narrative*,[5] in much the same way that Bibb revises his account of his reaction to the attack of the wolves in an attempt to make it conform to received popular opinion about religious orthodoxy.

Though Douglass certainly seems committed to Christian belief during his narrative, there is some reason to believe that he felt a more than passing hostility to Christianity. The distinction he makes in the Appendix between American Christianity and ideal Christianity, a distinction made by many others in antislavery polemic, is logically nice, so it seems to me, but in fact impossible. When Christ says to Peter, "Thou art Peter, and upon this rock I establish my church," the trope intends to connect an ideal church, a church whose existence is outside of time and history, with a material world. The similar distinction that Douglass and others make is based on the assumption that those logical categories have real existence. But if we agree with William James that "feeling is the deeper source of religion, and that philosophic and theological formulas are secondary products, like translations of a text into another tongue,"[6] then we might infer that Douglass's love for Christianity and his abhorrence of it both live in the same house, the former, perhaps, on a lower level than the latter.

The virulence of Douglass's characterization of American Christianity in the Appendix barely masks a deep-rooted anger and hostility, anger not only at the men who make up the church (I use the word "men" advisedly; there is not a single reference in the Appendix to Christians as women), but also at the vehicle that makes possible the hypocrisy of which he speaks. They may be separable on a logical level but not on an emotional one:

> I am filled with unutterable loathing when I contemplate the religious pomp and show, together with the horrible inconsistencies, which everywhere surround me. We have men-stealers for ministers, women whippers for missionaries, and cradle-plunderers for church members. The man who wields the blood-clotted cowskin during the week fills the pulpit on Sunday, and claims to be a minister of the meek and lowly Jesus. . . . He who sells my sister, for purposes of prostitution, stands forth as the pious advocate of purity. . . . We have men sold to build churches, women sold to support the gospel, and babes sold to purchase Bibles for the *poor heathen! all for the glory of God and the good of souls!*. . . . The dealer gives his blood-stained gold to support the pulpit, and the pulpit, in return, covers his infernal business with the garb of Christianity. Here we have

religion and robbery the allies of each other – devils dressed in angel's robes, and hell presenting the semblance of paradise. (*Narrative*, 153–4)

Douglass says, in effect, that whatever appears in the *Narrative* that could be read as anti-Christian is justified because of the church's participation in and support of slavery. He feels that he must defend himself because he knows that the distinction he and other abolitionists make between the "American" church and the "true" church is not a distinction acceptable to most, especially in a country where one might have been exiled or worse for saying the same thing less than 200 years before. He knows that he is expounding a radical doctrine, one that most Christians will not accept with equanimity. He is, after all, attacking the church and all its denominations, both North and South. "The religion of the South . . . is by communion and fellowship the religion of the North" (*Narrative*, 157).

By 1845, when Douglass was writing the *Narrative*, not one of the major denominations other than the Quakers held a strong antislavery position.[7] Earlier, this was not the case. In the eighteenth and early nineteenth centuries, antislavery sentiment was strong among Baptists, Methodists, and, of course, Quakers.[8] The course of the relations between the church and slavery was essentially similar among the various religious sects. The position of the Baptist church on the issue is illustrative:

> The Baptist appeal to and acceptance of blacks, both as equal members and as preachers [during the eighteenth-century Great Awakening], is the best evidence of the depth of their feelings about the spiritual equality of the races. . . . In a second wave of revivalism [roughly 1785–9] thousands of new parishioners were added to the Baptist churches – so that by 1790 the Baptists were the most numerous nonestablished sect. . . . During this period, Baptists became more conformist and less concerned with opposition to the establishment. . . . In 1793 the General Committee of Virginia [in a bellweather move] backtracked on its strong 1789 antislavery stand to allow each white Baptist the freedom to decide his individual position on slavery. (Sobel, 88–9)

The church was not always so passive; sometimes it was actively proslavery, as when the Methodist Episcopal Church in 1836 voted at its General Conference to oppose abolitionism and to avoid interference in the relations between slaves and slave owners.[9] The Presbyterians never disavowed slavery even in the eighteenth century, when it was safe to do so. They resolved in the late 1830s to postpone indefinitely any *discussion* of the issue.[10]

Douglass also has a vitriolic anger toward Christians and organized Christianity because his own experience and knowledge led him to believe that the more religious a slaveowner, the more mean, vicious, and cruel he is likely to be: "Were I to be again reduced to the chains of slavery, next to the enslavement, I should regard being the slave of a religious master the greatest calamity that could befall me. For of all slaveholders with whom I have ever met, religious slaveholders are the worst" (*Narrative*, 117). Douglass tells us that they are the worst because the license given them by a slaveholding society is buttressed by a religion that actively supports a system ultimately, it was claimed, sanctioned by God. After his conversion to Methodism in 1832, Thomas Auld, Douglass's owner at the time, was, indeed, not more humane and kind: "If it had any effect on his character, it made him more cruel and hateful in all his ways; for I believe him to have been a much worse man after his conversion than before. Prior to his conversion, he relied upon his own depravity to shield and sustain him in his savage barbarity; but after his conversion, he found religious sanction and support for his slaveholding cruelty" (*Narrative*, 97). Douglass particularizes his observation by describing Auld's bloody lashing of Henny, a young lame slave girl, whom he has tied up for that purpose. While he lashes her with a cowskin whip, he recites one of the two Bible verses used almost exclusively as texts for sermons preached to slaves. "He that knoweth his master's will, and doeth it not, shall be beaten with many stripes" (Luke 12:47). The other was "Servants, be obedient to them that are your masters according to the flesh, with fear and trembling, in singleness of your heart, as unto Christ" (Ephesians 6:5).[11]

Douglass is not the only witness to testify that Christians were the cruelest slaveholders. We have heard from Henry Bibb, who lists six "professors of religion" who sold him to other "professors of religion."[12] Harriet Jacobs, in her narrative, informs us that her tormenting owner was the worse for being converted.[13] Mrs. Joseph Smith, testifying before the American Freedmen's Inquiry Commission in 1863, tells why Christian slaveholders were the worst owners: "Well, it is something like this – the Christians will oppress you more."[14] Covey, the "nigger breaker," is also a "professor of religion"; and if he weren't, the struggle between Douglass and him would not be nearly so significant. The literal conflict between them, in Douglass's eyes, is a microcosmic conflict between all true religions and false ones, all slavery and freedom, all fathers and sons,[15] all black and white, all authority and liberty, all truth and error; for Douglass, in taking on Covey physically, takes on the full weight and range of the oppressors' strength and power, politically, religiously, and psychologically. To be free he need only defeat Covey, for Covey is, in Douglass's eyes, the literal embodiment of all that threatens his growth and well-being. Following Covey's defeat, Douglass tells us that Covey *is* slavery: "He only can understand the deep satisfaction which I experienced, who has himself repelled by force the bloody arm of slavery" (*Narrative*, 113), the whole bloody arm! Just as Douglass carried to the grave the scars of slavery, he also carried kinesthetically the significance of his victory over Covey. Although he might well have been influenced by abolitionists' views of Christianity, his own literally felt experience taught him his theology, taught him the belief system that would allow him to express the religious attitudes contained in the *Narrative* and spotlighted in the Appendix.[16]

To preserve religious belief, it was necessary for him to distance God from slavery.[17] On two occasions in the *Narrative* he raises the question of God's existence, the theodicy question that must have arisen in the mind of every slave exposed to Christianity: If there is a God, why am I a slave? and Is there a God?[18] Douglass asks the question once as he stands on the Maryland shore, looking out onto Chesapeake Bay, lamenting his condition: "Is there any God?" (*Narrative*, 106). Another time he raises the question as he remembers his beloved, yet still enslaved, companions who attended his sabbath school in Maryland before his escape: "Does a righteous God govern the universe?" (*Narrative*, 14).[19]

Very often it was most difficult for slaves to preserve religious faith, either because of the incredible contradictions between the two institutions or because of the conditions of slavery. Tortuous attempts to reconcile slavery and Christianity produced the most astonishing reasoning. At one point, the Savannah River Baptist Association in 1835 dealt with the question of whether slaves separated permanently by being sold and without the possibility of future reconciliation should be allowed to remarry, a question fundamentally about whether slaves, given their condition, can be true Christians. They resolved the issue in this way: "Such separation among persons situated as our slaves are, is civilly a separation by death, and we believe that in the sight of God it would be so viewed." Since "slaves are not free agents, they have no choice in the matter and have no more control over it than they would over death."[20]

The narrator of *Narrative of James Williams: An American Slave* relates an account of Uncle Solomon, an elderly and deeply pious slave, who frequently reminds other slaves of the necessity of concerning themselves with the welfare of their souls and states that their welfare rests in the hands of Christ the savior. These slaves, including Uncle Solomon, are cruelly driven, punished arbitrarily, and suffer at the whim of an overseer who is a drunkard and subject to frequent drunken rampages. Williams relates the responses of some of those whom Uncle Solomon exhorts:

> Some I have heard curse and swear in answer, and others would say that they could not keep their minds upon God and the devil

[whom they saw literally embodied in the sadistic overseer] at the same time; that it was of no use to try to be religious – they had no time. . . . Even Uncle Solomon, when he prayed, had to keep one eye open all the time to see if Huckstep [the malevolent overseer, who despised and mocked religion] was coming.[21]

In 1864 Charles C. Coffin sought the views of a freedwoman, Nellie, on religion. She responded: "It has been a terrible mystery to me why the good Lord should so long afflict my people, and keep them in bondage, to be abused and trampled down. . . . Some of my folks said there wasn't any God, for if there was he wouldn't let white folks do as they have done for so many years."[22]

Daniel Alexander Payne, later prominent as a bishop of the African Methodist Episcopal church, wrote candidly and convincingly in 1839 on the question of theodicy among slaves:

The slaves are sensible of the oppression exercised by their masters; and they see these masters on the Lord's day worshipping in his holy sanctuary. They hear their masters professing Christianity; they see their masters preaching the gospel; they hear these masters praying in their families, and they know that oppression and slavery are inconsistent with the Christian religion; therefore they scoff at religion itself – mock their masters, and distrust both the goodness and justice of God. Yes, I have known them even to question his existence. I speak not what others have told me, but of what I have both seen and heard from the slaves themselves.[23]

In order to deal with these vexing conundrums, Douglass finds himself, given his temperament, in the position of either denying God's existence or explaining the existence of slavery in such a way as to disallow God's participation in it. Early on, as he begins his reading of the Columbian Orator, he decides that slavery is the responsibility of men (Narrative, 84). His experience with Covey convinces him of several things. It teaches him, first, that he delivered himself out of the arms of slavery and, second, that God is not responsible for the evil that men do. He also learns that no root, such as that offered him by Sandy, his fellow slave, will be efficacious in protecting him from abuse. He becomes one of our early pragmatists (qualifiedly so) in that he comes to believe in a very practical Christianity, a world view that places politics ahead of religion insofar as the managing of the affairs of life is concerned.[24]

Such a practical bent ran throughout his thought during the course of his career. His early speeches found him saying that "he had offered many prayers for freedom, but he did not get it until he prayed with his legs."[25] During a period of intense debate about whether slaves should be sent the Bible, he said on more than one occasion: "Give them freedom first, and they will find the Bible for themselves."[26] At another time he responded scathingly that it would be "infinitely better to send them a pocket compass and a pistol!"[27]

The expression of such sentiments led to Douglass's reputation in some quarters, before and after the Civil War, as an infidel.[28] It was in part his reaction to such charges that lay behind the composition of the Appendix, where his declaration that "I love the pure, peaceable, and impartial Christianity of Christ" is a clear and direct denial of infidelity (Narrative, 153). His belief, expressed in the Appendix, that Christians would deny fellowship to a "sheep-stealer," yet harbor a "man-stealer, and brand me with being an infidel" for pointing it out, refers directly to the charge and implies that it was widespread indeed (156). This suggests that the apparently disjointed relation of the Appendix to the main text is due to the fact that the Appendix owes its existence to factors lying outside the narrative text and hence bears no organic relation to it. Thus one critic refers to the Appendix as a "slightly nervous apology," a not entirely apt description, from my perspective, but one clearly cognizant of the distance between main narrative and Appendix.[29]

The extent to which Douglass's religious thinking tended to be individualistic (in that it fell outside the limits of orthodoxy within black as well as white clerical and community thought of the time), and hence likely to be labeled "infidel," is revealed in his extraordinary but characteristic response on two occasions following ceremonies honoring the passage of the Fifteenth Amendment (allowing black male suffrage) in 1870. The overwhelming significance of the occasion lay in the fact that most people thought that the passage of the amendment signaled the final episode in the struggle, beginning with Quaker antislavery agitation in the seventeenth century, to end black oppression. Douglass's response is extraordinary not simply because of its provocativeness, but because of the character of mind it reflects. At the American Anti-Slavery Convention on April 19 of that year, Douglass, following a number of speakers, several of them religionists, said: "I like to thank men . . . I want to express my love to God and gratitude to God, by thanking those faithful men and women, who have devoted the great energies of their soul to the welfare of mankind. *It is only through such men and such women that I can get a glimpse of God anywhere* [my emphasis]."[30] The clear implication is that God is visible not through his handiwork, nature, but only through the good acts of humankind. Aptheker tells us that at a similar celebration in Albany, New York, shortly thereafter, Douglass again refused to thank God.[31] A few days later in Philadelphia, the stronghold of established black Christianity, Douglass was even more provocative: "I dwell here in no hackneyed cant about thanking God for this deliverance."[32]

The established Philadelphia clergy should be numbered among those who considered Douglass an infidel, an apostate, because he refused to place the responsibility for the fate of humankind in the hands of God. Had he done so, he would indeed in his own eyes have become an infidel, an atheist in fact. He could not make God responsible for slavery: "Those who defend slavery as an institution of the Almighty among men prove more than they would like to prove, for if they succeed in proving this, then out of the great heart of God, there is constantly springing all manner of torture and wrong and crime."[33]

Devolving from Douglass's sense of release, of freedom after his fight with Covey, came the sense that freedom belongs to those who seize it: "Hereditary bondsmen, know ye not who would be free, themselves must strike the blow?"[34] Such a sentiment comes directly out of Douglass's fight with Covey. Douglass personally captures and appropriates the whole of Western rebirth mythology and revises it to his own purposes. Consequently he is not Christ suffering on the cross; he is the risen Christ who seizes (as he "seized Covey hard by the throat," Narrative, 112), rather than lies subject to, the terms of the mythology: "It was a glorious resurrection from the tomb of slavery to the heaven of freedom" (Narrative, 113).

Out of his showdown with Covey emerges the expression of Douglass's strongest statement of conviction. The basis of the conviction is explained in his Appendix and also led to the expression of what to his Philadelphia brothers was apostasy. Douglass, the political person, knew that the achievement of political ends depends on the work of human hands. God must be distanced from the acts of men. Thus Douglass could be very much the pragmatist:

> If there is no struggle, there is no progress. Those who profess to favor freedom, and yet deprecate agitation, are men who want crops without plowing up the ground. They want rain without thunder and lightning. They want ocean without the roar of its many waters. The struggle may be a moral one; or it may be a physical one; or it may be both moral and physical; but it must be a struggle. Power concedes nothing without a demand. It never did and it never will.[35]

God does not free wo/man; only wo/man can!

"If there is no struggle, there is no progress" likewise distances God from social and political processes. The same line of thought, the same assumptions, underlay Douglass's thinking in "Self-Made Men," one of his most popular lectures. The point he makes is that "self-made men" are made by themselves and not God, fate, or destiny, by their own exertion of will. The pattern of utterance, the rhetoric, is the same as in the previous "freedom without agitation" quotation, statement through counterstatement: "growth," "knowledge," "progress," or "victory" are said to occur only through stress:

> There is no growth without exertion, no polish without friction, no knowledge without labor, no progress without motion, no victory without conflict. The man who lies down a fool at night, hoping that he will awake wise in the morning, will rise up in the morning as he laid down in the evening.[36]

No state of dynamic change is achieved without human endeavor. Perhaps Douglass did not know that he knew this in 1845, but he did. Otherwise he would not have felt the need to distance God from slavery, and there would have been no Appendix. The ministers who bridled when Douglass refused to thank God for the passage of the Fifteenth Amendment were not making the distinctions he made. Douglass saw that both proslavery and antislavery forces where busy using God for their own purposes, and that if God is responsible for whatever deliverance occurs, then He is also responsible for whatever deliverance does not occur. So, rather than saying that God supports or opposes slavery, Douglass said that He has nothing to do with it, except as His presence is made manifest in righteous human action. Charles Sanders Peirce's contemporary observations about doubt and belief are relevant. Douglass's doubt, occasioned by theodicy, results in an effort "to attain a state of belief," to destroy doubt.[37] The Appendix results from Douglass's desire to maintain psychological and intellectual integrity but not a literary, textual integrity. Douglass could not consider himself psychologically whole unless he connected his escape from slavery with the totality of his life. The Appendix is a testament to the understanding that simply flows from Douglass's experience that literature and life are very much the same in that they are inseparable, just as all aspects of life are inseparable from one another. The fight with Covey is not the literary center of the narrative; it is the psychological center of Douglass's whole life, as miraculous escapes from death and destruction at the end of adolescence are likely to be. Every issue that he later faces points back to the time he was born into adulthood, selfhood. The ending of the narrative reiterates the fight with Covey.[38] So does the Appendix insofar as it insists on the responsibility of humankind in determining the direction of history.

In 1890, five years before his death, Douglass made what appears to be his final statement about his basic beliefs, a statement whose essential meaning is prefigured in the Appendix's effort to distance God from slavery:

> It seems to me that the true philosophy of reform is not found in the clouds, in the stars, nor anywhere else outside of humanity

itself. So far as the laws of the universe have been discovered and understood, they seem to teach that the mission of man's improvement and perfection has been wholly committed to man himself. He is to be his own savior or his own destroyer. He has neither angels to help him, nor devils to hinder him. It does not appear from the operation of these laws, nor from any trustworthy data, that divine power is ever exerted to remove evil from the world, how great soever it may be.[39]

He wrote in the conclusion of the 1881 *Life and Times of Frederick Douglass*, revising *My Bondage and My Freedom* (1855), a similar statement:

I have aimed to assure them [blacks] that knowledge can be obtained under difficulties. . . . [T]hat neither institutions nor friends can make a race stand unless it has strength in its own legs – that there is no power in the world which can be relied upon to help the weak against the strong or the simple against the wise – that races, like individuals, must stand or fall by their own merits – that all the prayers of Christendom cannot stop the force of a single bullet, divest arsenic of poison, or suspend any law of nature.[40]

There is a measure of realism in Douglass's thinking that separates it from that of most people of his time and, at the same moment, makes him a man of his time. The hard, objective view he takes of religion, a view that allows him to consider it unsentimentally and dispassionately, caused him to be known as an unbeliever in a climate totally intolerant of anything suggesting doubt or unbelief. Such an appellation, however, he shared with the advanced thinkers of the nineteenth century, many of whom were beginning to see religion in its social and historical dimensions. Douglass saw it in its political dimension as well, as an institution inseparably bound to human affairs. The Appendix is one of Douglass's many efforts to see the church objectively, to drive a wedge between faith in God and support of the Christian church, which, as the Appendix conceives it, was the most "peculiar institution" of all.

NOTES

1 *Letters from an American Farmer* (New York: Penguin Classics, 1988), p. 169.
2 Quoted in Harriet Jacobs, *Incidents in the Life of a Slave Girl* in *The Classic Slave Narratives*, Henry Louis Gates, ed. (New York: New American Library, 1987), p. 399.
3 Du Bois poses this as a theoretical countermessage to that of the spirituals. The "devil of doubt . . . whispers these words." *W. E. B. Du Bois: Writings* (New York: The Library of American Literature, 1986), p. 542.

4   *Puttin' on Ole Massa: The Slave Narratives of Henry Bibb, William Wells Brown,
    and Solomon Northup*, Gilbert Osofsky, ed. (New York: Harper & Row,
    1969), pp. 53–171.
5   *Narrative of the Life of Frederick Douglass: An American Slave* (New York:
    Penguin Books, 1982). Subsequent references are to this edition.
6   *The Varieties of Religious Experience* (New York: Macmillan, 1961), p. 337.
7   This fact is what allowed Douglass and other antislavery advocates to attack
    the church as a whole. There were, of course, always *elements* of antislavery
    sentiment in all denominations.
8   Winthrop D. Jordan, *White Over Black: American Attitudes Toward the Negro
    1550–1812* (1968; rpt. Baltimore, Md.: Penguin, 1969), pp. 271–6, 293, 418;
    Kenneth M. Stampp, *The Peculiar Institution: Slavery in the Antebellum South*
    (New York: Random House, 1956), p. 157; Mechal Sobel, *Trabelin' On:
    The Slave Journey to an Afro-Baptist Faith* (1979; rpt. Princeton, N.J.: Princeton
    University Press, 1988), p. 87.
9   Philip B. Foner, *The Life and Writings of Frederick Douglass*, 5 vols. (New
    York: International Publishers, 1975), V, p. 127.
10 James Gillespie Birney, *The American Churches: The Bulwark of American
    Slavery* (Newbury Port, Mass.: Charles Whipple, 1842), p. 33. John Jay,
    Esq., in a pamphlet titled *Thoughts on the Duty of the Episcopal Church in
    Relation to Slavery*: "She [the church] has not merely remained mute and a
    careless spectator of the great conflict of truth and justice with hypocrisy
    and cruelty, but her very priests and deacons may be seen ministering at the
    altar of slavery." Birney, *The American Churches*, p. 39.
11 Frederick Law Olmsted quotes the "Southern Presbyterian" who says, in
    reporting comments made before a South Carolina Bible Society, that these
    "very passages which inculcate the relative duties of masters and servants
    . . . are *more frequently read* than any other portions of the Bible." *The Cotton
    Kingdom: A Traveller's Observations on Cotton and Slavery in the American Slave
    States* (1861; rpt. New York: Alfred A. Knopf, 1953), pp. 473–4. Interestingly,
    Luke 12:48, the passage following "He that knoweth his master's will," was
    probably not quoted at all: "But he that knoweth not [his master's will] and
    did commit things worthy of stripes, shall be beaten with few stripes."
12 Bibb, *Narrative*, p. 171.
13 Jacobs, *Incidents*, p. 403.
14 Albert J. Raboteau, *Slave Religion: The "Invisible Institution" in the Antebellum
    South* (New York: Oxford University Press, 1978), p. 166.
15 This facet of the narrative is explored at length by Eric Sundquist, "Frederick
    Douglass: Literacy and Paternalism," *The Raritan Review* 6 (Fall 1986):108–
    24.
16 Benjamin Quarles, *Frederick Douglass* (1948; rpt. New York: Atheneum,
    1969), attributes Douglass's religious attitudes to the influence of others:
    "The severe criticism he heard leveled against the church weaned him away
    from his religious bent and led him to go through life examining religious
    institutions from outside" (23). I will argue that Douglass's philosophical,
    religious, and political orientations are closely tied to his experience.
17 For Booker T. Washington the opposite was the case. Washington believed
    that God was responsible for everything, a belief that forced him into logical

absurdity worthy of Voltaire's Dr. Pangloss. God is responsible for the institution of slavery, which He established so that there could be emancipation. Benjamin E. Mays, *The Negro's God as Reflected in His Literature* (1938; rpt. New York: Atheneum, 1969), pp. 139–46.

18 For a general discussion of the theodicy question, especially in its American and English contexts, see James Turner, *Without God, Without Creed: The Origins of Unbelief in America* (Baltimore: Johns Hopkins University Press, 1985), pp. 204–7.

19 On an occasion when Douglass is speaking and seems less than optimistic about the ending of slavery, Sojourner Truth interrupts him, saying, "Frederick, is God dead?" Quoted in Frederick May Holland, *Frederick Douglass: The Colored Reformer* (New York: Funk and Wagnalls, 1891), p. 252. The obvious answer to the question is "no," but when Douglass asks it, it reflects true doubt, preceded as it is by "I am almost ready to ask . . ." Waldo M. Martin suggests that Douglass's religious skepticism increased as he was brutalized by Covey prior to resisting the tyrant. *The Mind of Frederick Douglass* (Chapel Hill: University of North Carolina Press, 1984), p. 12.

20 Birney, *The American Churches*, p. 27.

21 *Narrative of James Williams* (1838; rpt. New York and Boston: Historic Publications, 1969), pp. 70–1.

22 Raboteau, *Slave Religion*, p. 314.

23 Ibid., p. 313.

24 In a speech before the Ohio Anti-Slavery Society delivered on May 5, 1852, Douglass speaks to this point: "I will never be driven off the platform of the Christian religion in fighting slavery. But my heart goes out only to a practical religion." Quoted in Holland, *Frederick Douglass*, p. 203. See also Martin, *Mind of Frederick Douglass*, p. 177.

25 Reported in Holland, *Frederick Douglass*, p. 67.

26 Douglass expressed this thought on several occasions. See ibid., p. 167; *North Star*, June 1, 1849, quoted in Foner, *Frederick Douglass*, V, p. 130. This was a hotly debated antebellum issue especially among ministers, along with other religionists and abolitionists.

27 Benjamin Quarles, "Introduction," *Narrative of the Life of Frederick Douglass* (Boston: Harvard University Press, 1960), p. ix.

28 In a speech before the annual meeting of the American Anti-Slavery Society in New York on May 11, 1853, Douglass responds to the charge: "If the glory of American emancipation is to be given to infidels, it will be a killing sentence against the American church." Holland, *Frederick Douglass*, p. 219.

29 Michael Meyer, "Introduction," *Narrative of the Life of Frederick Douglass* (New York: The Modern Library, 1984), p. xxvi.

30 Herbert Aptheker, "An Unpublished Frederick Douglass Letter," *Journal of Negro History* 44 (July 1959):279–80. See also William L. Van DeBurg, "Frederick Douglass: Maryland Slave to Religious Liberal," *Maryland Historical Magazine* 69 (Spring 1974):27–43, who reads this quotation considerably differently and interprets Douglass's religious views differently as well.

31 Aptheker, "Letter," p. 280.

32 Ibid. Douglass tells why he chooses not to thank God. He points to those who were "always holding us back by telling us that God would abolish

slavery in his own good time." Of course, there were thousands of such
advisors, among them Henry Ward Beecher, who said, "All the natural laws
of God are warring upon slavery. We have only to let the process go on.
Let slavery alone. . . . Time is her enemy." To which Douglass replied,
"With a good cow-hide, I could take all that out of Mr. Beecher in five
minutes." Paxton Hibben, *Henry Ward Beecher: An American Portrait* (New
York: George H. Doran Company, 1927), p. 151. The black Philadelphia
church establishment met three weeks after Douglass's speech and resolved:
"That we will not acknowledge any man as a leader of our people who will
not thank God for the deliverance and enfranchisement of our race." Aptheker,
"Letter," p. 281.

33 *Manchester* [New Hamsphire] *Democrat*, reprinted in *Frederick Douglass' Paper*,
    February 10, 1854. See also Foner, *Frederick Douglass*, V, p. 311–12, and
    Martin, *Mind of Frederick Douglass*, pp. 178–9.

34 *Life and Times of Frederick Douglass* (New York: Collier Books, 1962), p.
    144. It is interesting and significant that this quotation appears in the later
    biography and not in the *Narrative*. I would argue that this change does not
    signify revision. Douglass after all, earlier claimed a hand in his self-eman-
    cipation in the *Narrative*. It was he, the man himself, who "repelled the
    bloody arm of slavery." He did indeed strike the blow. The quotation is
    from Byron, *Child Harold's Pilgrimage*, Canto II, stanza LXXIV, 11, 720–1.

35 Holland, *Frederick Douglass*, p. 261.

36 Ibid., p. 252. See also Holland's discussion of Douglass's speech, "Self-Made
    Men," p. 258.

37 Peirce sees intellectual doubt as an "irritant" that the mind will, of necessity,
    attempt to do away with. He assumes that all minds are intellectually curious
    and will not simply see doubt as one with the unknown or unknowable.
    He thinks that every doubter is like him, a being who will be intellectually
    irritated, unsettled, by the state of unknowing, clearly an assumption deriving
    from socioeconomic class. Douglass happens, anomalously, to be such a
    character, one who is irritated by not knowing, who requires intellectual
    consistency. Charles Sanders Peirce, "Illustrations of the Logic of Science,"
    The Popular Science Monthly 12 (November 1877):1–15.

38 See my article, "Reconciling Public and Private in Frederick Douglass's
    Narrative," *American Literature* 57 (1985):449–69. There I claim that the au-
    tobiography at its end returns to its beginning.

39 Letter of October 29, 1890, recorded in Holland, *Frederick Douglass*, p. 336.

40 *Life and Times*, p. 479.

Franklinian Douglass

The Afro-American as Representative Man

RAFIA ZAFAR

It is natural to believe in great men.

Ralph Waldo Emerson[1]

It has been said that Frederick Douglass can be seen as Benjamin Franklin's "specific shade," for "[i]n many ways, the black man in America is the white man's shadow."[2] "Alter ego" may prove to be a better appellation, or even *Doppelganger*, for Douglass's repeated inversions of the myth first articulated by Franklin represent more than imitation and simple reversal. The life of Douglass, in history and in print, operates as an extension and amplification of that of the ideal American set forth in Franklin's *Autobiography*. The white Protestant male would not be the only representative man in American society. To understand completely the achievement of the *Narrative of the Life of Frederick Douglass*,[3] one should apprehend the life structure it was, consciously or not, emulating and reversing. For Franklin's and Douglass's lives are remarkable for their similarities, which at times seem more abundant than their differences. The rise from obscurity to renown, the bondage to a kinsman, the education of the young man, and the attitudes toward self vis-à-vis the community are but some of many parallel events worthy of comment.

Franklin's life can be viewed as parallel and progenitor to many of the slave narratives, especially Douglass's first autobiography. The great emphasis on personal freedom, espousal of hard work and industriousness, and announcement of lowly origins are hallmarks of both works. Douglass scholars who have seen the Afro-American spokesman as "a sort of Negro edition of Ben Franklin"[4] have located him in a tradition originating with the Philadelphia Founding Father who, by the self-conscious act of writing his life, began the all-American genre of rags to riches. His self-styled movement from bondage to freedom, from powerlessness to power, provided a host of later autobiographers with a compelling ancestry.

Yet as recently as 1971, when critic James M. Cox observed that "an astonishingly large proportion . . . of so-called American classics" are autobiographies, he failed to include any pamphlets, memoirs, or books by an American of African descent.[5] Douglass and Cox's late contemporary, Malcolm X, are absent, for Cox apparently could not escape the embedded dictates of a cultural mode that predicated separate but equal as policy in more than just social organization.[6] In recontextualizing Douglass and Franklin within a framework that allows for their similarities as well as their differences, the critic takes on a task perhaps as "bold and arduous" as Franklin's own course of "moral Perfection:"[7]

> Having emerg'd from the Poverty and Obscurity in which I was born and bred, to a State of Affluence and some Degree of Reputation in the World, and having gone so far thro' Life with a considerable Share of Felicity, the conducing Means I made use of, which, with the Blessing of God, so well succeeded, my Posterity may like to know, as they may find some of them suitable to their own Situations, and therefore fit to be imitated. (1307)

At the opening of his *Autobiography* Franklin claims his "Poverty and Obscurity" as a kind of peculiar qualifying birthright, a prerequisite to the world of "Affluence and . . . Reputation." Franklin's quest for antecedents reveals land-owning but not high-born ancestors, successive generations of dyers, chandlers, and such. From the genealogical notations of his uncles, Franklin was provided with "several Particulars" in regard to the family tree:

> From those notes I learnt that the Family had liv'd in the same Village, Ecton in Northamptonshire, for 300 Years, & how much longer he [my uncle] knew not . . . – When I search'd the Register at Ecton, I found an Account of their Births, Marriages, and Burials, from the year 1555 only. . . . (1308–9)

Tradesfolk though they may be, Franklin can trace his male forebears back two and a half centuries to Northamptonshire.[8] Although a staunch republican, Franklin seeks to locate himself within a long line of descent, even though he may denote it as unremarkable. Pride of kin, if not of their actual achievements, retains its potency.

Frederick Douglass, in contrast, was born into the limbo of chattel slavery, where familial antecedents were likely to be either unacknowledged or absent. Secure in birth records and patrimony, a Franklin can address his memoirs to a son whose patrimony is assured.[9] Douglass, on the other hand, sums up his lineage in a few lines:

My mother was named Harriet Bailey. She was the daughter of Isaac and Betsey Bailey, both colored, and quite dark. My mother was of a darker complexion than either my grandmother or grandfather. . . . My father was a white man. He was admitted to be such by all I ever heard speak of my parentage. The opinion was also whispered that my master was my father. . . . (24)

Himself a father several times over by the year of the *Narrative*'s publication, Douglass could certainly have inscribed his autobiography to a son.[10] But he does not. Neither does he explicitly tell how a man of obscure origins can become a household word: In antebellum American society, Douglass could claim no meaningful origins and hence held meager authority. His own mother barely recalled, a grandmother from whom he was taken away as a child, his siblings fellow strangers – Douglass's genealogy is fractured, his individuality taken out of familial context. When Douglass complains that "white children could tell their ages. I could not tell why I ought to be deprived of the same privilege," he underscores the identityless state of the slave who "know[s] as little of [his] age as horses know of theirs" (23). No deeper obscurity existed in the United States than to be marked by slavery, to be both black and a slave was to be considered less than human. As Orlando Patterson has remarked in another context:

[The slave] was truly a genealogical isolate. . . . He had a past, to be sure. But a past is not a heritage. Everything has a history, including sticks and stones. Slaves differed from other human beings in that they were not allowed freely to integrate the experience of their ancestors into their lives, to inform their understanding of social reality with the inherited meanings of their natural forebears, or to anchor the living present in any conscious community of memory.[11]

Rather than inscribe his memoirs to his free children, Douglass prefers to confront his readers immediately with his "natal alienation," reminding them of their implicit participation in such a social system.[12] To break out of the "social death" of slavery, Douglass adopted the role of the self-made American man, already a powerful trope by the mid-nineteenth century.

Frequently, part of the journey from poor man to wealthy one involved a young man's physical arrival in a new world. Such a transition figures significantly in both Franklin's and Douglass's memoirs. In his anecdote of immigration the Philadelphia printer wastes no time in pointing out the moral:

I have been the more particular in this Description of my Journey, & shall be so of my first Entry into that City, that you may in your

mind compare such unlikely Beginning with the Figure I have since
made there. . . . I was dirty from my Journey; my Pockets were
stuff'd out with Shirts & Stockings; I knew no Soul, nor where to
look for Lodging. . . . [I went from the baker's] with a Roll under
each Arm, & eating the other. Thus I went up Market Street as far
as fourth Street, passing by the Door of Mr Read, my future Wife's
Father, when she standing at the Door saw me, & thought I made
as I certainly did a most awkward ridiculous Appearance. (1329)

A bedraggled and penniless visitor, Franklin goes on to build up a successful
business and win the hand of the very woman who once laughed at his
outlandishness. Even portrayed with all the mistakes, or errata, that
Franklin strategically leaves in, this portrait of a drive that cannot be
derailed becomes the prototypical American success story – the atypical
yet representative man.

In depicting himself as the essential yet providential slave, Douglass
also invokes a humble birth and the dirt of travel. As in the Franklin
memoir, a woman serves as the guardian of the new world's manners
and mores: "Mrs. Lucretia had told me . . . the people in Baltimore
were very cleanly, and would laugh at me if I looked dirty" (53). To
arrive truly was to remove all of the dirt identifying him as a country
slave:

I shall never forget the ecstasy with which I received the intelligence
that my old master [Anthony] had determined to let me go to
Baltimore. . . . I received this information about three days before
my departure. They were three of the happiest days I ever enjoyed.
I spent the most part of all these three days in the creek, washing
off the plantation scurf. . . . (52)

Held up as the model of all things desirable, Baltimore lived up to the
boy's expectations. As Douglass was to find out, the "city slave is almost
a freeman, compared with a slave on the plantation . . . [enjoying] privileges
altogether unknown to the slave on the plantation" (60). Able to hire his
own time, associate with white playmates and fellow workers, and attend
religious gatherings with his fellow blacks, Douglass takes the indispensable
first steps toward the self-made life. As he gratefully acknowledges:

[B]ut for the mere circumstance of being removed from that plantation
to Baltimore, I should have to-day, instead of being here seated by
my own table, in the enjoyment of freedom and the happiness of
home, writing this Narrative, been confined in the galling chains
of slavery. Going to live at Baltimore laid the foundation, and
opened the gateway, to all my subsequent prosperity. (56)

At the age of eight, Benjamin Franklin had been marked for college, for Josiah Franklin had intended his youngest son as "the Tithe of his Sons to the Service of the Church" (1313). As Franklin recalls, "My early Readiness in learning to read . . . encourag'd [my father] in this Purpose of his" (1313). Family finances necessitated the removal of the ten-year-old from school and his placement in a trade. From then on, the future printer, editor, and colonial leader was largely self-taught.

Franklin's first critic was his father, who came across an exchange of letters between his son and a friend, John Collins:

> [My father] took occasion to talk to me about the Manner of my Writing, observ'd that tho' I had the Advantage of my Antagonist in correct Spelling and pointing (which I ow'd to the Printing House) I fell far short in elegance of Expression, in Method and in Perspicuity. . . . (1319)

Franklin paid attention to his father's advice, for he had already envied Collins's greater ease in speaking and his broader vocabulary, believing that the points won by his friend were gained by elegance rather than facts. When Josiah Franklin pointed out, in response to two published poems of his son, that "Verse-makers were generally Beggars," Franklin was pleased that his father had saved him from being "most probably a very bad" poet (1318). His flair for versifying was channeled into rehearsals for his essays; to improve his vocabulary, he would cast prose from the London *Spectator* into verse and then rewrite his exercises as essays. If he lacked smoothness of presentation, he would seek to gain that fluency. Franklin properly linked a command of the written word with power.

Douglass discovered that the inquiring spirit of a Franklin was grounds for punishment in an Afro-American. When the bondsman first began his acquaintance with the written English language, he was about eight years old; a serendipitous turn of fate had sent him to the home of his owner's brother. There Douglass found in the presence of Sophia Auld, the wife of his new master, that a slave could not only be free of fear but even comfortable. Her "heavenly" disposition was further gilded by her naive belief that a young boy, whatever his color, should learn his letters:

> Very soon after I went to live with Mr. and Mrs. Auld, she very kindly commenced to teach me the A, B, C. After I had learned this, she assisted me in learning to spell words of three or four letters. (58)

At this point precisely, the real education of both Sophia Auld and Frederick Douglass began.

Upon discovering his wife's doings, Hugh Auld "at once forbade Mrs. Auld to instruct [Douglass] further, telling her, among other things, that it was unlawful, as well as unsafe, to teach a slave to read." Auld well knew the fruits of that forbidden tree of knowledge: "unmanageable . . . discontented and unhappy" servants (58). (James Franklin, dissatisfied with the increasing independence and "provoking" nature of his younger brother, had also found that a little knowledge in an inferior was a dangerous thing.[13]) A dismayed Douglass nevertheless appreciated the "new and special revelation . . . with which my youthful understanding had struggled": The continued enslavement of the black man to the white derived in large part from the former's illiteracy. Auld's harsh prescription impressed itself deeply on the boy, for the very vehemence of the ban gave him direction. This prohibition of education spelled out the means of Douglass's deliverance:

> Though conscious of the difficulty of learning without a teacher, I set out with high hope and a fixed purpose, at whatever cost of trouble, to learn how to read. The very decided manner with which he spoke, and strove to impress his wife with the evil consequences of giving me instruction, served to convince me that he was deeply sensible of the truths he was uttering. It gave me the best assurance that I might rely with the utmost confidence on the results which, he said, would flow from teaching me to read. (59)

Although master then of but a few written words, with this exchange the child leaped toward an adult's intellectual estate.

Writing, a pragmatic matter with Franklin, was initially to Douglass a literal means out of bondage. No youthful struggles with rewriting the high style of British periodicals are limned in the *Narrative*. Douglass would remember his schoolroom as a "board fence, brick wall, and pavement; my pen and ink a lump of chalk"; a careful study of the manner in which shipyard timbers were marked continued his ABCs (71, 70). The discarded workbook of his younger master gave him the opportunity to practice penmanship:

> By this time, my little Master Thomas had gone to school, and learned to write, and had written over a number of copy-books. . . . When left thus [alone], I used to spend the time in writing in the spaces left in Master Thomas's copy-book, copying what he had written. . . . [A]fter a long, tedious effort for years, I finally succeeded in learning how to write. (71)

Not only determination, but opportunity, was needed.

Free time, at a premium for any apprentice, was skillfully rearranged by Franklin so that he might turn any spare minute to his advantage.

Rather than go to the home of a neighbor for his supper, the apprentice preferred to have "a Slice of Bread, a Handful of Raisins . . . and a Glass of Water," saving his money and his time for education (1321). This hunger for information, which the printer invokes from his earliest conscious moments – "From a Child I was fond of Reading, and all the little Money that came into my Hands was ever laid out in Books" (1317) – young Frederick Douglass also exhibited. In going about his business, the young slave took along the Auld family's plentiful leftovers to bribe the local poor whites:

> When I was sent of errands, I always took my book with me, and by going one part of my errand quickly, I found time to get a lesson. . . . I used also to carry bread with me . . . I used to bestow [this bread] upon the hungry little urchins, who, in return, would give me that more valuable bread of knowledge. (65)

Along with their basic education, Douglass and Franklin sought works on which to model their own thoughts, if not the prose that would spring forth years later. Franklin lists Bunyan's *Pilgrim's Progress*, Plutarch's *Lives*, and volumes by Cotton Mather and Daniel Defoe as affecting his early development; John Locke's *Essay on Human Understanding*, Xenophon on Socrates, and a number of Enlightenment essays also fell into his hands (1317, 1321). Douglass could record few literary childhood influences. He does not mention the Bible, a great influence on his metaphoric style, perhaps because it seemed too obvious for a nineteenth-century Christian to point out. Yet echoes from the King James Bible are numerous, and the previously mentioned "bread of knowledge" passage (65), which echoes the New Testament's "Man shall not live by bread alone" (Matthew 4:4), is but one among many. The secular and popular *Columbian Orator*, which Douglass acquired at about the age of twelve, collected a number of essays in defense of human liberty. The young bondsman was particularly affected by the *Orator*'s inclusion of "a dialogue between a master and his [runaway] slave" and a speech for Catholic emancipation in Ireland. Still, a paucity of stylistic models remained the norm until he took up life as a free man.[14]

The Enlightenment ideals of liberty Douglass stumbled upon did a Maryland slave no good. He soon found gnawing at his soul "that very discontentment which Master Hugh had predicted would follow my learning to read." The horror of captivity was impressed upon him all the more by the awareness of another, free life. "In my moments of agony, I envied my fellow-slaves for their stupidity. . . . Anything, no matter what, to get rid of thinking!" (67). To the newly awakened, every word, every object, spelled independence – and tantalized with its elusiveness. A few years later, Douglass would see that the handwritten word could lead him to liberty: As the indentured Franklin had, the slave would attempt to use his master's own words against him. But as has already been noted, when the master was a relative, the battle lines were all the harsher.

As adolescents aspiring to "man's estate," Franklin and Douglass both used linguistic legerdemain in an attempt to free themselves from the control of an elder male. Having chafed for some time under the stern rule and iron rod of his brother, to whom he was apprenticed, Franklin decided to use to his advantage his elder brother's troubles with the Boston colonial government. James, already censured by the authorities for publishing libelous materials, sought to evade further punishment by allegedly placing the management of the *New England Courant* under his younger brother's direction. To do this, the elder Franklin "cancelled" the first set of indenture papers, while drawing up another to keep in reserve:

> A very flimsy Scheme it was, but however it was immediately executed, and the Paper went on accordingly under my Name for several Months. At length a fresh Difference arising between my Brother and me, I took upon me to assert my Freedom, presuming that he would not venture to produce the new Indentures. (1325)

As the younger man had guessed, James Franklin was not about to expose himself. Although the legitimacy of his brother's power had been successfully countermanded, the seventeen-year-old Franklin had little choice but to light out for the territories: With his father's support, James had blacklisted his brother in the area's printing establishments. Though free, the youngest son of Josiah Franklin faced the prospect of having a trade but no place to practice it, a situation faced then and later by thousands of freed blacks.

These "legitimate" rulers of the young Franklin and Douglass were not distant authorities. Franklin's brother James, who was intended to serve as his virtual master until Franklin was twenty-one, was no Edward Covey.[15] Nonetheless, Franklin felt that he merited more in the way of allowances from a master who also was his sibling. "Tho' a Brother, he considered himself as my Master," Franklin recalled, and he "was passionate and had often beaten me, which I took extremely amiss" (1324). Those blows led Benjamin to his indenture subterfuge, a maneuver worthy of Brer Rabbit and one that pointed to a republican moral: "I fancy his harsh and tyrannical Treatment of me, might be a means of impressing me with that Aversion to arbitrary Power that has stuck to me thro' my whole Life" (1324). Brother or no, unreasonable restraint was to be rejected.

Irresponsible power wielded by a blood relative was a threat with which Douglass and many other slaves were all too familiar. Part of slavery's torture for Douglass lay in the unfamilial purgatory in which he, along with countless other mulatto children, was placed. The heart of the matter lay in the slaveowner's "double relation of master and father" (26) that the institution of slavery permitted or encouraged. Slave children like Douglass frequently suffered greatly from their status as living proof of paternal indiscretions; as Werner Sollors has said, the great tragedy of American society is the denial of family on racial grounds.[16] Because the cursing, sadistic white man responsible for the torture of Douglass's beautiful Aunt Hester (Ester) is also represented as his probable father, every use of the title "master," when referring to Anthony, resounds with a peculiar chill.[17] When Douglass is sent to Baltimore, he gladly "looked for home elsewhere, and was confident of finding none which I should relish less than the one which I was leaving." No hardships loomed ahead of him that he had not already experienced, "[h]aving already had more than a taste of them in the house of my old master" (53). The final, cruellest hardship Douglass would encounter at the hands of his master came when Anthony died suddenly, leaving no will. Whereas the white children looked forward to receiving land and other goods, Douglass "was immediately sent for [from Baltimore], to be valued with the other property . . . pigs and [slave] children . . . holding the same rank in the scale of being" (73–4). In antebellum society, the role of the slaveholder's illegitimate black child was not to inherit but to *be* inherited. When intersected by racial boundaries, natural affinities between parent and child were obliterated. Paternal care or, for that matter, patrilineage of the kind claimed by Franklin, could not exist for Douglass.

Following the year meant to break him of his individualistic pursuits, Douglass was sent to work for William Freeland, a slaveowner who fed his workers well, allowed them ample rest, and gave all as fair treatment as a slave could expect. But this only further inspired in Douglass the desire to be "my own master" (115). To that end, he contrived to escape, with four friends, under the protection of false passes that he himself would write:

THIS is to certify that I, the undersigned, have given the bearer, my servant, full liberty to go to Baltimore, and spend the Easter holidays. Written with mine own hand, &c., 1835.

William Hamilton,
Near St. Michael's, in Talbot country, Maryland.
(119)

With this "official" letter, Douglass assumed the guise of his owner's father-in-law, bringing to fruition the hubristic deeds predicted nearly ten years before. In lettered whiteface, Douglass attempted to seize the withheld fire of independence. When his Promethean efforts were foiled by betrayal, the little group's capture led to a startlingly literal evasion: "Henry inquired of me what he should do with his pass. I told him to eat it with his biscuit, and own nothing; and we passed the word around, '*Own nothing*;' and '*Own nothing!*' said we all" (124). The act of eating one's words — reversing the original subterfuge by the destruction of these white-owned, if not precisely authored, letters — allowed Douglass and his friends to attain their liberty again. More than literal words were ingested: The figurative, false legality of slaveholding was consumed as well.

Early on in their respective searches for independence, both Franklin and Douglass exhibited a peculiar, perhaps American, form of egocentrism. By contemplating the treatment of interpersonal relationships in Franklin, we can see the ways in which Douglass both emulated and diverged from the prevailing model of self-made success. Despite the democratic ideals propounded by both autobiographers, their struggles do not often depict a community of equals combining against tyranny and oppression. Instead, both men couch their striking accomplishments in the unaided first-person singular. Franklin frequently speaks of the various flourishing ventures he undertook or proposed. Relating the story of an early press and a former co-worker, he notes: "I perceive that I am apt to speak in the singular Number, though our Partnership [of Franklin and Meredith] continu'd. The Reason may be, that in fact the whole Management of the Business lay upon me" (1364). The forming of the Junto Club, the public library, the university — all are depicted by Franklin as creations of his own, with almost no outside assistance. Analogously, when Douglass decides to make his first escape attempt, he is "not willing to cherish this determination alone," although he carefully shows himself to be the leader and guide who would later become so important. As he recalls, "I therefore, though with great prudence, commenced early to ascertain their views and feelings in regard to their condition, and to imbue their minds with thoughts of freedom" (116). However brave, his fellow bondsmen are shown as more or less intelligent followers.

In parallel developments, the steadfast helpmeet of Benjamin Franklin rates just a handful of lines in his memoirs, while Douglass's wife Anna, who helped to bankroll his second, successful escape attempt, is mentioned only twice in the *Narrative*. Fewer than ten references are made to Deborah Franklin in the *Autobiography*, and those few are hardly revelatory. The former Miss Read "prov'd a good & faithful Helpmate, assisted me [Franklin] much by attending the Shop, we throve together, and have ever mutually endeavour'd to make each other happy" (1371). Her diligence and thriftiness come in for commendation, too, for she "assisted me chearfully in my Business, folding and stitching Pamphlets, tending Shop, purchasing old Linen Rags for the Paper-makers, &c &c." (1381–2). But almost none of Deborah Franklin's personal qualities are revealed. Beyond the sketchy and infrequent details of their courtship and married life, Franklin does not care to expand.

Douglass mentions his wife even less frequently than does Franklin. Freeborn Anna Murray, who receives no credit for her efforts on behalf of her intended in the 1845 *Narrative*, merits only a couple of references. The two married in September 1838, shortly after Douglass's escape from Baltimore:

> At this time, Anna, my intended wife, came on; for I wrote to her immediately after my arrival at New York (notwithstanding my homeless, houseless, and helpless condition,). . . . In a few days after her arrival . . . [the Rev. J. W. C. Pennington] performed the marriage ceremony. . . . (145–6)

Murray functions as little more than a human interest element in Douglass's successful escape. Other than using the first-person plural to refer to their passage from New York City to New Bedford and celebrating the happiness of working "for myself and newly-married wife" (152), Mrs. Douglass remains practically invisible. Douglass, like Franklin, remains a husbandly isolato. In later versions of his autobiography Anna Murray Douglass would command a somewhat larger space, but in the critically acclaimed and best-selling *Narrative* she is little more than a cipher. Despite the resourcefulness, perseverance, and attractiveness Anna Murray Douglass undoubtedly possessed, we find her husband silent about her virtues. Because the help of Anna Murray Douglass in his second, successful escape attempt was not then acknowledged, we should place his published remarks on his spouse within the context of that era's cult of domesticity: Her sphere was delimited to the private, his to the public.

In Franklin's memoirs two men come in for particular attention. His boyhood friend John Collins, and his chum of Philadelphia and London, James Ralph, make quite an impression on both author and reader. Collins's true shortcomings are first hinted at when Franklin escapes from Boston, for his friend obtains pseudonymous passage for Franklin to New York "under the Notion of my being a young Acquaintance of his that had got a naughty Girl with Child, whose Friends would compel me to marry her" (1325–6). When Collins, hearing of Franklin's success in Philadelphia, follows his friend there, his presence proves a burden: A drunkard, gambler, and eventual reprobate, Collins finally moves on to Barbados, having borrowed all the money he could from Franklin. The figure of James Ralph similarly serves as an admonition to those who wish to imitate a worthy model: Franklin could not write much more clearly of the way *not* to improve one's station in life. Ralph, too, leaves his home town to travel to England in search of work and adventure with Franklin. Where Collins's unsavory dealings are merely hinted at by the recital of his escape ruse and his intemperate excesses, Ralph, with a wife and child, reveals himself to be a genuine rake. The perils of bad company become evident when the printer forgets his promises to Miss Read and in his compatriot's absence makes overtures to Ralph's new companion. Franklin's licentious bumbling ends the friendship, which he speaks further of only to say that the mistake afforded him relief from ever-growing financial obligations. Monetary matters overrule Franklin's affections and disguise his own moral failings.

In contrast to those of Franklin, the friendships of Douglass's young manhood are remarkable for their emotional tenor. Until his year with Edward Covey and his subsequent residence with Mr. Freeland, Douglass mentions no specific friends, only fellow slaves as a group. During the year with Covey, however, Douglass calls upon fellow slave Sandy Jenkins for aid:

> I found Sandy an old adviser. He told me, with great solemnity, I must go back to Covey; but [I must first harvest] a certain root, which, if I would take some of it with me, carrying it always on my right side, would render it impossible for Mr. Covey, or any other white man, to whip me. . . . To please him, I at length took the root. . . . (102)

Depicted as an "ignorant" and superstitious sort, Jenkins appears to be the fatal flaw in Douglass's first escape scenario. The lone slave who backs out of the freedom bid, Jenkins is the man to whom Douglass turns the moment he senses that they have been found out. "We are betrayed!" says the young mastermind to his co-worker. When Jenkins rather quickly answers that he has just had the same thought, a saddened Douglass realizes that his dream of freedom has been dashed (121). Whether fearful of the slaveowner's reprisals or desirous of whatever gain the betrayal would offer, the root man, Douglass believes, evidently had sold out his comrades.

But Jenkins was not the only friend Douglass had. The two Harris brothers, Henry and John, were also involved in the escape plan. Described by Douglass as "quite intelligent" (112–13), the two took reading lessons from Douglass and participated in his Sabbath school. In a group of "warm hearts and noble spirits" (116), the brothers impress Douglass with their manliness. When the arresting whites try to tie Henry up, the newly emboldened slave dares them to do their worst – "you can't kill me but once. Shoot, shoot, – and be damned! I won't be tied!" (123) Even though Mrs. Freeland insists that the Harrises would never have attempted to flee were it not for Douglass's baleful, mixed-blood's influence, the reader cannot be so sure. As Douglass says of himself: "You have seen how a man was made a slave; you shall see how a slave was made a man" (97). For Douglass, the worst part of the affair was a permanent parting from his friends. As the whites decided that Douglass was the ringleader, he alone would be punished:

> I regarded this separation as a final one. It caused me more pain than any thing else. . . . I was ready for any thing rather than [this]. . . . It is due to the noble Henry to say, he seemed almost as reluctant at leaving the prison as at leaving home to come to the prison. (126)

Henry Harris and his brother remained behind in rural Maryland when the ringleader was remanded to the Aulds of Baltimore. Fond remembrances though they may be, Douglass's reminiscences of his friends in bondage have a noticeable air of superiority. He alone was the superman able to will himself out, to help the deserving, to defeat Covey, Auld, and other masters, and triumph against all odds.

In the earliest version of his life, Douglass depicts himself primarily as a lone fighter, save for the good-luck charm of Sandy Jenkins's root. Yet all accounts of Douglass's autobiography recall the slavebreaker Covey asking for the assistance of another slave, Bill, in his struggle with Douglass. *My Bondage and My Freedom*, published ten years after the *Narrative*, amplifies this coworker's role. There Douglass reports Bill's sarcastic rejoinders to Covey: "With a toss of his head, peculiar to Bill, he said, 'indeed, Mr. Covey, I want to go to work. . . . My master [didn't hire me] to help you whip Frederick.' "[18] In this second version, another slave owned by Covey appears on the scene as well. Caroline, a physically powerful woman, also refuses to come to her master's aid and is beaten as a result. As Douglass remembers, "We were all in open rebellion, that morning" (*Bondage*, 244–6; cf. *Narrative*, 102–3). In both this and the virtually identical version in *Life and Times of Frederick Douglass* (1892), the *Narrative*'s image of Douglass as a man acting alone is contradicted.[19] Rightly regarded as the centerpiece of the *Narrative* for its epiphany on the connection between physical and psychological liberation, Douglass's fight with Covey must be read as the text of one who willed and portrayed himself as self-begotten:

> This battle with Mr. Covey was the turning-point in my career as a slave. It rekindled the few expiring embers of freedom, and revived within me a sense of my own manhood. It recalled the departed self-confidence, and inspired me again with a determination to be free. The gratification afforded by the triumph was a full compensation for whatever else might follow, even death itself. . . . My long-

crushed spirit rose, cowardice departed, bold defiance took its place; and I now resolved that, however long I might remain a slave in form, the day had passed forever when I could be a slave in fact. (104–5)

Depicted in the *Narrative* as a battle between two men, one white and free, one black and enslaved, the combat is portrayed in the later texts as a slavebreaker's attempt to intimidate physically one young slave; the effort was spoiled by the refusal of the other slaves to come to Covey's aid. To the young Douglass, it was critical to show himself as an actor alone, both to bolster his image as a self-reliant man and to improve the picture of slaves as a whole.

Although it may seem unbrotherly of Douglass to downplay or not report the loyalty of his fellow slaves, the reasons for doing so in the *Narrative* are straightforward. In this earliest version of his life, Douglass plays the role of isolato in order to win the approbation of his largely white audience, an audience weaned on such American heroes as Franklin and Andrew Jackson. For Douglass to win the laurels of a self-made man meant that slaves as a whole would benefit. Douglass's first autobiography paradoxically thus has as much to do with slaves as a class as it does with the author as one individual bondsman. The stereotypical image of the whipped and bleeding slave might serve to raise the audience's indignation, but not its admiration. A passage from *The Life and Times of Frederick Douglass* provides us with a gloss on his first incarnation: "Human nature is so constituted that it cannot honor a helpless man, although it can pity him; and even that it cannot do long, if the signs of power do not arise."[20]

Generally overlooked in favor of the more concise *Narrative*, the later autobiographies support the image of the manly isolato even as they celebrate a number of other individuals, such as young Douglass's spiritual leader, Uncle Lawson.[21] The successive renderings of Douglass's climactic fight with Covey, to which I have already referred, are the best examples of the maturing Douglass's willingness to share the stage.[22] Amplifications of his life in New Bedford, from the first relation in the *Narrative* to the *Life and Times*, similarly reveal Douglass's revisions of the past, his position in it and among his people. Yet his place in the Afro-American community retains its ambiguities. Douglass's attitudes toward other men maintain the air of a leader speaking of the masses. Remarks in the middle autobiography praising the "promise of great usefulness" among various "colored young men of New Bedford" give way to the elderly statesman's left-handed estimation of the men of his race:

[While working with Mr. Howland in New Bedford] I was fortunate in my workfellows. I have seldom met three working men more intelligent than were John Briggs, Abraham Rodman, and Solomon Pennington. . . . They taught me that all colored men were not light-hearted triflers, incapable of serious thought or effort.[23]

The grand old man may have been writing with the pique of the elderly for an apparently feckless younger generation. But we may also consider that an older Douglass, much in the way of the elderly Franklin, wanted to revise the "errata" of his youthful estimations.[24]

Not only interpretation and revision were necessary to the great abolitionist; self-mythologizing was called for as well. The reader of Douglass's autobiographies comes away with the feeling, doubtless intentional, that Douglass was an *un*representative Afro-American. For in order to win the undivided attention of his white audiences, to gain the day for man and race alike, Douglass had to tap into the cultural myths already prevalent in mid-nineteenth-century America. The image of a self-made man – a Franklinian Douglass – resulted.

Properly speaking, there are in the world no such men as self-made men. That term implies an individual independence of the past and present which can never exist.[25]

In the last part of his life, Frederick Douglass toured the country giving speeches and lectures on a variety of subjects, from the treatment of the Negro to the legacy of the Civil War. One of his most popular speeches, "Self-Made Men," focused on the meaning and uses of the individual who created himself out of nothing.[26] In this speech, Douglass finds a standard in such historical figures as Abraham Lincoln and the black mathematician Benjamin Bannecker. Both men had the requisite humble beginnings, the "Obscurity" that Franklin had invoked; both fit well under Douglass's rubric for such achievers:

Self made men . . . are the men who owe little or nothing to birth, relationship, friendly surroundings; to wealth inherited or to early approved means of education; who are what they are, without the aid of any of the favoring conditions by which other men usually rise in the world and achieve great results. (6–7)

By employing this definition, Douglass could place himself within a tradition of American representative men beginning with Benjamin Franklin. If any person could count himself as having owed "little or nothing to birth, relationship, [or] friendly surroundings," it was the American slave.

Most apparently in the *Narrative*, Douglass succinctly and repeatedly portrayed himself as a self-created being. This literary maneuver presents

precisely the image of the manly isolato acting "without the aid of any
. . . favoring conditions." What figured most significantly to the *Narrative*'s
author about self-made men was not simply that they rose almost single-
handedly, but that they did so "in open and derisive defiance of all the
efforts of society and the tendency of circumstances to repress, retard,
and keep them down" (7). As a black, Douglass was excluded from the
definition of human being, much less man; he was property. Under such
a formulation, the invoked character of Benjamin Bannecker would be
even more heroic than that of his white counterparts because of the nearly
insurmountable obstacle of race prejudice. The dual purposes of the
Narrative's author – to depict Douglass as an heir to Franklin and other
white American models and to improve the reputation of Afro-Americans
among white Americans – conflate into ambiguity, presenting the twentieth-century reader with an interpretive puzzle. Can the reader extend
the lessons of the *Narrative* to all of the enslaved, or should Douglass's
story be read as the story of a single extraordinary man? Manifestly,
Douglass means for us to think of him as an American individual as
much as he paints himself as a synecdochic Afro-American.

Forever poised between black society and the larger national scene,
Douglass embodied the psychic split identified by Afro-America's next
great leader, W. E. B. Du Bois. Writing of the doubly conscious men
and women of African descent,[27] Du Bois can be said to have paved the
way for Victor Turner's identification of those marginal actors like Douglass
whose liminality, marginality, and structural inferiority are conditions
in which are frequently generated myths, symbols, rituals, philosophical
systems, and works of art.[28] Such people, Turner asserts, often come to
represent society's most human aspects. The very precariousness of the
nineteenth-century Afro-American's position anticipated his eventual status
as an arbiter of moral direction and purveyor of literary taste and comment.
Deprived of status and property, natally alienated and structurally inferior,
Frederick Douglass's extraordinary success as a self-made man seems
almost unsurprising.

Finally, if we agree that the self-conscious act of writing the *Narrative*
makes Douglass the prototypical yet new American, we are acceding to
Benedict Anderson's hypothesis that the modern citizen means one con-
versant with and master of its written means of power. Anderson has
indicated that the rise of "print-capitalism," or vernacular literacy on a
mass scale, "made it possible for rapidly growing numbers of people to
think of themselves, and to relate themselves to others, in profoundly
new ways."[29] Douglass's appropriation of the memoir of the self-made
man must be understood from the vantage point of the "socially dead"
seizing upon literate means as an act of resurrection, if not of birth.[30]
Because "[w]riting always increases the power at the disposal of a civilization, but who wields this power toward what ends is a cultural vari-

able,"[31] Douglass's literacy, and subsequent scaling of the heights of nineteenth-century rhetorical excellence, signal the coming of a new order – albeit one that is literary rather than social. Whether Douglass specifically takes on the shade of Franklin becomes moot when placed next to the larger issue of his writing himself into a tradition then limited to white males. Franklin's memoirs, in circulation by the time of Douglass's manhood, could well have served as a template for the *Narrative*. More meaningfully for this endeavor, correspondences between the two autobiographies can now be seen where they were previously obscured by restrictive definitions of what makes American and Afro-American literature. The "unreconciled strivings" of Douglass to be the representative American man, as well as an Afro-American, produce much of the ambiguity and tension in his work. But ambivalence and strain may only prove that Douglass's struggles with the limitations of self-presentation are, after all, those of a genuinely representative man.

NOTES

1   Ralph Waldo Emerson, *Representative Men*, in *Essays and Lectures* (1850; rpt. New York: Library of America, 1983), p. 615.
2   John Seelye, "The Clay Foot of the Climber: Richard M. Nixon In Perspective," in *Literary Romanticism in America*, ed. William L. Andrews (Baton Rouge: Louisiana State University Press, 1981), p. 125.
3   Frederick Douglass, *Narrative of the Life of Frederick Douglass, An American Slave, Written by Himself*, ed. Benjamin Quarles (1845; rpt. Cambridge, MA: Harvard University Press, 1960). Future references will be cited parenthetically.
4   Alain Locke, cited in Rayford Logan's introduction to the *Life and Times of Frederick Douglass* (New York and London: Collier Macmillan, 1962), p. 16. See also Peter F. Walker, *Moral Choices: Memory, Desire, and Imagination in Nineteenth Century Abolition* (Baton Rouge: Louisiana State University Press, 1978), p. 213, and Benjamin Quarles, *Frederick Douglass* (Washington, DC: The Associated Publishers, 1948).
5   James M. Cox, "Autobiography and America," *Virginia Quarterly Review*, 47, No. 2 (Spring 1971), p. 253. Further references will be cited parenthetically.
6   By the same token, I do not wish to exclude earlier black proponents of the self-made man. In *The Interesting Narrative of the Life of Olaudah Equiano, or Gustavus Vassa, the African. Written by Himself* (1792; rpt. Leeds, England: James Nichols, 1814) and *A Narrative of the Life and Adventures of Venture a Native of Africa, But Resident Above Sixty Years in the United States of America. Related by Himself* (1798; rpt. Middletown, CT: Wesleyan University Press, 1971) the writers assert themselves to be both capitalists *and* Afro-Americans.
7   Benjamin Franklin, *The Autobiography* (1771–1790), in *Writings*, ed. J. A. Leo Lemay (New York: The Library of America, 1987), p. 1383. Further references will be cited parenthetically.
8   Many slave memoirs call attention to a missing patrilineage by the placement of the writer in a black matrilineal genealogy, along with the absence, or

apathy, of a white father. In contrast, Franklin discounts his maternal forebears
(at least in the *Autobiography*), choosing instead to select his father's clan as
the significant line. His mother rates a handful of words, and his wife,
adoptive mother to the addressed son, a handful of mentions.

9   Although Franklin's oldest son was not born to him and Deborah Read, but
of an earlier liaison "with an unidentified mother" (LeMay, in Franklin,
Writings, p. 1474), he was nevertheless the presumptive heir. Following the
Revolutionary War, however, Franklin and his oldest son split over the issue
of loyalties, with the son remaining Tory; this matter of misplaced patriotism
was to cost William Franklin his legacy.

10 The Douglasses' first child, Rosetta, was born in 1839; Anna Murray Douglass
than gave birth to three sons before 1845: Lewis Henry (1840), Frederick,
Jr. (1842), and Charles Remond (1844). See Waldo E. Martin, *The Mind of
Frederick Douglass* (Chapel Hill: University of North Carolina 'Press, 1984),
p. 15.

11 Orlando Patterson, *Slavery and Social Death: A Comparative Study* (Cambridge,
MA: Harvard University Press, 1982), p. 5.

12 Douglass was still a fugitive slave at the time of the *Narrative*'s publication.
His children, paradoxically, did "exist" because their mother and his wife,
Anna Murray Douglass, was a free black. On the concept of natal alienation,
see Patterson, *Slavery*, pp. 5–9.

13 See Franklin, *Writings*, p. 1324n.

14 In his *Black Autobiography in America* (Amherst: University of Massachusetts
Press, 1977), Steven Butterfield writes that the "white influences [on writers
such as Douglass] came from the Bible and other Christian literature, abolitionist newspapers, Websterian and Garrisonian oratory, the expectations
of the white reading public, and the antithetical prose style inherited from
eighteenth-century England." See Butterfield, *Black Autobiography*, pp. 32,
47–64.

15 Frederick Douglass knew that his poor white friends would· be free "when
they got to be men." An Irish immigrant whom Douglass had aided urged
the young boy to run off once he realized that such "a fine little fellow as
[yourself] should be a slave *for life*" (emphasis added; Douglass, *Narrative*,
65, 69).

16 Werner Sollors, " 'Never Was Born': The Mulatto, An American Tragedy?",
Massachusetts Review, 27, No. 2 (Summer 1986), p. 305 and passim.

17 See Dickson J. Preston's *Young Frederick Douglass* (Baltimore: Johns Hopkins
University Press, 1980), especially pp. 22–40, for a discussion of the relationship
between Frederick Douglass and his alleged father, Aaron Anthony. Successive
versions of Douglass's autobiographies alter the original picture; see, for
example, "I say nothing of *father*, for he is shrouded in a mystery I have
never been able to penetrate." *My Bondage and My Freedom* (1855; rpt. New
York: Arno Press and the New York Times, 1968), p. 51.

18 Douglass, *My Bondage and My Freedom*, p. 245.

19 Valerie Smith has remarked that although Douglass's *Narrative* criticized
"American cultural practices . . . [he affirmed] its definitions of manhood
and power." Smith, *Self-Discovery*, p. 21.

20 This particular sentence was brought to my attention by Orlando Patterson in his *Slavery and Social Death*, p. 13; the complete passage can be found in *The Life and Times of Frederick Douglass*, edited and with an introduction by Rayford W. Logan (1892; rpt. New York and London: Collier Macmillan, 1969), p. 143. The popular antebellum illustrated motto of a chained, supplicating slave – "Am I not a man and a brother?" – may have served to incite as much disdain for the bondsman's unmanliness as sympathy with his lot.

21 For a spirited defense of Douglass's second autobiography, see William L. Andrews, *To Tell a Free Story: The First Century of Afro-American Autobiography, 1760–1865* (Urbana: University of Illinois Press, 1986), especially pp. 214– 39.

22 Andrews has trenchantly discussed the variations of the Covey fight. See *Free Story*, pp. 226–8.

23 Compare Douglass, *My Bondage and My Freedom*, p. 350, with *Life and Times*, p. 212.

24 Compare Franklin: "I should have no Objection to a Repetition of the same Life from its Beginning, only asking the Advantage Authors have in a second Edition to correct some Faults of the first. So Would I if I might . . . change some sinister Accidents & Events of it for others more favourable. . . ." Franklin, *Writings*, p. 1307.

25 Frederick Douglass, "Self-Made Men" (n.d.), in the papers of Frederick Douglass, Library of Congress, volume 29, microform reel 18, p. 5. Of the many variants of this speech included in the Douglass papers, I have used the pamphlet commemorating an address of Douglass to the students of the Carlisle Indian School. Further references will be cited parenthetically.

26 For a further discussion of Douglass's postbellum speeches, see David Blight, " 'For Something Beyond the Battlefield': Frederick Douglass and the Struggle for the Memory of the Civil War," *Journal of American History*, 75, No. 4 (March 1989), pp. 1156–78. Waldo E. Martin has explored the great black abolitionist's relation to the ideology of self-made men; see his "Self-Made Man, Self-conscious Hero," in *The Mind of Frederick Douglass*, pp. 253–78.

27 W. E. B. Du Bois, *The Souls of Black Folk. Essays and Sketches* (Chicago: A. C. McClurg and Company, 1903), pp. 3–5.

28 Victor Turner, "Liminality and Communitas," in *The Ritual Process: Structure and Anti-Structure* (1969; rpt. Ithaca, NY: Cornell University Press, 1977), passim.

29 Benedict Anderson, *Imagined Communities* (London: Verso Editions, 1983), p. 40.

30 Under the formulation of George Devereux and Edwin Loeb, Douglass's autobiography can be viewed as a supreme feat of antagonistic acculturation for its adoption of the literary genres of the white mainstream the better to denounce it. See Devereux and Loeb, "Antagonistic Acculturation," *American Sociological Review*, 8, No. 2 (April 1943), passim.

31 Robert Pattison, *On Literacy: The Politics of the Word from Homer to the Age of Rock* (New York: Oxford University Press, 1982), p. 62.

Reading Slavery

The Anxiety of Ethnicity in Douglass's Narrative

DAVID VAN LEER

In the tenth chapter of the *Narrative of the Life of Frederick Douglass, An American Slave, Written by Himself*, Douglass says of the "nigger-breaker" Edward Covey that "his comings were like a thief in the night."[1] The simile accurately describes Covey's tendency to sneak up on the slaves, attempting to take them by surprise. But as a literary allusion it seems less appropriate. The phrase comes from the New Testament, specifically from Paul's characterization of the unpredictability of Christ's second coming and the judgment it initiates: "For yourselves know perfectly that the day of the Lord so cometh as a thief in the night."[2] This comparison of Christ to a slave master might seem merely one more instance of Douglass's general ambivalence toward Christianity throughout the *Narrative*, especially in the Appendix. Yet the allusion raises more complicated issues of rhetoric and audience. For Christianity is only the most obvious of the many white discourses Douglass must appropriate if he is to have any audience in the North, even among generally sympathetic abolitionists. And although irony is surely one way Douglass controls these superimposed languages, the variety of devices he uses to position both himself and his white audience within his text suggests a far more subtle understanding of the political, and finally epistemological, problems of the slave narrative as a mode of communication.

The oddity of Douglass's allusion to Christ points to more widespread tensions in the metaphoric language throughout the crucial tenth chapter of the *Narrative*.[3] In general, of course, this chapter is patterned on the traditional conversion narrative, with its descent toward a despairing "true sight of sin" and its subsequent climb to sanctification.[4] Douglass explicitly invokes this structure in his famous summaries of the conflict with Covey. Dividing his account into equal segments of six months each, Douglass labels the first "how a man was made a slave"; the second, "how a slave was made a man" (68). Moreover, he appropriates the traditional phrase for religious despair in calling his turning point "the dark night of slavery" (66).[5]

The general Christian structure of the sequence is reinforced by the specific imagery Douglass uses to describe both Covey and himself. Repeatedly presented as an animal, Covey is nicknamed "the snake" and depicted in the traditional posture of the postlapsarian Satan, "crawl[ing] on his hands and knees" (63).[6] In contrast, Douglass plays the Christic role. His initial beating takes place at "about three o'clock" on Friday (68). On route to his master, Thomas Auld, his legs are torn by "briers and thorns." Appearing before Auld "like a man who had escaped a den of wild beasts," Douglass becomes Daniel, himself a type of Christ (70).[7] And most explicitly, his final triumph over Covey is "a glorious resurrection, from the tomb of slavery, to the heaven of freedom" (74).

Yet the Christian shape and imagery of the confrontation with Covey merely raise the question of the structural differences between slavery and sin – the ways in which Douglass's "freedom" is not heaven, or manhood, or even in any strict sense freedom. The inexact parallel of the time scheme – Douglass fights Covey not in the sixth month but in the eighth, and on Monday, not Sunday – is probably factually accurate.[8] Yet it makes for oddly inconsistent storytelling. Douglass's failure to complete either the religious or the seasonal pattern he explicitly attributes to the experience, like his depiction of Covey as simultaneously Satan and Christ, suggests his desire to problematize the relation of his experience as conversion. The whole account is as striking for its omissions as for its inclusions. And the more we examine this crucial turning point, the less clear becomes the nature of the turn.

The central irony, of course, is that the Monday confrontation with Covey does not result in a beating: Covey's mathematical claim that had Douglass not resisted he would not have whipped him "half so much" is immediately exploded by Douglass's wry observation that he "had not whipped me at all" (74). The literal absence of whipping in the fight scene, moreover, calls attention to the figurative absence of such beatings elsewhere: Even those whippings that Covey administered earlier are not fully represented in the account. The chapter begins with a description of the "first" of Covey's attacks, the only physical abuse of himself Douglass depicts anywhere in the *Narrative*. Yet the actual beating is reduced to two sentences: the graphic description of the "bloody ridges" that opens the account and a more clinical mention of the "visible marks" of Covey's "savagery" that closes it (61–2). The two pages of "details" offered between these two sentences mostly treat the plowing accident that occasioned the whipping. Of the ensuing punishment, both Covey's preparation of the switch and Douglass's refusal to strip are dealt with at greater length than the actual beating.

There are surely sociological reasons for this reticence, and perhaps Douglass's silence about some of his youthful experiences can be entirely attributed to this need as an adult to present a nonthreatening persona to his audience. Although violence against male slaves did not undermine their authorial reliability as fully as did that against female slaves, some of the same standards of decorum would apply. At the very least, as Wendell Phillips suggests in his introduction, Douglass had to prove that his account was not merely one of "wholesale complaints," an act of personal vengeance against former persecutors (xxii).[9] Yet, however clearly sanctioned by Douglass's sociological situation, this reticence does alter significantly the nature of his account as a conversion experience. After all, the traditional Puritan narrative succeeded by being explicit and public about its sinful experiences; reticence in this context would be read not as decorousness but as false pride.

Moreover, audience expectations cannot account for all the irregularities of Douglass's mode of presentation; some, in fact, run counter to the requirements of conversion. Even the section's most famous lines – the celebrated apostrophe to the ships – seem to fight against the generic conventions. The soliloquy represents the low point in Douglass's development, structurally parallel to the moment of near despair just before the saint begins to remark evidences of his justification. Yet emotionally, the speech is the antithesis of religious despair. Traditionally, the true sight of sin is a moment of humility, even of silence.[10] For Douglass, however, it is virtually a celebration of its own eloquence, in Garrison's analysis "thrilling" and "sublime" (xv). Though acknowledging the character's social entrapment, the language displays a rhetorical balance that contradicts Douglass's own reading of his condition as "goaded almost to madness" (68). Even his more temperate characterization of the passage as "my soul's complaint, in my rude way, with an apostrophe to the moving multitude of ships" undercuts itself (66). The alliteration of "moving multitude" and the use of the word "apostrophe" show the author's "way" to be anything but rude; in fact, "rude" is itself paradoxical, a sophisticated word for a lack of sophistication.

The conclusion of the apostrophe is equally anomalous. The final optimism may reflect the traditional end to the dark night of the soul: the recognition that the vision of absolute depravity is also the beginning of self-knowledge and progress. Yet the confidence of the passage undercuts Douglass's claim that he is at that stage of his development being made a slave. In this otherwise reticent chapter, the passage explicitly announces not only the narrator's intention to escape but a projected escape route, the central omission of most slave narratives:

> It cannot be that I shall live and die a slave. I will take to the water. This very bay shall yet bear me into freedom. The steamboats

steered in a north-east course from North Point. I will do the same; and when I get to the head of the bay, I will turn my canoe adrift, and walk straight through Delaware into Pennsylvania. When I get there, I shall not be required to have a pass; I can travel without being disturbed. Let but the first opportunity offer, and, come what will, I am off. (68)

Moreover, "reconciliation" to his "wretched lot" seems neither reconciled nor wretched (68):

Meanwhile, I will try to bear up under the yoke. I am not the only slave in the world. Why should I fret? I can bear as much as any of them. Besides, I am but a boy, and all boys are bound to some one. It may be that my misery in slavery will only increase my happiness when I get free. There is a better day coming. (67)

We need not take too seriously the rationalizations about the universal enslavement of youth or the masochistic embrace of pain as preparation for pleasure. Yet Douglass's clear sense that his misery is of limited duration suggests more dawn than dark to his night of slavery. And it is hard to imagine from this passage what more confidence could be learned from the subsequent "conversion" to manhood after the fight with Covey.

One should not overinvest in the narrative irregularities of what is, after all, a basically factual account. Yet the tension between the actual events and the form of the conversion narrative in which Douglass recasts them suggests his ambivalence about the genre and the religion that underwrites it. Both the conversion narrative and Douglass's version of it are based on an ironic reversal of fortune. Yet the reasons for this reversal differ. In the religious conversion, the irony measures the human inability to anticipate God's actions: In Shepard's famous paradox, "And now when I was worst he began to be best unto me."[11] In Douglass, however, the irony does not reassert a hierarchy of knowledge but undercuts it. His appeal to the higher authority of his true master, Thomas Auld, does not intentionally result in more lenient treatment; Auld sends his slave back to Covey, believing that he will receive more of the same. That he does not is an irony directed as much against Auld and Covey as against Douglass himself. And the reversal, rather than establishing an absolute standard of divine knowledge, suggests the relativism of power and the ways in which the canny slave can exploit it.

By inverting the traditional meanings of these conventions, Douglass implicitly denies the divine origin of his conversion, turning it from "God's plot" into just one among many ways of structuring a narrative. And indeed, the rest of the tenth chapter continues this secularization of

religion. The lesson the "converted" Douglass most immediately learns
is not of his own justification but of the hyprocrisy of southern religion.
After recounting the fight with Covey, Douglass launches into a series
of harangues: against the invidiousness of the Christmas holidays, the
brutality of slaveholding ministers, and the prohibition of black Sunday
schools. However seriously we take Douglass's apology for these
"digressions" (82), they follow oddly on what had been cast as a religious
conversion.

Even more suggestive is the role of religion in the biographical events
that conclude this longest chapter of the book – the formation of a black
Sunday school and the escape attempt that follows from it. The first
(brief) event is striking for its introduction into the *Narrative* of a community
experience often missing. Yet the meaning of the episode is unclear: Does
Douglass intend to instruct his fellow slaves in religion or in reading and
writing? This ambiguity becomes more apparent when Douglass's account
is contrasted to a similar moment in *The Interesting Narrative of the Life
of Olaudah Equiano, or Gustavus Vassa, the African. Written by Himself*
(1789).[12] Shortly after his own conversion to Christianity, Equiano sails
with four Musquito Indians, one of them an eighteen-year-old prince.
During the voyage he undertakes to teach the prince religion under the
guise of teaching him to read and write:

> In our passage I took all the pains that I could to instruct the Indian
> prince in the doctrines of Christianity, of which he was entirely
> ignorant; and, to my great joy, he was quite attentive, and received
> with gladness the truths that the Lord enabled me to set forth to
> him. I taught him, in the compass of eleven days, all the letters;
> and he could put even two or three of them together, and spell
> them.[13]

Teased by his fellow pagans, however, the prince increasingly wants
to distinguish between writing and righteousness:

> At last he asked me, – "How comes it that all the white men on
> board, who can read and write, observe the sun and know all things,
> yet swear, lie, and get drunk, only excepting yourself?" I answered
> him, *the reason was that they did not fear God; and that if any one of
> them died so, they could not go to, or be happy with, God.* He replied
> *that if a certain person went to hell, he would go to hell too. . . .* Then
> I told him if he and these people went to hell together, their pains
> would not make his any lighter. This had great weight with him;
> it depressed his spirits much; and he became ever after, during the
> passage, fond of being alone. (154)

Equiano's moral position is clear. But the prince, as a proleptic Huck
Finn, makes a telling point about the independence of reading and religion.

Why must knowledge be located within a particular moral system, especially if individuals inside that system seem flawed and those outside it admirable? It may not be only guilt that keeps the prince away from the proselytizing Equiano for the rest of the voyage.[14]

What is striking about Douglass's recapitulation of this moment is that the uneasiness in Equiano's account is eliminated by a corresponding elimination of the religious element that generated it. Although the Bible becomes the medium for lessons, there is no indication that religious issues are in any way central to the slaves' education. Admitting only once that "we were trying to learn how to read the will of God," Douglass more often claims that they simply "availed themselves of the little opportunity to learn to read" (81). In retrospect, the experience becomes an occasion for near blasphemy: "When I think that these precious souls are to-day shut up in the prison-house of slavery, my feelings overcome me, and I am almost ready to ask 'Does a righteous God govern the universe?' " (82). More generally, the experience remains a wholly secular one, with reading a means not of spiritual purification but of bodily freedom, through the intervention not of Christ but of Douglass himself. "And I have the happiness to know that several of those who came to Sabbath school learned how to read; and that one, at least, is now free *through my agency*" (83; emphasis added)

The demystification of the conversion narrative begun by secularizing religious education is completed in the account of the failed escape. For here it becomes clear, as it was implicit throughout the chapter, that Douglass uses the structure of conversion not to reaffirm religion but to empower his story. Throughout the chapter, Douglass's ability to shape his language measures his ability to control his fate.[15] Even before his fight with Covey, Douglass distances himself from "Covey's reputation as a 'nigger-breaker' " (59). The quotation marks around the offending phrase register the difference between the community's way of talking and his own. The fight shows Douglass how to exploit this difference. Wondering why Covey did not have him arrested, he concludes:

> The only explanation I can now think of does not entirely satisfy me; but such as it is, I will give it. Mr. Covey enjoyed the most unbounded reputation for being a first-rate overseer and negro-breaker. It was of considerable importance to him. That reputation was at stake; and had he sent me – a boy about sixteen years old – to the public whipping-post, his reputation would have been lost; so, to save his reputation, he suffered me to go unpunished. (75)

Whether or not fully convincing, this explanation marks a development in Douglass's narrative strategies. Not only does Douglass speak exclusively in his own voice, calling Covey a "nigger"-breaker. In his growing ability to distinguish between Covey's actions and his reputation – and even

between his own explanations and the characters' possible motivations –
Douglass discovers a literary power that frees him psychologically and
finally even physically.

Although a practical failure, the escape succeeds even more than the
fight as a lesson in the liberating potential of the imagination. This triumph
is clearest, ironically, in the slaves' anticipation of the terrors of freedom:

> Upon either side we saw grim death, assuming the most horrid
> shapes. Now it was starvation, causing us to eat our own flesh; –
> now we were contending with the waves, and were drowned; –
> now we were overtaken, and torn to pieces by the fangs of the
> terrible bloodhound. We were stung by scorpions, chased by wild
> beasts, bitten by snakes, and finally, after having nearly reached
> the desired spot, –after swimming rivers, encountering wild beasts,
> sleeping in the woods, suffering hunger and nakedness, – we were
> overtaken by our pursuers, and, in our resistance, we were shot
> dead upon the spot! (85–6)

Like the apostrophe to the ships, this writerly passage undercuts its own
content. For all the horrors of cannibalism, disememberment, and exe-
cution, the description offers a powerful sense of group identity, embodied
in the communal "we" imagining these horrors. The imaginative effort
is so vital, in fact, that it is hard to remember that such an escape, like
the similar one at the end of the apostrophe, never occurs. It is, at least,
not surprising that this fictionalizing moment ends in a doubly literary
gesture, Douglass's quotation of Hamlet and of Patrick Henry to characterize the slaves' willingness to proceed despite their terror.[16]

This newfound linguistic power is epitomized in the pun of possession
that structures the final sequence of capture and release:

> I told [Henry] to eat his [pass] with his biscuit, and own nothing;
> and we passed the word around, "*Own nothing*;" and "*Own nothing!*"
> said we all. Our confidence in each other was unshaken. (90)

Douglass's advice, of course, makes good sense. The passes (in Douglass's
neologism, "protections") are the only concrete evidence that an escape
has been planned; and if their masters cannot find the actual slips of
paper, the slaves are much less likely to be punished severely. Yet, as
they "pass" the "word" around, they activate the pun on "own." Their
denial of the category of ownership is an implicit act of rebellion against
the system that makes them another man's property. By making this
denial a mark of their own community, they assert the strength that lies
within their shared identity as slaves and rebels.

Within this highly literary context, the white characters take on a
significantly lower status. Earlier in the chapter, Douglass's pun about
wanting "to live *upon free land* as well as with *Freeland*" reduces his master,

William Freeland, to a word (83–4). The planned rebellion effects a similar but more complicated transformation in William Hamilton. Hamilton is first mentioned in passing as the owner of Charles. Although in the legal sense this relation subordinates Charles to Hamilton, in terms of the story it makes Hamilton a satellite of Charles.[17] Hamilton's second appearance is equally circumscribed: His is the name forged by Douglass at the bottom of the "protections" (87). Only after these two subordinate appearances does the man himself, "with a speed betokening great excitement," scurry into the text (88). Without denying the legal hold that all white characters exert over the slaves in the text, then, one must still acknowledge how Douglass's retelling limits this control: Quite simply, the hierarchy of power in his narrative is not identical to the hierarchy of power in slave society.

The real mark of this power shift, however, lies not in its disenfranchisement of white figures but in the creation of a black figure whose presence virtually overturns the moral of Douglass's own story – the problematic Sandy Jenkins. Sandy stands apart from the central events of the chapter, commenting on them, and in his inscrutability takes on mythic proportions matched in the tenth chapter only by the satanic Covey. In the sequence with Covey, Sandy represents that authentic African experience to which Douglass himself is attracted despite a residual skepticism. Offering on Saturday a sanctuary from the cruelties of Covey and Auld, Sandy speaks of a magic "root," which epitomizes for Douglass Sandy's allegiance to a black religious tradition not reconciled to Judeo-Christian practices.

Douglass's relation to the root is ambiguous.[18] Generally, he views it with scorn and implies (much later in a footnote) that superstition is one of the ways in which whites keep blacks enslaved (81n). Yet these "mature" views are superimposed on the sixteen-year-old Frederick's belief that the root may in fact be powerful. When Covey at first offers no reprimand, Douglass states:

> Now, this singular conduct of Mr. Covey really made me begin
> to think that there was something in the *root* which Sandy had given
> me; and had it been on any other day than Sunday, I could have
> attributed the conduct to no other cause than the influence of that
> root; and as it was, I was half inclined to think the *root* to be
> something more than I at first had taken it to be. (72).

Nor does Covey's subsequent anger lessen the adolescent's faith; and the fight becomes an occasion on which "the virtue of the *root* was fully tested" (72).

All readings of the fight see Douglass quickly outgrow his need for (and interest in) the root as a psychological crutch. Surely Douglass's final explanation of Covey's failure to punish him in terms of his "rep-

utation" implicitly denies the root's importance. At the same time that
the root cannot be seriously said to cause Douglass's victory, however,
its symbolic role in his recovery of his manhood should not be underestimated. A synecdoche for folk medicine (as religion), the root more
generally represents Douglass's black heritage, those "roots" that slavery
repeatedly silences. In later retellings of the fight, Douglass himself activates
this pun in the ironic claim that "I now forgot my *roots*, and remembered
my pledge to *stand up in my own defense.*"[19] Wanting to deny simultaneously
all extraneous assistance from magical herbs and the subordination of his
race in the South, Douglass implicitly acknowledges that the root does
stand for his roots. And his decision to take up "his own defense," though
cast in wholly individualistic terms, is also the acceptance that his roots
(and his root) should be a source not of shame but of pride.

   If in the first half of the chapter Sandy stands as a black counterexample
of the self-confidence Douglass seeks, his role in the escape plot is even
more disruptive. For here he seems to play simultaneously the role of
chief confident and betrayer. Although there is no historical evidence
that it was Sandy who informed on the group, he is the most logical
suspect, the only nonparticipant who knew of the plot.[20] Moreover, the
scene in which Douglass anticipates the betrayal casts Sandy symbolically
as the informant. The exchange between the two men as they spread
manure – "We are betrayed!" "Well, . . . that thought has this moment
struck me" (88) – recalls Christ's predictions of His betrayal, with Sandy
playing the role of either Judas at the Last Supper or Peter at Gethsemane.
Whatever Sandy's real part in the escape, moreover, at least his unexplained
refusal to participate implicitly questions the value of escape. And in the
second half of the chapter, as in the first, he stands as the symbol of
something that Douglass cannot fully assimilate to the reconstruction of
his personal history – a challenge that Douglass suspects may be even
more authentically black than his own individualistic rebellion.

The tensions within the tenth chapter – between the traditional coversion
and Douglass's revised version, between historical fact and narrative
reshaping, even between the characters of Frederick and Sandy – suggest
the range of literary and epistemological issues Douglass must confront
in casting his life as a slave narrative. Some are rhetorical problems
endemic to the genre – questions of plot motivation, authorial tone, and
audience response faced by every writer of slave narratives. But some
are more particular to Douglass's personal situation and his narrative
decisions about the best way to portray slavery and himself.

   The central generic paradox of Douglass's *Narrative*, of course, derives
from the inappropriateness of the conversion paradigm Douglass uses to
shape his experience of slavery. After all, although the escape from Maryland

can be compared to that from sin, enslavement is not itself sinful. Slavery is not primarily a problem of psychological purification, of "weaned affections." Slaves need not mend their ways, but must merely free themselves from a repressive social situation. Unlike sin, slavery has no divine sanction; this fall is wholly unfortunate. At the same time that slavery is not so bad as sin, moreover, escape is not so good as salvation. As Sandy stands to remind Douglass, some of the things one leaves behind are valuable – home, family, friends, and, at least during the early stages of relocation, cultural solidarity. Although few would present this sacrifice as a sufficient reason for remaining enslaved, one can regret the loss as one should not regret anything left behind in sin.

Yet the dissimilarities between slavery and sin cannot account for all the *Narrative*'s irony. However central the conversion motif is in the tenth chapter, in the other chapters Douglass generally employs a more secular model: the rags-to-riches success story best represented in American literature by the works of Benjamin Franklin and Horatio Alger. The effect of this generic shift on Douglass's ironic presentation is evident in the differences between the "converting" fight with Covey and the other celebrated moment of growth – Mrs. Auld's reading lessons.[21] The two scenes share many structural elements, especially the triangulation that positions Douglass in the reading scenes between Mr. and Mrs. Hugh Auld, much as it later places him between Covey and Thomas Auld. And the intervention of the second figure in both cases is equally ineffectual. Just as Thomas's sending Douglass back to Covey ironically protects Douglass from further beatings, so Hugh's reprimand to his wife ironically reinforces Douglass's desire to learn.

Yet these apparent similarities mask a more fundamental difference in the character of the reversals. In the conversion setting, Douglass changes with the changed situation; having been made a slave, he becomes once again a man. In the more secular setting, the reversal involves no corresponding reversal in Douglass but merely hastens his progress along a road already taken. And in this absence of reversal lies the second, greater irony of Hugh Auld's position. Not only does Auld choose exactly the wrong tactic to keep Douglass illiterate, his angry prediction that Douglass will "misuse" learning to become dissatisfied and forge his way to freedom is fundamentally correct. Far from reversing Douglass's direction, Auld not only speeds him along but accurately prophesies his destination and means of travel.

This second kind of irony – of a nonreversing intervention – is perhaps characteristic of all rags-to-riches stories. Certainly Benjamin Franklin regularly masks his machinations by recasting political payoffs as lucky coincidences. Similarly, Alger's heroes customarily triumph through a fortuitous event that, however merited, is not quite earned.[22] Moreover, in duping only the white characters, not the black, this illusory reversal is closely linked with the traditional double-voiced discourse of slavery.[23] As Douglass explains such apparent dishonesty, in slave society harsher enslavement could easily be "the penalty of telling the truth, of telling the simple truth, in answer to a series of plain questions." As a result, slaves hold it a maxim "that a still tongue makes a wise head. They suppress the truth rather than take the consequences of telling it, and in so doing prove themselves a part of the human family" (20). Nor is there any reason to doubt that Douglass would find surveillance by his abolitionist sponsors sufficient reason for continuing the circumspection and veiled discourse taught him in the South.[24]

Yet the tensions within the text mark more than the predictable irony of secular autobiography or slave discourse. For the secular rags-to-riches motif, like the conversion paradigm it supersedes, oddly limits the ways in which the slave can conceptualize his experience. The characterization of slave culture as poverty or "rags" is no less problematic than its vilification as sin. The negative construction of the plot as an "escape from" dictates that the narrative center of interest will lie almost exclusively in that which must be left behind: Audience interest in the plot ends just as the slave's life of "riches" begins. These narrative inconsistencies are matched by an even more troubling political paradox. The model of individual triumph over adversity tends to undermine the plea for social reform at the heart of all antebellum slave narratives. If the liberation is effected through exceptional intelligence and perspicacity, those who remain enslaved might seem flawed, lacking the requisite strengths to earn and merit freedom. Just such an implication cripples our appreciation for Sandy – and Uncle Tom.

The conflict between the representative and exceptional characteristics of the protagonist is a problem in all slave narratives, arguably in all American narratives.[25] Yet the problem may be especially strong in Douglass. For the *Narrative* is, at least in part, Douglass's "proof" that he was formerly a slave.[26] And to prove personal identity, his text relocates all the general paradoxes of the genre within himself. Douglass does not simply choose to present himself as a Franklinesque entrepreneur. His political position requires as credential a narrative of slavery as a personal experience. Not only does the success of that narrative as literary statement undermine its believability as historical document, it inevitably distances Douglass from the self he authenticates: The personal story validates the politician by establishing the existence of a self from which, by definition, he has "escaped."

It is this epistemological paradox that one critic has called the "black hermeneutic circle," a "declaration of the arbitrary relationship between a sign and its referent, between the signifier and the signified."[27] Douglass summarizes the problem in his description of the slaves' songs. Wishing to overturn the slaveholders' argument that these songs demonstrated the blacks' contentment, Douglass problematizes the relation between form and content, tone and sentiment, pathos and rapture (13). At first, his deconstruction seems to open the songs to a plurality of meanings: The slaves sing lyrics that "seem unmeaning jargon, but which, nevertheless, were full of meaning to themselves." Yet in fact the meaning for Douglass, though full, is univocal: "every tone was a testimony against slavery, and a prayer to God for deliverance from chains." Moreover, this meaning is available only to those who do not sing: "I did not, when a slave, understand the deep meaning of those rude and apparently incongruent songs. I was myself within the circle; so that I neither saw nor heard as those without might see and hear" (14).

The passage epitomizes the troubling subordination in many slave narratives, especially Douglass's, of personal experience to political point: the rapidity with which the various meanings of the songs reduce to the single meaning of slavery. And Douglass's dichotomy between participation and knowledge theorizes the narrative irony by which the flight from slavery becomes a flight from culture. Yet the passage does not merely internalize these tensions; it critiques them. Here, more explicitly than anywhere else in the *Narrative*, Douglass distinguishes between his youthful experiences "when a slave" and his mature reconsideration of those experiences. The contrast between the two voices confers full authority on neither. The mature narrator's greater understanding is balanced by a clear nostalgia for that time "within the circle" of the black community. Nor is the knowledge of "those without" really determinate: Although inarticulate, the singers know the songs to be "full of meaning to themselves." Rather than contrast experience and knowledge, then, the passage compares an unarticulated meaning of experience and an articulable meaning of distance. Douglass's apparent preference for the latter over the former is merely his recognition that in the slave narrative (as in the North) only the latter is available to him. And he experiences the black hermeneutic circle not as semantic inevitability but as a measure of his loss of group identity – an anxiety of ethnicity.[28]

The dual focus of Douglass's understanding of the slave songs, in fact, characterizes his whole conceptualization of slavery as the prohibition of knowledge. The work, of course, begins with the absence of knowledge:

> I have no accurate knowledge of my age, never having seen any authentic record containing it. By far the larger part of the slaves know as little of their ages as horses know of theirs, and it is the wish of most masters within my knowledge to keep their slaves thus ignorant. I do not remember to have ever met a slave who

could tell of his birthday. . . . A want of information concerning my own was a source of unhappiness to me even during childhood. The white children could tell their ages. I could not tell why I ought to be deprived of the same privilege. (1)[29]

Perhaps Douglass believes that an "authentic record" might "contain" his age, although both Emerson and Wittgenstein show this proposition to be false.[30] Yet more generally, the passage illustrates the paradox that what the youthful slave "could not tell" is itself the subject of the mature Douglass's account. And his telling of this untellability becomes the ironic proof that in his inability to tell he formerly was a slave. His punning "want" of information registers both the former lack and the nascent desire that would overcome that deficiency. And the claim that "most masters within my knowledge" keep slaves "ignorant" concentrates the paradox of the slave narrative into a single contradictory phrase: Not only does his knowledge "of" slaves deny the universal ignorance "of" slaves, but the very master–slave hierarchy is circumscribed "within" that paradoxical slave knowledge.

The strongest instance of this epistemological exclusion rests, however, not in the paradoxes of Douglass's voice but in the doubly excluded enslavement of those characters to whom even Douglass's mature understanding is immune – the female slaves. In one sense, women cut as poor figures in Douglass's highly individualized retelling as they do in Franklin's. Yet however understated, such figures as Douglass's mother, his grandmother, his aunt, and Mrs. Auld occupy central roles in Douglass's transformation. Although Mrs. Auld is the most obvious mentor, his mother the most touching, the role of Douglass's almost invisible wife Anna is, as one critic suggests, even more representative. Although not characterized, scarcely even mentioned, Anna stands silently at the center of the narrative's climax: She is the means by which, in his marriage certificate, Douglass "repossesses himself."[31]

Douglass's use of female guides to chart the progress of male development may show no real interest in the engendered individuality of their experience as women. Anna seems objectified in the liberating marriage certificate in roughly the same way Hamilton is in the earlier pass to freedom, the failed "protection." The narrative strategy involving Aunt Hester (Esther), however, is more complex. In his prefatory letter, Phillips defines slavery as that which "starves men and whips women" (xxi). Douglass's depiction of Hester's beating might seem to reduplicate the sexual insensitivity of Phillips's definition. At the end of the first, introductory chapter, the scene formally initiates Douglass into the horrors of slavery:

It was the first of a long series of such outrages, of which I was doomed to be a witness and a participant. It struck me with awful force. It was the blood-stained gate, the entrance to the hell of slavery, through which I was to pass. It was a most terrible spectacle. (5)

The scene stands synecdochally for all those female beatings that he does not mention, much as, in the fourth chapter, Demby's slaughter represents all the male murders he similarly omits. As his aunt, however, Hester is in more direct relation than Demby to Douglass himself. Her beating not only anticipates that of his cousin Henny but also foreshadows both the partial stripping and beating Douglass himself receives from Covey and the later beating whose absence commences his psychological liberation.[32]

This exemplary dimension of Hester's beating might seem to reduce her personal pain to a symbol of more general exploitation. But in fact, the very fullness of the depiction fights against its representative status. Most obviously, the description insists on the gender specificity of the beating. Although the narrator prudishly leaves the master's previous relations to Hester "to conjecture," he explicitly states that the punishment was not for general disobedience but for the specific act of visiting her black lover. Moreover, as the detailed description of the stripping makes clear, the violence has a sexual, even sadistic, dimension. The narrative almost echoes this ambivalence: When divorced from the "heart rending shrieks" that permeate the scene, the phrases about Hester's "neck, shoulders, and back, entirely naked" and her "warm red blood" seem surprisingly sensual (6). And if the scene dramatizes the youth's discovery of slavery as rape, it does so within the context of another archetypal moment: that of the child's breaking in upon parents engaged in the apparently violent act of sexual intercourse.

The youthful Douglass's failure to understand all the implications of the event he witnesses is not in any simple sense a failure of knowledge: He rightly labels the scene as one of the horrors of slavery. What he does not understand is that this particular horror is not and never will be his. "I was so terrified and horror-stricken at the sight, that I hid myself in a closet, and dared not venture out till long after the bloody transaction was over. I expected it would be my turn next" (6–7). The mature narrator knows the youth to be wrong. Not only does the boy's "turn" never come – at least, not quite in this way[33] – but the sexual undercurrents in the passage clearly indicate the narrator's implicit understanding of the different power dynamics in male and female beatings. His failure to comment more directly on this difference marks his tacit admission that as a male he is shut out from a knowledge of this uniquely female experience.

Thus, finally, Hester's beating is in one sense not exemplary at all. She does not "stand in" to illustrate something Douglass too experienced. Instead, much like the songs understood too late, her beating represents

not identity but difference, something Douglass once again sees from
"outside the circle." Despite the youth's claim to be "doomed to be a
witness and a participant," the passage emphasizes the former through
repeated images of observation and performance. He is regularly characterized as a "witness," with the event itself being a "spectacle" or
"exhibition." Moreover, observation quickly degenerates into voyeurism.
The scene is presented twice: first in terms of the boy's participatory
stance, and once more through a detailed delineation of the violation of
Hester's body. During the second telling the boy disappears from the
narrative, only at the end to admit his presence hidden in the closet. The
repetition emphasizes his fascination with, virtually his enjoyment of,
the brutal details. His placement in the second telling – spying from a
position of relative safety – suggests the prurience of any such description.
And we begin to suspect that he is "doomed" to witness and participate
in slavery because his participation as witness is itself morally suspect.

Douglass's voyeuristic participation in Hester's beating epitomizes the
ambiguity of his position throughout the *Narrative*. His proof that he
was once a slave recasts the escape story as a narrative of cultural
betrayal and redefines freedom as the "guilt" that he is a slave no
longer. The attempt to recapture that lost self only broadens the gap
– between who he was and what he is, between who they were and
who he never was. Description requires distance, and the pursuit of
knowledge, whatever it says about Douglass's personal identity, turns
his narration into a subtle form of pornography. This complex of
interconnected paradoxes constitutes what I called earlier Douglass's
"anxiety of ethnicity" – his recognition of the impossibility of knowing
the self as Other without opening an epistemological chasm between
the knowing subject and the known self.

Yet finally, the work is directed not inward but outward: Like all slave
narratives, Douglass's account wants chiefly to elicit an emotional and
political response from its readers. This readerly aspect of the text is
implied even in the customary subtitle of slave narratives: "written by
him/herself." The phrase primarily asserts the existence and narrative
authenticity of the autobiographical voice: "Frederick Douglass is a real
person; and his words have not been substantially altered by his editors,
Wm. Lloyd Garrison and Wendell Phillips, Esq." Yet the importance of
the phrase's pronoun should not obscure the significance of its preposition.
That the narrative is written "by" himself marks the extent to which it
is not written "for" himself. Ben Franklin can attribute his autobiographical
urge to simple vanity or even the garrulity of old men; the slave narrator
is allowed no comparably selfish motives, but writes to inform and
reform others.[34]

Yet Douglass's understandable interest in his readers raises the question of their somewhat more problematic interest in him. In part the nineteenth-century reader of slave narratives merely wants information on a topic insufficiently understood. Ignorance about the actual details of oppression is one of the ways in which those complicit in exploitation traditionally avoid confronting their complicity. Yet, as Douglass suggests in his view of Hester's beating, the gathering of data can itself be an intrusion, and in some situations it is difficult to distinguish between an honest wish to understand and a prurient desire to see.[35] Douglass exposes the mixed motives of his readers in the wryly sexualized language used to describe their need to know his escape route, even at the expense of closing off that route to subsequent fugitives. "It would afford me great pleasure indeed, as well as materially add to the interest of my narrative, were I at liberty to gratify a curiosity, which I know exists in the minds of many" (99). Not even to sell more books will he "please" readers by "gratifying" this curiosity.

In denying the "pleasures" of this particular text, Douglass does more than expose the hegemonic complacency underlying his readers' curiosity. He suggests through his own anxiety of ethnicity the even greater paradoxes informing white knowledge of blacks. First, of course, there is the quantitative difference in their ignorance: if Douglass can know slavery only in terms of what he is not, his belief in the incompatibility of knowledge and experience doubly excludes his readers – neither slaves nor on this point knowledgeable. This exclusion, moreover, may be logical as well as empirical. Douglass's characterization of his own epistemological dilemma, when reapplied to his readers, leaves them no means to understand slavery. On the one hand, to know black culture as difference, as Douglass himself does, seems racist in a white audience. And indeed, the tendency of much abolitionist rhetoric to reinforce a notion of racial hierarchy now appears condescending at best. On the other hand, knowing black culture as essentially the same as white inevitably collapses into knowing it *as* white. Even if his readers do not think that Douglass needs their assistance, racial guilt still leads them to coopt his pain. Recognizing their role in black persecution, whites make that persecution "their" problem. The result may not deny outright the difference between black and white. It does, however, tend to assimilate that difference to a cultural context that remains largely unchanged.

The white belief that slavery is "knowable," then, reduces a problem of epistemological difference to one of insufficient data. Douglass's insistence on his own inability to "read" difference relocates the philosophical question of unknowability at the heart of a genre that its white sponsors intended merely as a means of gathering and disseminating facts.[36] Garrison's difficulties in colonizing his protégé testify to the effectiveness of Douglass's

problematization of white ways of knowing. Garrison's attribution of
Patrick Henry's phrase to Douglass attempts to assimilate him to a white
tradition of rebellion, one culminating in midcentury America not with
Douglass but with Garrison himself. Yet Douglass's *Narrative* implicitly
redefines – and in its own quotation of the phrase explicitly tropes on –
the character of that assimilation. Douglass of course recognizes that the
Founding Fathers are not conspicuous for their interest in racial equality.[37]
More important, Garrison fails to realize that by offering Henry's phrase
to Douglass as black fugitive, he loses it himself as white abolitionist.
And in the context of the *Narrative*'s epistemological ambivalence, the
different positioning of the two men toward slavery reduces virtually to
the issue of utterability. Whatever the relation between Douglass and
Patrick Henry, Garrison himself cannot authorize the continuity: There
is simply no way in which Garrison could credibly cry at the end of
Douglass's speech, "Give him liberty or give him death."

Beneath the question of knowledge, then, lies the thornier question
of power. Slavery may be wholly the white man's shame; it is not so
exclusively his subject. And anxiety of ethnicity in the *Narrative* is experienced most fully not by the fugitive narrator but by his white readers.
Whatever Douglass's geographical distance from the slave culture he
deserted, it is far less than their ontological distance from it as members
of the persecuting other race. White northerners may sympathize with
Douglass's persecution, feel guilt for their complicity, even want to effect
a change, immediate or gradual. But however authentic and moral these
reactions, they all reinscribe structurally the white privilege they try
practically to overturn. The desire for knowledge presupposes the right
to know. The possibility of knowledge precludes the possibility of difference. And, outside the circle or in the closet, Douglass only stands in
for his white readers, whose very eagerness to know marks their disbelief
in the autonomy of the ethnicity they wish to defend.[38]

This final version of the anxiety of ethnicity has not diminished with
time. As it confounded the white audience of Douglass's generation, so
it confronts us. Slave narratives in general and Douglass's *Narrative* in
particular have taken on special significance for the modern black reader,
for whom they occupy an important position early in the tradition of
Afro-American literature, perhaps at its head.[39] Nonblack readers of the
Narrative – female or male, gay or straight – remain, however, as fully
problematized as ever by Douglass's paradoxes of knowledge. No longer
motivated by a practical political project like emancipation, we wish to
know the Afro-American literary tradition much as our forefathers wanted
to know slavery. But our need to read the books, like theirs to know
the facts, is morally ambiguous and epistemologically embattled. To
welcome the *Narrative* into "our" canon, of course, merely repeats the

act of colonization that helped generate so ironic a text in the first place. Yet to read fully Douglass's distancing strategies is in some sense to acknowledge our inability to "read" the work at all. Knowledge is not only power, but a power move as well. Douglass continues to remind us today, as he warned white readers then, that our sympathy is welcome but our interest must be earned. And although we are invited to listen, like Garrison we may not be in a position to speak.

NOTES

1   *Narrative of the Life of Frederick Douglass, An American Slave, Written by Himself* (Garden City, N.Y.: Anchor Press/Doubleday, 1973), p. 64. The characterization of Covey as a "nigger-breaker" is on p. 59. Subsequent references cite this edition parenthetically in the text. In preparing this essay, I have profited from the expert advice of Michael J. Colacurcio, Valerie Smith, Clarence E. Walker, and the students in my graduate seminar on the American Renaissance, especially Lori Lindgren Voorhees.

2   1 Thessalonians 5.2. See also 1 Thessalonians 5.4; 2 Peter 3.10; Revelation 3.3; and Revelation 16.15. The phrase derives from Christ's comparison of the coming of the Son of Man to that of a thief, for whom the wise householder will watch; see Matthew 24.43 and Luke 12.39. The comparison leads, in Matthew, to the parable of the ten virgins, an important source for the Puritan notion of preparation. For possible Old Testament anticipations, see Job 24.14 and Jeremiah 49.9.

3   For readings of Douglass that pay particular attention to this chapter, see Houston A. Baker, Jr., *The Journey Back: Issues in Black Literature and Criticism* (Chicago: University of Chicago Press, 1980), pp. 32–46, and his *Blues, Ideology, and Afro-American Literature: A Vernacular Theory* (Chicago: University of Chicago Press, 1984), pp. 39–50; Donald B. Gibson, "Reconciling Public and Private in Frederick Douglass's *Narrative*," *American Literature* 57 (1985), 549–69; David Leverenz, *Manhood and the American Renaissance* (Ithaca, N.Y.: Cornell University Press, 1989), pp. 108–34; Robert G. O'Meally, "Frederick Douglass' 1845 *Narrative*: The Text Was Meant to Be Preached," *Afro-American Literature: The Reconstruction of Instruction*, ed. Dexter Fisher and Robert B. Stepto (New York: Modern Language Association, 1979), pp. 192–211; and Bernd Ostendorf, "Violence and Freedom: The Covey Episode in Frederick Douglass' Autobiography," *Mythos und Aufklarung in der amerikanischen Literatur*, ed. Dieter Meindl and Friedrich W. Horlacher (Erlangen: Universitatsbund Erlangen-Nurnberg, 1985), pp. 257–70.

4   On the American tradition of spiritual autobiography, see Daniel B. Shea, Jr., *Spiritual Autobiography in Early America* (Princeton, N.J.: Princeton University Press, 1968), and Patricia Caldwell, *The Puritan Conversion Narrative: The Beginnings of American Expression* (New York: Cambridge University Press, 1983). For an account of the Augustinian paradigm lying behind the tradition, see William C. Spengemann, *The Forms of Autobiography: Episodes in the History of a Literary Genre* (New Haven, Conn.: Yale University Press,

1980), pp. 1–33. For a brief review of the stages of preparation and sanctification, see Edmund S. Morgan, *Visible Saints: The History of a Puritan
Idea* (Ithaca, N.Y.: Cornell University Press, 1965), pp. 67–8.

5 The phrase "the dark night of the soul" is the title of a work by the sixteenth-
century Spanish mystic St. John of the Cross. The relative unavailability of
the text before the late nineteenth century suggests that Douglass's allusion
is only to the notion of mystic passivity embodied in the work. Yet even
so general an allusion is interestingly at odds with the empiricist tone of
most American conversion narratives.

6 The later tellings of the incident emphasize even more the snake imagery.
See, for example, *The Life and Times of Frederick Douglass* (1892; rpt. New
York: Collier, 1962), pp. 122, 134. On this point the texts of the *Life and
Times* and *My Bondage and My Freedom* do not differ significantly; if anything,
My Bondage has slightly more snake imagery. See Frederick Douglass, *My
Bondage and My Freedom*, ed. Philip Foner (1855; rpt. New York: Dover, 1969),
p. 142. For general discussions of the place of Christianity in the *Narrative*,
see Baker, *The Journey Back*, pp. 36–8; Ann Kibbey, "Language in Slavery:
Frederick Douglass's *Narrative*," *Prospects* 8 (1983), 163–82; and Lucinda H.
MacKethan, "From Fugitive Slave to Man of Letters: The Conversion of
Frederick Douglass," *Journal of Narrative Technique* 16 (1986), 55–71.

7 For a representative Puritan use of Daniel as a type of Christ, see Mrs.
Rowlandson's captivity narrative *The Sovereignty and Goodness of GOD . . . ,
Narratives of the Indians Wars, 1675–1699* ed. Charles H. Lincoln (New York:
Barnes & Noble, 1966), pp. 156, 161. Douglass repeats the Daniel metaphor
to characterize as well his final escape to the North (106).

8 For an attempt to reconstruct the factual circumstances, see Dickson J. Preston,
Young Frederick Douglass: The Maryland Years (Baltimore: Johns Hopkins
University Press, 1980), pp. 117–30.

9 On the parallel but greater difficulties in representing persecution of females,
see Harriet Jacobs, *Incidents in the Life of a Slave Girl Written by Herself*
(Cambridge, Mass.: Harvard University Press, 1987), pp. 1, 53–5, et passim.
Most commentators on Jacobs emphasize the problem of propriety in the
female slave narrative. See, for example, Hazel V. Carby, *Reconstructing
Womanhood: The Emergence of the Afro-American Woman Novelist* (New York:
Oxford University Press, 1987), pp. 20–61; Henry Louis Gates, Jr., ed.,
The Classic Slave Narratives (New York: New American Library, 1987), pp.
xv–xviii; Annette Niemtzow, "The Problematic of Self in Autobiography:
The Example of the Slave Narrative," *The Art of Slave Narrative: Original
Essays in Criticism and Theory*, ed. John Sekora and Darwin T. Turner (Macomb:
Western Illinois University Press, 1982), pp. 105–8; and Valerie Smith, *Self-
Discovery and Authority in Afro-American Literature* (Cambridge, Mass.: Harvard
University Press, 1987), pp. 28–43.

10 See, for example, Thomas Shepard's account of his despair:
And I drank so much one day that I was dead drunk, and that upon a
Saturday night, and so was carried from the place I had drink at and did
feast at unto a scholar's chamber, one Basset of Christ's College, and knew
not where I was until I awakened late on that Sabbath and sick with my

beastly carriage. And when I awakened I went from him in shame and confusion, and went out into the fields and there spent the Sabbath lying hid in the cornfields where the Lord, who might justly have cut me off in the midst of my sin, did meet me with much sadness of heart and troubled my soul for this and other my sins which then I had cause and leisure to think of. *God's Plot: The Paradoxes of Puritan Piety, Being the Autobiography and Journal of Thomas Shepard*, ed. Michael McGiffert (Amherst: University of Massachusetts Press, 1971), p. 41.

11   *God's Plot*, p. 41.

12   Some scholars think Douglass writes with conscious reference to Equiano. Baker calls Douglass's *Narrative* a "palimpsest"; Gates labels Equiano Douglass's "second silent text." See Baker, *Blues, Ideology, and Afro-American Literature*, p. 39; and Gates, ed., *Classic Slave Narratives*, p. xiv. Even those who do not argue for conscious influence see a thematic and rhetorical continuity. See Smith, *Self-Discovery and Authority in Afro-American Literature*, pp. 20, 26–8.

13   Gates, ed., *Classic Slave Narratives*, p. 153. Subsequent references to Equiano cite this edition parenthetically in the text.

14   There is no reason, of course, to insist that Equiano as author is unaware of the limitations of his narrator's morality. The power of the prince's alternative viewpoint, like that of the more obvious ambiguities in Douglass's narrative, may suggest that Equiano too embeds subversive elements in his apparently conventional account.

15   The relation between storytelling and identity is central to both Stepto's and Smith's readings of the Afro-American tradition. For Douglass in particular, see Robert B. Stepto, *From Behind the Veil: A Study of Afro-American Narrative* (Urbana: University of Illinois Press, 1979), pp. 16–26; and Smith, *Self-Discovery and Authority in Afro-American Narrative*, pp. 20–6. The entrapping power of language is discussed in Baker, *The Journey Back*, pp. 32–46, and in Kibbey, "Language in Slavery."

16   The quotation of Patrick Henry may be doubly ironic. According to his introduction, Garrison quoted the same lines to lend his support to Douglass's first public speech (p. xi). The introduction of a white text to validate a black experience that needs no validation may itself be an ironic gesture. The choice of the same text that Garrison used may register even further his hostility to Garrison's patronization. On Douglass's problems with Garrison, see Waldo E. Martin, Jr., *The Mind of Frederick Douglass* (Chapel Hill: University of North Carolina Press, 1984), pp. 31–48; and, for a more theoretical view, Stepto, *From Behind the Veil*, pp. 17–20.

17   Hamilton's lack of an autonomous identity is reinforced by his other relation as "my master's father-in-law" (p. 86). It is amusing, though probably not significant, that Douglass misspells Hambleton's name. His retention of the mistake in all three versions of the autobiography suggests that he may never have recognized the error. The misspelling does, at least, make the forged "protection" even less efficacious: Presumably, anyone checking the pass would immediately notice the error. On Hambleton more generally, see Preston, *Young Frederick Douglass*, pp. 130–40.

18 For thoughtful accounts of the root, though ones generally less sympathetic
than mine, see Baker, *Blues, Ideology, and Afro-American Literature*, pp. 46–
7; and Leverenz, *Manhood and the American Renaissance*, pp. 110–12. Niemtzow
discusses the root pun in "The Problematic of Self in Autobiography," p.
103.

19 *My Bondage*, p. 242. The phrase in the *Life and Times* differs only incidentally,
p. 138.

20 Douglass, of course, never indicated any doubt of Sandy's loyalty, and
instead insisted that the informant must have been someone unknown to
all. On the limitations of Douglass's interpretation, see Preston, *Young Frederick
Douglass*, pp. 135–9.

21 Like the fight, this famous scene is treated by most scholars. For particularly
detailed readings, see Baker, *Journey Back*, pp. 32–5; Baker, *Blues, Ideology,
and Afro-American Literature*, pp. 42–4; O'Meally, "Douglass' 1845 *Narrative*,"
pp. 201–3; and Smith, *Self-Discovery and Authority in Afro-American Narrative*,
pp. 23–5. MacKethan resituates this scene within a conversion tradition in
"From Fugitive Slave to Man of Letters," pp. 60–4. The relation between
freedom and literacy is widely discussed; see especially Henry Louis Gates,
Jr., *The Signifying Monkey: A Theory of Afro-American Literary Criticism* (New
York: Oxford University Press, 1988), pp. 127–72.

22 See, for example, Franklin's disingenuous surprise when his essays in favor
of paper currency result in his firm being offered the contract to print the
money; *The Autobiography of Benjamin Franklin*, ed. Leonard W. Labaree et
al. (New Haven, Conn.: Yale University Press, 1964), p. 124. On Alger's
use of miraculous reversals, see, for example, *Mark the Match Boy*, where
the protagonist is discovered in the final chapters to be the long-lost heir of
a wealthy man.

23 The fullest account of this double-voiced discourse is Gates's treatment of
"Signifyin(g)" throughout *The Signifying Monkey*. Gates discusses Douglass's
role as "trickster" in "Binary Oppositions in Chapter One of *Narrative of
the Life of Frederick Douglass an American Slave Written by Himself*"; rpt. in
his *Figures in Black: Words, Signs, and the "Racial" Self* (New York: Oxford
University Press, 1987), p. 93; see also pp. 105–7. Kibbey deals with related
issues in "Language in Slavery," pp. 176–80. Focusing not on signification
but on a "vernacular" theory of the blues, Baker characterizes the double
voices of the *Narrative* as moral and economic; see *Blues, Ideology, and Afro-
American Literature*, pp. 39–50.

24 The pressures exerted on authors of slave narratives by their white editors
is a repeated theme throughout the scholarship. See, for example, William
L. Andrews, *To Tell a Free Story: The First Century of Afro-American Autobiography, 1760–1865* (Urbana: University of Illinois Press, 1986) pp. 19–
22; James Olney, " 'I Was Born': Slave Narratives, Their Status as Autobiography and as Literature," *The Slave's Narrative*, ed. Charles T. Davis
and Henry Louis Gates, Jr. (New York: Oxford University Press, 1985),
pp. 148–75; and Marion Wilson Starling, *The Slave Narrative: Its Place in
American History*, 2nd ed. (Washington, D.C.: Howard University Press,
1988), pp. 221–48.

25   For discussions of the paradox with respect to slave narrative in general, see Olney, " 'I Was Born,' " pp. 150–5; and Frances Smith Foster, *Witnessing Slavery: The Development of Ante-Bellum Slave Narratives* (Westport, Conn.: Greenwood Press, 1979), pp. 3–23. For treatments of this problem in the *Narrative*, see Gibson, "Reconciling Public and Private in Frederick Douglass' *Narrative*"; Niemtzow, "The Problematic of Self in Autobiography," pp. 98–104; and Smith, *Self-Discovery and Authority in Afro-American Narrative*, pp. 26–8. For biographical discussions of Douglass's troubled sense of self, see Martin, *The Mind of Frederick Douglass*, pp. 253–84; and Peter F. Walker, *Moral Choices: Memory, Desire, and Imagination in Nineteenth-Century American Abolition* (Baton Rouge: Louisiana State University Press, 1978), pp. 207–61. That the tension between individuality and representativeness may be built into our notion of America is apparent in our terminology: "Exceptionalism" is the name given to the belief in the Americanness of America.

26   Douglass tells of the disbelief of his slave origins, and his resulting decision to write the *Narrative*, in *My Bondage and My Freedom*, pp. 362–4; cf. *Life and Times*, pp. 218–19.

27   Gates, *Figures in Black*, pp. 96–7. Gates's reading of the songs in this passage has strongly influenced my own, which I take to be identical to his in all but its final turn. For other readings of the scene, see Kibbey, "Language in Slavery," pp. 165–7; Smith, *Self-Discovery and Authority in Afro-American Narrative*, pp. 26–8; and Stepto, *From Behind the Veil*, p. 23.

28   For a warning against the treatment of race as merely one form of a difference called "ethnicity," see Richard Yarborough's review of Werner Sollors's *Beyond Ethnicity*, "Breaking the 'Codes of Americanness,' " *American Quarterly* 38 (1986), 860–5. Although I agree with Yarborough's argument, I cannot think of a less problematic term for Douglass's experience of difference. I can only hope that since (by my reading) the true center of this difference is that between black author and white reader, my phrase does not reinscribe the kind of racism Yarborough fears. For my similar strictures against premature conflation of minorities, see "The Beast of the Closet: Homosociality and the Pathology of Manhood," *Critical Inquiry* 15 (1989), 603–5.

29   Again, the fullest reading of the ironies of the opening paragraph is Gates, *Figures in Black*, pp. 88–91. See also Gibson, "Reconciling Public and Private in Frederick Douglass' *Narrative*," pp. 551–2; and Olney, " 'I Was Born,' " pp. 152–7. The apparent differences between Gates's reading and mine derive from our focuses: Gates emphasizes the political and sociological differences of the black text; I emphasize Douglass's positioning of the narrator's voice as a way of positioning his audience. These emphases do not disagree in substance.

30   See Ludwig Wittgenstein, *Philosophical Investigations* (New York: Macmillan Publishing Co., Inc., 1968), sec. 265. I have discussed what such skepticism would look like in the nineteenth century in terms of Emerson's "Experience," published a year before the *Narrative*. See my *Emerson's Epistemology: The Argument of the Essays* (New York: Cambridge University Press, 1986), pp. 150–87.

31   See Baker, *Blues, Ideology, and Afro-American Literature*, p. 48. Baker talks
     more generally about the position of women in the triangulations of the
     text, pp. 39–43.

32   For a reading of the nonbeating as a revision of the earlier beating of Hester,
     see Smith, *Self-Discovery and Authority in Afro-American Literature*, pp. 22–
     6. For other treatments of the scene, see Baker, *Blues, Ideology, and Afro-
     American Literature*, p. 40; and Kibbey, "Language in Slavery," pp. 168–9.

33   During the beating that opens the tenth chapter, there is some indication of
     a submerged homosexual threat in Covey's repeated orders – and Douglass's
     repeated refusals – to strip. This implication, even if intended, is far more
     masked, however, than the clear representation of Hester's rape.

34   For Franklin's motives, see *Autobiography*, pp. 43–4. None of Franklin's
     other three overt motives, in fact, finds an exact parallel in Douglass. Franklin's
     intention to offer posterity a suitable model for imitation is closest to Douglass's
     own wish to educate his reader. The desire to glorify God, an afterthought
     in Franklin, is a possible motive for the slave narrator, but not one that
     Douglass himself embraces. And Franklin's "pleasure" in ancestral anecdotes
     finds only a vague parallel in Douglass's more melancholy sense of cultural
     banishment.

35   On the pornographic dimensions of the slave narrative, see Foster, *Witnessing
     Slavery*, p. 20. Her characterization of the "cultural matrix" of the narratives
     helpfully reviews the variety of reasons for the genre's popularity. The
     continuity between piety and pornography persists today, especially in the
     literature of child abuse.

36   For a recent examination of whether slavery is knowable, see Deborah E.
     McDowell, "Negotiating between Tenses: Witness Slavery After Freedom –
     Dessa Rose," *Slavery and the Literary Imagination*, ed. Deborah E. McDowell
     and Arnold Rampersad (Baltimore: Johns Hopkins University Press, 1989),
     pp. 144–63. For a critique of the category of race in terms of the philosophical
     problem of reidentifiability, see Anthony Appiah, "The Uncompleted Ar-
     gument: Du Bois and the Illusion of Race," *Critical Inquiry* 12 (1985), 21–
     37, especially p. 27.

37   On the attempt more generally of antebellum rhetoric to rewrite racial strife
     in the language of the Founding Fathers, see Eric J. Sundquist, "Slavery, Rev-
     olution, and the American Renaissance," *The American Renaissance Reconsidered*,
     ed. Walter Benn Michaels and Donald E. Pease (Baltimore: Johns Hopkins
     University Press, 1985), pp. 1–33. The recovery of Jefferson's racism is, of
     course, one of the major projects of recent Afro-Americanist theory.

38   For a similar reading of the desire to invent white ethnicity at the turn of
     the century, see Walter Benn Michaels, "The Souls of White Folk," *Literature
     and the Body: Essays on Populations and Persons*, ed. Elaine Scarry (Baltimore:
     Johns Hopkins University Press, 1988), pp. 185–209.

39   The role of the slave narrative as the foundation of Afro-American literature
     has recently been challenged by Hazel V. Carby; see "Ideologies of Black
     Folk: The Historical Novel of Slavery," *Slavery and the Literary Imagination*,
     pp. 125–43. McDowell's "Negotiating between Tenses" in the same volume
     is constructed in part as a response to Carby.

The Punishment of Esther

Frederick Douglass and the Construction of the Feminine

JENNY FRANCHOT

During the forty-seven-year course of his autobiographical career, Douglass often situated the image of the victimized – often "whipped" – female body at the emotional center of his critique on slavery. A conventional feature of slave narratives and abolitionist fiction, the sexual and physical abuse of the slave woman is especially apparent in the two antebellum versions of Douglass's autobiography, for these contain relatively little information about his postslavery career. The atrocities of slavery find their most powerful synecdoche in the silenced figure of the slave mother forced to endure rape, concubinage, and the theft of her children. Douglass's continued rhetorical exposure of the black woman's suffering body is crucial to his lifelong mission of disclosing the sins of the white fathers by turning slavery's hidden interiors into the publicized exterior of prose – an exposure that claims for itself a metaphysical power. As he declares in his disturbing account of Aaron Anthony's whipping of Aunt Esther (Hester), his stunned childhood witness of the whipping has the force of "revelation"; in diabolic imitation of Christ's manifestation of the concealed divinity, Esther's punishment appears as the "blood–stained gate" into the hitherto disguised interior of slavery, in whose secret being resides the punitive white father.[1] Douglass's narrative construction of Esther's punishment fixes upon her body, which in all its stark and abruptly damaged materiality ("Her shoulders were plump and tender. Each blow . . . brought screams from her as well as blood") stands as a condemnatory sign for an otherwise elusive patriarchy. Esther's back covers over, with violent materiality, the void at the base of Douglass's identity and in so doing perversely completes the denied connections that rendered Douglass's filial status little more than a lifelong conjecture.

A surrogate figure for Douglass's mother, Aunt Esther provides the author retrospective access to the recalcitrant interior of the past that closed within itself the parental relation. If slavery leaves him "without an intelligible beginning in the world,"[2] Esther's punishment, which

141

"struck . . . with awful force" (N, 25), obliterates any integral selfhood and imposes the new ontology of slavehood. Her degradation signals his loss of identity. Reconstructing what Anthony inflicted upon his mother's sister some two decades before, Douglass controls the memory (as he would many others) by converting it into a text conveying information from the otherwise silenced void of slavery. Grimly positioning the boy behind the white father, who himself stands behind the black woman, the scene invites the boy to read through the father to the mother-surrogate beyond. But Douglass does not arrive at Esther but rather reads through the father into the "system" behind him. Esther's punished back, a "most terrible spectacle" (N, 25), emits a virtual iconic power that resists the metaphorization designed to situate it as one more event in Douglass's teleological pursuit of literacy. Evading Douglass's interpretive strategies, the episode displays instead the conundrum of his family identity that would make any progressive self-development a simultaneous loss. Starkly opposing the white father-owner to the black mother-surrogate, the scene outlines bitterly conflicted racial and gender identifications. If the masculine is vitiated by its identification with the white slaveholder, so is blackness contaminated by its identification with the exposed and degraded woman. To achieve "manhood," then, is to forsake not only the mother but her race, whereas to achieve "blackness" is to forsake the father and his virility.

It is not only the episode's brutality but also its paradigmatic display of this intractable origin that makes it unforgettable. For Douglass, the subjectivity born of Esther's whipping (like the punishment itself) encloses an enslaved black femininity within a punitive white masculinity, forcing radical difference into union. Douglass's later and much advertised identification with a transracial masculine subjectivity provided him a complete identification otherwise unavailable to his privileged mulatto status, enabling him to suppress these contaminated dialectics of race and class beneath a discourse of self-reliant virility. But as Douglass's autobiographies continually suggest, that masculinized subjectivity remains linked to the black feminine through the very narratives that mark his literate virility. Abruptly introduced to slavery by the sight of the whipped Esther, Douglass's narrative construction of the event privileges it as originating moment, and thus lodges a memorial urge inside his rhetoric of indictment aimed at exposing slavery's "foul embrace" (N, 47).[3]

Esther's punishment visualizes this developmental conundrum and in so doing enacts slavery's prohibition against the growth of the self. From Douglass's vantage point in the closet adjoining the kitchen, where "through the cracks of its unplanned boards, I could distinctly see and hear what was going on, without being seen by old master" (MB, 87), the whipping tableau only partially manifests its figures, aptly staging Douglass's half-revealed origins. Again unseen by the white father and the even more distanced black mother, the "hushed" child experiences the dreadful fixity that is Esther's (*MB*, 88). Once translated into narrative, her punishment (and to a lesser extent the descriptions of the whippings of Nelly and Cousin Henny) disorders the progressive movement of the autobiography, which Douglass neatly enumerates in his final version of *Life and Times* as "first, the life of slavery; secondly, the life of a fugitive from slavery; thirdly, the life of comparative freedom; fourthly, the life of conflict and battle; and fifthly, the life of victory, if not complete, at least assured."[4] Lodged within that progressive self is the child-witness who, "stunned" into commodity status, resists autobiography's generic obligations to celebrate the changing self and exposes the limits (and limitations) of Douglass's self-transformational ideology. Confessing that "I never shall forget it whilst I remember anything" (*N*, 25), Douglass uncovers the impediment at the base of memory that makes the very act of remembering paradoxical. If memory serves as the means by which the self is constituted, he inevitably returns to that which denies the possibility of autonomous development. That denial is further registered by the loss of literary power in the later autobiographies. As "story," Douglass's autobiography threatens to stop at the punishment of Esther, unable to rival the aesthetic power achieved in the indictment of slavery's iniquities.

Douglass links his subsequent renamings that mark his acquisition of "manhood" and celebrity status to Esther's suffering and thus diminishes the static power of the memory by forcing it to participate in his developmental narrative. The whipping provokes his eventually emancipatory inquiry into the "nature and history of slavery" (*MB*, 89). This imposed genealogy fails to seal the rupture between her remembered degradation and his triumph. The opposition remains and suggests that Douglass acquired his virile autonomy somewhat at her expense. Receiving "some thirty or forty stripes" (*MB*, 88) and suffering repeated whippings thereafter, Esther plays the sacrifice to his redemption. As he admits in his less incriminating second autobiography, he receives different punishment from Aaron Anthony, "a regular whipping from old master, such as any heedless and mischievous boy might get from his father" (*MB*, 129) – punishments meant to signal his filial rather than enslaved status. Thus, although the "fate of Esther might be mine next," recalls Douglass of his terrified boyhood reaction, his destiny proves entirely otherwise (*MB*, 88). Indeed, his success as abolitionist orator depends uneasily upon his recurrent invocation of the whipped woman, for "she" is capable of provoking in his readers and listeners the same "palpitating interest" that Nelly's whipping does in the young Frederick (*MB*, 94). If, as he writes in his public letter to Thomas Auld, the "transition from degradation to respectability was indeed great, and to get from one to the other without

carrying some marks of one's former condition, is truly a difficult matter,"
the accounts of the marking of the slave woman enable Douglass to effect
that transition.[5] Her suffering provides him with his credentials as victim –
critical to his self-authentication as fugitive slave-orator; her femininity
enables him to transcend that very identification – a transcendence critical
to his success as the "Representative Colored Man of the United States."

Douglass was not unaware of the uneasy connection between his
exposure and that of the enslaved woman. The sensation caused by the
exhibition of his subversively claimed manhood drew upon his exposé
of the slaveholder – an unmasking most effectively achieved through the
publication of the slavewoman's degradation with the very powers of
literacy that marked his emancipation. Reported one Irish newspaper of
Douglass's 1845 speech in Limerick: "Mr. Douglas[s] then proceeded to
exhibit some of the implements used in torturing the slaves, among which
was an iron collar taken from the neck of a young woman who had
escaped from Mobile. It had so worn into her neck that her blood and
flesh were found on it (sensation)."[6] It was an avenue unavailable to
female abolitionists. In a gracious letter of commendation to Harriet
Tubman, for example, he owned the benefits accrued form his highly
public masculinity: "The difference between us is very marked. Most
that I have done and suffered in the service of our cause has been in
public, and I have received much encouragement at every step of the
way. You, on the other hand, have labored in a private way."[7] Although
acknowledging that black women were denied the benefits of an uninvidious
publicity, he continued to argue that his self-exhibition could provide
an imitable model for women. Reported one listener to Douglass's 1850
speech, "Let Women Take Her Rights": "He had been its victim [of
public opinion], and the lesson he had learned was to *take* his rights
wherever he could get them – to assume them, at any rate, as properly
his. . . . Let Woman take her rights, and then she shall be free."[8]

Other evidence suggests that Douglass's model of aggressive individualism signaled not so much the potential for female emancipation as for
continued female subordination. Reporting for the *New York Daily Graphic*
in 1874 of her attempt to land a position as assistant editor for a Washington
weekly, writer Celia Logan encountered Douglass in the editor's office;
he encouraged her to apply. Logan's description of their exchange reveals
the unstable line between "example" and "specimen," between Douglass's
projection of self-made literate virility and the spectacle of himself as
unique instance:[9]

"Look at me – not that I offer myself as an example, but I have
overcome by preseverance [sic], obstacles that even women do not
have to contend with. . . . Thirty years ago I did not know a single

letter, and I was then a man." He rose from his chair, his eyes blazing with indignation, and he tossed back his white locks.

The play of his fine features made a little thrill run through me. The dignity of his attitude, the majesty of his stature made Frederick Douglass look every inch a man.

As Logan reports it, Douglass's abrupt invitation to "Look at me" shows him well practiced at provoking and managing the admiration of white onlookers and suggests that his insistent denial of difference ("There is no difference, except of colour, between us"[10]) depended upon the potential duplicities of sentimental sympathy whose rapt focus upon the suffering object did not necessarily induce empathy, much less political action. Recalling that he "was called upon to expose even my stripes, and with many misgivings obeyed the summons and tried thus to do my whole duty in this my first public work" (LT, 512), Douglass did not submit to this exhibitionism but rather aggressively publicized it in order to control the potentially contaminatory relation between the eroticized punishment of the black woman and the acquisition of his virile rhetoric of exposure. Douglass typically deflected audience attention from the "feminine" exposure of his body (taking off his shirt to reveal his scars) to the "masculine" display of his face. Thus Douglass proffered his features on the podium as evidence against the racist pseudoscience of the new ethnology:[11]

> We have heard all that can be said against the humanity of the negro, from one who deals with the matter scientifically. He (Mr. Grant) does not come here to browbeat, nor to arouse your prejudice; no, he appeals to your understanding; but look at me – look at the negro in the face, examine his woolly head, his entire physical conformation; I invite you to the examination, and ask this audience to judge between me and that gentleman (Mr. Grant). Am I a man?

If Douglass invoked his scarred back as synecdoche for the hidden body of slavery, his face – as unconcealed body – obscured any easy decipherment of slavery; although the inscriptions of the whip on his back unambiguously portrayed the slavebreaker's brutality, his face denied that victimization, registering instead a "standing accusation" (MB, 59) against the slaveholder fathers and their concealed sexual crimes. But although his features signified paternal criminality, they also manifested the uniqueness and freedom born from that corrupted genealogy. According to one biographer, Douglass preserved a newspaper clipping describing him as "perhaps the only perfectly pronounced and complete specimen in the world of his color, kin, and kind. Mount Caucasus [and] the mountains of the Moon were joined with our Indian wilderness to mix the strain of blood from three races in his veins and produce a peculiar individuality with no antecedent or copy of his traits."[12] Affectionately called "my little Indian boy" by his first owner and probable father, Aaron Anthony, Douglass likely inherited his distinctive "Indian" features through the maternal line, for his venerated grandmother was reportedly part Cherokee. Douglass enjoyed the subversive potential of his face, for its racial ambiguity beckoned prejudiced whites to draw closer – close enough to see not him but themselves. Like his narrative procedure of sardonically redisguising himself as silenced black man, which concluded his incisive exposé of life on the Lloyd plantation ("But, let others philosophize; it is my province here to relate and describe; only allowing myself a word or two, occasionally, to assist the reader in the proper understanding of the facts narrated" [*MB*, 106]), Douglass's face enabled him to elude and hence mock racial categories. In the *Life and Times*, he recorded one such subversive episode:

> A passenger on the deck of a Hudson river steamer, covered with a shawl, well-worn and dingy, I was addressed by a remarkably-religiously-missionary-looking man in black coat and white cravat, who took me for one of the noble red men of the far West, with "From away back?" I was silent, and he added, "Indian, Indian?" "No, no" I said; "I am a Negro." The dear man seemed to have no missionary work with me, and retreated with evident marks of disgust. (463)

Elsewhere, he exploited the rhetorical power of a suspended self-disclosure that functioned as vicarious exposure of the body. "My back is scarred by the lash – that I could show you. I would, I could make visible the wounds of this system upon my soul."[13] Both displayed and retracted, Douglass's scarred back claims the advantages of a publicity that avoids the degradation of visual exposure. Such a rhetorical transaction, skillfully containing the feminine power of the lacerated back within the masculine confines of the heroic face, pointedly inverted slavery's invasive exposure of black bodies and proved invariably successful in performance. "I was subject to all the evils and horrors of slavery," said Douglass to one Irish audience, "and even as I stand here before you I bear on my back the marks of the lash (sensation)."[14] Offering himself as both suffering object and virile subject, Douglass protects not only his exterior but also the undisclosed "wounds . . . upon [his] soul" from any infection by the diseased interior of slavery, thus fending off undue readerly (or audience) intimacy invited by his rhetoric of self-exposure by offering them the spectacle of his penetration of slavery. Declaring to an English audience that "I need not lift up the veil by giving you any experience of my own,"[15] he can then give his own experiences under another guise. Refusing to unveil himself, he personifies the slave system as the depraved feminine who "could only live by being permitted to grope her way in darkness"[16] and whom he, as depersonalized "representative man," must expose. Douglass returned time and again to these potentially incriminating problematics of self-exposure; in the concluding pages of his final autobiography he again disavows the self-feminizing aspect of his exemplary status, insisting that "I have written out of my experience here, not in order to exhibit my wounds and bruises and to awaken and attract sympathy to myself personally, but as a part of the history of a profoundly interesting period in American life and progress" (LT, 478).

If the slavewoman, as represented by abolitionist prose, articulated middle-class white woman's resentful complicity in her own subordination to white patriarchal power and lack of ownership of her body, she did so as well for Douglass, who as favored mulatto child endured a liminal status structurally analogous to that of the middle-class white woman, neither brutally subjugated nor granted equality. Douglass's Maryland biographer, Dickson Preston, convincingly argues that it was "precisely because he was a privileged child rather than an abused one, because he was spared slavery's burdens rather than being crushed by them, that he remained sensitive to the damning effect of abuse on others."[17] As Douglass's later comments about his own whippings indicate, such punishment (enforcing his black over his white status) deflected attention from his ambiguously favored status. "I feel at liberty to speak on this subject. I have on my back the marks of the lash."[18] A key 1852 speech, "The Internal Slave Trade," memorably characterizes the segregation bound into his ambiguous filial status as Tommy Auld's companion: "I lived on Philpot Street, Fell's Point, Baltimore, and have watched from the wharves the slave ships in the basin, anchored from the shore, with their cargoes of human flesh, waiting for favorable winds to waft them down the Chesapeake." The reminiscence strikingly recalls his famous description of watching ships sail to freedom on the Chesapeake. Like his stepson status with Hugh and Sophia Auld, the two shorebound passages reveal him as headed neither north nor south. Like the autobiographies, "The Internal Slave Trade" answers the anxiety of this suspended racial and filial status by appealing to the punitive contact of the whip that enables Douglass and his audience to come closer to slavery and to one another:[19]

> Suddenly you hear a quick snap, like the discharge of a rifle; the fetters clank, and the chain rattles simultaneously; your ears are saluted with a scream that seems to have torn its way to the center of your soul. The crack you heard was the sound of the slave whip; the scream you heard was from the woman you saw with the babe.

The stasis of that observer, caught between the two "races," lies beneath the text of Esther's punishment: In describing the whipped woman, Douglass sublimates his own fixity to the reimagined horror of her bondage, sentimentally reinhabiting the body of the enslaved and absolving (if only temporarily) his liminal status. As symbol and instrument of excess and the breaking of boundary, the whip assumes a charismatic authority in Douglass's discourse. Sufficient in its excess to create a suffering narrator and reader, the punishment of Esther bridges the black person's status elsewhere described by Douglass as that of being "aliens . . . in our native land."[20] But of course, in witnessing Esther's terrible suffering, Douglass is drawn not only into terrible communion with her but with Aaron Anthony as well, for he observes the scene from his father's point of view. And like Stowe's sentimental narrative technique, which produces identification while enforcing hierarchy and difference, Douglass's description of Esther's whipping serves finally to make visible his heroic attainment of control, irony, and distance in the narrative voice. As his interpolated references to the struggles of writing subordinate her punishment to his authoring, so Esther's punishment provides him a temporary membership in the suffering body whose final function is to afford him a permanent escape from it. As the spectacle created and in turn transcended by the narrative of his "several lives in one" (LT, 479) and as the great antagonist in his autobiographical quest, "slavery" functions as feminized antithesis to a narrative whose insistence upon linear progress and aggressive individuation testifies to its masculine credentials. Thus his descriptions betray a paradoxical exploitation of the very feminine that they seek to rescue, advertising an identification strategically dependent upon maintaining a superior (if agonized) distance. Guarding his ever progressive virility from undue identification with the stasis of the bound Esther, Douglass authenticates his credentials as victim while transcending the contamination of victimized femininity. It becomes the measure of that virility to touch, even manipulate, the contamination of victimage at the height of his oratorical performances.

Although largely silent about his adult domestic life in his autobiographies, Douglass writes at length about the women he knew when a slave. Grandmother Betsey Bailey, his mother Harriet, his Aunt Esther, cousin Henny, "Aunt" Katy, and the white women, Lucretia Auld (his half sister) and Sophia Auld (his Baltimore mistress), memorably demonstrate slavery's capacity to punish or to corrupt. Douglass's white and black female characters form the measure of slavery's otherwise uncontrollable masculine power and hence serve as the means to expose, if not fully decipher, the inscrutable male, who through the unpredictable agency of the father-owner "committed outrages, deep, dark and nameless"

(*MB*, 79). Once Douglass shifts from discussing his life as a fugitive slave to his career in the North, however, he relegates women to the periphery of his text. This marginalization in one sense reflects a partial normalizing of sexual and racial relations in the North, where rape and concubinage did not enjoy institutional sanction. However, that relative degree of improvement ironically facilitates Douglass's suppression of women in his account of life as an "ex-slave." The subsidence of women into the ambiguously privileged domain of middle-class domesticity enables Douglass's elision of women to appear as the sign of freedom and autonomous control over the household.

In the final three autobiographies, the intensified and frequently punitive relations between men and women under slavery – be it the sexual sadism of the master toward his slave Esther, or young Frederick's vulnerability to the tyrannical maternal power of "Aunt" Katy and his anxious attachment to his half sister, "Miss Lucretia" (whom he must serenade in order to be fed) – yield to a self-parented hero occupied with male rivals and the conquest of the public, avowedly masculine worlds of journalism and oratory. As the autobiographies extend to Douglass's postslavery experiences, the absence of women becomes increasingly noticeable. As if to say that one knows women in slavery and men in freedom, the final autobiography condenses any extended acknowledgment of female influence into one chapter ("Honor to Whom Honor") out of fifty-three while expansively discussing heroic encounters with such masculine model/ rivals as William Lloyd Garrison, Abraham Lincoln, and John Brown. Trenchant descriptions of his precarious position within the largely female household world of slavery issue to depictions of an invincible (and nomadic) autonomy designed to demonstrate that his self-reliance as a "man" can untangle the knotted strands of being a "black man." Douglass's claim that "races, like individuals, must stand or fall by their own merits" (*LT*, 479), by personalizing the question of race, converts its intractable problems into the claimed simplicities of gender.[21]

This shift from often impassioned descriptions of women in slavery to virtual silence about them in the comparative freedom of the North testifies to the repression of the feminine required by the middle-class virility that Douglass emulated.[22] Situating himself in the American Revolutionary tradition of self-reliant opposition to tyranny, Douglass strove to negate the vestiges of any "effeminate" dependence or vulnerability. His final autobiographical version of the death of his daughter Annie tellingly illustrates this suppression of the domestic:

> Though disappointed in my tour of the Continent, and called home by one of the saddest events that can afflict the domestic circle, my presence here was fortunate, since it enabled me to participate in

the most important . . . presidential canvass ever witnessed in the
United States, and to labor for the election of a man who in the
order of events was destined to do a greater service to his country
. . . than any man who had gone before him in the presidential
office. (*LT*, 325)

The syntactical subordination of the lost daughter to his participation
in Lincoln's first presidential campaign dramatizes the extent of Douglass's
attachment to the narrative conventions of the white masculine world.
If his accounts of slavery vehemently indict the father–owner Aaron
Anthony, and the Auld brothers who subsequently owned and "fathered"
him, Douglass does not abandon the treacherous dynamics of filial subordination to white patriarchal power. With reference to Garrison, he
describes himself as "something of a hero-worshiper by nature" (*LT*,
213); of John Brown, he writes that he was "not long in company with
the master of this house before I discovered that he was indeed the master
of it, and was likely to become mine too if I stayed long enough with
him" (*LT*, 272). The later autobiographies, as they recount his separation
from Garrison, his refusal to join with John Brown, and his penetrating
indictment of Lincoln (trenchantly summarized in his 1876 "Oration . . .
at the Unveiling of the Freedmen's Monument"), display his expropriation
of their charismatic patriarchal authority. Since his resistance to male
power is effected by suppressing the role of women in his own life, the
critique paradoxically increases rather than diminishes the presence of
the paternal.[23]

   With disturbing ease, then, the silence of the slave that figures prominently in Douglass's account of his Maryland past yields to the subordination of the feminine in his account of life in the North. Silence
conventionally functions in the autobiographies as the principal index of
slavery's blighting impact:[24]

> But ask the slave – *what* is his condition? – *what* his state of mind? –
> *what* he thinks of enslavement? and you had as well address your
> inquiries to the *silent dead*. There comes no *voice* from the enslaved.
> We are left to gather his feelings by imagining what ours would
> be, were our souls in his soul's stead.

But as Douglass insists, the voicelessness of the slave is born of strategic
reticence. The silence of women, however, is more profound, for it
implies no language held back in wary reserve. Douglass's autobiographies
advertise themselves both as the slave's "voice" and as its imaginative
equivalent – a voice whose abrasiveness and plentitude powerfully disrupt
racist theories asserting illiteracy to be the racial inheritance of the African.[25]
Plausible surrogate for the male slave, Douglass's voice belies its implied

claim to speak for the enslaved woman as well. Although presupposing a universal applicability, Douglass's discourse of vicarious identification, of imagining himself into the position of the suffering other, does not uncover women's voice. Esther is granted brief speech in *My Bondage* (" 'Have mercy; Oh! have mercy' she cried; 'I won't do so no more' " [88]. But free women, black or white, rarely speak at all. Even in his accolade for women's contribution to the antislavery movement, Douglass recollects Lucretia Mott as presence rather than speech: "Seated in an antislavery meeting, looking benignantly around upon the assembly, her silent presence made others eloquent, and carried the argument home to the heart of the audience" (*LT*, 469). Women's voice in slavery becomes virtually their only voice. Douglass's campaign, then, against the "concealment" that is the "constant care of slaveholders"[26] recapitulates its gestures by concealing his adult interactions with women, whether inside or outside of the domestic.

Douglass's suppression of the feminine, recorded in his novella *The Heroic Slave*, as well as in his autobiographies, occurred alongside his lifelong support for women's rights. One of thirty-two men who attended the 1848 Seneca Falls convention, Douglass spoke throughout his career for "Woman" and had as the slogan for *The North Star* "Right is of no sex Truth is of no color." While evacuating his autobiographical texts of any adult relations to women, he devoted many speeches and editorials to their rights. Throughout his career as abolitionist and "woman's rights man," he held up his progress from enslaved to emancipated masculinity as a model for women by which to overcome their subjugation. The emancipatory rhetoric of these feminist speeches, however, bears little relation to the autobiographical portraits of women in slavery, for his oratorical discourse about "Woman" flattens the narrative terrain inhabited by a series of women enacting various aspects of Douglass's personal crisis of miscegenated, illegitimate, and enslaved origin. In this shift from autobiographical prose to rhetorical polemic, the representation of women evades more than resolves the crisis of miscegenation and dependence encoded within the autobiographies and the novella. Notwithstanding the evident rupture between the two manifested by these separate and unequal representations, Douglass frequently asserted that his suffragism stemmed naturally from his abolitionism and that the connection between enslaved women on the one hand and "woman" on the other was an unproblematic one:[27]

> It may be that there is something in our position, in this country –
> something in the injustice of which we are the subjects – something
> in the hatred of slavery and proscription, either natural or acquired

by the hard circumstances of our early life – at any rate, from some
cause – this whole woman question is exceedingly plain and simple,
and commends itself at once to our mind.

The statement is a striking one not only because it records frank male
advocacy of women's rights but also because, having done so, it attempts
to obscure the support it offers. Explaining that his own slave experience
has enabled him to intuit the plight of women (of whatever race), he
declares himself unsure as to the reasons for his feminist convictions.
That Douglass couches his support in such mystified language ("it may
be," "something," "at any rate, from some cause") argues for his difficulty
in maintaining a relationship between the black and the white feminine.
Can "woman" as rhetorical category equally include black and white
women? His statement posits a natural continuum from his powerful
identification with black women when an enslaved child (and with his
two white "mothers," Lucretia and Sophia Auld) and his later political
support for "woman" when a free man. This latter "woman," favored
but denied recognition, functions as an abstracted version of himself,
whose own ambiguously privileged background as son of Anthony and
member of the well-known Bailey clan distanced the slave child from
complete identification and burdened him with a vicarious more than
actual relation to any one family, race, and class. That he should sufficiently
obscure his original connections with black women so that his later
support for "woman" emerges, finally, only "from some cause" suggests
that his desire to rid himself of the "marks of one's former condition"
("Letter to His Old Master" [*MB*, 421]) was chiefly effected through an
autobiographical discourse acknowledging the black woman and an oratorical discourse acknowledging the white. This splintering of the feminine
enables him to separate his otherwise contradictory agendas of gender
dominance and racial equality. Through the victimized figure of the black
woman he asserts his transcendent malehood; through the figure of the
(white) "woman" he asserts his claim to racial equality.

In the immediate postbellum years, the precarious workings of this
strategy broke down. Douglass insisted that suffrage be extended to black
men before "woman," since black men stood in more critical need of
the protection afforded by enfranchisement. Feminists such as Susan B.
Anthony and Lucy Stone refused to accept what they viewed as Douglass's
subordination of women to the special case of slavery. The punitive
conditions of Reconstruction existed in the North as well, argued Stone,
where "Ku-Kluxes . . . in the shape of men . . . take away the children
from the mother and separate them as completely as if done on the block
of the auctioneer."[28] To Stone and other feminists who urged the joint
advancement of blacks and women, Douglass's position belied the iden-

tification between his enslavement and woman's subjugation previously asserted by his antebellum abolitionist rhetoric:[29]

> Woman is not excluded with a view to her degradation, or out of a spirit of hate. Nobody will pretend that she is. On the contrary, a sentiment quite opposite to malice dictates her exclusion. It is an error, and one which is to be met with light and truth. Far otherwise is the case of the black man's exclusion from public halls. . . . the very spirit of the pit is here manifest, and against which no rebuke is too stringent.

Situating the question of women's suffrage "upon another basis than that on which our right rests,"[30] Douglass's subordination of his identification with women (black or white) to an alliance with black men ironically entangled him in a dubious defense of the family and the very paternalist myth whose fraudulence he had exposed in his public indictment of Thomas Auld and his critique of Abraham Lincoln. At the 1869 American Equal Rights Association meeting, for example, he argued that "in some ways the men are *compelled* to protect the women; they protect them from the motives both of politeness and affection, but my race is hated, and in proportion to the measure of the dislike is the necessity of defense before and in the law."[31] Insisting upon a hierarchy of exclusions, Douglass subordinated any equivalence between his and women's subjugation to the claims of his gender. And in arguing that such masculine compulsion need not sully masculine "affection" for women, Douglass implicitly invoked his problematic origins that so bitterly confused the affectional and the coercive as justification for his subordination of "woman."

With the passage of the Fifteenth Amendment enfranchising black men, Douglass returned to supporting women's rights and was even given to declaring the superiority of the latter cause over his own abolitionism: "When I ran away from slavery, it was for my people; but when I stood up for the rights of women, self was out of the question, and I found a little nobility in the act."[32] Traveling through Egypt with his second wife, he recorded his objections to the Islamic subordination of women in a diary entry that shows him returning to his antebellum formulations of equivalence between racial and gender oppression, but only within the context of a foreign culture and religion: "It is sad to think that one-half of the human family should be thus cramped, kept in ignorance and degraded, having no existence except that of minister[ing] to the pride and lusts of the men who own them as slaves are owned."[33]

Because "manhood" and "freedom" function throughout Douglass's discourse as coincident terms, his shift from the obscurity of enslavement to the publicity of being the "Representative Colored Man of the United

States" marks a transition from the afflicted feminine to the empowered masculine. Ironically applying the vernacular of evangelical rebirth, which traditionally records the ecstatic loss of selfhood, to convey his abrupt acquisition of an independent identity, Douglass describes his conquest of the slavebreaker Covey: "I was a changed being after that fight. I was *nothing* before; I was A MAN NOW" (*MB*, 247). This gendered conversion paradigm unavoidably situates the feminine within the *"nothing"* that precedes the acquisition of virile autonomy; as the principal sign of the annihilated world of the captive, the feminine comes to share in its nothingness and, in so doing, anticipates the postenslavement dynamic by which the substantial female characters known in slavery ephemeralize into a residual, abstracted "effeminacy" within the ex-slave.

Douglass's subsequent advertisement of this conversion to the masculine suggests that his newfound exposure as famed abolitionist speaker depended upon a rhetorical exploitation of slavery that simulated the slaveholder's sexual abuse of female slaves. Resisting the paternalist Garrisonian injunction to just "give us the facts," Douglass claims the white man's prerogative to critique his own self-exhibit: "It did not entirely satisfy me to *narrate* wrongs. I felt like *denouncing* them" (*LT*, 217). Narration and denunciation together constitute what he characteristically terms his "exposure" of slavery. "I expose slavery in this country, because to expose it is to kill it," announced Douglass at the beginning of his extraordinarily popular lecture tour of Great Britain. Aiming to unveil slavery's interior, "opening the dark cell, and leading the people into the horrible recesses of what they are pleased to call their domestic institution,"[34] Douglass's oratory gains its force through the unmasking of slavery's concealed atrocities. In constructing his first account of Esther's whipping, he writes that Anthony "stripped her from neck to waist" and tied her so that she "now stood fair for his infernal purpose" (*N*, 26); in a similar fashion, the fugitive slave strips slavery, enunciating his manhood by forcing the "system" to yield "her" secrets. If slavery links language and violence in a depraved symbiosis personified by the overseer for whom "it is literally a word and a blow" (*MB*, 103), Douglass's indictment, as it punitively exposes the slaveholder ("I want the slaveholder surrounded as by a wall of anti-slavery fire, so that he may see the condemnation of himself and his system glaring down in letters of light"),[35] vicariously enjoys that perverse connection.

As suggested by Douglass's famous assertion that his "feet have been so cracked with frost, that the pen with which I am writing might be laid in the gashes" (*MB*, 132), his wounded body serves as arbiter of his literary performance. It is not just that only by having been whipped can one speak, but that the whip itself performs a type of authoring that, in converting body into text ("The overseer had written his character on the living parchment of most of their backs" [*MB*, 177]), permits that body to author in turn. At times Douglass even personalizes this penmanship of the whip into dialogue: "In the sacred name of Jesus we beg for mercy, and the slave-whip, red with blood, cracks over us in mockery."[36] Language as promptly metamorphoses into a weapon; Hugh Auld's "iron sentences – cold and harsh – sunk deep into my heart" (*MB*, 146). Such reiterated assertions of equivalence between the whip and the word dramatically contrast to his struggles elsewhere over the issue of identification. Although the whipping scenes unforgettably register the crucially important narrative and psychological structures of disparity that fuel Douglass's writings, the consequent convergence between the whip and the word that typically occurs in these episodes offsets the felt sense of difference and approximate identity that destablilzed Douglass's feminist discourse. Although ostensibly opposed, language and physical violence identify, even recognize, one another. And to the extent that they speak to each other, the whip and its accompanying language (both as recollected "fact" and as "fictional" elaboration) offer a model of surrogate kinship otherwise denied the slave son.[37]

Douglass's recurrent use of the trope of rhetorical impotence serves as virtual signal for the production of language and hence as progenitor of the text. Like the deity of mystical discourse, slavery functions in his autobiographical discourse as that which resists language – a resistance that, in turn, instigates verbal exposure. Douglass caps his detailed, re-velatory description of Esther's whipping with an assertion of his failure: "language has no power to convey a just sense of its awful criminality" (*MB*, 88). In all its versions, however, the passage on Esther's punishment implies a symbiosis between her body, tied to the joist and streaming with blood, and his text memorializing that body some two decades later. The screams of the "gory victim" and the "most terrible spectacle" generate a linguistic impotence ("I wish I could commit to paper the feelings with which I beheld it" [*N*, 25]) that, by its eloquent confession of inadequacy, articulates its indignation by focusing attention on Douglass's own procedures of authoring.[38] Although his rhetorical helplessness is meant to measure Esther's radical abjection, the narrator's plight is con-tinuously belied by his narrative powers, which adroitly produce a searing but genteel text whose absences mark the atrocity of the "other" rather than its own deficiencies.

The contagion between his language and her punishment emerges not only in self-reflexive references to the operations of writing but in the recollected structure of the episode itself. Supplying more locational detail in his revised version of the episode for *My Bondage*, Douglass suggests that Esther's punishment was already framed for him by his position in the closet. Like the fugitive Harriet Jacobs, who witnesses her tormentor,

Dr. Flint, through her "peephole," Douglass's position as voyeur articulates
the silenced slave's subversive powers of observation. The closet cracks
affix a frame to Aaron Anthony and in so doing both label his barbarity
and prevent what was "revolting and shocking, to the last degree" (*MB*,
88) from exceeding its boundaries. Such framing, as it aestheticizes Anthony
and Esther, works then to seal off the revelation from the child observer.
The experience is, in a sense, already made text in its unfolding, for the
spatial boundary imposes an order upon the episode's distorted temporality.
Awaking to the dawn scene, Douglass is deprived of "preliminaries" that
might have explicated what was to occur. As slavery withholds from
him an "intelligible beginning" (*MB*, 60), so does Esther's punishment
begin without him. It is not only its barbarity but also its confusion that
makes it such an unforgettable cameo of slavery. Like Douglass himself,
the punishment is unique and mysterious, *and* is a fully iterable example
of the system.

Douglass's slight but telling emendations of the passage in his successive
autobiographies speak to that dual construct; the revisions attest to a
disturbing instability surrounding the primal memory that threatens to
expose the scene as malleable narrative convention rather than unique
and indelible memory. In the first version, Douglass massively incriminates
Aaron Anthony by situating himself as witness to the tying up: "He then
told her to cross her hands . . . he tied them . . . he made her get upon
the stool, and tied her hands to the hook" (*N*, 26). He is no longer
witness to those preliminaries in *My Bondage*, which presents Esther
already bound, the punishment in progress. In likely response to the loss
of intelligibility implied by this adjusted memory, Douglass inserts in
the second version three additional sentences that protract the actual
description of the whipping by supplying a new motivational hypothesis
for the father's behavior.[39] Yet even that newly supplied preliminary is
lost by the fourth version of the autobiography: there, Anthony is already
"pursuing his barbarous work" rather than, as in *My Bondage*, "preparing"
for it. Although Anthony's malevolent agency is diminished by our no
longer witnessing the tying up, and by Douglass's suppression of his
"father's" language ("Now, you d_____d b_____h, I'll learn you how
to disobey my orders!" becomes, in the second version, "all manner of
harsh, coarse, and tantalizing epithets"), Anthony is not demystified, for
his sadistic pleasure in the episode still marks him as part of slavery's
unreason.

That rhetorical manipulation of the slaveholder's punitive proximity
is perhaps nowhere more powerfully registered than in Douglass's 1848
public "Letter to His Old Master," which, in practicing upon Thomas
Auld the licentious intimacy of the "most complete exposure"[40] that
imitates the "all in all" of the whip, can be read as a companion text to

the punishment of Esther. Already skilled in the narration of woman-whipping scenes, Douglass, in his public indictment of Auld, removes the woman and proceeds to punish his former owner directly. The transaction discloses the depth of Douglass's identification with the sexualized fury of the father-owner. Known for his gift of mimicry (he was especially good at imitating the southern clergy), Douglass tests the subversive implications of parodic identification in his "advertisement" of Thomas Auld, who functions as the third version of the father-owner after Aaron Anthony and Hugh Auld. Such filial obedience to the ways of the fathers enables Douglass to situate himself as the father and transform Auld into the feminized object of his assault: "In thus dragging you again before the public, I am aware that I shall subject myself to no inconsiderable amount of censure." Declaring to Auld that he intends to "make use of [him] as a weapon," Douglass neatly consents to Auld's former conversion of Frederick Bailey into an instrument of labor. Playing the male aggressor, Douglass appropriates the slaveholder's role and, admitting that he will "probably be charged with an unwarrantable, if not a wanton and reckless disregard of the rights and proprieties of private life," deftly mimics the slaveholder's nonchalant appraisal of any possible retribution for his crimes. A "dragging," a shaming, a destruction of the privacy of character, the "Letter" grafts the perverse sexuality of slavery's "foul embrace" (N, 17) onto the master – son bond.[41] If the discourse of vicarious suffering that inflects the description of Esther's punishment and Douglass's feminist oratory finally serves to disguise rather than eradicate the patriarchal and in so doing exposes the limitations of Douglass's quest to eradicate difference, the "Letter," frankly speaking the masculine language of abduction and rape, enables the son to vanquish the father's power.

> *The whip we can bear without a murmur, compared to the idea of separation. . . . The agony of the mother when parting from her children cannot be told.*
> ("I Have Come to Tell You
> Something about Slavery," 1841)

With ironic enjoyment, Douglass converted slavery into his parent: As the principal antagonist in his quest for identity, slavery generated his famed career as journalist, lecturer, and autobiographer. Against its chaos, violence, and deprivation, Douglass fashioned his order, rhetorical prowess, and achievement – a progeny constituting an ironic ancestry to replace the void left by slavery. Dryly remarking of his concealed origins that "genealogical trees do not flourish among slaves" (MB, 34), Douglass forces slavery's deprivation to serve as his self-constitution and symbolically reproduces himself from its negation. Having silenced his mother, its silences are made to assume the maternal function, giving birth to his autobiographical language of successful genesis and indictment through its mute female victims who catalyze the eventual rhetorical display of the observer. Imagining that his literacy derives genetically from the "native genius of my sable, unprotected, and uncultivated *mother*" (*MB*, 58), Douglass forges a symbolic identity between text and mother that overshadows the hero's self-fathering. Hugh Auld's repression, then, is as fruitful as Sophia Auld's encouragement. "In learning to read, therefore, I am not sure that I do not owe quite as much to the opposition of my master, as to the kindly assistance of my amiable mistress" (*MB*, 147). Such deftly sarcastic acknowledgment of indebtedness – one that coolly undercuts the pretensions of the master class to omniscient control – only barely contains a volatile interior drama of continuing allegiance to the mute, suffering, "feminine" world of slavery. The birth of the ex-slave from his past depends upon his continued link to the malignant "domestic institution," and as a maternal linkage resists the witty inversions that form the language of self-fathering. To "conceive" of himself as slavery's child, rather than as the son of Harriet Bailey and Aaron Anthony, sufficiently abstracts his genealogy for him to endure (even humorously) its contradictions; and it enables him to indict slavery rather than his father and hence purify that ancestry. But in extricating himself from his contaminated paternal heritage, Douglass endows slavery with the static, charismatic power of his lost maternal heritage. In the final version of his autobiography, he confesses to a "strange and, perhaps perverse feeling" at the Civil War's conclusion:

> I felt that I had reached the end of the noblest and best part of my life; my school was broken up, my church disbanded, and my beloved congregation dispersed. . . . The antislavery platform had performed its work, and my voice was no longer needed. (*LT*, 373)

For Douglass, slavery remains disturbingly implicated with the punished black woman, surrogate for the lost mother by whom he is both thoroughly infiltrated and abandoned. As he views the whipping of Esther through the cracks in the closet, a view that, in foreclosing full understanding, intensifies the enormity of Anthony's inhumanity, Douglass's meager memory of his mother magnifies her inscrutable influence: "The side view of her face is imaged on my memory, and I take few steps in life, without feeling her presence; but the image is mute, and I have no striking words of her's treasured up" (*MB*, 57). The view of Esther's back and the side view of the mother's face serve as companion images for the undisclosed feminine that remains beyond the reach of language, a partial "image" whose obscurity silhouettes the plenary masculine voice.

When Douglass singled out the portrait of Ramses the Great from Prichard's *The Natural History of Man* (London, 1845) as most like his memory of his mother, he selected a face for her that deftly placed her at the origin of civilization and provided him with a royal ancestry while simultaneously attacking the racist ideology of polygenesis.[42] Seeking an equivalence for the "side view" of Harriet Bailey, Douglass's chosen image of royal manhood (which itself appears on three-quarter profile in Prichard's text) reveals again the impediment of the masculine in any recovery of the feminine and, in so doing, the presence of the punitive within any imagined redemptive space. As a primary Christian symbol of racial and religious oppression, the pharaoh, after all, is a dual figure: Douglass's selection of "him" to impersonate "her" reimposes the slaveholder on the figure of the mother. The recovery of origin would always speak of duplicity rather than union.[43] Able to attain only a stunned view of Esther's back and a "side view" of his mother, Douglass fashioned a comprehensive perspective on slavery. As malign but visible substitute, slavery provides that feminine object with which his subjectivity could commune and assert its necessary mastery:

Why are some people slaves, and others masters?. . . . How did the relation commence?. . . . Once, however, engaged in the inquiry, I was not very long in finding out the true solution of the matter. . . . The appalling darkness faded away, and I was master of the subject. (*MB*, 89, 90)

NOTES

1   *Narrative of the Life of Frederick Douglass, an American Slave, Written by Himself* (New York: New American Library, 1968 [1845]), p. 25, hereafter cited in the text as *N*. William L. Andrews briefly discusses the relation between Douglass's witness of Esther's punishment and his initiation into the character of the father in *To Tell a Free Story The First Century of Afro-American Autobiography, 1760–1865* (Urbana and Chicago: University of Illinois Press, 1988), pp. 222–3.

2   *My Bondage and My Freedom*, ed. Philip S. Foner (New York: Dover Publications, 1969), p. 60, hereafter cited in the text as *MB*.

3   For treatments of the role of the punished female slave in women's antislavery fiction, see Carolyn L. Karcher, "Rape, Murder and Revenge in 'Slavery's Pleasant Homes': Lydia Maria Child's Antislavery Fiction and the Limits of the Genre," *Women's Studies International Forum*, v. 9, no. 4 (1986), 323–82; Karen Sanchez-Eppler, "Bodily Bonds: The Intersecting Rhetorics of Feminism and Abolition," *Representations*, no. 24 (1988), 28–59. Both essays stress the unavoidable complicity of antislavery writing in the very evils they sought to expose and explore the implications of that complicity for white female abolitionist authors.

4   *Life and Times of Frederick Douglass* (New York: Macmillan Publishing Co., 1962 [1892]), p. 479, hereafter cited in the text as *LT*.

5   "Letter to His Old Master," reprinted in *My Bondage and My Freedom*, ed. Foner, p. 425. Speaking to an Irish audience in 1845, Douglass acknowledged the disorienting impact of his startling transformation: "When I think of the situation I once filled, and of the one I now fill, I can scarcely believe my own identity." *The Frederick Douglass Papers*, 4 vols., ed. John W. Blassingame (New Haven, CT: Yale University Press, 1979), v. 1, p. 56.

6   *Frederick Douglass Papers*, ed. Blassingame, v. 1, p. 86.

7   *The Life and Writings of Frederick Douglass*, 5 vols., ed. Philip S. Foner (New York: International Publishers, 1955), v. 4, p. 211.

8   *Frederick Douglass Papers*, ed. Blassingame, v. 2, p. 129.

9   Celia Logan, "Three Distinguished Men," *The New National Era* (May 14, 1874), in *Frederick Douglass on Women's Rights* ed. Philip Foner (Westport, CT: Greenwood Press, 1976), p. 104.

10 Douglass, "Farewell to the British People: An Address Delivered in London, England, on 30 March 1847" in *Frederick Douglass Papers*, ed. Blassingame, v. 2, p. 129.

11 Douglass, "Men and Brothers: An Address Delivered in New York, New York, on 7 May 1850," in *Frederick Douglass Papers*, ed. Blassingame, v. 2, p. 238.

12 As quoted by Dickson J. Preston, *Young Frederick Douglass: The Maryland Years* (Baltimore and London: Johns Hopkins University Press, 1980), p. 214, n. 25. Douglass extended his symbolic reading of his own physiognomy to include all individuals in his major speech, "The Claims of the Negro Ethnologically Considered: An Address Delivered in Hudson, Ohio, on 12 July 1854": "A man is worked upon by what *he* works on. He may carve out his circumstances, but his circumstances will carve him out as well" (*Frederick Douglass Papers*, ed. Blassingame, v. 2, p. 520). On his 1846 British tour, Douglass wrote to Francis Jackson: "I find that I am hardly black enough for British taste, but by keeping my hair as wooly as possible I make out to pass at least for half a Negro" (as quoted in *Frederick Douglass Papers*, ed. Blassingame, v. 1, p. 144).

    My essay is indebted to Preston's fascinating discussion of Douglass's deeply felt connection to his Maryland past. See also Peter F. Walker, *Moral Choices: Memory, Desire, and Imagination in Nineteenth-Century Abolition* (Baton Rouge: Louisiana State University Press, 1978), ch. 8. Walker subordinates any question of gender to an interesting but oversimplified argument that Douglass's conflicted search for his lost patrimony reveals his "hopeless secret desire to be white and the absurdity of selecting abolition as the instrument to blot out his blackness" (p. 247). Based on Preston's study, Allison Davis, *Leadership, Love, and Aggression* (New York: Harcourt Brace Jovanovich, 1983) argues for the "central paradox in Douglass's personality – the conflicting hatred and love for the powerful father who treated him as a son at times, but never emancipated or publicly acknowledged him" (p. 19). Unlike his nurtured hatred for Thomas Auld, Douglass, according to Davis, "actually got along well with his father, who often beat Hester and the others, but never Fred" (p. 40). Although Davis points out that Douglass's childhood relations with Lucretia and Sophia established his lifelong affection for white women, he does not explore issues of narrative representation or, for that matter, the implications of this disparity between the black and the white feminine.

13 Douglass, "American Slavery Is America's Disgrace: An Address Delivered in Sheffield, England, on 25 March 1847," in *Frederick Douglass Papers*, ed. Blassingame, v. 2, p. 16.

14 Douglass, "My Experience and My Mission to Great Britain: An Address Delivered in Cork, Ireland, on 14 October 1845," in *Frederick Douglass Papers*, ed. Blassingame, v. 1, p. 37.

15 Douglass, "Reception Speech," as reprinted in *My Bondage and My Freedom*, ed. Foner, p. 409.

16 Douglass, "An Account of American Slavery: An Address Delivered in Glasgow, Scotland, on 15 January 1846" in *Frederick Douglass Papers*, ed. Blassingame, v. 1, p. 137.

17 Preston, *Young Frederick Douglass*, p. 66.

18 Douglass, "Reception Speech" in *MB*, p. 418.

19 Douglass, "The Internal Slave Trade" reprinted in *MB*, p. 447.

20 Douglass, "Excerpt" in *Autographs for Freedom*, ed., Julia Griffiths (Auburn, N.Y.: Alden, Beardsley & Co., 1854), p. 253.

21 Douglass's 1853 novella, *The Heroic Slave*, similarly clears the impediment of the black feminine from the masculine terrain by killing off the slave hero's wife on the verge of obtaining her freedom. Unlike the autobiographies that are bent on demonstrating the cleanness of the break with the past, Douglass's only work of fiction unfolds a protracted and conflicted process of disaffiliation from the plantation world of white owners and black women. Supplying a domestic history for the developing black revolutionary, the novella supplants Madison Washington's connection to his wife with an improbable connection to a white man, Mr. Listwell, who had "long desired to sound the mysterious depths of the thoughts and feelings of a slave" (*The Heroic Slave* in *Life and Writings*, ed. Foner, v. 5, p. 476) and who becomes linked to the black hero through three coincidental meetings. The narrative demonstrates how Douglass relies upon the ideology of masculinity to resolve the problematics of racial identity. Male bonding to the white man enables the hero to break the problematic connection to the black woman while venerating her memory. For an account of the filial dynamics at work in *The Heroic Slave*, see Eric J. Sundquist, "Frederick Douglass: Literacy and Paternalism" *Raritan*, v. 6, no. 2 (Fall, 1986), 108–24.

22 For a recent account of Douglass's "preoccupation with manhood and power" see David Leverenz, *Manhood and the American Renaissance* (Ithaca, NY, and London: Cornell University Press, 1989), ch. 4. Although agreeing with Leverenz's general argument about the centrality of "manliness" and its consequent suppression of the feminine (and the working class) in Douglass's adoption of bourgeois gentility, this essay takes issue with Leverenz's unwitting compliance in the very discourse of "manliness." His analysis assumes the entire success of this masculinist ideology, for it avoids any careful discussion

of Douglass's abundant narrative representations of the feminine and chooses instead to indict Douglass for his appropriation of white middle-class male culture. For a more sympathetic account of Douglass's restrictions "by the system he adopts" see Houston A. Baker, Jr., "Autobiographical Acts and the Voice of the Southern Slave" in Charles T. Davis and Henry Louis Gates, Jr., eds., *The Slave's Narrative* (New York: Oxford University Press, 1985), pp. 242ff. See also Waldo E. Martin, Jr., *The Mind of Frederick Douglass* (Chapel Hill: University of North Carolina Press, 1984), for a discussion of Douglass's feminism. Martin rather uncritically accepts Douglass's repeated assertions of uncomplicated identity between his and women's subjugation.

23   Douglass's posthumous praise of John Brown represents the nation as a degraded, intemperate body in critical need of such a virile and punitive asceticism: "Posterity will owe everlasting thanks to John Brown for lifting up once more to the gaze of a nation grown fat and flabby on the garbage of lust and oppression, a true standard of heroic philanthropy, and each coming generation will pay its installment on the debt" (as quoted in *Life and Writings*, ed. Foner, v. 2, p. 459). As Leverenz argues in *Manhood and the American Renaissance*, such revolutionary virility was significantly qualified by Douglass's admiring acceptance of the white male capitalist ethos. Writing to Harriet Beecher Stowe in 1853 on how she might "contribute to the improvement of blacks" who had "become free by their own exertions," Douglass advocated industrial rather than agricultural training, since the latter called for a self-reliance that the blacks allegedly lacked: "It is a fact then, and not less so because I wish it were otherwise, that the colored people are wanting in self-reliance – too fond of society – too eager for immediate results – and too little skilled in mechanics or husbandry to attempt to overcome the wilderness" (*Life and Writings*, ed. Foner, v. 2, p. 232). In *Leadership, Love, and Aggression*, Allison Davis provides an extended discussion of Douglass's relationships to both Garrison and Brown.

24   Douglass, "Slavery and The Slave Power: An Address Delivered in Rochester, New York, on 1 December 1850," in *Frederick Douglass Papers*, ed. Blassingame, v. 2, p. 259.

25   For a succinct summary of Western European assumptions about African illiteracy, see H. L. Gates, Jr., "Editor's Introduction: Writing "Race" and the Difference It Makes," in *"Race," Writing, and Difference*, ed. H. L. Gates, Jr. (Chicago and London: University of Chicago Press, 1985), pp. 1–20.

26   Douglass, "The Key to Uncle Tom's Cabin," *Frederick Douglass' Paper* (April 29, 1853), in *Life and Writings*, ed. Foner, v. 2, p. 242.

In *My Bondage and My Freedom*, a single sentence serves to describe his married life: "In the meantime, my intended wife, Anna, came on from Baltimore – to whom I had written, informing her of my safe arrival at New York – and, in the presence of Mrs. Mitchell and Mr. Ruggles, we were married" (p. 341). His wife for forty-eight years, Anna Murray Douglass shared neither her husband's interracial background nor his evident ease with white culture. Although Douglass hired a tutor for her, she refused instruction and, in stark contrast to her heroic mother-in-law, remained illiterate throughout her life. Virtually unmentioned in the latter two autobiographies, she surfaces at one point in Douglass's correspondence as a verbally aggressive invalid: "I am sad to say she is by no means well – and if I should write down all her complaints there could be no room even to put my name at the bottom, although the world will have it that I am actually at the bottom of it all" (Letter to Mrs. Lydia Dennett [April 17, 1857], as quoted in *Frederick Douglass on Women's Rights*, ed. Foner, p. 22).

Eighteen months after Anna's death, Douglass married his white secretary, suffragist Helen Pitts. Acknowledging that his first wife "was the color of my mother, and the second, the color of my father" (as quoted in *Life and Writings*, ed. Foner, v. 4, p. 116), Douglass read his two marriages as an allegorical reenactment of his interracial origins otherwise rendered inaccessible by maternal loss and paternal repudiation. As a free version of a coercive parental union that received its only visualization in Esther's punishment, Douglass saw his controversial second marriage as replacing his father's crime with a model of affectional union. Such a revision still did not resolve the underlying alienation. As he wrote to Elizabeth Cady Stanton of his second marriage:

> Circumstances have during the last forty years thrown me much more into white society than in that of colored people. While true to the rights of the colored race my nearest personal friends owing to association and common sympathy and aims have been white people and as men choose wives from friends and associates, it is not strange that I have so chosen my wife and that she has chosen me. (*Life and Writings*, v. 4, p. 410)

Frankly confessing a consciousness divided between its convictions and affections, Douglass tellingly concluded his letter by alluding to his first wife's illiteracy: "How good it is to have a wife who can read and write, and who can as Margaret Fuller says cover one in all his range." The reference to Fuller, America's high priestess of reformed heterosexual relations and "elective affinity," suggests not only that he identified with liberal white female culture but that his heroic literacy – a sign of the black man's emancipation – rested upon an uneasy disaffiliation from black women.

27 *Frederick Douglass on Women's Rights*, ed. Foner, p. 59.
28 Ibid., p. 33. Douglass's disputes with the women's rights movement began with his split from the Garrisonians. Their dislike for the British abolitionist Julia Griffiths led Garrison to insinuate that there was a sexual liaison between Douglass and Griffiths, "whose influence over him," wrote Garrison in *The Liberator*, "has not only caused much unhappiness in his own household, but perniciously biased his own judgment; who, active, futile, mischievous, has never had any sympathy with the American Anti-Slavery Society, but would doubtless rejoice to see it become extinct" (*Frederick Douglass on Women's Rights*, ed. Foner, p. 20). Douglass was deeply angered by Garrison's invasion of his privacy, and although his wife publicly protested any such domestic discord to Garrison, the episode split the women's rights movement. See also Ellen Carol DuBois, *Feminism and Suffrage: The Emergence of an Independent Women's Movement in America 1848–1869* (Ithaca, NY, and London: Cornell University Press, 1978), for an account of postbellum struggles

between advocates of black male suffrage and feminist demands for universal suffrage. DuBois notes: "Those who considered woman suffrage agitation itself a betrayal of the ex-slave, for instance Phillips and Douglass, sometimes ignored or minimized women's grievances to make their position. Stone, Stanton, and others recognized and criticized this antifeminist tendency" (p. 177).

29 *Frederick Douglass on Women's Rights*, ed., Foner, p. 72.
30 Ibid., p. 78.
31 Ibid., p. 80. To this Stanton retorted: "Mr. Douglass talks about the wrongs of the negro; but with all the outrages that he to-day suffers, he would not exchange his sex and take the place of Elizabeth Cady Stanton" (ibid., p. 88). Douglass's attack upon the feminist Lucy Stone's effort to gain Stephen A. Douglas's endorsement showed him capable of indulging in the language of sexual oppression to fight racism. Converting the suffragist into the seductress, Douglass condemned Stone for "flinging the network of her notes of invitation about the neck of Stephen A. Douglas, as notorious for his contempt for Women's Rights as Brigham Young is for the number of his wives!" (ibid., p. 76). Shortly after his second marriage, Douglass again voiced the masculinist orientation of his antislavery thinking: "I have held all my life . . . that the fundamental and everlasting objection to slavery, is not that it sinks a Negro to the condition of a brute, but that it sinks a *man* to that condition. I base no man's right upon his color, and plead no man's rights because of his color. My interest in any man is objectively in his manhood and subjectively in my own manhood" (*Life and Writings*, ed. Foner, v. 4, p. 117).
32 *Frederick Douglass on Women's Rights*, ed. Foner, p. 14.
33 *Life and Writings*, ed. Foner, v. 4, p. 125.
34 Douglass, "Reception Speech" (May 1846) in *MB*, pp. 418, 409.
35 Ibid., p. 418.
36 Douglass, "Extract" in *Autographs for Freedom*, ed. Griffiths, p. 254.
37 See John Sekora, "The Dilemma of Frederick Douglass: The Slave Narrative as Literary Institution," *Essays in Literature*, v. 10, no. 2 (Fall 1983), 219–26, and "Comprehending Slavery: Language and Personal History in Douglass' *Narrative* of 1845," *College Language Association Journal*, v. 29, no. 2 (December 1985), 157–70, for the "collectivizing forces" through which Douglass came to speak the "language of abolition" (p. 161).
38 James Olney, " 'I Was Born': Slave Narratives, Their Status as Autobiography and as Literature," in *The Slave's Narrative*, ed. Davis and Gates, pp. 29–48, argues that such self-reflexive narrative moments powerfully convey Douglas's central ideological assertion that literacy and freedom are one and the same. My reading of such self-reflexivity stresses its more competitive aspects.
39 The added sentences read: "He was cruelly deliberate, and protracted the torture, as one who was delighted with the scene. Again and again he drew the hateful whip through his hand, adjusting it with a view of dealing the most pain-giving blow. Poor Esther had never yet been severely whipped, and her shoulders were plump and tender" (*MB*, pp. 87–8).

40   Douglass, "Letter to His Old Master" in *MB*, p. 421.

41   Thus, to extract himself from his suffering vulnerability, Douglass does not abandon but rather, through language, usurps the position of the father. Such usurpation, however, could not eradicate the rooted affection for the Auld family, toward whom, as he wrote to Hugh Auld in 1859, "I feel nothing but kindness" (as quoted in Preston, *Young Frederick Douglass*, p. 168). If language serves as his means of getting back at Thomas Auld, it is also his means of getting back to him. The "Letter," like the autobiographies, testifies to this conflicted urge to memorialize and accuse: "Among these [the abolitionists] I have never forgotten you, but have invariably made you the topic of conversation – thus giving you all the notoriety I could do" ("Letter" in *MB*, p. 428).

42   For an account of nineteenth-century black historians' attack upon theories of polygenesis, see Clarence E. Walker, "The American Negro as Historical Outsider, 1836–1935," *The Canadian Review of American Studies*, v. 17, no. 2 (Summer 1986), 137–54. Douglass's "The Claims of the Negro Ethnologically Considered" is an important contribution to this historiography.

43   For a brief discussion of the importance of the Egyptian captivity for nineteenth-century black Christians, see Ernest Bradford, "Towards a View of the Influence of Religion on Black Literature," *College Language Association Journal*, v. 27, no. 1 (September 1983), 18–29.

The view of the tormented and punitive owner-father is, of course, partial and covert as well. Of the cursing Aaron Anthony, Douglass recollects. "He little thought that the little black urchins around him, could see, through those vocal crevices, the very secrets of his heart" (*MB*, p. 81). But Douglass immediately undercuts his claimed taboo knowledge, for his understanding of the father can reach no further than the father's own truncated self-understanding: "I really understand the old man's mutterings, attitudes and gestures, about as well as he did himself" (*MB*, p. 81). Douglass's language of exposure increases its vehemence in direct proportion to the obdurate inscrutability of the parents.

Race, Violence, and Manhood

The Masculine Ideal in Frederick Douglass's "The Heroic Slave"

RICHARD YARBOROUGH

Sir, I want to alarm the slaveholders, and not to alarm them by mere declamation or by mere bold assertions, but to show them that there is really danger in persisting in the crime of continuing Slavery in this land. I want them to know that there are some Madison Washingtons in this land.

Frederick Douglass[1]

In 1877 the Afro-American author Albery A. Whitman published an epic poem called "Not a Man, and Yet a Man." At one level, his apparently contradictory title refers to the fact that although relegated to the category of chattel, of brute property, slaves possessed the ability to maintain their own humanity. At another level, Whitman's articulation of black heroism in male terms typifies a great deal of the discourse in nineteenth-century Afro-America surrounding the slave experience. We encounter a more telling example of this tendency in Whitman's preface to a later work, *The Rape of Florida*:

> Amid the rugged hills, along the banks of Green River in Kentucky, I enjoyed the inestimable blessings of cabin life and hard work during the whole of my early days. I was in bondage, – I was never a slave, – the infamous laws of a savage despotism took my substance – what of that? Many a man has lost all he had, except his manhood.[2]

With its focus on "manhood," Whitman's proud self-representation recalls one of the most eloquent testaments to the slave's capacity to transcend attempts at dehumanization – *Narrative of the Life of Frederick Douglass, an American Slave, Written by Himself* (1845). In this text, Douglass first describes how he fell into the depths of slavery, becoming, in his words, "transformed into a brute"; then he makes one of the most often-quoted statements in Afro-American literature: "You have seen how a man was made a slave; you shall see how a slave was made a man."[3] The key step in this latter transformation involves Douglass's physical confrontation with a white slavebreaker:

> This battle with Mr. Covey was the turning-point in my career as a slave. It rekindled the few expiring embers of freedom, and revived within me a sense of my own manhood. It recalled the departed self-confidence, and inspired me again with a determination to be free. . . . It was a glorious resurrection, from the tomb of slavery, to the heaven of freedom. My long-crushed spirit rose, cowardice departed, bold defiance took its place; and I now resolved that, however long I might remain a slave in form, the day had passed forever when I could be a slave in fact. I did not hesitate to let it be known of me, that the white man who expected to succeed in whipping, must also succeed in killing me.[4]

These lines are replete with fascinating rhetorical turns, but I want to focus particularly on, first, the extent to which the term "manhood" comes to stand for the crucial spiritual commodity that one must maintain in the face of oppression in order to avoid losing a sense of self-worth and, second, the connection established between manhood and violent resistance.

One might argue that when writers like Douglass say "man" they mean "human," that when they say "manhood" they mean "humanity." It would follow then that David Walker, for instance, is addressing all blacks, regardless of gender, when he asks in 1829, "Are we MEN!! – I ask you, O my brethren! are we *MEN*? Did our creator make us to be slaves to dust and ashes like ourselves?"[5] Quite often, however, the broader rhetorical contexts of such statements reveal the gender-specific nature of the discourse. Thus Henry Highland Garnet's paraphrase of Walker's angry question in 1843 is prefaced by statements directed exclusively to his male listeners:

> You act as though you were made for the special use of these devils. You act as though your daughters were born to pamper the lusts of your masters and overseers. And worse than all, you tamely submit, while your lords tear your wives from your embraces, and defile them before your eyes. In the name of God we ask, are you *men*?[6]

Even a superficial survey of nineteenth-century writing and oratory reveals the extent to which Afro-American spokespersons like Whitman, Douglass, Walker, and Garnet saw the crucial test of black fitness to be whether or not black men were, in fact, what was conventionally considered "manly." As Calvin Hernton puts it:

> Historically, the battle line of the racial struggle in the United States has been drawn exclusively as a struggle between the men of the races. Everything having to do with the race has been defined and counter-defined by the men as a question of whether black people were or were not a race of Men. The central concept and the universal metaphor around which all aspects of the racial situation revolve is "Manhood."[7]

In this essay, I want to examine some of the complex ramifications of this obsession with manhood as manifested in early Afro-American fiction – in particular, in Frederick Douglass's "The Heroic Slave."

Contemporary scholars have focused on the obstacles that nineteenth-century black women encountered in convincing white society that they were little different from their middle-class white counterparts, that they embodied the attributes of True Womanhood with only slight adjustments.[8] Social scientists have noted for some time that black men have confronted related problems in meeting white society's criteria for male status. Indeed, one can identify a mythology of masculinity analogous to the Cult of True Womanhood and partially grounded, like the feminine ideal, in the nineteenth-century sentimental tradition. The Anglo-American bourgeois paradigms of both masculinity and femininity were equally imaginary in nature, essentially ideologically charged constructions serving, first, to bolster the self-image of privileged whites who endorsed and propagated them through their control of major acculturating institutions and, second, to keep marginalized those "others" who – on account of their appearance, speech, family background, class, religion, behavior, or values – did not measure up.

In striving to counter racist charges of inferiority, early Afro-American authors understandably sought to shape their portrayal of black male heroes in accord with middle-class definitions of masculinity. Such definitions contained the following crucial ingredients: nobility, intelligence, strength, articulateness, loyalty, virtue, rationality, courage, self-control, courtliness, honesty, and physical attractiveness as defined in white Western European terms. Furthermore, as Robert Staples puts it, "Masculinity . . . has always implied a certain autonomy over and mastery of one's environment."[9] As if the need to have their black male protagonists embody these characteristics were not a daunting enough task, early Afro-American writers were also aware of the extent to which many of the white readers whom they wished to reach would have agreed with proslavery commentator John Campbell's characterization of blacks:

The psychical attributes that peculiarly belong to man are adoration, benevolence, conscientiousness, intellectual appetite, fame, speech, prudence, admiration, and reason, or causality. In the Caucasian, these attributes are developed harmoniously, and he is *warlike*, but not cruel nor destructive. In the negro, on the contrary, these attributes are equally undeveloped: he is neither originative, inventive nor speculative; he is roving, revengeful and destructive, and he is *warlike*, predatory and sensual.[10]

Campbell's telling use of the term "warlike" here captures perfectly the dilemma confronting black authors. That is, whites were quite capable of viewing the same trait that signified heroism in whites as signifying degradation and inferiority in blacks.

Afro-American writers were fully aware of both the arbitrary way in which white middle-class standards of behavior were applied to blacks and also of how the environment in which most blacks lived prevented the full development of those very capacities that white readers appeared to value so highly. Accordingly, in 1860 the black abolitionist H. Ford Douglass qualified his claim for black manhood this way: "Now, I want to put this question to those who deny the equal manhood of the negro: What peculiar trait of character do the white men of this country possess, as a mark of superiority, either morally or mentally, that is not also manifested by the black man, *under similar circumstances*?[11] His phrase "under similar circumstances" would appear to allow him to attribute any alleged lack of manhood among slaves to the oppressive conditions of servitude. At the same time, however, such a stance acceded to racist contentions that the masses of blacks were, in fact, inferior; as far as many whites were concerned, whether this inferiority resulted from heredity or environment constituted a rarely meaningful distinction. In an attempt to shore up this weakness in his racial defense, H. Ford Douglass takes his argument in a somewhat different direction: "After all, I say that the negro is a man, and has all the elements of manhood, like other men; and, by the way, I think that, in this country, he has the *highest* element of manhood."[12] By claiming the "*highest* element of manhood" for blacks, he turns his back on his environmentalist position and seems to welcome the application of the most exacting white bourgeois criteria in the evaluation of black abilities.

By hook or by crook (and occasionally through a disorienting wrenching of our credulity), mid-nineteenth-century Afro-American writers found ways to discover black male figures who could stand up to the most rigorous scrutiny and thereby substantiate H. Ford Douglass's lofty pronouncement. For example, in the 1853 edition of William Wells Brown's *Clotel*, currently recognized as the first novel published by an Afro-

American, we have two heroic male slave characters, William and George Green. Brown describes the former as "a tall, full-bodied Negro, whose very countenance beamed with intelligence."[13] In speech and manner, he is hardly distinguishable from bourgeois whites, expressing himself in proper English for most of the novel. Brown's portrayal of George Green is even more striking. Like Harriet Beecher Stowe's George Harris in *Uncle Tom's Cabin*, he is virtually white in appearance: "His hair was straight, soft, fine, and light; his eyes blue, nose prominent, lips thin, his head well formed, forehead high and prominent."[14] Green resembles the typical middle-class Anglo-American male hero in terms of achievement as well, for Brown locates his ultimate fate firmly in what later became known as the Horatio Alger myth of success: Having emigrated to England after escaping slavery, George works his way up to a clerkship and is eventually reunited with his ex-slave sweetheart.

Although Brown would seem to be giving ground to stereotypes and stock images here without much of a struggle, he and other black authors were often too committed to capturing in their writing the reality of the slave experience as they knew it to concede completely to convention. (Brown himself was an ex-slave.) That is, incongruities in their characterizations frequently reflect some degree of ambivalence on their part toward the social values and literary images they felt constrained to endorse in their fiction. Thus, although Brown's George Green is nearly white in appearance, William is clearly black. Even more revealing developments occur in the 1864 edition of *Clotel* – entitled *Clotelle; A Tale of the Southern States* – where we see significant differences in the appearances of both leading men. In the initial version of the novel, Brown describes William as "a tall, full-bodied Negro"; in *Clotelle*, however, he is "a tall, full-blooded African."[15] This change, although apparently minor, in fact manifests Brown's rejection of some of the racist ideological assumptions that supported popular white conceptions of blacks.

A more dramatic shift occurs in his recasting of George Green, now named Jerome Fletcher. In *Clotel* this character is "as white as most white persons"; in the 1864 edition, he is "of pure African origin, . . . perfectly black, very fine-looking, tall, slim, and erect as any one could possibly be."[16] Unfortunately, this flattering portrait is marred by Brown's inability to transcend all racist physical standards: "His features were not bad, lips thin, nose prominent, hands and feet small. . . . His hair which was nearly straight, hung in curls upon his lofty brow."[17] The significance of Brown's hasty qualification of this black image is brought home when we consider his depiction of another dark-skinned figure, Pompey, whose job is to disguise the ages of his master's slaves before they are put on the market. In sharp contrast to Jerome, Pompey is, in his own words, "de ginuine artikle."[18] Not only does he speak dialect, but his features are stereotypically "black." The differences between the two characters are directly related to their roles in the novel. The primary male lead in Brown's sentimental melodrama, Jerome must look the part; a partially comic embodiment of the degradation of slavery, Pompey is not intended to arouse our admiration or identification. Although Brown's emphasis upon Jerome's undiluted African heritage represents a small but significant move away from the nearly white male hero and thus an important step toward artistic self-determination, the problematic assumptions underlying Brown's strategy here are evident. Furthermore, he feels no need whatsoever to call into question the paradigms of male heroism that so inform his characterizations.

Perhaps the most pressing task confronting early Afro-American writers who sought to establish the manhood of their black slave heroes lay in determining how to depict their male protagonists' responses to slavery, especially given what Marian Musgrave calls the "interdiction, perhaps unconscious, perhaps deliberate, upon even mentioning the fearful possibility of black violence visited upon whites."[19] In the initial edition of Clotel, William Wells Brown attempts to solve this problem by locating George Green's bravery and militant resistance to slavery in both a black and a white context. Thus, immediately after Green is introduced, we learn that he is the sole surviving member of Nat Turner's group of rebels. Then, in a dramatic trial scene, this articulate and well-educated slave endorses armed resistance to injustice by invoking the ideals of the American War of Independence; at one point he declares, "Did not American revolutionists violate the laws when they struck for liberty? They were revolters, but their success made them patriots – we were revolters, and our failure makes us rebels."[20] In a quite calculated move, Brown links two violent acts of liberation – one that many of his white readers would instinctively reject and one that many of them would readily endorse. Brown cannot go much further than this lest the crucial link he is forging between the American Revolution on the one side and the Nat Turner rebellion on the other be broken.[21] Consequently, for all of his militant background and patriotic talk, George does not come close to committing a violent act in the novel. Even his freedom is won not through any assertion of force but rather through the intervention of his slave lover, Mary, who exchanges clothing and places with the imprisoned George in one of the novel's less credible plot twists.

In the final edition of the novel – entitled Clotelle: or, the Colored Heroine (1867) – history provides Brown with something of a way out of this conceptual cul-de-sac – the Civil War, an event that most black leaders saw as the opportunity to fulfill what David Blight terms the "quest for the irrevocable recognition of manhood and citizenship."[22] For possibly the only moment in United States history, black men were provided with a socially sanctioned opportunity to bear arms against their white American oppressors. It is hardly surprising, then, that Brown has his fictional hero, Jerome, return to the United States toward the end of the novel and eventually lose his life in the bloody engagement at Port Hudson. What is unexpected, however, is the fact that Jerome does not die in an attack upon Confederate forces; rather, he is decapitated by a shell while attempting to retrieve the corpse of a fallen (presumably white) officer. In one fell swoop, Brown skillfully identifies the male slave's militant struggle for freedom with the Union's struggle for survival and simultaneously strengthens his hero's claim upon the respect due one embodying the best of American manhood without forcing his readers to confront a dramatization of black violence against whites.

In November 1841, a slave named Madison Washington played a key role in a revolt aboard the American ship *Creole* while it was enroute from Virginia to New Orleans. After commandeering the vessel, he and his fellow blacks sailed to Nassau, where they gained their freedom. Although Washington's story is relatively little known today, in antebellum circles his name was often mentioned in the same breath with those of other black heroes. Henry Highland Garnet, for example, extols Washington as "that bright star of freedom" and ranks him with the likes of Denmark Vesey, Nat Turner, and Cinque.[23] Thus, in 1853, when Douglass published a fictionalized version of the *Creole* revolt entitled "The Heroic Slave," his audience was probably already familiar with his protagonist and his remarkable story.[24] No nineteenth-century Afro-American thinker was more concerned with the issue of manhood than Frederick Douglass, and the manner in which he transforms Madison Washington from a historical personage into a fictional epitome of militant slave resistance vividly reveals the representational strategies he adopted in attempting to dramatize black male heroism.

Just as William Wells Brown does in depicting his protagonists, Douglass initially focuses upon Washington's attractive physical appearance:

> Madison was of manly form. Tall, symmetrical, round, and strong. In his movements he seemed to combine, with the strength of the lion, a lion's elasticity. His torn sleeves disclosed arms like polished iron. His face was "black, but comely." His eye, lit with emotion, kept guard under a brow as dark and as glossy as the raven's wing. His whole appearance betokened Herculean strength.[25]

In sharp contrast to Brown's relatively unadorned treatment of George and Jerome, however, Douglass conveys the superhuman stature of his hero through explicit allusions to both Greek legend ("Herculean strength") and the Old Testament ("black, but comely" from the Song of Solomon).

Douglass is also quick to qualify Washington's seeming ferocity: "Yet there was nothing savage or forbidding in his aspect. A child might play in his arms, or dance on his shoulders."[26]

This elaborate description differs radically from Douglass's celebration of Madison Washington in a speech that he delivered in April 1849 – four years before the publication of "The Heroic Slave":

> About twilight on the ninth day, Madison, it seems, reached his head above the hatchway, looked out on the swelling billows of the Atlantic, and feeling the breeze that coursed over its surface, was inspired with the spirit of freedom. He leapt from beneath the hatchway, gave a cry like an eagle to his comrades beneath, saying, *we must go through.* . . . Suiting the action to the word, in an instant his guilty master was prostrate on the deck, and in a very few minutes Madison Washington, a black man, with *woolly head, high cheek bones, protruding lip, distended nostril, and retreating forehead,* had the mastery of that ship.[27]

In a characteristic use of irony here, Douglass contrasts the racist connotation of certain black physical attributes with the fact that Washington has just taken control of both the *Creole* and his fate. In "The Heroic Slave," however, Douglass forgoes the sarcastic thrust at racist conceptions of black physiognomy so that his protagonist's appearance will fall more in line with conventional Anglo-American conceptions of ideal masculinity. Unfortunately, in so doing, Douglass retreats from his attack upon the racist stereotypes that he had earlier successfully undercut.

One year after the publication of "The Heroic Slave," Douglass indirectly reveals his tendency to link physical appearance with mental capacity as he describes Irish peasants whom he encountered on a trip to Europe:

> I say, with no wish to wound the feelings of any Irishman, that these people lacked only a black skin and woolly hair, to complete their likeness to the plantation negro. The open, uneducated mouth – the long, gaunt arm – the badly formed foot and ankle – the shuffling gait – the retreating forehead and vacant expression – and, their petty quarrels and fights – all reminded me of the plantation, and my own cruelly abused people. . . . The Irishman educated, is a model gentleman; the Irishman ignorant and degraded, compares in form and feature, with the negro![28]

Douglass then asks, "But what does it all prove?. . . [I]t raises the inquiry – May not the condition of men explain their various appearances? Need we go behind the vicissitudes of barbarism for an explanation of the gaunt, wiry, ape like appearance of some of the genuine negroes?"[29] Douglass's argument here – what Waldo Martin terms "an ambiguous environmentalism" – is flawed in a number of ways, not the least of which is his tacit endorsement of the assumption that "form and feature" are accurate indications of psychological development.[30] As a result, he lets stand one of the fundamental assertions of the racist, proslavery position: that the appearance of most blacks signified inferiority. Thus, for Douglass, the heroic stature of his fictional Madison Washington is directly related to the fact that his protagonist is not a "genuine negro," despite his apparently undiluted black pedigree and harsh experiences as a slave. Madison's manner reinforces his uniqueness even further, for as soon as he opens his mouth, he reveals himself to be extremely articulate and formally educated – hardly the typical slave. A white sailor in the story later notes, "His words were well chosen, and his pronunciation equal to that of any schoolmaster. It was a mystery to us *where* he got his knowledge of the language." It is likewise a mystery to the reader, but one upon which Douglass offers no comment.[31]

Like William Wells Brown in *Clotel*, Douglass confronted an especially troublesome dilemma in depicting black violence. He had encountered a similar challenge several years earlier when he sought to trace his own evolving rebelliousness in his 1845 narrative. There, in describing his battle with Covey, he goes to extraordinary lengths to portray himself as having exhausted every reasonable alternative before resorting to force. And he makes it quite clear that when he at last turns to violence, he is not the aggressor; rather, he presents his goal as solely to keep Covey from beating him.[32] The emotionally controlled, rational, and physically restrained persona Douglass meticulously constructs serves both to establish his narrator's genteel, bourgeois credentials and to render his violence palatable to his white audience. Douglass's job would have been far simpler had the speaker in his *Narrative* been a white man, for most readers would have been quite prepared to endorse his use of force. In fact, they would likely have criticized the narrator for not vigorously resisting Covey from the outset. Simply put, blacks were not granted the same freedom of action as whites, and yet they were condemned for not meeting popularly held norms of behavior. Black men were viewed as unmanly and otherwise inferior because they were enslaved; at the same time, they were often viewed as beasts and otherwise inferior if they rebelled violently. Moreover, black writers like Douglass must have realized at some level that to make their heroic figures too independent, too aggressive, might permit white readers to evade acknowledging that they themselves must intervene in order to end the horrors of slavery. Many Afro-American authors saw no easy way to make their black male characters deserving of sympathy and at the same time to celebrate their manhood.

Given Douglass's complex sculpting of his own violence in his autobiography, it is hardly surprising that in his fiction he emphasizes not

Madison Washington's use of physical force but rather his restraint after taking command of the vessel. In his 1849 comments on the *Creole* incident, Douglass makes it clear that Washington encouraged if not actively participated in the attack that resulted in the death of several whites. In contrast, because the white sailor through whose eyes we witness the revolt is conveniently knocked unconscious at the outset of the uprising, in "The Heroic Slave" we see Washington neither commit nor directly urge any acts of physical violence whatsoever. When the white man awakens, the fighting has ended, and Washington is doing his utmost to prevent further bloodshed.[33]

Despite Madison Washington's exemplary behavior during the insurrection, however, Douglass takes no chances and has his protagonist justify what violence has been used:

> You call me a *black murderer*. I am not a murderer. God is my witness that LIBERTY, not *malice*, is the motive for this night's work. I have done no more to those dead men yonder, than they would have done to me in like circumstances. We have struck for our freedom, and if a true man's heart be in you, you will honor us for the deed. We have done that which you applaud your fathers for doing, and if we are murderers, *so were they.*[34]

Washington's phrasing reflects Douglass's conscious attempt to exploit the parallels between the rebellion on board the *Creole* and the American Revolution and thereby to gain reader approval of his protagonist's implied violence. Like William Wells Brown in *Clotel*, Douglass turns a backward glance to the early days of the American republic to find socially approved examples of violent male action, and the name of his chosen hero doubtless makes this tactic seem especially appropriate. As the white sailor who narrates the final chapter of the story puts it, the name "Madison Washington" was one "ominous of greatness."[35] Accordingly, Douglass from the outset emphasizes the links between Washington and two especially well-known white American political leaders – James Madison and George Washington.

If Douglass sensed that his white audience might experience some discomfort with the means adopted by his slave hero to win his freedom, his concern was well grounded. As Ronald Walters points out, a resolution put forward by one antislavery group in support of the *Creole* revolt manifests the ambivalence felt by many abolitionists:

> The society decided that while we would deprecate a resort to arms for the emancipation of the enslaved population of the south, yet we rejoice in the fact proved, by the recent strike for freedom of the slaves of the *Creole*, that slaves are not indifferent, as our opponents have often declared, to the inestimable blessings of civil liberty.[36]

That Douglass was struggling with his own mixed feelings regarding the appropriateness of violent resistance to slavery and his solidifying opposition to Garrisonian pacifism at the time he wrote "The Heroic Slave" also contributes to the tensions we find in the text surrounding this issue.[37]

Douglass's sensitivity to and absorption of the values and expectations of his target audience inform his depiction of Madison Washington in other important ways as well. For example, Douglass's fascination with self-reliance and heroic male individualism thoroughly shapes his conception of Madison as a leader.[38] Thus, although there were reportedly several key instigators of the *Creole* revolt, Douglass omits mention of all but Washington, thereby highlighting the individual nature of his protagonist's triumph as well as the man's superiority in comparison to his fellow blacks.[39] Furthermore, Douglass's celebration of solitary male heroism leaves little room for women. In his 1845 narrative, critics have noted, he downplays the role played by females slaves in his life. As David Leverenz points out, Douglass's wife, Anna, "seems an afterthought. He introduces her to his readers as a rather startling appendage to his escape and marries her almost in the same breath."[40] At first glance, Douglass's treatment of black women in "The Heroic Slave" would appear to differ considerably from that in his narrative. Not only does Madison allude frequently to his wife, Susan, but it is her support that enables him to hide in the wilderness for five years. In addition, he is recaptured after his successful flight from slavery because he decides to return to Virginia to rescue her. However, not only do we receive no description of Susan whatsoever but, more significantly, she is rendered voiceless in a text marked, as Henry Louis Gates notes, by "a major emphasis on the powers of the human voice," on the potency of speech acts.[41] Finally, Douglass has Susan murdered during her attempt to escape with her husband. Her disappearance from the text at this point simply reinforces Washington's heroic isolation.

One way to appreciate fully the strategies underlying the characterization of Madison Washington in "The Heroic Slave" is to compare the novella not just with Douglass's own comments in his 1849 speech but with three other literary dramatizations of the incident – by William Wells Brown in 1863, by Lydia Maria Child in 1866, and by Pauline E. Hopkins in 1901.[42] The most significant ways in which Brown, Child, and Hopkins revise Douglass's rendering of the *Creole* revolt involve the handling of violence in the story, the depiction of Susan, Madison's wife, and the role of whites.[43]

First, Brown, Child, and Hopkins all treat Madison Washington's violence more directly than does Douglass in "The Heroic Slave." In describing Washington's recapture, for example, Brown does not qualify the slave's fierce resistance:

> Observed by the overseer, . . . the fugitive [was] secured ere he could escape with his wife; but the heroic slave did not yield until he with a club had laid three of his assailants upon the ground with his manly blows; and not then until weakened by loss of blood.[44]

In depicting the revolt itself, both Brown and Douglass stress Washington's determination to shed no more blood than is absolutely necessary. However, Brown differs sharply from Douglass by locating his hero at the very center of the violence:

> Drawing his old horse pistol from under his coat, he [a white "negro-driver"] fired at one of the blacks and killed him. The next moment [he] lay dead upon the deck, for Madison had struck him with a capstan bar. . . . The battle was Madison's element, and he plunged into it without any care for his own preservation or safety. He was an instrument of enthusiasm, whose value and whose place was in his inspiration. "If the fire of heaven was in my hands, I would throw it at these cowardly whites," said he to his companions, before leaving their cabin. But in this he did not mean revenge, only the possession of his freedom and that of his fellow-slaves. Merritt and Gifford, the first and second mates of the vessel, both attacked the heroic slave at the same time. Both were stretched out upon the deck with a single blow each, but were merely wounded; they were disabled, and that was all that Madison cared for for the time being.[45]

Like Douglass in "The Heroic Slave," Brown, Child, and Hopkins all portray Madison Washington as a superman, but their hero is one whose strength, courage, and power find unmistakably violent outlet.

In their treatment of Susan, Madison's wife, Brown, Child, and Hopkins again revise Douglass quite extensively. In contrast to the faceless character we encounter in "The Heroic Slave," William Wells Brown's Susan receives an even more elaborate description than does Washington himself:

> In the other cabin, among the slave women, was one whose beauty at once attracted attention. Though not tall, she yet had a majestic figure. Her well-moulded shoulders, prominent bust, black hair which hung in ringlets, mild blue eyes, finely-chiselled mouth, with a splendid set of teeth, a turned and well-rounded chin, skin marbled with the animation of life, and veined by blood given to her by her master, she stood as the representative of two races. With only one eighth of African, she was what is called at the south an "oc-

toroon." It was said that her grandfather had served his country in
the revolutionary war, as well as in both houses of Congress. This
was Susan, the wife of Madison.[46]

Furthermore, Brown arranges for Susan to be among the freed blacks
when her husband takes over the *Creole*. Susan's death *before* the revolt
in "The Heroic Slave" reflects both Douglass's lack of interest in incor-
porating a sentimental reunion into his happy ending and his conception
of Washington as an isolated male protagonist. In Brown's vision of
Washington's successful heroic action, liberation leads to a restoration of
the integrity of the domestic circle, the black family unit; in Douglass's,
it does not.[47]

Although similar in phrasing to Brown's, Child's depiction of Susan
manifests an added concern with the beautiful slave as the embodiment
of endangered womanhood. Child describes Susan's peculiar plight this
way: "[A] handsome woman, who is a slave, is constantly liable to insult
and wrong, from which an enslaved husband has no power to protect
her."[48] Hopkins, in turn, both corrects and elaborates on Child's comment
not only by showing that Madison Monroe (as she calls her hero) *does*,
in fact, save his wife from sexual assault but also by making Susan almost
as much the protagonist of the story as Madison. In Hopkins's rendering,
most of the drama on board the *Creole* centers not on the revolt but on
the white captain's attempted rape of Susan, which coincidentally occurs
on the same night that Madison has planned his uprising.[49] Even the
syntax of the emotional reunion scene reinforces Hopkins's focus on
Susan: "*She* was locked to his breast; *she* clung to him convulsively.
Unnerved at last by the revulsion to more than relief and ecstasy, *she*
broke into wild sobs, while the astonished company closed around them
with loud hurrahs."[50] On the one hand, Hopkins implicitly rejects Douglass's obsession with masculine heroism as she gives Susan not only a
voice in the text but also force – the first act of black violent resistance
aboard the *Creole* is Susan's striking the white captain when he kisses
her in her sleep. On the other hand, by having Madison fortuitously
appear and interrupt the assault on Susan like some white knight rushing
to the aid of his damsel, Hopkins ultimately falls back on the conventions
of the sentimental romance. Hopkins does succeed in reinserting the black
female into a field of action dominated, in Douglass's fiction, by the
male. However, in claiming for Susan a conventional role generally
denied black women, she necessarily endorses the accompanying male
paradigm in her depiction of Madison, a paradigm drawn from the same
set of gender constructions that provides Douglass with his heroic model.

Finally, of the four versions of the *Creole* incident under consideration
here, Douglass's places the greatest emphasis upon the role played by

whites in the protagonist's life. Granted, for much of "The Heroic Slave,"
Madison Washington is the epitome of manly self-reliance. At key points
in the text, however, Douglass qualifies the isolated nature of the protagonist's liberatory struggle not by creating ties between Madison and
a black community but rather by developing a close relationship between
Washington and a white northerner named Listwell. As Robert Stepto
suggests, Douglass probably modeled Listwell on the abolitionist James
Gurney.[51] Yet, Douglass claims in his 1849 speech on the *Creole* incident,
another abolitionist, Robert Purvis, also played an important role as
Washington's friend and advisor. Douglass's decision to incorporate the
white Gurney and not the black Purvis into his story reflects his desire
to reach and move white readers. Like George Harris's former employer,
Mr. Wilson, in *Uncle Tom's Cabin*, Listwell gives the white audience a
figure with whom to identify; as Listwell comes to endorse Washington's
behavior – to evolve literally before our eyes into an abolitionist – Douglass
hopes that the white reader will too.

In none of the three later versions of the revolt do we encounter a
white character who plays the central role that Listwell does in "The
Heroic Slave." Brown, Child, and Hopkins all depict a sympathetic white
named Dickson, who employs Madison after he first escapes; but there
is no great intimacy between the two. Furthermore, where as Douglass
has Listwell slip Washington the files and saws that he subsequently uses
to free himself and his fellow slaves on board the *Creole*, Brown, Child,
and Hopkins each tells us that Madison obtains these implements on his
own, before he returns to Virginia in the ill-fated attempt to free his
wife. By having Listwell provide Washington with the means of his escape, Douglass doubtless intends the white audience to see that they
should not only sympathize with the slaves' plight but work actively to
help them gain their freedom. As a result, however, he implies that even
the most self-reliant and gifted black male slave needs white assistance.

In composing "The Heroic Slave," Frederick Douglass could have easily
taken a strictly documentary approach. The unadorned story of Madison
Washington's exploits certainly contained sufficient drama and courageous
action to hold an audience. Moreover, Douglass's writing to that point
had been primarily journalistic; the novella would have hardly seemed
the form with which he would have felt most comfortable. In depicting
Washington in fiction, however, Douglass ambitiously set out to do more
than demonstrate the slave's determination to be free; he sought to transform
his black male protagonist into a heroic exemplar who would both win
white converts to the antislavery struggle and firmly establish the reality
of black manhood. The route that Douglass chose in order to achieve
these goals was to master the codes of Anglo-American bourgeois white

masculinity, and his own internalization of the values informing mainstream masculine paradigms made this strategy relatively easy to adopt. In addition, as Robert Stepto observes, the act of fictionalizing this story of successful violent male resistance to slavery offered Douglass the opportunity not only to express his ideological independence from Garrison but also to present a potent alternative to the model of the black male hero as victim promoted so successfully in Stowe's *Uncle Tom's Cabin*.[52] Ultimately, however, Douglass's ambitious agenda was undermined by his intuitive sense that he could challenge white preconceptions regarding race only so far without alienating the audience that he sought to win and by problems inherent in the masculine ideal that he so eagerly endorsed.

Douglass's strategies for appealing to white readers in "The Heroic Slave" were flawed in at least three important ways. The first involves the extent to which his representation of Madison Washington as the embodiment of black manhood inevitably emphasizes the distance between his hero and the average slave. In celebrating this unusually self-aware, courageous, aggressive, conventionally educated, and charismatic figure, Douglass never explains his attractive capacities in terms that would encourage the reader to extrapolate a general sense of the black potential for heroic action from the extraordinarily endowed Washington. The gap between Douglass's protagonist and less gifted blacks is widened even further by the presence of Listwell. That the one character both emotionally and intellectually closest to Washington is white indicates the extent to which Madison's strengths and capabilities, training, and manner distinguish him from other slaves and thereby weaken his usefulness as a counterargument against claims that most blacks were inferior to whites.

A second problem derives from Douglass's attempt, in William Andrews's words, "to domesticate a violence that easily could have been judged as alien and threatening to everything from Christian morality to the law of the high seas."[53] Employing a common abolitionist gambit, Douglass works to establish a link between Washington's rebellion and the American War of Independence. However, doing so, Andrews contends, precipitates Douglass and other antislavery writers into a troublesome conceptual trap: "Even as they violate the ideals of Uncle Tom's pacifism and declare blacks free from bloodguiltiness for killing their masters, they justify such actions by an appeal to the authorizing mythology of an oppressive culture."[54] That is, the very figures whose patriotic heritage Douglass claims for his hero won their fame by working to establish a social order in which the enslavement of blacks like Madison was a crucial component.

In his careful packaging of Washington's manly heroism, Douglass also chooses not to dramatize a single act of physical violence performed by his protagonist. One might argue that this approach reinforces the statesmanlike quality that Douglass may have been striving to imbue in his portrayal of Washington – after all, how often do depictions (literary and otherwise) of George Washington fully convey the violent nature of his heroism? Ultimately, however, Douglass's caution here strips his fictional slave rebel of much of his radical, subversive force. As Douglass knew from personal experience, revolution usually entails violence, and black self-assertion in the face of racist attempts at dehumanization often necessitates a direct and forceful assault upon the very structures of social power that provide most whites (especially white males) with a sense of self-worth, security, and potency.

In his public statements regarding the *Creole* revolt both before and after he wrote "The Heroic Slave," Douglass apparently felt little need to undermine the implications of the black militancy that Madison Washington embodied. We have already examined his celebration of Washington's heroism in his 1847 speech. In commenting on West Indian emancipation ten years later, Douglass goes even further:

> Joseph Cinque on the deck of the Amistad, did that which should make his name dear to us. He bore nature's burning protest against slavery. Madison Washington who struck down his oppressor on the deck of the Creole, is more worthy to be remembered than the colored man who shot Pitcairn at Bunker Hill.[55]

Granted, the exhaustion of Douglass's patience with the limited efficacy of moral suasion as an antislavery tactic surely informs this quite remarkable repudiation of the popular appeal to an American patriotic past as a way to validate black slave violence. I would argue, however, that there was something about the mode of fiction itself (and possibly about autobiography as well) that stifled the radical nature of Douglass's anger. The "controlled aggression" that Donald Gibson sees as informing every aspect of Douglass's *Narrative* underlies the depiction of Madison Washington in "The Heroic Slave" as well.[56] The key may lie in what Houston Baker describes as the "task of transmuting an authentic, unwritten self – a self that exists outside the conventional literary discourse structure of a white reading public – into a literary representation." Baker continues: "The simplest, and perhaps the most effective, way of proceeding is for the narrator to represent his 'authentic' self as a figure embodying the public virtues and values esteemed by his intended audience."[57] Baker's argument applies with particular force to "The Heroic Slave," for it appears that the freer rein the form offered Douglass in his depiction of the exemplary black male hero paradoxically also confronted him more directly than possibly ever before with the restrictions imposed by the expectations of the whites to whom he was appealing.

The third weakness in his attempt to use fiction to shape his white reader's attitudes toward slavery is structural in nature. That is, by rendering the *Creole* revolt through the recollections of a white sailor, Douglass cuts us off not just from Washington's heroic violence but from his emotional responses to the dramatic events in which he plays such a crucial part. William Wells Brown's straightforward depiction of Washington's rebellious behavior in his sketch dramatizes by contrast the extent to which Madison's role in "The Heroic Slave" is primarily catalytic, as Douglass emphasizes through shifts in point of view his impact upon the whites around him. Such elaborate formal manipulations result in what Raymond Hedin terms "an emphatically structured fiction," which serves to convey a sense of the writer's control and thus to permit a release of anger in a rational and somewhat unthreatening manner.[58] As one result of this strategy, at the end of the novella Washington stands not as the embodiment of expressive, forceful self-determination, but as an object of white discourse, a figure whose self-assertive drive to tell his own story – to reclaim, in a sense, his own subjectivity – is ultimately subordinated by Douglass to a secondhand rendition by a white sailor who did not even witness the full range of Washington's heroic action. This decentering of the black voice in "The Heroic Slave" may be the greatest casualty of Douglass's polemical appeal to white sympathies.

Finally, like the majority of nineteenth-century black spokespersons. Douglass was unable or unwilling to call into question the white bourgeois paradigm of manhood itself. Consequently, his celebration of black heroism was subverted from the outset by the racist, sexist, and elitist assumptions upon which the Angle-American male ideal was constructed and that so thoroughly permeated the patriarchal structure of slavery. As Valerie Smith points out, "Within his critique of American cultural practices, then, is an affirmation of its definitions of manhood and power." That is, "Douglass . . . attempts to articulate a radical position using the discourse he shares with those against whom he speaks. What begins as an indictment of mainstream practice actually authenticates one of its fundamental assumptions."[59] It should go without saying that one can scarcely imagine how Douglass might have extricated himself from the conceptual briar patch into which he had fallen, given both the political purposes to which he directed his fiction and the extent to which he sought validation in the most conventional, gender-specific terms for himself in particular and for black men in general from a white society unwilling to acknowledge the complex humanity of blacks in any unqualified way.

The dilemma so powerfully rendered in Douglass's attempt to dramatize the Madison Washington story in fiction is one that has plagued most Afro-American fiction writers – and, indeed, most Afro-American thinkers – over the past century and a half.[60] His failures do not qualify the boldness of his attempt, and one can argue that the short-term benefits of his approach must be taken into account in assessing the overall success of his enterprise. Ultimately, however, Douglass's "The Heroic Slave" may be most valuable insofar as it enables us to understand better the complex internal and external obstacles to a balanced, complex depiction of black men and women in Afro-American fiction. If nothing else, it leaves us wondering whether the tools of the master can ever be used to achieve the complete liberation of the slave.

NOTES

I am grateful to a number of people whose comments and criticisms have been useful in my work in this essay. In particular, I want to thank King-Kok Cheung, Kimberle Crenshaw, and Mary Helen Washington.

1 "Great Anti-Colonization Meeting in New York," *The North Star*, 11 May 1849, 2.

2 Albery A. Whitman, *The Rape of Florida* (1885; reprint, Upper Saddle River, NJ: Gregg, 1970), 8.

3 Frederick Douglass, *Narrative of the Life of Frederick Douglass, an American Slave, Written by Himself*, ed. Houston A. Baker, Jr. (1845; reprint, New York: Penguin, 1982), 105, 107.

4 Ibid., 113.

5 David Walker, *Walker's Appeal* (1829; reprint, New York: Arno, 1969), 27.

6 Henry Highland Garnet, *An Address to the Slaves of the United States of America* (1848; reprint, New York: Arno, 1969), 96 (emphasis added). Garnet first delivered this speech in 1843; in 1848 he published it bound together in one volume with Walker's *Appeal.*

7 Calvin Hernton, *The Sexual Mountain and Black Women Writers: Adventures in Sex, Literature, and Real Life* (New York: Anchor/Doubleday, 1987), 38.

8 Barbara Welter, "The Cult of True Womanhood," *American Quarterly* 18 (September 1966): 151–74. For more on nineteenth-century black women's ongoing engagement with this feminine ideal, see Paula Giddings, *When and Where I Enter . . . .: The Impact of Black Women on Race and Sex in America* (New York: William Morrow, 1984). Also see the work of, among other scholars, Hazel V. Carby, Barbara Christian, Frances Smith Foster, Deborah McDowell, Valerie Smith, and Mary Helen Washington.

9 Robert Staples, *Black Masculinity: The Black Male's Role in American Society* (San Francisco: Black Scholar, 1982), 2.

10 Review of *Negro-Mania*, by John Campbell, *Southern Quarterly Review* (January 1852): 163–6; emphasis added.

11 James M. McPherson, *The Negro's Civil War* (New York: Vintage, 1965), 101; emphasis added.

12 Ibid., 102.

13 William Wells Brown, *Clotel; or, The President's Daughter* (1853; reprint, New York: Citadel), 171.

14 Ibid., 224.
15 Ibid., 171; William Wells Brown, *Clotelle; A Tale of the Southern States* (1864), reprinted in *William Wells Brown and Clotelle*, by J. Noel Heermance (Hamden, CT: Archon, 1969), 46.
16 Brown, *Clotel*, 224; Brown, *Clotelle*, 57.
17 Brown, *Clotelle*, 57–8.
18 Ibid., 11.
19 Marian E. Musgrave, "Patterns of Violence and Non-Violence in Pro-Slavery and Anti-Slavery Fiction," *College Language Association Journal* 17 (1973): 426–37. Also see John Demos, "The Antislavery Movement and the Problem of Violent 'Means,' " *New England Quarterly* 37 (1964): 501–26. The literary event before the Civil War that brought the issue of black heroism and violence to center stage was the publication and astounding success of Harriet Beecher Stowe's *Uncle Tom's Cabin*. For a survey of the diverse black literary responses to Stowe's novel, see Richard Yarborough, "Strategies of Black Characterization in *Uncle Tom's Cabin* and the Early Afro-American Novel," in *New Essays on Uncle Tom's Cabin*, ed. Eric J. Sundquist (New York: Cambridge University Press, 1986), 45–84.
20 Brown, *Clotel*, 226.
21 This appeal was complicated by what Eric Sundquist terms "the ambivalence that pre–Civil War generations felt and expressed toward the legacy of the founding fathers" (Eric J. Sundquist, "Slavery, Revolution, and the American Renaissance," in *The American Renaissance Reconsidered: Selected Papers from the English Institute, 1982–83*, ed. Walter Benn Michaels and Donald Pease [Baltimore: Johns Hopkins University Press, 1985], 2).
22 David W. Blight, *Frederick Douglass's Civil War: Keeping Faith in Jubilee* (Baton Rouge: Louisiana State University Press, 1989), 14. Douglass was an especially powerful spokesperson for this view of the war. See, for instance, his "Men of Color, To Arms!", *Frederick Douglass' Monthly*, 5 (March 1863):801; and "Another Word to Colored Men," *Frederick Douglass' Monthly*, 5 (April 1863):817–18. For a detailed look at black military involvement in the Civil War, see Mary Frances Berry, *Military Necessity and Civil Rights Policy: Black Citizenship and the Constitution, 1861–1868* (Port Washington, NY: Kennikat, 1977).
23 Garnet, *Address*, 96.
24 Douglass's novella was serialized in his *North Star*, beginning in March 1853; Julia Griffiths also included it in her *Autographs for Freedom* of that year.
25 Frederick Douglass, "The Heroic Slave," in *Autographs for Freedom*, ed. Julia Griffiths (Boston: John P. Jewett, 1853), 179.
26 Douglass, "Slave," 179.
27 "Anti-Colonization Meeting," *North Star*, 2; second emphasis added.
28 Frederick Douglass, *The Claims of the Negro, Ethnologically Considered* (Rochester, NY: Lee, Mann, 1854), 30.
29 Ibid., 31.
30 Waldo Martin, *The Mind of Frederick Douglass* (Chapel Hill: Univ. of North Carolina Press, 1984), 237. For a thorough discussion of Douglass's ethnological views, see 197–250. Much later in life, Douglass called this speech "a very

defective production," but Martin argues that Douglass's ethnological views did not change substantially over time (Martin, *Mind*, 230).

31 Douglass, "Slave," 233. In the most thorough modern examination of the *Creole* revolt, Howard Jones reports that Washington was "the slaves' head cook" ("The Peculiar Institution and National Honor: The Case of the *Creole Slave Revolt*," *Civil War History* 21 [March 1975]:29). If Jones's information is correct, it is understandable that Douglass would refrain from mentioning this somewhat undignified aspect of his hero's life. It should be noted that Jones draws primarily upon testimony provided by white witnesses at an inquiry after the revolt. (See *Senate Documents*, 27th Cong., 2nd sess., January 21, 1842, no. 51, 1–46.) One must not take for granted the objectivity of such individuals, most of whom had reasons to create their own fictional versions of the *Creole* incident. For a southern proslavery reading of the event, see the article entitled "Mutiny and Murder" from the *New Orleans Daily Picayune* (December 3, 1841), in which the author notes with admiration how the captain's dog "fought furiously against the negroes" until he was killed.

32 A number of scholars have examined the strategies that Douglass adopts in shaping the narrator's persona in his autobiographies in general and in this scene with Covey in particular. See, for example, William L. Andrews, *To Tell a Free Story: The First Century of Afro-American Autobiography, 1760–1865* (Urbana: University of Illinois Press, 1986); Houston A. Baker, Jr., *The Journey Back: Issues in Black Literature and Criticism* (Chicago: University of Chicago Press, 1980); Frances Smith Foster, *Witnessing Slavery: The Development of Ante-bellum Slave Narratives* (Westport, CT: Greenwood, 1979); Donald B. Gibson, "Reconciling Public and Private in Frederick Douglass' *Narrative*," *American Literature* 57 (December 1985):549–69; David Leverenz, *Manhood and the American Renaissance* (Ithaca, NY: Cornell University Press, 1989); Valerie Smith, *Self-Discovery and Authority in Afro-American Narrative* (Cambridge, MA: Harvard University Press, 1987); Robert B. Stepto, *From Behind the Veil: A Study of Afro-American Narrative* (Urbana: University of Illinois Press, 1979); Peter F. Walker, *Moral Choices: Memory, Desire, and Imagination in Nineteenth-Century American Abolition* (Baton Rouge: Louisiana State University Press, 1978).

33 Howard Jones notes, "Casualties were light on both sides because there was little resistance to the revolt and because Washington and another mutineer, Elijah Morris, restrained the others from killing the whites" (Jones, "*Creole*," 30).

34 Douglass, "Slave," 234–5.

35 Ibid., 232.

36 Ronald G. Walters, *The Antislavery Appeal: American Abolitionism after 1830* (Baltimore: Johns Hopkins University Press, 1976). One also wonders if it is mere coincidence that the version of Douglass's speech published in the *Liberator* (run by the pacifist William Lloyd Garrison) matches that in the *North Star* exactly, except for the striking omission of Douglass's comments on the *Creole* episode ("Great Anti-Colonization Mass Meeting," *Liberator*, 11 May 1849, 74). This speech contains some of Douglass's most openly

militant statements. Perhaps the best known is his prediction that "unless the American people shall break every yoke, and let the oppressed go free, that spirit in man which abhors chains . . . will lead those sable arms that have long been engaged in cultivating, beautifying and adorning the South, to spread death and devastation there." This portion of Douglass's comments was, in fact, carried in the *Liberator* in full.

37   For Douglass's stance on violence as an antislavery weapon, see, among other studies, Allison Davis, *Leadership, Love, and Aggression* (New York: Harcourt Brace Jovanovich, 1983); Philip S. Foner, *Frederick Douglass* (1950; reprint, New York: Citadel, 1969); and Martin, *Mind*.

38   Douglass's speech on "Self-Made Men" was one of his most often-delivered presentations. See Martin, *Mind*, 253–78.

39   See Jones, "*Creole*," 30 n7.

40   Leverenz, *Manhood*, 128. Frances Smith Foster suggests that Douglass's with-holding information regarding Anna enables him to suppress certain positive aspects of his slave experience (Foster, *Witnessing*, 113). Also see Gibson, "Public and Private," 551.

41   Henry Louis Gates, Jr., *Figures in Black: Words, Signs, and the "Racial" Self* (New York: Oxford University Press, 1987), 107. The closest we get to hearing Susan speak is Madison's explanation that in his extreme concern for her safety after his flight to Canada, he "could almost hear her voice, saying, 'O Madison! Madison! will you then leave me here? can you leave me here to die? No! no! you will come! you will come!' " (Douglass, "Slave," 219).

42   William Wells Brown, "Madison Washington," in *The Black Man, His Antecedents, His Genius, and His Achievements* (1863; reprint, New York: Arno, 1969), 75–83; Lydia Maria Child, "Madison Washington," in *The Freedmen's Book* (Boston: Ticknor and Fields, 1866), 147–54; and Pauline E. Hopkins, "A Dash for Liberty," *Colored American Magazine* 3 (August 1901):243–7.

43   Some of the minor distinctions among these four versions are revealing as well. For example, Brown's description of Washington is far more ethnically specific than Douglass's: "Born of African parentage, with no mixture in his blood, he was one of the handsomest of his race" (Brown, "Washington," 75). This emphasis on Washington's African background recalls Brown's treatment of Jerome in the 1864 *Clotelle*, published one year after *The Black Man* appeared.

It must be noted that there are several instances where Brown, Child, and Hopkins employ remarkably similar phrasing. Brown had appropriated material from Child before, in the first edition of *Clotel*. There is evidence of extensive borrowing here as well – either by Brown from an earlier version of Child's sketch or by Child from Brown's in *The Black Man*, or by both Brown and Child from an earlier text by another writer. In a letter written in 1865, Child had this to say regarding the composition of *The Freedman's Book*:

The reason my name appears so often in the Index is that I re-wrote all the Biographies. They are not only interspersed with remarks of my

own, but are so completely and entirely told in my own way, that I
cannot, with an propriety ascribe them to anyone else. . . .

You will find William and Ellen Crafts the most interesting. I collected
it from various sources; some of it verbal information. James Madison
Washington is also very romantic, and every word of it true. (Child to
James T. Fields, 27 August 1865, *Lydia Maria Child: Selected Letters,
1817–1880*, ed. Milton Meltzer and Patricia G. Holland, assoc. ed. Francine
Krasno [Amherst: University of Massachusetts Press, 1982], 458–9.)

Pauline Hopkins was familiar with the work of both Brown (whom she
had met personally) and Child, and thus would likely have encountered their
versions of the *Creole* revolt. To complicate matters, Hopkins cites neither
Brown nor Child as her primary source, but rather an article by Thomas
Wentworth Higginson.

44   Brown, "Washington," 80.

45   Ibid., 83.

46   Ibid., 81. Brown's portrayal of Susan closely resembles the sentimental
depiction of his light-skinned heroines in *Clotel.*

47   We find what is perhaps the first suggestion that Madison Washington's wife
may have been aboard the *Creole* in "Madison Washington: Another Chapter
in his History," *Liberator*, June 10, 1842. In his recent article on "The Heroic
Slave," William Andrews quite rightly suggests:

> This effort by the *Liberator* to infer a romantic plot underlying the *Creole*
> incidents testifies to the strong desire of American abolitionism for a
> story, if not *the* story, about Washington that would realize him as a
> powerful symbol of black antislavery heroism. ("The Novelization of
> Voice in Early African American Narrative," *PMLA*, 105 [January 1990],
> 28.)

48   Child, "Washington," 147.

49   Characteristically, Hopkins provides an extensive discussion of Susan's mixed
racial pedigree. For a look at the role of ancestry in her most important
fictional work, see Yarborough, Introduction to *Contending Forces*, by Pauline
E. Hopkins (1900; reprint, New York: Oxford University Press, 1988),
xxvii–xlviii.

50   Hopkins, "Liberty," 247; emphasis added.

51   Robert B. Stepto, "Storytelling in Early Afro-American Fiction: Frederick
Douglass's "The Heroic Slave," *Georgia Review* 36 (Summer 1982): 363 n8.

52   For a further discussion of what Robert B. Stepto calls the "antislavery textual
conversation" between Stowe's *Uncle Tom's Cabin* and Douglass's "The
Heroic Slave," see Stepto's "Sharing the Thunder: The Literary Exchanges
of Harriet Beecher Stowe, Henry Bibb, and Frederick Douglass," in *New
Essays on Uncle Tom's Cabin*, 135–53. Stepto contends that Washington's
revolt also appealed to Douglass because it "in some measure revises his
own story" (Stepto, "Thunder," 359).

53   Williams L. Andrews, *To Tell a Free Story: The First Century of Afro-American
Autobiography, 1760–1865* (Urbana: University of Illinois Press, 1986), 186.

54   Ibid., 187.

55 Philip S. Foner, *The Life and Writings of Frederick Douglass*. Vol. 2, *Pre–Civil War Decade, 1850–1860* (New York: International, 1950), 438.

56 Gibson, "Public and Private," 563. See also David Leverenz's discussion of the tension between Douglass's "genteel self-control and his aggressiveness" in the 1855 edition of his narrative (Leverenz, *Manhood*, 114).

57 Baker, *Journey*, 39.

58 Raymond Hedin, "The Structuring of Emotion in Black American Fiction," *Novel* 16 (Fall 1982):37.

59 Smith, *Self-Discovery*, 20, 27. Also see Baker, *Journey*, 32–46; Lorenz, *Manhood*, 108–34; and Annette Niemtzow, "The Problematic of Self in Autobiography: The Example of the Slave Narrative," in *The Art of Slave Narrative*, ed. John Sekora and Darwin T. Turner (Macomb: Western Illinois University Press, 1982), 96–109.

60 In a forthcoming essay entitled "In the First Place: Making Frederick Douglass and the Afro-American Narrative Tradition," Deborah McDowell examines how the tendancy to give Douglass's *Narrative*, with its uncritical inscription of sexist Anglo-American concepts of gender, a central position in constructing the Afro-American literary tradition marginalizes black women's texts.

"We Hold These Truths to Be Self-Evident"

The Rhetoric of Frederick Douglass's Journalism

SHELLEY FISHER FISHKIN AND
CARLA L. PETERSON

On August 22, 1844, the young Frederick Douglass wrote to J. Miller McKim. "Though quite unaccustomed to write anything for the public eye, and in many instances quite unwilling to do so, in the present case I cannot content myself to take leave of you . . . without dropping you a very hasty, and of course very imperfect sketch of the Anti-slavery meetings."[1]

Little did Douglass then suspect that over the next fifty years he would do little else but "write for the public eye" on antislavery and other related topics. Indeed, under the aegis of such white abolitionists as William Lloyd Garrison, Douglass had started what would become a long and illustrious career in journalism in the early 1840s, writing for *The Liberator* as well as other antislavery newspapers. Chafing under constraints imposed by the white abolitionist leadership, however, Douglass gradually broke away to create his own journalistic organs, first *The North Star*, followed by *Frederick Douglass' Paper* and, still later, by *Douglass' Monthly*. After the Civil War, Douglass maintained his prolific journalistic output, writing on all the major issues confronting blacks in postbellum America for *The New National Era*, as well as such mainstream journals as *The North American Review*, *The Atlantic Monthly*, and *Harper's Weekly*.

How did a piece of property transform himself into a speaking subject? How did a young man who had spent the first twenty-odd years of his life in slavery become the most articulate spokesman for his race and the foremost black journalist of the nineteenth century? In his autobiographical *Narrative*, Douglass tells his readers that "you have seen how a man was made a slave; you shall see how a slave was made a man," and proceeds to locate this transformative moment in an act of physical resistance, his battle with the slave breaker, Covey.[2] And yet, the events of Douglass's life that frame this moment make it clear that for Douglass, manhood and freedom could not be purely physical states of being, just as resistance could never simply be of a physical nature. Indeed, Douglass's language specifies that his emergence into manhood was not a new event in his life, but rather a revival of feelings formerly felt, of thoughts formerly held: "This battle with Mr. Covey was the turning-point in my career as a slave. It rekindled the few expiring embers of freedom, and revived within me a sense of my manhood. It recalled the departed self-confidence, and inspired me again with a determination to be free" (74).

Douglass locates these earlier intimations of freedom and manhood in his acquisition of reading skills and in the act of reading itself, in particular in his reading of a volume entitled *The Columbian Orator*. Compiled by Caleb Bingham and first published in 1797, *The Columbian Orator* contained a variety of pieces designed to instruct "in the ornamental and useful art of eloquence"[3]; and, according to Douglass, it was these pieces that first "gave tongue" to thoughts that Douglass himself did not yet have the language to articulate (42). From them, Douglass was for the first time exposed to contemporary notions of oratory – both to the Enlightenment discourse of freedom and independence, and to the oratorical situation itself established between speaker and audience – which would greatly influence his antebellum journalism. Indeed, it is from these pieces that Douglass first became familiar with the rhetoric of John Locke and the Founding Fathers, which invokes the inalienable rights of man to freedom and happiness; appeals to the natural principles of liberty, equality, and justice; and inveighs against all forms of tyranny and oppression. In the speeches the oratorical voices of national leaders – Roman, English, and American – ring out with great authority. These men were able to assert themselves self-confidently as speaking subjects because they spoke both out of personal experience and on behalf of an entity larger than their individual "I," be it an entire nation, an oppressed group within the nation, or a broad principle such as freedom.

Most importantly, perhaps, the pieces in *The Columbian Orator* underscored for Douglass the importance of the orator's relationship to his audience. In his introductory remarks, Bingham offers his readers some "particular rules for the voice and gesture" (24). But he focuses especially on the movement of the eyes as the "most active and significant" part of the body, since, according to Cicero, " 'all the passions of the soul are expressed in the eyes, by so many different actions' " (22). More than any part of the body, the orator's eyes express the passion of his convictions. How to direct one's eyes upon one's audience in order to catch *its* eyes and compel *its* attention becomes, then, a crucial question for the orator. For Douglass this question would in later years become that of translating this visual strategy into a verbal one, of figuring out how to direct the writing eye of the journalist most effectively to the reading eye of public newspaper readers.

The most prominent oratorical devices used to attract the public eye in *The Columbian Orator* are techniques of the dialogic that, as Bakhtin has pointed out, most often function as a subversive strategy designed to undermine the monologic official discourse of the dominant class.[4] In many of the reproduced pieces, the orator appeals directly to his audience, asking it rhetorical questions that he then proceeds to answer himself. In addition, however, many of the pieces are actual dialogues that stage a confrontation between two antagonists who hold opposing points of view and must use their rhetorical skill to persuade the other of the rightness of his position. The "Dialogue between a Master and Slave," singled out by Douglass in his *Narrative*, exemplifies many of the rhetorical strategies that he was to make good use of in later years. In it, master and slave confront one another directly, face to face, making eye contact. The master, who prides himself on being kind and humane, berates the slave for having attempted to run away for a second time. The slave construes the mere fact of this master's talking to him as an acknowledgment that he is a man and, taking full advantage of this admission, constitutes himself as a speaking subject in order to press home his points. Speaking from his own experience as a man, he argues that liberty and the full exercise of his free will are what are most precious to him. Constituting himself as spokesman for all other slaves, he assures his master that they will not hesitate to resort to violence in order to obtain these same rights. He decries the injustice of slavery, pointing out that no man has the right to dispose of another man. When the master attempts to argue that it is the order of Providence that one man be the slave of another, the slave skillfully points out that the argument in favor of providential design can be made for just about any situation, to the point where Providence simply becomes another form of human agency: " 'Providence . . . gave my enemies a power over my liberty. But it has also given me legs to escape with; and what should prevent me from using them?' " (241). The entire dialogue thus constitutes a bold assertion of the power of human agency through both physical and verbal resistance.

Douglass's antebellum journalism owes much to his reading of *The Columbian Orator*. For, as a result of this reading, Douglass was able to create what Foucault has called a "counter discourse," by means of which an oppressed minority begins "to speak on its own behalf," demanding "that its legitimacy or 'naturality' be acknowledged."[5] As Foucault has pointed out, the oppressed group most often asserts itself, not by creating a new discourse, but by "using the same categories [of the dominant discourse] by which it was . . . disqualified" and simply reversing these categories or the values that had been assigned to them. In addition, as we have seen, the dialogic can function as an important element of a counter discourse as it creates a variety of other voices – parodic, ironic, and so on – designed to subvert the official monologic discourse of the dominant class. In his early writings, Douglass relies heavily on such techniques of reversal and the dialogic to fashion a powerful counter discourse for black Americans. He does so by forcing his opponents to enter into dialogue with him, by wresting the principles of the Declaration of Independence out of the exclusive possession of the dominant class and applying them to oppressed Afro-Americans, and finally, by repeatedly and subversively reversing the categories that it had so carefully assigned both to itself and to those it held in bondage. With emancipation and the acquisition of citizenship, however, Douglass would be forced to rethink the effectiveness of such rhetorical strategies and to recast them in new ways.

From his earliest days in the abolitionist movement, Douglass recognized the particular difficulty of constituting himself as a speaking and writing subject, since one of the major goals of slavery had been to reduce the slave to the level of animal or property, denying him all sense of humanity. and moral life. In an article published in *The North Star* on September 29, 1848, Douglass laments that "Shut up in the prison-house of bondage – denied all rights, and deprived of all privileges, we are blotted from the page of human existence, and placed beyond the limits of human regard. Death, moral death, has palsied our souls in that quarter, and we are a murdered people" (I, 332). And ten years later, he was to complain that "*slavery has bewitched us* [the American people]. It has taught us to read history backwards" (V, 402). The pressing question facing Douglass in the antebellum period was, then, how to raise a murdered people, how to reinsert blacks – both slave and free – back on the page of human existence, how to rewrite history so that it could once again be read forward. And Douglass knew that he could do so only by asserting himself as a man, that is, as a speaking and writing subject.

To do so, Douglass had, first of all, to prove that he was literally – biologically and physiologically – a man. In his early years of lecturing and writing in England, he made this argument by contrasting British recognition of his manhood to American ignorance. He sarcastically commented that even British dogs recognized him to be a man and wondered why the American people were unable to do so. When *The New York Sun*, in a hostile article of May 13, 1847, referred to him as a man, he ironically complimented the newspaper for having perceived that he was indeed a man as opposed to a monkey. Even as late as 1855,

Douglass found it necessary to defend his manhood. In an article published that year, Douglass demonstrated the archimedean nature of his claim to being a man: He might be regarded either as a man or as a thing, an object of property, but he could not be regarded as both. If a person, he maintained, he was entitled to all "the rights sacred to persons in the constitution" (II, 368).

Following the example set by the slave in *The Columbian Orator*'s dialogue, Douglass also asserts an existential claim to manhood, arguing that the mere fact of being addressed constitutes evidence of his manhood, as it implicitly recognizes his ability to talk back. To illustrate his point, he makes use of the incident on board the *Cambria* in which "mobocratic" American slaveholders had attempted to deny him the right to speak. He insists that the passengers on board the ship had every right to ask him to speak on the subject of slavery, since "to deny that they had such right, would be to deny that they had the right to exchange views at all," a point that not even the slaveholders would uphold. Thus, Douglass continues, "if they had the right to ask, I had the right to answer, and to answer so as to be understood by those who wished to hear." Again following the lead of the slave in the dialogue, Douglass claims the right to speak on the subject of slavery, since he himself has been a slave and can thus effectively represent not only himself but "three million of my brethren . . . in chains and slavery on the American soil" (I, 124, 189). Douglass's claim to speak on behalf of his enslaved brethren rests on memories of his own enslavement, as well as on his acute awareness that the prejudice under which they labor extends to free blacks as well.

Having thus asserted his manhood, Douglass then turned to the Enlightenment discourse of liberty and equality – the discourse of the dominant culture – to shape it into a powerful counter discourse that would challenge the proslavery arguments of the period. He grounded the force of his argument and the sweep of his eloquence on a vision of human rights – self-evident, universal, and inalienable – that he had first come across in the pages of *The Columbian Orator* and later found in the rhetoric of the Declaration of Independence. As political theorists like Harry Jaffa have suggested, the Declaration is a clear embodiment of Locke's philosophy in *The Second Treatise of Civil Government*, which argues that all men are naturally in "a state of perfect freedom to order their actions . . . without asking leave, or depending upon the will of any other man. A state also of equality, wherein all power and jurisdiction is reciprocal, no one having more than another; there being nothing more evident than that creatures of the same species and rank . . . should also be equal one amongst another without subordination or subjection."[6] Jaffa further suggests that the Founding Fathers intended the Declaration to be a universalistic document and the American Revolution a war that was to secure these inalienable rights for some men while holding out the promise that they would one day be enjoyed by all.

Douglass understood the Declaration in just such a sense as well and felt that the time had finally come for these promises to become realities. In a speech reprinted in the August 2, 1858, issue of *The New York Times*, Douglass affirmed that the Declaration of Independence was the great act that gave the American Republic its existence. In it the Founding Fathers asserted that "all men are entitled to life, liberty, and to an equal chance for happiness." They regarded slavery as a transient rather than a permanent feature of American society, and nowhere made provision for blacks to be enslaved or for the principles asserted in the document to be unequally applied: "They nowhere tell us that black men shall be slaves and white men shall be free. . . . They say, 'we, the people,' never we, the white people" (V, 402).

By midcentury, Douglass had further extended his interpretation of the Declaration of Independence to include more revolutionary and self-empowering efforts to achieve black liberation and independence. In the aftermath of the raid on Harper's Ferry, Douglass praised John Brown's heroic actions as perfectly consistent with the principles of the Declaration of Independence: "He believes the Declaration of Independence to be true, and the Bible to be a guide to human conduct, and acting upon the doctrines of both, he threw himself against the serried ranks of American oppression" (II, 459–60). And in increasingly militant terms, Douglass exhorted blacks to work for their own elevation and that of their enslaved brethren: "We must rise or fall, succeed or fail, by our own merits" (I, 314). In so doing, Douglass, like the slave in *The Columbian Orator*'s dialogue, was affirming his belief in the power of human agency over that of Providence. In this he differed quite strikingly from other black leaders of the period, particularly clergymen, whose liberatory rhetoric was at all times interwoven with appeals to Providence and divine intervention. Although never totally abandoning the rhetoric of providentiality, Douglass remained more suspicious of the promiscuous uses to which it had been put over time and more inclined to rely on the power of human agency to achieve the goals of freedom and full citizenship.

In further analyzing the historical situation of the Declaration of Independence, however, Douglass found that he had good reason to reproach the Founding Fathers, for he came to believe that the very men who had framed the document were at the same time "trafficking in the blood and souls of their fellow men" (I, 207). To Douglass, then, America was one great falsehood, containing a fundamental contradiction: On the one hand, it professed equality and liberty for all people; on the other, it practiced slavery, thereby denying those rights to many. To illustrate the extent to which slavery perverts the ideals on which the Republic was founded, Douglass repeatedly resorts to rhetorical schemas of antithesis. He asserts that slavery "has given us evil for good – darkness for light, and bitter for sweet" (V, 402), and underscores the contradiction between America's "profession of love of liberty" and its "statute-book so full of all that is cruel, malicious, and infernal" (I, 212). In fact, Douglass argues, slavery has replaced the Declaration of Independence as "the only sovereign power in the land." It has so permeated the entire fabric of American society that it "gives character to the American people. It dictates their laws, gives tone to their literature, and shapes their religion" (I, 168).

To reinforce his condemnation of proslavery discourse and practice, Douglass relied on a wide variety of techniques of reversal. These techniques were designed to show that the "reality" asserted by the dominant class is in fact often the exact opposite of that claimed and that, similarly, the effects sought by this dominant class often result in the exact opposite, thus reversing the system of values it has tried so hard to impose and maintain. Thus Douglass mocks the use of such "honeyed words" as the "peculiar" or "patriarchal" institution to describe the slave system. In particular, he calls attention to the sexual abuses created by the slave system; a slaveholder is not an uncle or brother but rather "a keeper of a house of ill-fame," and his "kitchen is a brothel" (I, 271). Douglass shows that the system of slavery works not because it is "benevolent" but because it relies on the cold fact of "the whip": "To ensure good behavior, the slaveholder relies on *the whip*; to induce proper humility, he relies on *the whip*; to rebuke what he is pleased to term insolence, he relies on *the whip*" (II, 135). After the passage of the Fugitive Slave Act, he repeatedly refers to slaveholders as robbers, manstealers, highwaymen, and kidnappers. Tearing away their mask of gentility, he mocks southern gentlemen and ladies who appear at Saratoga Springs, New York, "arrayed in purple and fine linen, . . . covered with silks, satins and broadcloth," but who are in reality "naked pirates before God and man" (II, 242). And he sarcastically refers to those politicians in the federal government who have southern sympathies as manstealers, thieves, and robbers.

Returning to his analogy of blacks as animals, Douglass once again manages to reverse the terms of the dominant discourse to point out how slavery's dehumanization of slaves dehumanizes slaveholders even more. He shows how, under the slave system, slaves are "registered with four footed beasts and creeping things" and are reduced to a level of brutishness that justifies the accusations of degradation so often leveled against them (I, 282). Through skillful manipulation of rhetoric, however, he also illustrates how the slaveholders themselves become animals. He likens their cruelty toward their slaves to "the kick of a jackass, or the barking of a bull-dog" (III, 182) and asserts that, in their greed, slaveholders have become worse than pigs, for "your genuine American Negro hater surpasses the pig in piggishness" (IV, 229). To entrust the well-being of slaves to slaveholders is, finally, tantamount to suggesting that "wolves may be trusted to legislate for themselves and . . . for lambs" (II, 329).

In yet another ironic reversal, Douglass shows how supposedly tyrannical countries are in fact resolutely advancing the causes of liberty and equality while democratic America is eagerly trampling on the principles of the Declaration of Independence: "The fact is, while Europe is becoming republican, we are becoming despotic; while France is contending for freedom, we are extending slavery. . . . While humanity, justice, and freedom are thawing the icy heart of Russia into life, and causing, even there, the iron hand of despotism to relax its terrible grasp upon the enslaved peasantry . . . we of the United States are buried in stone-dead indifference" (I, 305; II, 440). And of all ironies, England, the erstwhile oppressor, has now become the champion of the slave. "Monarchical freedom," Douglass bitterly concludes, "is better than republican slavery" (I, 172).

The most important rhetorical strategy of Douglass's counter discourse in the antebellum period was, perhaps, his use of dialogic techniques that allowed him to make eye contact not only with his audience but with his opponents as well, with those "masters" from whom he had had to wrench his freedom. In particular, he made use of the form of the "open letter" in order to engage in dialogue some of the most important men of his time. Although the term "open letter" did not come into use until the 1860s and 1870s, the form had existed for hundreds of years, in kind if not in name. It was most often used by a society's elite to challenge an opponent's point of view in a political or religious controversy. Probably the first black American to make use of this form, Douglass fashioned it into a particularly effective counter discourse, claiming as his own a form that had proven useful to popes, bishops, noblemen, and political leaders over the last 300 years. By adopting this form, Douglass was implicitly asserting his claim to equal status with all those who had used it before him.

As the most personal of literary forms, the letter implies by its very nature a back-and-forth, a give-and-take, a dialogue between two parties. With few exceptions, Douglass's open letters are addressed to individuals who would never deign to engage him in conversation, let alone answer him by letter. By means of this technique, Douglass was able to create hypothetical dialogues in which he invented his opponents' speeches or letters so that he could respond to them. The open letter thus became yet another effective means of entering into dialogue with those who wished to blot blacks from the page of human existence. Moreover, although each of Douglass's open letters is addressed to a particular individual, each is also addressed to a larger public concern, allowing Douglass to personify and concretize larger issues that his readers might remain insensitive to in the abstract. By adopting the open letter format, then, Douglass used it, much as the slave in *The Columbian Orator* used the dialogue form, to constitute himself as a speaking and writing subject, engage his opponents in dialogue, and concretely claim for himself and all blacks the principles of liberty and equality inscribed in the Declaration of Independence.

Douglass makes use of the open letter as early as 1846 in a series of letters to Garrison in which he diverges at given points from addressing his antislavery friend in order to address an antislavery opponent. Thus, in a letter dated January 27, 1846, Douglass turns away from Garrison to enter into dialogue with Mr. A. C. C. Thompson of Wilmington, who had attempted to invalidate Douglass's testimony against those slaveholders whose names were mentioned in the *Narrative*. Much like the slave in *The Columbian Orator*'s dialogue, Douglass responds to Thompson, thanking him profusely for the attention he has paid him, which proves that he is in fact the man he claims to be, "an *American slave*," rather than an imposter. He then proceeds ironically to compliment Thompson for doing "a piece of anti-slavery work, which no anti-slavery man could do" (I, 131). In another open letter, this one addressed to Samuel H. Cox, Douglass once again takes advantage of the fact that Cox has addressed him to engage him in dialogue, this time reclaiming Cox's words of insult and turning them into words of praise. In particular, he redefines the term "*abolition agitator and altruist*" to mean "simply . . . one who dares to think for himself – who goes beyond the mass of mankind in promoting the cause of righteousness – who honestly and earnestly speaks out his soul's conviction" (I, 192).

Douglass's boldest use of the open letter form may be found in two letters written in the late 1840s: one to Henry Clay, published in *The North Star* on December 3, 1847, the other to his former master, Captain Thomas Auld, published in *The Liberator* on September 14, 1849. In his letter to Clay, Douglass incorporates Clay's language into his own discourse, by quoting from it at length, and then proceeds to answer his points on the spot. The letter itself thus constitutes a kind of dialogue between master and slave. In it Douglass points out Clay's ideological inconsistencies. On the one hand, Clay calls slaves "unfortunate victims," but on the other, he continues to call for the perpetuation of slavery. Likewise, he purports to be a lover of liberty, but at the same time he insists that each state should have the power to decide whether it wants slavery within its borders or not. Faced with such an intellectual muddle, Douglass feels compelled to offer Clay advice, something that he would never have the opportunity to do in person; and his advice is "Emancipate your own slaves" (I, 290). In his letter to Auld, Douglass adopts a more informal tone, audaciously asserting his intellectual and moral superiority over his old master. Intimating that his own antislavery activities have influenced Auld, he graciously compliments the latter on his emancipation of his slaves and goes on to suggest that he make his conversion to antislavery public. In effect, in this open letter Douglass re-creates the scene between master and slave in *The Columbian Orator*, in which the slave, having gained his freedom, turns around to lecture and warn his master.

In the March 11, 1853, issue of *The North Star*, Douglass published a short story entitled "The Heroic Slave," which also appeared the same year in Julia Griffith's *Autographs for Freedom*. Based on events surrounding the slave revolt on board the *Creole* in 1841, the story is important for the ways in which Douglass both continues and extends the themes and strategies of his antebellum journalism, turning in particular to techniques of fiction to accomplish what factual writing would not allow him to do. Douglass was already aware of the power of fiction when, in his "Farewell Speech to the British People" published in *The London Times* in 1847, he imputed certain statements to Daniel Webster concerning Madison Washington, which then allowed him to underscore the basic contradictions at the heart of the slave system. In Webster's hypothetical speech, he was made to praise Washington's courage and nobility while at the same time demanding that the slave be returned to the chains of slavery. In fictionalizing Washington's story in "The Heroic Slave," Douglass took full advantage of the freedom that fiction allowed him further to point out the contradictions inherent in the slave system and to press home the abolitionists' cause.[7]

Many of the themes and rhetorical devices that Douglass employs in the story continue those of his journalism. In particular, Douglass is most effective in adapting certain of his journalistic techniques to the manipulation of voice and point of view in the story. First of all, he creates a powerful black hero who, through soliloquy, speeches, and storytelling, is granted full status as speaking subject. In addition, Douglass's technique of the hypothetical dialogue comes into its own here, as Douglass is able to create not only dialogues but full-blown characters – black and white – who interact dramatically in scenes spun from his imagination. In Part III, for example, Douglass's narrator moves the action to a tavern in Virginia and creates a series of dialogues between a white proslavery "loafer" and the abolitionist Listwell, as well as among the loafers themselves. The main point of these dialogues is to expose the foolishness of the loafers' perceptions, their inability to read Listwell properly and ultimately to achieve any semblance of narrative authority. They are reduced to telling each other "stories" that the narrator, as controlling authority, refuses to record, considering them unworthy of the reader's attention. Listwell, in contrast, remains very much in control, able both to withhold information about himself and to achieve an invisible, omniscient perspective so that, unknown to them, he may learn a good deal about them. If Listwell disappears in Part IV of the story, it is so that the narrative may record a second conversation among a group of white men, this time southern sailors. Amplifying once again the technique of the hypothetical dialogue, Douglass's narrator creates a conversation between a sailor and the first mate of the *Creole*, who, goaded by the former, ends up praising Washington's heroic act of self-assertion, defending his essential dignity and nobility, and unwittingly underscoring the contradiction inherent in white America's refusal to apply the principles of 1776 to the black man.

In "The Heroic Slave" Douglass also extends the narrative techniques of his journalism in his efforts both to transcend the highly personal perspective of the "I" and to develop the broader perspective of a third-person narrator. In portraying Madison Washington, Douglass creates a character who, although a fictional projection of himself in many ways, is nonetheless historically distinct from him. In so doing, Douglass initiates a process whereby he attempts to distance himself from his autobiographical and factual "I."

Moving beyond the autobiographical "I," Douglass creates a third-person narrator who is especially important to the development of the Washington–Listwell relationship. A primary function of Listwell, who is converted to abolitionism after hearing Washington's soliloquy in the forest, is to *listen well*. He listens well both to Washington and to the white loafers at the Virginia tavern. This is clearly the role that Douglass, the journalist and public speaker, wants white abolitionists to play: to listen well to what the black slave has to say. But Listwell's function as listener has other implications as well. For without Listwell's position as overhearer of Washington's soliloquy or as recipient of his stories, Washington would not be able to tell his tale. A mutual interdependence is thus established between Washington and Listwell, between slave and abolitionist: Without Washington, there is no story to tell; without Listwell, there is nobody to receive and relay the story. Most importantly, however, both Madison and Listwell are dependent on the narrator, who is the controlling authority of the story, who organizes, shapes, and comments on it according to his own ideological perspective. Douglass here creates in his fiction a narrative situation that he must have desired in his journalistic career both before and after the Civil War: an interdependent relationship between the black slave as speaking and experiencing subject, on the one hand, and the white abolitionist, who both listens well and takes an active role in his cause, on the other, guided by an authoritative black leader whose role it is to write the black back on the page of human existence.

Although Douglass would never again experiment with writing fiction, his achievement in this story marks a key transitional phase in his rhetorical stance as a journalist. Just as his third-person omniscient narrator in the story moves back and forth from one point of view to another, Douglass the journalist will soon allow his own work to move back and forth between several points of view – those of black and white, of "we" and "they" – as the exigencies of the Civil War, Reconstruction, and the post–Reconstruction debacle demand departures from the rhetorical strategies that had proven to be so effective before the war.

During the Civil War, rapid shifts in political events gradually came to dictate shifts in Douglass's journalistic rhetoric. In one article, for example, Douglass follows a dramatic, searing condemnation of government policy toward slaves who escape across Union lines with a retraction based on just-received information that reflects a change in policy. Given such rapid changes of events, generalizations and abstract explanations were perhaps a wiser rhetorical strategy than an invocation of specific charges and ad hominem attacks. In addition, Douglass found that he could rely less frequently on his own experiences in slavery as the foundation on which to ground his arguments, and instead had to find ways to broaden both his perspective and the issue of slavery itself. Thus the brutal facts and concrete metonyms of Douglass's journalism of the 1840s give way to such abstract comments as "Self-deception is a chronic disease of the American mind and character. . . . We are masters in the art of substituting a pleasant falsehood for an ugly and disagreeable truth, and of clinging to a fascinating delusion while rejecting a palpable reality" (III, 126).

Looking ahead to the end of slavery and the beginning of a new social system, Douglass suddenly found himself confronted with the question of how those who had for so long been outside of the social system could now become part of it. He alternates between his earlier rhetorical mode of castigating the federal government for its complicity with slavery, rebuking it for its hypocrisy, dishonesty, and failure of nerve, and a new impulse to see himself and other blacks as part of the government, which he now sometimes refers to as "we" and "our rulers" instead of "they." Shifting between references to *the* government and *our* government, Douglass's stance is more constrained than it was in the antebellum period, when the object of his criticism was quite clearly the slaveholding class and the government that supported it. As Douglass's own view of his place – and the place of other blacks – in America's democratic experiment changes, his strategies as a journalist change as well.

In this period, for example, Douglass still occasionally reverts to the form of the open letter, but with less and less frequency. The difference between his open letter to Postmaster General Blair, dated October 1862, and the earlier ones to Henry Clay and Thomas Auld is instructive: The latter letter is a response to an actual letter sent to Douglass by a person in a position of power, who addresses him with respect and courtesy. Responding to Blair's arguments in favor of colonization, Douglass appeals to analogies from abroad to drive home his point, arguing that if the free colored populations of Cuba and Brazil are not being subjected to expatriation schemes, why should the free black man in the United States be? The most interesting part of the letter is, however, the epistolary situation itself, in which Douglass is acutely aware that a man of Blair's stature has actually written to him and given him the occasion to respond. To underscore his sense of its importance, Douglass in the letter self-consciously places himself in a tradition of black men who have been addressed by great national leaders, recalling, for example, Jefferson's letter to Benjamin Banneker, in which the president "warmly commend[ed] his talents and learning" (III, 284).

During the Civil War period, buried among articles addressed to specific issues, such as black enlistment or colonization schemes, are several articles in which Douglass looks ahead to what lies in store for black Americans. In 1863, he had referred to "slavery and its twin monster prejudice" (III, 38). But although exposing slavery was something Douglass had honed into a highly developed art, exposing its "twin monster" – especially after Reconstruction – proved to be more complicated. Douglass may well have sensed this fact when in 1862 he pondered the question: "What shall be [the slaves'] status in the new condition of things? Shall they exchange the relation of slavery to individuals, only to become slaves of the community at large, having no rights which anybody is required to respect, subject to a code of black laws, denying them school privileges, denying them the right of suffrage, denying the right to keep and bear arms, denying them the right of speech, and the right of petition? Or shall they have secured to them equal rights before the law?" (III, 40–1).

After the Civil War, with slavery officially abolished, Douglass struggled to reframe this question. It was a troubling and difficult task. Whereas slavery was a clear and present evil, the postwar evil was often too murky and complex to name: "The thing worse than rebellion is the thing that causes rebellion," he wrote. "What that thing is, we have been taught to our cost. It remains now to be seen whether we have the needed courage to have that cause entirely removed from the Republic" (IV, 201). The "we" that Douglass invokes here is an inclusive "we," a "we" that situates itself squarely among the citizenry that give the government its legitimacy and its power. Douglass often employs this "we" to shame his fellow citizens into sharing his revulsion at the activities of former rebels. For example, in 1871 he writes: "The spread of the lynch law at the South, the wholesale slaughter of loyal men, the open defiance by the people of the General Government, the organization of secret bands sufficiently powerful in every rebel State to control its policy and defeat the ends of justice, prove how foolish and practically wicked has been the impunity with which we have treated their crimes" (IV, 258).

From the end of the Civil War until his death, Douglass struggled to find ways to describe and expose the realities of postwar race relations in America. In a series of articles in mainstream, predominantly white publications such as *The North American Review* and *Harper's Weekly*, Douglass endeavored to explain the current state of blacks in America by reminding his audience of the degradation of a slave system from which blacks had so recently been liberated.

Much of Douglass's writing during this period gives policy advice. and social analysis of the kind he had given in the past. But there is often a restraint, keyed perhaps to his efforts to withhold judgment during a period of enormous transition. Although the articles are clear and well argued, they lack the passion of his antebellum writing. Much of the fire that characterized his earliest triumphs as a journalist is absent. His analysis is often more abstract than previously, such as his vague recommendation that "time and endeavor must have their perfect working before we shall see the end of the effect of slavery and oppression in the United States" (IV, 227).

In his most important articles, however, Douglass was able once again to find his stride as a masterfully eloquent journalist when he reclaimed as fact and metaphor the subject that had fueled his writing from the start: slavery. That which he had expressed as a hypothetical fear in 1862 had come to pass by the end of Reconstruction: Black people had exchanged slavery to individuals for slavery to "the community at large." As he reclaimed slavery both as symbol and as reality, retelling the horrors of the past to reframe the horrors of the present, Douglass broadened his perspective on his country's social ills and ascended to new heights of rhetorical intensity and passion. He achieves his effectiveness of old when he recalls and extends those images that had served him in the antebellum period. He reminds his audience that slavery still scars the free black and does not hesitate to detail its brutal and gory facts: "he has scarcely been free long enough to outgrow the marks of the lash on his back and the fetters on his limbs. He stands before us, to–day, physically, a maimed and mutilated man. . . . Slavery has twisted his limbs, shattered his feet, deformed his body and distorted his features" (IV, 194). Douglass is also compelling in his use of slavery as a metaphor, as he reminds his audience that slavery is not only a bondage of the body, but an even "more terrible bondage of ignorance and vice" (IV, 224).

In article after article, Douglass reaches new heights of moral indignation as he effectively shows how slavery has left a legacy of barbarism hanging like a black cloud over the slave states. This legacy, Douglass claims, burdens ex-slaves and slaveholders alike. Slave labor has been replaced by cheap labor that is motivated by "the same lust for gain, the same love of ease, and loathing of labor, which originated that infernal traffic." Like slave labor, cheap labor brings "ease and luxury to the rich, wretchedness and misery to the poor" (IV, 264–5). For slaveholders, the barbarism of slavery has left a "brutalizing, stupefying, and debasing effect upon their natures" (IV, 243). Blind to their own interests, slaveholders are expelling northern emigrants from the South, engaging in burnings, lynchings, and wholesale murders. Such is the legacy of "besotted madness" that slavery has pinned upon the old ex-slaveholding oligarchy of the South.

Douglass is equally effective in his postbellum journalism as he intensifies his efforts on behalf of women's suffrage. Aware that all his prior actions have been either on behalf of himself or his people, Douglass notes that in supporting women's suffrage "self [is] out of the question" and that a broader perspective than that of the personal "I" is necessary (IV, 452). Douglass achieves this broader perspective as he once again reclaims the arguments and images of his antislavery journalism and applies them to women's causes. He asserts that women are human beings and do not need "protection" in the ways that animals do; he insists that if women are indeed human beings, they must be intellectual and moral, and therefore capable of making their own choices; finally, he argues that the true doctrine of American liberty demands that women, like blacks, be allowed to represent themselves.

Throughout his journalism of this period, then, Douglass's "I" is at its most authoritative when he once again positions himself as an outsider, pressing arguments for reasons why blacks – and women – should become part of the "we." His rhetoric is most effective in those instances when he is most acutely aware that blacks still remain outside the "we" and must continue their fight to become a part of it, to break down the "color line" whose origins are rooted in the slave system. Against those who assert that race prejudice is both universal and natural, Douglass retorts that it is neither. In a tightly reasoned article entitled "The Color Line," he argues that prejudice is in fact a learned response that exists neither worldwide nor at all times. In the United States it is the result of a social system that had effectively sought "to enslave [the black man], to blot out his personality, degrade his manhood, and sink him to the condition of a beast of burden" (IV, 347). The shadow of this system still lingers over the country, poisoning the moral atmosphere of the Republic and preventing genuine emancipation.

The "we" who hold those famous "truths to be self-evident" is, in several ways, a different "we" after the war than before. It is a "we" that now includes millions of former slaves, and it is a "we" that is sobered and chastened by the pain and death of strife. But rather than abandon the habits that animated his antebellum journalism, Douglass now recasts them in a new light. The dialogic power of his rhetoric is now trained not on one class and the government's support of it, but on the society as a whole. For the new "we," as Douglass well understands, embraces not only former slaves but also the forces of history that allowed them to be enslaved. Facing up to that history requires a constant vigilance toward all people and institutions that exploit, defraud, and degrade in the name of "civilization." The society Douglass wants to bring into being is a self-reflective political culture in which first principles are frequently invoked, deep questioning is both accepted and expected, and probing the gaps between the country's stated ideals and the actual condition of its people is the responsibility of every citizen. It is to membership in this new "we" that Douglass would have all of us aspire.

NOTES

1   Philip S. Foner, *The Life and Writings of Frederick Douglass*, 5 volumes (New York: International Publishers, 1950–75), V, p. 3. All further references to Douglass's journalism will be to this edition and will be cited parenthetically in the text.

2   Frederick Douglass, *Narrative of the Life of Frederick Douglass, an American Slave, Written by Himself* (New York: Anchor Books, 1973), p. 68. All further references to the *Narrative* will be to this edition and will be cited parenthetically in the text.

3   Caleb Bingham, *The Columbian Orator* (New York: E. Duyckinck, 1816), title page. All further references to *The Columbian Orator* will be to this edition and will be cited parenthetically in the text.

4   M. M. Bakhtin, *The Dialogic Imagination*, trans. Michael Holquist (Austin: University of Texas Press, 1981), especially pp. 324–35.

5   Michel Foucault, *The History of Sexuality* (New York: Vintage Books, 1980), I, p. 101.

6   Locke quoted in Harry V. Jaffa, *Crisis of the House Divided* (Seattle: University of Washington Press, 1959), pp. 314–15.

7   For another analysis of "The Heroic Slave," see Robert B. Stepto, "Storytelling in Early Afro-American Fiction: Frederick Douglass's 'The Heroic Slave,'" in *Black Literature and Literary Theory*, ed. Henry Louis Gates (New York: Methuen, 1984), pp. 175–86.

The Frederick Douglass–Gerrit Smith Friendship and Political Abolitionism in the 1850s

JOHN R. MCKIVIGAN

It was an unusual friendship: a runaway slave and a wealthy New York landholder. Frederick Douglass and Gerrit Smith were drawn together by a shared commitment to ending slavery and guaranteeing equal rights to all. Their friendship began tentatively in the late 1840s at about the time Douglass launched his first newspaper, the *North Star*, in Rochester, New York. It solidified in the early 1850s and contributed to Douglass's acrimonious break with his original abolitionist associates, the followers of Boston editor William Lloyd Garrison.

Douglass's friendship with Smith was a turning point in his career, and it illuminates the whole history of abolitionism. Smith's financial assistance put Douglass's newspaper on a more secure footing and gave him the opportunity to improve his journalistic skills. Smith also drew Douglass into antislavery political circles at the moment when the northern public finally began to consider the issues of slavery and sectionalism seriously. The friendship with Smith also marked an important stage in Douglass's personal development. After escaping from slavery, he struggled to win acceptance as an equal from his white abolitionist colleagues. Since, the 1960s, historians have noted that the paternalism of white Garrisonians played a leading role in causing Douglass's alienation from that faction.[1] This essay explores the extent of Smith's influence on Douglass's political ideology and behavior during the crucial decade of the 1850s and shows why Douglass found his new allegiances in the abolitionist movement, particularly his close and abiding friendship with Smith, more acceptable to his growing sense of personal self-confidence and racial pride.

Thanks to his own autobiographical writings and the dedicated work of his biographers,[2] the details of Douglass's early life are better known than those of any other antebellum black. He was born on a tobacco plantation on the eastern shore of Maryland in 1818. His mother was a slave, but the identity of his father was unknown to Douglass – a common situation among slaves. Sent to Baltimore to be trained as a craftsman, Douglass seized an opportunity to escape from slavery in 1838. Fearful of recapture, he settled far north in New Bedford, Massachusetts. In August 1841, Douglass was invited to recount his slave experiences at a convention of abolitionists in Nantucket, Massachusetts. He spoke in such clear and moving terms that the Massachusetts Anti-Slavery Society immediately hired him as a lecturer.[3]

By the time Douglass joined the abolitionist movement, it had already experienced a significant splintering of its never large ranks. The modern abolition campaign in the United States emerged during the early 1830s as a by-product of the upsurge of revivalism popularly known as the "Second Great Awakening." Early abolitionists condemned slavery as the product of personal sin and demanded immediate emancipation as the price of repentance, but the rejection of their emancipation and antiracial discrimination program by slaveholders and by national institutions, including the churches and political parties, forced abolitionists to reconsider their original "moral suasion" strategy. Many followed the lead of veteran antislavery editor William Lloyd Garrison of Boston and abandoned institutions such as the churches as hopelessly corrupted by slavery. Many of these Garrisonians also adopted pacifistic or "nonresistant" political practices and counseled northerners that the Constitution was a proslavery document and that voting therefore indirectly lent moral sanction to slavery. Adhering to an extreme brand of perfectionistic philosophy, Garrisonians became leading champions of many antebellum reform causes ranging from sexual equality to dietary reform.[4]

In 1840, following several years of acrimonious debate, the followers of Garrison won control of the abolitionists' national organization, the American Anti-Slavery Society. Their opponents, including Gerrit Smith, immediately quit the group. Although some non-Garrisonian abolitionists continued to devote their energies to activities in the religious sphere,[5] most shifted their efforts from religious to political antislavery reform. Down to the Civil War, the gulf between Garrisonian and non-Garrisonian abolitionist groups remained wide and bitter.

Recruited into the abolitionist movement by the Garrisonians, Frederick Douglass initially espoused all of that faction's principal tenets. He told audiences that slavery had "spread a dark cloud over the intellect of the nation, corrupting the channels of morality, poisoning the fountains of religion and perverting the beneficial objects of government."[6] He even advocated the unpopular Garrisonian call for the dissolution of the federal union to separate the North from the guilt of sustaining a proslavery Constitution. Douglass condemned not only the two major political parties, the Whigs and Democrats, which refused to act against slavery, but also the political efforts of Garrison's abolitionist opponents.[7]

Although Douglass had no ideological quarrels with other Garrisonians in his early years as a lecturer, signs of personal tensions with that faction's white leaders began to surface. Douglass soon tired of repeating personal anecdotes about his years of a slave and began to offer a more ideological denunciation of the institutions. His white coadjutors, however, warned Douglass that his true asset to the movement was not his rhetorical skill but his status as a fugitive slave.[8]

Even though this advice might have been well intentioned, it revealed a paternalistic attitude that many white abolitionists from all factions displayed toward their black colleagues. Although the antislavery societies endorsed equal rights, they rarely allowed black members to reach policy-making positions. Only a few white abolitionists treated blacks as more than child-like beings who needed benevolent but firm guidance.[9]

Although Douglass resented the close supervision by the Garrisonians of his antislavery activities, he continued to lecture in their employ.[10] After the publication in 1845 of his immensely popular first autobiography, *The Narrative of the Life of Frederick Douglass*, Douglass's abolitionist friends warned him that his safety was in jeopardy and helped him flee to Great Britain, where U.S. fugitive slave laws could not reach him. From August 1845 to April 1847, Douglass lectured in Ireland, Scotland, and England and became a celebrity who drew large audiences to his speeches. His enthusiastic reception by all levels of British society greatly elevated Douglass's self-confidence.[11] In late 1846, Douglass's British admirers purchased his freedom from his Maryland master, causing some Garrisonian abolitionists to complain that he had sanctioned a transaction that acknowledged the "right to traffic in human beings."[12]

Another controversy developed on this overseas tour when British admirers gave Douglass $2,175 to start his own newspaper when he returned to the United States in 1847. American Garrisonians labored hard to discourage Douglass's journalistic ambitions. They noted that black-edited newspapers already existed, and that another one could not possibly succeed financially, but Douglass also sensed that the editors of the various publications of the American Anti-Slavery Society feared the competition his new paper would provide. Most significantly, some white Garrisonians advised Douglass that he lacked the prerequisite education to be an editor and should stick to lecturing. Underlying all of these arguments was a belief that Douglass, only a few years away from slavery, still required close tutelage. The fact that Douglass refused to acknowledge his continued dependence on those who had originally sponsored and guided him in the abolitionist movement angered many white Garrisonians and made them interpret Douglass's motivation for desiring to become an editor as willful and mercenary.[13]

These arguments only temporarily dissuaded Douglass. In the fall of 1847, he publicized his decision to launch his own newspaper. After his personally liberating experiences in Britain, Douglass could not bear to return to the subservient position that white Garrisonians expected of a paid black itinerant lecturer. In becoming an editor, he confessed that he sought to become "a principal, and not an agent."[14] Douglass also believed that founding a newspaper would aid not only his personal development but the cause of abolition as well. A successfully managed black newspaper, he felt, would help dispel the racist assumptions of most American whites. Such a paper could also set a good example for fellow blacks and guide them down the road to self-reliance.[15]

Douglass selected Rochester in western New York as the site for his newspaper. That rapidly expanding city along the Erie Canal and its immediate surroundings had an energetic reform community, including both Garrisonian and politically inclined abolitionists. Rochester also had an established free black community numbering over 300. Douglass had visited Rochester on speaking tours in the mid-1840s and recalled a warm welcome by all segments of the antislavery constituency. A final consideration for choosing Rochester was that it was too far away from Garrison's Boston *Liberator* or the New York *National Anti-Slavery Standard* to be a direct competitor.[16]

On December 3, 1847, the first issue of Douglass's newspaper, the *North Star*, was published. The second issue was published on January 7, 1848, and the paper appeared regularly as a four-page weekly for the next twelve and a half years. With an initial subscription list of only around 700 and weekly costs of over $50, the *North Star* lost money from the start. To survive, Douglass had to devote much of his time to traveling and lecturing to drum up new subscriptions. The purse from his English friends was soon depleted, and Douglass had to place a mortgage on his own house to keep afloat financially. He did receive some monetary assistance from the Garrisonians' Western New York Anti-Slavery Society, but he flatly refused the group's request to oversee his bookkeeping. Neither subsidies nor a significant number of subscriptions were forthcoming from East Coast Garrisonians.[17]

A crucial figure in the survival of the *North Star* was English abolitionist Julia Griffiths, who had befriended Douglass during his tour of the British Isles. She came to Rochester to join his staff as informal business manager in 1849. She reorganized the office, separated Douglass's personal finances from the paper's, and lifted the mortgage from his house. Within two years, Griffiths reduced the paper's debt by $800 and doubled its subscription list.[18]

As they struggled to bring their books into balance, Douglass and the *North Star*'s small staff each week managed to fill their four pages with news, editorials, correspondence, announcements, ads, fiction, and poetry, usually dealing with the antislavery campaign. Just as Douglass copied his format from that of other abolitionist weeklies, the *North Star*'s editorials echoed the major tenets of the Garrisonian ideology. Douglass lambasted schemes to colonize blacks in Africa and branded the churches proslavery.[19] The *North Star* likewise condemned the U.S. Constitution as a proslavery document and advocated the disunion of North and South as the morally correct strategy for abolitionists.[20]

Douglass also used the *North Star* to report on events of concern to northern blacks. The paper carried reports and announcements of the activities of black churches and other institutions. Several prominent blacks, including Samuel R. Ward, Amos G. Beman, Henry Bibb, James McCune Smith, and William J. Wilson, became regular contributors to the *North Star*. The paper editorialized against the racial discrimination that free blacks faced in the North and preached a doctrine combining agitation and self-help to overcome it. This policy mirrored Douglass's increased personal involvement in the affairs of the free black community in Rochester, where he helped lead a fight to integrate the city's public schools.[21]

The Garrisonians remained suspicious about Douglass's motivation for operating his own paper and scrutinized his every issue for evidence of deviance. They regarded Douglass's announcement that the *North Star* was intended as "an organ for the oppressed in this land, through which all may speak, no matter how widely any party may differ from each other"[22] as dangerous impartiality. The unsuccessful attempt in 1849 by Rochester Garrisonians to gain some control over the *North Star* in exchange for further financial assistance may have been motivated by doubts about Douglass's ability to resist the temptation to switch allegiance to the more affluent political abolitionists. Most alarming, however, were clues that Douglass had befriended the most powerful of all local political abolitionists, Gerrit Smith.[23]

Gerrit Smith was born in Utica, New York, in March 1797, but resided most of his life in the small community of Peterboro in Madison County, New York. Heir to nearly a quarter-million acres of undeveloped land scattered across New York, Vermont, Michigan, and Virginia, Smith's annual income in the 1840s and 1850s typically exceeded $60,000.[24] Smith used his great fortune to become a leading philanthropist as well as a leader and major financial sponsor of state and national organizations promoting temperance, prison reform, women's rights, international peace, and land reform. But the cause to which he was most devoted was the campaign to end slavery. Smith supported the goal of immediate emancipation and many other reforms advocated by the Garrisonians, but he disagreed strongly with their political views. He quit the American Anti-Slavery Society when it fell under their control in the spring of 1840.[25]

By that time, Smith was supporting efforts to launch an independent political party on an abolitionist platform. In April 1840, Smith played a prominent part in the convention that nominated a presidential ticket headed by former slaveholder James G. Birney.[26] The new Liberty Party condemned not only slaveholding but also the nation's pervasive racial prejudice as an affront to God's laws. It conceded that the Constitution protected slavery in the southern states but called for immediate abolition in all territories under direct control of the federal government.[27] Birney's small totals of just 7,000 votes (0.29 percent) in 1840 and 62,000 votes (2.31 percent) when he ran again in 1844, however, showed that the issue of slavery was not yet strong enough to win significant support from the electorate.[28] However, although weak nationwide, the Liberty Party played a stronger role in New York politics. In New York State elections in the mid-1840s, where Smith was its most prominent leader, the Liberty Party vote usually reached 5 percent of the total cast, sometimes double that figure in western New York.[29] Smith's home county of Madison generally returned the highest percentage for the party. Smith's political influence derived largely from the more than $50,000 he contributed to the national and state Liberty Party.[30]

A contest for control of the Liberty Party, following Birney's second defeat in 1844, destroyed the unity of the political abolition movement. As early as 1845, Smith, Birney, and a few other political abolitionists proposed broadening the Liberty Party's platform to a program of "universal reform." Calling themselves the "Liberty League," this faction also argued that the Constitution did not sanction slavery and that therefore Congress had the power to abolish slavery everywhere in the Union.[31]

A second faction led by Salmon P. Chase, Gamaliel Bailey, and Henry B. Stanton advocated electoral cooperation with moderate antislavery elements in the major parties. In a complicated series of interparty battles sparked by the Mexican War, the procoalition forces merged the Liberty Party with Whigs and Democrats opposed to the western extension of slavery, creating the new Free Soil Party and nominating former president Martin Van Buren for president in 1848. Unlike the Liberty Party, the Free Soilers gave no endorsement to immediate abolition or to equal rights for blacks. In fact, many Free Soilers held strong negrophobic sentiments and supported antiextensionism as a means of keeping black labor – free or slave – from the territories.[32] Although the Liberty League failed to prevent the Free Soil merger, its members vowed to continue to work for their undiluted abolitionist program. In June 1848, the Liberty League renamed itself the National Liberty Party and ran Smith for president in opposition to the Free Soil and major party candidates. Smith attracted only 2,500 votes, however, compared to Van Buren's 290,000.[33]

In addition to his work with the Liberty Party, Smith engaged in many nonpolitical efforts to assist northern free blacks. He financially assisted the schools, newspapers, and temperance societies of New York blacks;[34] and he denounced efforts to return fugitive slaves to their masters and made his estate in Peterboro an underground railroad stop.[35] Smith's most generous act of philanthropy toward blacks was his program to distribute land grants to New York blacks. Almost 3,000 took advantage of Smith's generosity, but only a small minority settled on his land. By the mid-1850s, many of the grants had been abandoned and confiscated for unpaid taxes.[36] One motivation for Smith's land distribution plan was to enable as many blacks as possible to meet the state's $250 property qualification for the right to vote, required of black men alone according to the state constitution adopted in 1821. After the founding of the Free Soil Party, Smith was one of the few prominent white politicians to continue to battle for equal rights as part of the struggle against slavery. By the time Frederick Douglass was establishing himself in Rochester, Smith had won a nationwide reputation as an uncompromising abolitionist and friend to blacks.[37]

The Douglass–Smith friendship started soon after the founding of the *North Star* in Rochester. When the two men met for the first time is uncertain. Although Smith infrequently ventured far from his Peterboro home, he might have heard Douglass speak during tours of New York. Douglass certainly knew Smith by reputation and occasionally listed him as a wealthy patron of abolitionist activities in speeches in England in the mid-1840s.[38]

A letter Smith sent Douglass during the first month of the *North Star*'s operation might have been their first direct communication. If so, Smith introduced himself to Frederick Douglass in a flamboyant manner. Along with $5 to pay for a two-year subscription to the *North Star*, Smith sent Douglass a deed to forty acres of land from the lots he was distributing to New York blacks. Smith wished Douglass: "In this, your new home, may you and yours, and your labours of love for your oppressed race, be all greatly blessed of God."[39] Douglass responded with effusive praise in the *North Star* for Smith's land distribution scheme, calling it a "generous and magnificent donation." For the next several years, he publicized Smith's offer and called on blacks to accept it as a means to combat racial prejudice by becoming successful farmers.[40]

The *North Star* also reported on Smith's antislavery activities. In January failed to prevent the Free Soil merger, its members vowed to continue to work for their undiluted abolitionist program. In June 1848, the Liberty League renamed itself the National Liberty Party and ran Smith for president in opposition to the Free Soil and major party candidates. Smith attracted only 2,500 votes, however, compared to Van Buren's 290,000.[33]

Douglass also took note of Smith's political career. The first political convention that Douglass attended was that of the National Liberty Party at Buffalo on June 14–15, 1848, which nominated Smith for president. Douglass praised its "strong and radical character," comparing it favorably to Garrisonian meetings. Douglass particularly commended Smith's call to northern free blacks "to prove their superiority to the whites in industry, economy, temperance and education, in order to disprove the frequently repeated charge that Negroes were fit only for slavery."[42]

A month later, Douglass attended the convention in Buffalo, which created the Free Soil Party. He was invited to address the assembled delegates, but hoarseness prevented a long speech. Douglass simply bade the gathering "God speed your noble enterprise."[43] Throughout the fall, Douglass wavered about the propriety of voting and the best candidate to support. He said that he could not vote because of Garrisonian principles but used his editorial column to advise blacks and abolitionists who could vote to support Van Buren. In early September, however, he withdrew his backing of Van Buren and counseled only nonvoting. At the same time, he rejected Samuel Ward's pleas to support Smith and the Liberty Party. He did praise the determination of that small band to drag the Free Soilers to the "summit of the anti-slavery hill."[44] By the end of September, Douglass resumed his quasi-endorsement of the Free Soilers and continued it until the election.

In his postelection assessment, Douglass acknowledged the shortcomings of the Free Soil movement, particularly its attitude toward racial equality. Nonetheless, he argued that the group had "done some good" and that he "would not find fault with political action, in a party formed against slavery."[45] Douglass also stated that he could no longer counsel blacks to give up their right to vote voluntarily to conform to the principles of nonresistance.

Other signs began to appear in the *North Star* that Douglass was moving away from Garrisonian political positions. In editorials early in 1849, Douglass conceded that the governing principles of the U.S. Constitution were antislavery, but he still contended that the framers' intention had been to protect slavery.[46] Smith wrote Douglass that his new stand was ambivalent but had "cheer[ed] me with the hope that you are on the eve of wielding the Federal Constitution for the Abolition of American Slavery."[47]

Smith sent Douglass Liberty Party literature on the Constitution. Douglass nonetheless maintained a relatively orthodox Garrisonian position in a good-natured public debate with Ward, who argued for the antislavery nature of the Constitution, in May 1849.[48] Douglass and Smith debated the issue of the Constitution head to head the following January in Syracuse. When Douglass said he regretted that he could see no way over the "great gulf" to Smith's position, the latter cryptically replied that it could be "very easily bridged."[49] In a report to his readers on this convention, Douglass expressed doubt that either side had won a single convert to its position.[50]

Douglass continued to weigh the ideological issues dividing abolitionists and, the next year, wrote Smith that he had made significant changes in his views. Douglass confessed to Smith that he was "sick and tired of argueing [sic] on the slaveholder side" and had "about decided to let the Slaveholders and their Northern abettors have the labouring *oar* in putting a proslavery interpretation on the Constitution." He acknowledged that he had "thought much since [his] personal acquaintance" with Smith and been "much impressed by your reasoning." Although he still had doubts about how "legal rules of interpretation" could be made to override the "wicked intentions of our constitution makers," Douglass suspected that he had "conceded all that you require."[51]

Although this friendly exchange over the U.S. Constitution slowly moved Douglass closer to Smith's position, there is evidence that non-ideological factors also drew Douglass to the white abolitionist. In particular, Douglass was attracted to Smith's liberal racial attitudes. Besides his philanthropies to blacks and his antislavery work, Smith actively battled racial discrimination. He frequently attended black churches rather than condone the segregated "negro pew" found in most churches.[52] When Douglass reported in the *North Star* that he had been accosted for accompanying Julia Griffiths on a New York City street, Smith wrote him a revealing letter:

> Think not, my dear Douglass, that is is you colored men alone who suffer from this insane and rampant prejudice. The wound it inflicts on you, it inflicts on us who sympathize with you, and who have identified ourselves and made ourselves colored men with you. In your sufferings, we suffer. – In your afflictions, we are afflicted. . . . How can I enjoy that in which my equal brother is permitted no participation? Even the attempt to enjoy it, I feel to be traitorous to him; and if enjoyment begin, the rising of such a feeling arrests and withers it.[53]

Years later, Douglass fondly recalled an incident when Smith personally encouraged and assisted him in confronting racial prejudices. In his third autobiography, *Life and Times*, Douglass wrote: "Invited to accompany

Hon. Gerrit Smith to dine with Mr. E[dward] C. Delavan at Albany
many years ago, I expressed to Mr. Smith my awkwardness and embarrassment in the society I was likely to meet there. 'Ah!' said that good
man, 'you must go Douglass; it is your mission to break down the walls
of separation between the two races.' "[54] The two men attended together,
and the wealthy friends of Delavan soon warmed to their black dining
companion.

Other antebellum blacks had similar experiences with Smith and testified
that he demonstrated little of the fear of social intimacy that many white
abolitionists revealed to blacks.[55] Like other blacks, Douglass found himself
a welcome guest when he visited Smith's Peterboro estate.[56] In their
correspondence, Douglass and Smith regularly exchanged information
and inquiries about the well-being of their families. When Smith sent
Douglass a copy of a memorial book he had written for his son, Fitzhugh,
the entire Douglass family signed a letter of thanks, "Your affectionate
friends."[57]

An important clue that Douglass looked to Smith as a friend and
confidant can be seen in a letter written in March 1849. In response to
Smith's inquiry about the financial health of the *North Star*, Douglass
confessed that he had spent most of the money given him by British
abolitionists "foolishly." He also complained that the East Coast Garrisonians thought him "far more serviceable as a public speaker than I
can be as an editor." Because he "started the paper against their wishes –
and against their advice, they feel therefore little or no interest in its
support," he wrote.[58] Douglass might have hoped for additional monetary
assistance from Smith in response to this letter, but he also seemed to
be searching for moral support from a fellow abolitionist. All indications
are that the Douglass–Garrison friendship was fully established by the
start of the 1850s.

In April 1851, two months after Douglass informed Smith of his
altered views on the Constitution and political action, the Peterboro
abolitionist responded with a proposal that would transform Douglass's
subsequent career as an abolitionist journalist. Smith offered to help
finance a merger between the *North Star* and the official organ of his
political faction, the *Liberty Party Paper*, edited by John Thomas. He also
hoped that Samuel Ward of Cortland, New York, would merge his own
struggling journal, the *Impartial Citizen*, with the new paper under
Douglass's editorial leadership.[59]

The *Liberty Party Paper* in early 1851 definitely needed help. Begun
by Thomas in Syracuse, New York, in August 1849, the paper sought
to be the voice of political abolitionists dissatisfied with the new Free
Soil Party. Thomas's paper never attracted more than 1,100 subscribers,
however, and survived largely on Smith's financial subsidies.[60] Smith

had always been dissatisfied with Thomas's editorial skills. By 1851 he believed that under a better editor, particularly one as well respected as Douglass, the *Liberty Party Paper* might help revive the moribund Liberty Party. Smith felt that Free Soilers benefited greatly from the high quality and appearance of their Washington, D.C.-based *National Era*, edited by Gamaliel Bailey. Smith also hoped that uniting the *Liberty Party Paper* with the *North Star* would solidify Douglass's new political views.[61]

Douglass quickly replied to Smith's offer: "You want a good looking – as well as a good paper, established in western N.Y. & have a plan to accomplish that object. *I like the plan.*" Douglass wanted the new paper based in Rochester because he did not want to "leave an important work incomplete – the breaking down of prejudice." He felt that Smith's promise of a subsidy of $100 a month for two years would guarantee the new paper the resources to compete with the *National Era* in attracting paying subscribers. "Money must be at hand," he informed Smith, "or the Editor will have his brains more puzzled about the means – than about the ends." He warned Smith, however, that his subsidy should be kept secret or few others would contribute to the paper's support.[62]

Douglass took pains to make it clear to Smith that he did not need his money to keep his newspaper going. According to Douglass, "the 'North Star' sustains itself, and partly sustains my large family. It has just reached a living point." He gave much of the credit for the *North Star*'s hard-won financial stability to Julia Griffiths, who he proposed to put in charge of the "money matters" of the new paper.[63] Rather than relying indefinitely on Smith's assistance, Douglass hoped that the improved quality of the new paper would gather sufficient subscribers to become profitable. Douglass strove for self-reliance but Griffiths often appealed to Smith directly for extra financial assistance, causing Douglass to apologize for his business manager and to assure Smith that "I am anxious to set an example of ability to take care of myself which shall prove grateful to your feelings."[64]

Smith deferred to Douglass in arranging the merger. The final terms of these negotiations made it clear that Douglass intended to make the new newspaper unmistakably his vehicle. Before the first issue appeared, Douglass wrote Smith that "you may hold me – morally, intellectually, and mechanically responsible for the character of the paper."[65] Although offered generous financial inducements, Ward was not willing to become Douglass's junior partner and soon suspended his *Impartial Citizen*.[66] Thomas agreed to the merger on the condition that he remain in Syracuse and serve as corresponding editor of the new paper at a salary of $6 per week. Douglass guaranteed Thomas the freedom to write editorials of his own choosing. Friction over Thomas's stand on land reform soon developed, however, and Douglass printed disavowals of his extreme colleague's views. After just one year, Thomas severed his ties with Douglass and later edited temperance newspapers.[67] To make his editorial control clear to all, Douglass gave the new newspaper, which debuted on June 26, 1851, his own name, the *Frederick Douglass Paper*.

Douglass had had few doubts about how the Garrisonians would regard his new newspaper. When the issue of a merger was first raised, Douglass wrote Smith: "The leaders in the American Antislavery Society are strong men – noble champions in the cause of human freedom – and yet they are not after all the most charitable in construing the motives of those who see matters in a Different light from themselves."[68]

As Douglass predicted, the Garrisonian press, led by the *Liberator*, launched what Douglass dubbed a "war of destruction" on his new newspaper.[69] They assaulted Douglass's new positions on the Liberty Party, the Constitution, and voting. Most of the attacks had a personal rather than an ideological character. Garrison accused Douglass of "roguery" and of selling himself to the political abolitionists. The title of the new newspaper was treated as evidence of Douglass's overreaching ego. At the controversy's most vicious point, Garrison's *Liberator* published unsubstantiated rumors about discontent that "a certain person," implying Julia Griffiths, was causing in Douglass's household. Douglass responded with growing bitterness. Within a few years, his estrangement from his former colleagues was complete.[70]

During this difficult period, Smith stood closely by his new friend. Some scholars have portrayed Garrison as a white father figure for Douglass, a surrogate for his unknown male parent. Other historians, analyzing Smith's personality, have noted his keen ability to respond to the emotional needs of his abolitionist associates. So, when Douglass and Garrison parted ways, the generous and supportive Smith can be pictured as replacing the Bostonian as a father surrogate.[71] For those less inclined to a psychological interpretation, there is a simpler explanation of why the Douglass–Smith friendship solidified in these years. Although Smith was disinclined to venture from Peterboro, his wife became a frequent visitor to Douglass's Rochester home and put a lie to the rumors of discord there by befriending both Douglass's wife, Anna, and Julia Griffiths. Both the Smiths became close confidants of Julia and assured her that they dismissed the "home trials" gossip begun by Garrison. Even in Rochester, close interracial friendships were quite rare, and the emotional bond between the Douglass and Smith families in these years was a remarkable occurrence and goes far to explain the strength of the political alliance between the two men during the rest of the decade.[72]

The Liberty Party that Douglass joined in 1851 was a shell of what it had been in the 1840s. Election results in 1848 reveal that a large majority of the original Liberty Party members had joined the Free Soilers. The small band clinging to the Liberty Party's name were able to keep active largely because of the generous contributions of Smith. In 1855, Smith's associates and such black leaders as James McCune Smith, Henry H. Garnet, and Jermain Loguen created the American Abolition Society and its companion, the Radical Abolition Party, in a effort to resuscitate the moribund non-Garrisonian wing of the abolitionist movement.[73]

As the National Liberty Party, the group adopted a wide-ranging reform platform. In addition to declaring slavery illegal under the U.S. Constitution, they condemned import tariffs and the liquor traffic and endorsed land reform. But as the Radical Abolitionist Party, the group returned to a concentrated attack on slavery, which it denounced as "sinful, illegal, and unconstitutional." Under both names, the small band lobbied the churches to condemn slavery and gave strong endorsements to equal rights for blacks.[74]

The *Frederick Douglass Paper* began its life by giving energetic support to the struggling Liberty Party movement. Douglass publicized the group's activities at the local, state, and national levels. His paper also carried detailed articles by the party's leading theorists, including Lysander Spooner, William Jay, James G. Birney, and William Goodell, who argued for the unconstitutionality of slavery. In the fall of 1851, a convention in Buffalo aimed at revitalizing the Liberty Party selected Douglass to join its national committee.[75] Douglass gave strong editorial endorsement to the antislavery positions of the Liberty Party, but he also criticized efforts by some of its leaders, including Smith and Thomas, to broaden the party's platform to include land reform, free trade, and other causes.[76]

In addition to publicizing the activities of the Liberty Party, Douglass's new paper served as a mouthpiece for the views of its generous patron, Smith. Sometimes Douglass asked Smith to explain his views on current issues, but more often Smith sent Douglass lengthy, unsolicited essays that filled many columns of the *Frederick Douglass Paper*. Douglass occasionally rejected a roughly written piece, but letters or articles by Smith on diverse topics appeared frequently in the early years of the new paper.[77]

The *Frederick Douglass Paper* prospered moderately in its early years. Departing Garrisonian subscribers were replaced by new Liberty Party readers. Griffiths's fund-raising skills also were at their peak in the early 1850s. Nonetheless, it was Smith's monthly subsidy that allowed the paper to generate a satisfactory living for Douglass and his family and small staff. In the spring of 1852, Douglass assured Smith that he was not "looking for one cent more from you, in support of the *"Frederick Douglass' paper"* than you kindly offered to give at the first." A year later,

Douglass bragged to Smith that "Our paper is getting on well. Subscribers are renewing their subscriptions – and a career of usefulness seems to unfold before it."[79]

Prosperity, however, eluded Douglass's newspaper. After the two years initially agreed upon, Smith ceased his regular subsidy to the *Frederick Douglass Paper*. Thereafter he sent occasional contributions in cash and sometimes in goods, including a new suit for Douglass to wear at an important antislavery convention.[80] The loss of Smith as a reliable revenue source for the *Frederick Douglass Paper* forced Douglass to pay greater attention to financial considerations in deciding on political stands during the remainder of the decade.

Douglass's loyalty to the Liberty Party and Smith were put to the test during the 1852 election campaign. Popular support for the Free Soilers had declined since 1848, especially in New York, where many Democrats had followed Martin Van Buren back to their old partisan allegiances. Douglass began the year with the hope that the remaining Free Soilers might be won over to the uncompromising platform of the Liberty Party.[81] A trip to Cincinnati in May 1852, however, persuaded Douglass that, at least in the West, there were Free Soilers with firm enough antislavery beliefs for Liberty men to support. Douglass persuaded Smith to accompany him to the national convention of the Free Soilers, who were now calling themselves the Free Democrats. Douglass told Smith that he was the only man who might convince the Free Democrats to adopt a sufficiently principled antislavery platform "that the Liberty party may properly vote for its candidates."[82] Douglass was chosen as one of the convention's secretaries and found it refreshingly free of racial prejudice. Smith got a respectful hearing from the Free Democrats but failed to persuade them to adopt his platform planks, which declared slavery illegal and demanded equal political rights for "all persons – black white, male and female."[83] Smith received a few votes for president, but the convention delegates overwhelmingly nominated New Hampshire Senator John P. Hale for president and U.S. Representative George Julian of Indiana for vice president.[84]

The initial reaction of both Douglass and Smith to the Free Democratic ticket was positive. In his newspaper, Douglass praised Hale and Julian and called the Free Democratic platform "a long step in the right direction."[85] Smith called Hale and Julian "earnest and generous philanthropists" and indicated that he would support them.[86] A few Liberty Party men, however, opposed any compromise of principle and nominated minister and journalist William Goodell as their presidential candidate. Disturbed that Hale and Julian had ignored his request for an endorsement of his rejected platform planks, Smith belatedly backed Goodell. Douglass's position was more ambiguous. He was a vice president of the Liberty Party convention on

September 30, 1852, that ratified Goodell's nomination. However, the *Frederick Douglass Paper*, which had recently gained many Free Democrats as subscribers, continued to carry Hale's name on its masthead until election day. Trying not to alienate either antislavery political camp, Douglass trod such a fine line in the remaining weeks of the campaign that historians, examining the same scant sources, still disagree about his final position in the election. In any case, the 1852 election results were disappointing to all antislavery groups, with Hale winning barely half of Van Buren's 1848 total and Goodell receiving so few votes that they went unreported.[87]

The question of which presidential candidate to support produced no discernible breach between Douglass and Smith. By mid-fall, the attention of both men shifted away from the national race to Smith's campaign for Congress. In September, a coalition of abolitionists and more moderate antislavery voters nominated Smith to run against the Democrat and Whig candidates for the U.S. House seat representing Madison and Oswego counties. In early October, Douglass took to the field and delivered at least eighty speeches on Smith's behalf. Douglass initially had little optimism about Smith's chances. He wrote him: "The people say they are going to vote for Gerrit Smith – and say he shall be elected. This however, I deem unreasonable."[88] However, the local popularity of Smith's stand on issues like free trade, the endorsement of prominent Free Democrats, and the untiring campaigning of Douglass and other political abolitionists combined to give Smith a plurality in the election.[89] A genuinely surprised and elated Douglass congratulated Smith and pronounced his election the beginning of a new era in the antislavery struggle because, "for the first time, a man will appear in the American Congress completely infused with the spirit of freedom."[90]

Douglass visited Smith at Peterboro shortly before the new congressman departed for Washington. He advised Smith to master parliamentary procedure in order to counter proslavery politicians. Unfortunately, Smith ignored his advice. Smith opposed the Kansas–Nebraska Bill that proposed to open more western land to slavery, pending the approval of the territory's settlers. He refused to join a maneuver by Free Democrats and other antislavery congressmen to table the measure, however, and was condemned by many northerners when the bill passed and became law. Most painful was a resolution passed by a black convention in Cincinnati that declared that Smith had failed "to serve the cause of the oppressed."[91]

By contrast, Smith received warm applause from the *Frederick Douglass Paper* for his performance in Congress. Douglass reprinted Smith's congressional speeches and praised them effusively. Douglass was particularly impressed that Smith, a lifelong land reformer, fought a homestead bill because it barred blacks from receiving land. As to the Kansas–

Nebraska measure, Douglass called Smith's speech opposing the bill "the mightiest and grandest production – ever before delivered in the House or Senate of this nation."[92] The columns of the *Frederick Douglass Paper* reveal that Douglass kept a promise he had made Smith that "You have only to vote and speak the convictions of your head and heart to have my earnest, though feeble support."[93] When Douglass disagreed with Smith's support for efforts to annex Cuba, he kept silent rather than join that "swarm of hungry birds . . . pecking at you – with no other apparent motive than to prove Gerrit Smith as weak as themselves."[94]

Despite the loyal backing of Douglass and a few others, Smith grew less and less happy with his congressional office, particularly when criticized by blacks and other abolitionists. In the summer of 1851 Smith resigned his seat, telling his friend Goodell that the criticism and frustration with the "fixed routine" of Congress, which caused him to be constantly called out of order, had made him feel that his "talents were being wasted" in Congress.[95] Douglass voiced deep regret at Smith's resignation and once again praised his performance in Congress:

> To say that Mr. Smith has been true to his anti-slavery principles, is superfluous to those who understand him and his position. His words and his votes have been given faithfully and industriously on the side of justice and freedom; but he has condescended to no tricks in parliamentary tactics, and we are not sorry that he has not. That was something, not in his line, and he would scarcely have looked well in it, besides the event showed, that no evil was removed, and no good secured by such kind of opposition.[96]

Douglass was a firm supporter of Smith, but he displayed much less loyalty to the Liberty Party. For example, in March 1853, Douglass in his editorial columns announced that "though we take exception to [the Free Democrats'] 'sectionalize and denationalize' slavery philosophy, we judge them abolitionists, and stand ready to cooperate with such men, and the Free Democrats in general."[97] The next fall, however, Douglass attended the state's Liberty Party convention and accepted its nomination for New York's secretary of state on a ticket headed by Goodell for governor. Smith wrote Douglass: "My heart would leap for joy at your election. It would be the greatest blow yet struck for the emancipation of the slave."[98] The party made a poor showing in the election, however, as antislavery sentiment generated by the recent passage of the Kansas–Nebraska Act went overwhelmingly to the new Republican Party, which had replaced the Free Democrats.

Douglass supported the creation of the American Abolition Society in 1855, but his relations with its political arm proved as ambivalent as those with the Liberty Party. Douglass praised the prominent roles that blacks played in the Radical Abolitionist Party and the group's condemnation of the antislavery character of the U.S. Constitution. Perhaps because of Douglass's history of wavering political loyalties, the new society selected a periodical edited by Goodell, renamed the *Radical Abolitionist*, rather than Douglass's newspaper as the group's official organ. Douglass nonetheless assured Smith that he would "try to uphold the great principles of freedom – as laid down by yourself and Mr. Goodell."[99]

As he had four years earlier, Douglass began 1856 by giving Smith brave promises that he would support his political faction. He wrote Smith in April:

> The coming presidential campaign will severely try, and perhaps break down my paper. Radical abolitionism is too far ahead of these degenerate times to be well supported. I shall, however, nail my colors to the mast – and if I go down – it will be with all colors flying.[100]

Douglass had genuine grounds for concern about the survival of his paper. The *Frederick Douglass Paper* had been financially hard pressed since Griffiths had returned to England the previous year and had failed to raise funds there. Douglass believed that his political isolation was the chief source of his financial problems. He wrote Smith that the *Frederick Douglass Paper* was $1,500 in debt because "My paper is not Republican – and therefore Republicans look coldly on it. It is not Garrisonian and therefore Garrisonians hate and spare no pains to destroy it. Meanwhile the colored people do very little to support."[101] The largest indication of Douglass's despair was his confidential proposal to Smith to merge his paper with Goodell's and accept a junior editor's position.

Whether Smith assisted Douglass at this crisis is not known. Douglass nonetheless attended the Radical Abolitionists' national convention at the end of May and editorially endorsed its nomination of Smith for president. He announced: "This, certainly, is not the hour in which we should desert our standard, and thrust aside our well-tried men, because others who have little or no sympathy with our principles, are deemed more available."[102] After the Republicans' nomination of John C. Frémont, however, Douglass reassessed his position and switched allegiance from the Radical Abolitionists to the more moderate antislavery party. He rationalized his change as "a difference of Policy, not of Principle."[103]

Worried that his behavior had angered Smith, Douglass wrote: "I have done what seemed to me right & proper to be done in this crisis – and can afford to be calm under the censure of those who cannot approve my course. I support Frémont as the best thing I can do *now* – but without losing sight of the great doctrines and measures, inseparable from your great name and character."[104] Douglass's actions probably did not greatly offend Smith, who had himself contributed $500 to the Frémont campaign. Smith regarded his candidacy primarily as a prod to move the Republicans to higher antislavery ground. On election day Smith received only 165 votes in New York state and, at most, a few hundred nationally.[105]

Any ill-will on Smith's part certainly ended soon after the election because he sent Douglass a badly needed $20 for his newspaper. Douglass wrote of his gratitude to Smith: "I am happy to know by this expressive sign, that you still desire to see my paper afloat. You ought to, for you have watched over it with almost paternal interest. No, my Dear Sir. I am not a member of the republican party. I am still a radical abolitionist – and shall as ever, work with those whose antislavery principles are similar to your own."[106] Over the next few years, Douglass frequently commended Smith for his antislavery work. When the Radical Abolitionists and a "People's State Ticket" nominated Smith for governor in 1858, Douglass supported him unequivocally in speeches and editorials. Privately Douglass told Smith that he wished that the campaign had focused more on black rights, but because he knew the candidate so well, "I lose no sleep because you touched it lightly." Despite an energetic campaign financed largely from his own pocket, Smith received only 5,000 out of nearly 500,000 votes cast.[107]

Douglass's and Smith's activities at this point were interrupted by events surrounding John Brown's unsuccessful attempt to foment a slave uprising at Harper's Ferry, Virginia, in October 1859. The two men had encountered Brown in the 1840s and became entangled in his plotting in the next decade. Brown regarded Smith as essential to his plans because of his great wealth. Brown likewise hoped that Douglass would become an active participant and a role model for the slaves. He visited the homes of Douglass and Smith several times while making final preparations for his ill-fated expedition.[108] After Brown's capture at Harper's Ferry, letters were found in his baggage implicating Smith and Douglass in the planning for the raid. To escape possible arrest and prosecution, Douglass fled to Canada and then to Great Britain. He returned to Rochester in May 1860 after the furor died down. Smith remained in this country, but his extreme anxiety over his involvement with Brown required several months of hospitalization at the New York State Lunatic Asylum at Utica.[109]

In the initial panic after Harper's Ferry, both Smith and Douglass had asked relatives to destroy documents linking them with Brown.[110] Although intended to thwart possible prosecution, this loss of materials makes it hard to determine the extent to which Smith and Douglass influenced each other's decision to support Brown. Surviving correspondence between Douglass and Smith during the 1850s reveals that events such as the Fugitive Slave Law and the armed struggle between free and slave state supporters in the Kansas territory had pushed each man to abandon the abolitionists' traditional pacifist stance and instead to sanction violent antislavery tactics. That both men aided Brown's scheme to initiate a slave rebellion is further evidence, albeit circumstantial, of the close link between Douglass and Smith in thinking about antislavery tactics.[111]

The reverberations from Harper's Ferry were still felt at the start of the next presidential campaign. The 1860 election added a final, and characteristically confusing, chapter to the story of the relationship between Douglass the political journalist and Smith the political candidate. Financial problems finally forced Douglass to suspend his weekly newspaper in July 1860, despite last-minute contributions from Smith and other friends. In January 1858, Douglass began another periodical, *Douglass's Monthly*, which became his principal voice in antislavery politics.[112] The issue that concerned Douglass most as the 1860 election approached was the failure of the Republican Party to guarantee equal rights for blacks in the states under their control, including New York. Nonetheless, when the Republicans nominated Abraham Lincoln of Illinois for president in May 1860, *Douglass's Monthly* endorsed him, although voicing the wish that the Republicans had subscribed "Death to Slavery" instead of "No More Slave States" on their banners.[113]

Privately Douglass had doubts about the Republicans. He wrote to Smith in July: "I can't support Lincoln – but whether there is life enough in the Abolitionists to name a Candidate I cannot say – I shall look to your letter for light on the pathway of duty."[114] When Smith wrote back to Douglass in the form of a printed circular, he deeply disappointed the black journalist by emphasizing that intemperance, not slavery, was the most important ground from which to launch a presidential candidacy independent of the Republicans.[115] Douglass responded with an editorial criticizing abolitionists who failed to see that in its "origin, history, and pretensions, the Republican party is the anti-slavery party of the country."[116]

A rapid reconciliation between Douglass and Smith occurred by the end of that summer, largely due to the effort to rally New York State blacks and their white friends behind a referendum to remove the property qualification for nonwhite voters. As in 1846, Smith was a generous financial backer of this drive. By contrast, many leading New York Republicans distanced themselves and their party from the suffrage referendum, drawing angry protests from blacks.[117]

Disenchanted with the temporizing spirit of the Republicans, Douglass went to the Radical Abolitionists' convention in late August. Once again Smith was nominated for president. Douglass endorsed Smith's campaign and was chosen an elector on his ticket. He campaigned for Smith as the only candidate who represented "sound anti-slavery principles and doctrines."[118] When Goodell and some other Radical Abolitionists refused to support Smith because of the latter's alleged recent deviance from religious orthodoxy, Douglass labeled the quarrel extraneous and called for unity behind the ticket. Privately both Douglass and Smith hoped that the Republicans would win.[119] Although Lincoln carried 53.7 percent of the New York ballots, the equal suffrage referendum attracted the support of only 36.4 percent of the voters. A disappointed Douglass branded the outcome a triumph of "blind intelligence and prejudice, hardly less destitute of manly intelligence than the kick of an ass."[120] His experience in this election left Douglass suspicious about the racial attitudes and antislavery convictions of most Republicans throughout most of the Civil War years.

Douglass and Smith remained friends until the latter's death in 1874, but the period of the 1850s marked their closest association. As one of the most intimate alliances formed between a black and a white abolitionist, the Douglass–Smith relationship, a product of the crisis Douglass had reached over his own role in the abolitionist movement, is of great historical significance. Garrisonian opposition to Douglass's launching of his own newspaper had left him dissatisfied with many Garrisonian ideological tenets, especially political ones. What Douglass sought was a principled antislavery alternative to the Garrisonians, and he found it in Gerrit Smith's Liberty and Radical Abolitionist parties, whose belief that the Constitution did not sanction slavery meant that political action could lead directly to immediate emancipation.

Garrisonians charged that Douglass had defected from the American Anti-Slavery Society to become a paid client of the wealthy Smith; they also implied that a black could not be intellectually independent and that Douglass had been corrupted by Smith's superior mind, as well as by his money.[121] An examination of the two men's interaction during the 1850s largely refutes such charges. Smith's financial assistance helped Douglass improve the quality of his newspaper and sustained it during periods of financial difficulty, but both Douglass and Smith believed in the importance of black self-reliance and viewed the monetary assistance as a means of helping the *Frederick Douglass Paper* ultimately to become self-sufficient. Rather than money, it was the principled abolitionist stands and the enlightened racial attitudes of Smith and his close associates that attracted Douglass. Smith's continued moral and financial support, despite Douglass's wavering loyalty to the Liberty and Radical Abolition parties, shows that the white philanthropist did not demand subservience from the black editor. In Smith, Douglass had found an understanding friend who could overlook minor points of disagreement in their shared commitment to the cause of freedom.

NOTES

1   William H. Pease and Jane H. Pease, "Boston Garrisonians and the Problem of Frederick Douglass," *Canadian Journal of History*, 2 (September 1967), 29–48; Tyrone Tillery, "The Inevitability of the Douglass– Garrison Con-

flict," *Phylon*, 37 (June 1976), 137–49; Benjamin Quarles, "The Breach Between Douglass and Garrison," *Journal of Negro History*, 23 (April 1938), 144–54; Lawrence J. Friedman, *Gregarious Saints: Self and Community in American Abolitionism, 1830–1870* (Cambridge: Cambridge University Press, 1982), pp. 187–92.

2 Douglass, *The Narrative of the Life of Frederick Douglass* (1845; New York: Penguin Books, 1982); idem, *My Bondage and My Freedom* (1855; Urbana: University of Illinois Press, 1987); idem, *The Life and Times of Frederick Douglass* (1892; New York: Collier Books, 1962); Benjamin Quarles, *Frederick Douglass* (1948: New York: Atheneum, 1968); Philip S. Foner, *The Life and Writings of Frederick Douglass*, 5 vols. (New York: International Publishers, 1950–75); Peter Walker, *Moral Choices: Memory, Desire and Imagination in Nineteenth-Century American Abolition* (Baton Rouge: Louisiana State University Press, 1978), pp. 207–61.

3 Douglass, *Life and Times*, pp. 215–16; John W. Blassingame et al., *The Frederick Douglass Papers* (New Haven, Conn.: Yale University Press, 1979), 1:1xxxvii–xcv.

4 Aileen S. Kraditor, *Means and Ends in American Abolitionism: Garrison and His Critics on Strategy and Tactics* (New York: Pantheon, 1967), pp. 79–82, 102–8; Ronald G. Walters, *The Antislavery Appeal: American Abolitionism After 1830* (Baltimore: Johns Hopkins University Press, 1976), pp. 86–89, 104–6; Lewis Perry, *Radical Abolitionism: Anarchy and the Government of God in Antislavery Thought* (Ithaca, N.Y.: Cornell University Press, 1973), pp. 55–63, 65.

5 John R. McKivigan, *The War Against Proslavery Religion: Abolitionism and the Northern Churches, 1830–1865* (Ithaca, N.Y.: Cornell University Press, 1984), pp. 56–73.

6 Cork *Examiner*, October 20, 1845, and Cork *Southern Reporter*, October 18, 1845, as quoted in Blassingame, *Frederick Douglass Papers*, 1:46.

7 Blassingame, *Frederick Douglass Papers*, 1:79, 187, 364; Kraditor, *Means and Ends*, pp. 33, 106; Friedman, *Gregarious Saints*, pp. 59–61.

8 Douglass, *Life and Times*, p. 218; also Pease and Pease, "Boston Garrisonians and the Problem of Frederick Douglass," 31–2.

9 Benjamin Quarles, *Black Abolitionists* (New York: Oxford University Press, 1969), pp. 48–9, 51–2; Friedman, *Gregarious Saints*, pp. 163, 166–78; Pease and Pease, "Boston Garrisonians and the Problem of Frederick Douglass," 46–8; Tillery, "Douglass–Garrison Conflict," 139–40.

10 Tillery, "Douglass–Garrison Conflict," 139–40; Pease and Pease, "Boston Garrisonians and the Problem of Frederick Douglass," 31–3.

11 Douglass, *Narrative*, "Introduction," pp. 19–20, 23; R. J. M. Blackett, *Building an Antislavery Wall: Black Americans in the Atlantic Abolitionist Movement* (Baton Rouge: Louisiana State University Press, 1983), pp. 40–1, 42–3, 106–14; Quarles, *Frederick Douglass*, 35–7; Blassingame, *Frederick Douglass Papers*, 1:xcvi–cii, 2:xvii–xviii; Tillery, "Douglass–Garrison Conflict," 140–1.

12 As quoted in Foner, *Life and Writings*, 1:72; Tillery, "Douglass–Garrison Conflict," 141–2; Quarles, "Breach Between Douglass and Garrison," 145; Blackett, *Building an Antislavery Wall*, pp. 112–13.

13 Douglass, *Life and Times* pp. 259–60; Friedman, *Gregarious Saints*, pp. 188–92; Quarles, "Breach Between Douglass and Garrison," 147–8; Tillery, "Douglass–Garrison Conflict," 142; Quarles, *Frederick Douglass*, p. 80.

14 Douglass, *Life and Times*, p. 264; Quarles, "Breach Between Douglass and Garrison," 147; Tillery, "Douglass–Garrison Conflict," 142–3.

15 Rochester *North Star*, December 3, 1847, and January 8, 1848 (hereafter cited as *NS*); Waldo E. Martin, Jr., *The Mind of Frederick Douglass* (Chapel Hill: University of North Carolina Press, 1984), p. 30.

16 Less fortunate was the *Anti-Slavery Bugle*, published by western Garrisonians in Ohio, whose editors deeply resented Douglass's intrusion into their limited circulation market. Douglass, *Life and Times*, pp. 255, 260, 263; [New York State], *Census of the State of New York for 1855, etc.* (Albany: n.p., 1855), pp. 1–17; Paul Johnson, *A Shopkeepers' Millennium: Society and Revivals in Rochester, New York, 1815–1837* (New York: Hill and Wang, 1978), pp. 102–15; Nancy A. Hewitt, *Women's Activism and Social Reform: Rochester, New York, 1822–1872* (Ithaca, N.Y.: Cornell University Press, 1984), pp. 4–25, 66–7, 118, 139–76; Howard W. Coles, *The Cradle of Freedom: A History of the Negro in Rochester, Western New York and Canada*, 2 vols. (Rochester, N.Y.: Oxford Press, 1941), 1:123, 126–30; Mary L. McMillan, "Mr. Editor If You Please: Frederick Douglass in Rochester, 1847–1852" (Senior honor thesis, Mount Holyoke College, 1985), 13–14, 7–28; Pease and Pease, "Boston Garrisonians and the Problems of Frederick Douglass," 36– 7.

17 *NS*, June 29, November 30, 1849; Douglass, *Life and Times*, pp. 259, 263; Frederick Douglass to Gerrit Smith, March 30, 1849, Gerrit Smith Papers, George Arents Research Library, Syracuse University (hereafter cited as Smith Papers); McMillan, "Mr. Editor," 9–10, 19–23, 7–30; Quarles, *Frederick Douglass*, pp. 88–9; Blassingame, *Frederick Douglass Papers*, 2:446–7, 512– 13.

18 Douglass to Smith, March 30, 1849, Smith Papers; Erwin Palmer, "A Partnership in the Abolition Movement," *University of Rochester Library Bulletin*, 26 (1970–1), 1–19; Hewitt, *Women's Activism and Social Change*, pp. 150–1; Coles, *Cradle of Freedom*, p. 131; McMillan, "Mr. Editor," 58–9.

19 *NS*, January 14, February 18, July 21, 1848.

20 *NS*, March 17, July 7, 1848; Douglass, *Life and Times*, pp. 260–2; McMillan, "Mr. Editor," 23– 6.

21 James McCune Smith to Gerrit Smith, July 28, 1848, as quoted in Martin, *Mind of Frederick Douglass*, p. 58; *NS*, August 25, September 15, October 27, 1848, May 4, 1849; McMillan, "Mr. Editor," 40–1, 44–5.

22 *NS*, February 11, 1848, as quoted in McMillan, "Mr. Editor," 35.

23 Douglass to Smith, March 30, 1849, Smith Papers; Palmer, "Partnership in Abolition Movement," 11–12.

24 Ralph Volney Harlow, *Gerrit Smith: Philanthropist and Reformer* (New York: Henry Holt and Co., 1939), pp. 1–45; L. M. Hammond, *History of Madison County, State of New York* (Syracuse, n.p., 1872), pp. 717–26; Stephen B. Oates, *To Purge This Land with Blood: A Biography of John Brown* (New York: Harper & Row, 1970), p. 193.

25 Harlow, *Gerrit Smith*, pp. 154–9.

26 Utica (N.Y.) *Friend of Man*, February 8, 1840; Alan M. Kraut, "The Forgotten Reformers: A Profile of Third Party Abolitionists in Antebellum New York," in *Antislavery Reconsidered: New Perspectives on the Abolitionists*, eds. Lewis Perry and Michael Fellman (Baton Rouge: Louisiana State University Press, 1979), p. 136; Harlow, *Gerrit Smith*, pp. 146–8.

27 James B. Stewart, *Holy Warriors: The Abolitionists and American Slavery* (New York: Hill and Wang, 1976), pp. 97, 104–5; Merton L. Dillon, *The Abolitionists: The Growth of a Dissenting Minority* (De Kalb, Ill.: Northern Illinois University Press, 1974), pp. 141–4; Richard H. Sewell, *Ballots for Freedom: Antislavery Politics in the United States, 1837–1860* (New York: Oxford University Press, 1976), pp. 81–2, 95–6.

28 John R. McKivigan, "Vote As You Pray and Pray As You Vote: Church-Oriented Abolitionists and Antislavery Politics," in *Crusaders and Compromisers: Essays on the Relationship of the Antislavery Struggle to the Antebellum Party System*, ed. Alan M. Kraut (Westport, Conn.: Greenwood Press, 1983), p. 186.

29 Alan M. Kraut, "The Liberty Men of New York: Political Abolitionism in New York State, 1840–1848" (Ph.D. diss., Cornell University, 1975), 159–63.

30 Harlow, *Gerrit Smith*, pp. 149, 169, 170–1; Kraut, "Liberty Men of New York," 91, 163, 160–9; Gerald Sorin, *New York Abolitionists. A Case Study of Political Radicalism* (Westport, Conn.: Greenwood Press, 1971), pp. 34–5.

31 William Goodell, *Slavery and Antislavery: A History of the Struggle in Both Hemispheres* (New York: William Harned, 1852), pp. 571–2; Bertram Wyatt-Brown, *Lewis Tappan and the Evangelical War Against Slavery* (Cleveland: Press of the Case Western Reserve University, 1969), pp. 332–4; Friedman, *Gregarious Saints*, pp. 117–20; Sewell, *Ballots for Freedom*, pp. 167–9; Harlow, *Gerrit Smith*, pp. 176–80.

32 Frederick Blue, *The Free Soilers: Third Party Politics, 1848–1854* (Urbana: University of Illinois Press, 1974), pp. 8–9; Kraditor, *Means and Ends*, pp. 153–4; Sewell, *Ballots for Freedom*, pp. 117–21, 131–69; Stewart, *Holy Warriors*, pp. 119–20; Harlow, *Gerrit Smith*, pp. 180–2.

33 Goodell, *Slavery and Antislavery*, pp. 571–2; Wyatt-Brown, *Lewis Tappan*, pp. 332–4; Blue, *Free Soilers*, pp. 2, 103, 233–4, 243–7; Friedman, *Gregarious Saints*, pp. 117–20; Sewell, *Ballots for Freedom*, pp. 167–9; Harlow, *Gerrit Smith*, pp. 183–5, 187.

34 Jane H. Pease and William H. Pease, *They Who Would Be Free: Blacks' Search for Freedom, 1830–1861* (New York: Antheneum, 1974), pp. 132, 138; Douglass to Smith, March 30, 1849, Smith Papers; Benjamin Quarles, "Letters from Negro Leaders to Gerrit Smith," *Journal of Negro History*, 27 (October 1942), 432–53; Quarles, *Black Abolitionists*, pp. 33–4, 95; John R. McKivigan and Madeleine L. McKivigan, " 'He Stands Like Jupiter': The Autobiography of Gerrit Smith," *New York History*, 65 (April 1984), 188–200; Pease and Pease, "Boston Garrisonians and the Problem of Frederick Douglass," 36–7; Hewitt, *Women's Activism and Social Change*, pp. 143–4, 151; McMillan, "Mr. Editor," 23–6, 55, 60–1.

35 Quarles, *Black Abolitionists*, pp. 154, 157; Harlow, *Gerrit Smith*, pp. 266–9.

36 Smith to Douglass, February 24, 1849, reprinted in *NS*, March 2, 1849; Zita Dyson, "Gerrit Smith's Efforts in Behalf of the Negroes in New York," *Journal of Negro History*, 3 (October 1918), 354–9; Phyllis F. Field, *The Politics of Race in New York: The Struggle for Black Suffrage in the Civil War* (Ithaca, N.Y.: Cornell University Press, 1982), pp. 138, 236; McKivigan and McKivigan, " 'He Stands Like Jupiter'," 194; Quarles, *Black Abolitionists*, p. 182; Sorin, *New York Abolitionists*, p. 37.

37 Eric Foner, *Free Soil, Free Labor, Free Men: The Ideology of the Republican Party Before the Civil War* (New York: Oxford University Press, 1970), pp. 261–71; Field, *Politics of Race*, pp. 35–7, 64, 96, 138; Harlow, *Gerrit Smith*, pp. 175–7.

38 Blassingame, *Frederick Douglass Papers*, 1:290–1, 2:40–1, 66–8; Friedman, *Gregarious Saints*, p. 116.

39 Smith to Douglass, December 8, 1847, reprinted in *NS*, January 7, 1848.

40 *NS*, February 18, 1848; also *NS*, February 25, 1848, January 5, 1849; Smith to Douglass, February 24, 1849, reprinted in *NS*, March 2, 1849.

41 *NS*, January 5, 19, 1849; also see McKivigan, *War Against Proslavery Religion*, pp. 95, 142, 144.

42 *NS*, June 23, July 7, 1848; Smith to Douglass, March 16, 1849, Peterboro, N.Y., reprinted in *NS*, March 23, 1849; Charles H. Wesley, "The Participation of Negroes in Antislavery Political Parties," *Journal of Negro History*, 29 (January 1944), 32–64; Pease and Pease, *They Who Would Be Free*, pp. 200–1; Martin, *Mind of Frederick Douglass*, pp. 33–4; Quarles, *Frederick Douglass*, pp. 143–4.

43 As quoted in Wesley, "Participation of Negroes in Antislavery Political Parties," 53; Pease and Pease, *They Who Would Be Free*, pp. 198–9; Quarles, *Frederick Douglass*, p. 145.

44 *NS*, September 15, 1852, also September 1, November 10, 1848; Wesley, "Participation of Negroes in Antislavery Political Parties," 56–7; Pease and Pease, *They Who Would Be Free*, pp. 198–201; Martin, *Mind of Frederick Douglass*, pp. 33–4; Quarles, *Frederick Douglass*, p. 146.

45. *NS*, November 10, 1848, also March 25, 1849; Martin, *Mind of Frederick Douglass*, p. 34.

46 *NS*, January 23, February 9, March 16, 1849; *Anti-Slavery Bugle*, February 23, 1849; Smith to Douglass, June 20, 1848, reprinted in *NS*, June 7, 1848; Martin, *Mind of Frederick Douglass*, p. 36; Blassingame, *Frederick Douglass Papers*, 2:194–5; Quarles, *Frederick Douglass*, p. 146.

47 As quoted in Blassingame, *Frederick Douglass Papers*, 2:194–5.

48 Smith to Douglass, March 16, 1849, reprinted in *NS*, March 23, 1849; Smith to Douglass, March 30, 24, 1849, reprinted in *NS*, April 7, 1849; Douglass to Smith, March 18, 1849, Smith Papers; Blassingame, *Frederick Douglass Papers*, 2:194–7.

49 Blassingame, *Frederick Douglass Papers*, 2:217–35.

50 *NS*, January 25, 1850.

51 Douglass to Smith, January 31, 1851, Smith Papers; McMillan, "Mr. Editor," 66–7.

52 Smith to Douglass, June 20, 1848, reprinted in *NS*, June 7, 1848; Smith to Douglass, June 1, 1850, reprinted in *NS*, June 13, 1850.

53 Smith to Douglass, June 1, 1850, reprinted in *NS*, June 13, 1850.

54 Douglass, *Life and Times*, p. 453.

55 Douglass to Smith, March 30, November 19, 1849, June 10, 1851, Smith Papers; Palmer, "Partnership in the Abolition Movement," 9–10, 11.

56 Douglass to Smith, March 30, 1849, Smith Papers; Pease and Pease, *They Who Would Be Free*, p. 92; Friedman, *Gregarious Saints*, p. 176.

57 Douglass to Smith, November 19, 1850 [?], Smith Papers.

58 Douglass to Smith, March 30, 1849, Smith Papers.

59 Douglass to Smith, May 1, 1851, Smith Papers.

60 Dwight H. Bruce, ed., *Onondaga's Centennial: Gleanings of a Century*, 2 vols. (N.P.: Boston History Company, Publishers, 1896), 1:574; Harlow, *Gerrit Smith*, pp. 187–8, 380.

61 Douglass to Smith, May 1, 1851, Smith Papers; McMillan, "Mr. Editor," 67–8; Harlow, *Gerrit Smith*, pp. 187–8.

62 Douglass to Smith, May 1, 1851, Smith Papers.

63 Ibid.; Palmer, "Partnership in the Abolition Movement," 9–10; McMillan, "Mr. Editor," 68–9.

65 Douglass to Smith, May 29, 1851, also June 4, 10, 1851, Smith Papers; *FDP*, October 30, 1851.

66 *FDP*, October 30, 1851; Douglass to Smith, May 29, June 4, 10, 18, 1851, Smith Papers.

67 Douglass to Smith, May 15, 28, 1851, Smith Papers; Rochester *Frederick Douglass Paper*, June 26, September 4, October 30, November 20, 1851, February 5, 1852 (hereafter cited as *FDP*); McMillan, "Mr. Editor," 74.

68 Douglass to Smith, May 21, 1851, Smith Papers.

69 *FDP*, September 9, 30, December 1853; Douglass to Smith, June 18, 1851, Smith Papers.

70 As quoted in Quarles, *Frederick Douglass*, p. 106; also Martin, *Mind of Frederick Douglass*, pp. 38–8, Quarles, "Breach Between Douglass and Garrison," 150–4; Pease and Pease, "Boston Garrisonians and the Problem of Frederick Douglass," 39–46.

71 Friedman, *Gregarious Saints*, pp. 101–2, 187–95; Martin, *Mind of Frederick Douglass*, p. 47; Walker, *Moral Choices*, pp. 248–59.

72 Douglass to Smith, February 5, 1852, July 18, 1854, May 1, 1856, April 20, 1857, Smith Papers; Palmer, "Partnership in the Abolition Movement," 11; Hewitt, *Women's Activism and Social Change*, pp. 41–2, 143, 239–41.

73 Blue, *Free Soilers*, p. 233; Pease and Pease, *They Who Would Be Free*, pp. 202–23; McKivigan, *War Against Proslavery Religion*, pp. 149, 151, 157–8, 160; Harlow, *Gerrit Smith*, pp. 190–1, 341–3.

74 *Radical Abolitionist*, 1 (October 1855), 35, 3 (August 1857), 2; Jane Grey Swisshelm, *Half a Century* (Chicago: n.p., 1880), pp. 199–200; McKivigan, *War Against Proslavery Religion*, pp. 157–8; Harlow, *Gerrit Smith*, pp. 190–1, 341–3; M. Leon Perkal, "American Abolition Society: A Viable Alternative to the Republican Party," *Journal of Negro History*, 65 (Winter 1980), 57–71.

75 *FDP*, July 31, October 2, 30, 1851, April 8, August 27, 1852; Douglass to Smith, July 27, 1852, Smith Papers; Smith to Douglass, September 27, 1851, reprinted in *FDP*, October 2, 1851; Foner, *Life and Writings*, 2:73–5; Blue, *Free Soilers*, p. 233.

76 *FDP*, July 24, October 2, 1851, April 8, 1852; Pease and Pease, *They Who Would Be Free*, pp. 200–1.

77 *FDP*, July 31, October 2, December 25, 1851, March 4, May 24, June 3, August 6, 1852; Douglass to Smith, August 4, 1851, February 27, 28, May 25, July 7, 1852, June 1, 1853, Smith Papers.

78 Douglass to Smith, July 14, 1852, also September 2, 1851, Smith Papers; Smith to Douglass, November 11, 1852, General Correspondence File, Reel 32, Frame 002, Douglass Papers, Library of Congress.

79 Douglass to Smith, January 14, 1853, Smith Papers.

80 Douglass to Smith, April 6, 1853, May 1, 1856, Smith Papers; Quarles, *Frederick Douglass*, p. 91.

81 *FDP*, April 8, June 3, 24, 1852; Douglass to Smith, February 13, 18, 1852, Smith Papers.

82 Douglass to Smith, July 15, 1852, Smith Papers; also Douglass to Smith, May 7, July 17, 20, 30, 1852, Smith Papers; *FDP*, July 23, 1852.

83 Quoted in Blue, *Free Soilers*, p. 248; *FDP*, August 20, 1852.

84 Sewell, *Ballots for Freedom*, pp. 245–7; Quarles, *Black Abolitionists*, pp. 186–7; Blue, *Free Soilers*, pp. 246–9.

85 *FDP*, August 20, September 17, 1852.

86 Quoted in Sewell, *Ballots for Freedom*, p. 246; also Harlow, *Gerrit Smith*, p. 191.

87 Douglass to Smith, January 14, 1853, Smith Papers; *FDP*, September 10, October 15, 1852; Harlow, *Gerrit Smith*, p. 191; Martin, *Mind of Frederick Douglass*, p. 34; Pease and Pease, *They Who Would Be Free*, pp. 201–2; Sewell, *Ballots for Freedom*, p. 47; Quarles, *Black Abolitionists*, p. 187; Blue, *Free Soilers*, pp. 248–9.

88 Douglass to Smith, October 21, 1852, Smith Papers; also *FDP*, October 29, 1852.

89 Harlow, *Gerrit Smith*, pp. 312–14; Quarles, *Black Abolitionists*, p. 187; Friedman, *Gregarious Saints*, p. 120; Sewell, *Ballots for Freedom*, p. 249.

90 Douglass to Smith, November 6, 1852, Smith Papers; *FDP*, November 12, 1852.

91 As quoted in Jeffrey S. Rossbach, *Ambivalent Conspirators: John Brown, the Secret Six, and a Theory of Slave Violence* (Philadelphia: University of Pennsylvania Press, 1982), pp. 99–100; also Douglass to Smith, August 18, 1853, Smith Papers; *FDP*, July 22, 1853; Harlow, *Gerrit Smith*, pp. 326–31.

92 Douglass to Smith, May 6, 1854, also December 23, 1853, March 6, April 29, May 19, 1854, Smith Papers; Smith to Douglass, June 12, 1854, Reel 32, Frame 3, Douglass Papers, Library of Congress; *FDP*, December 30, 1853, March 3, 17, May 5, 1854.

93 Douglass to Smith, March 13, 1854, Smith Papers.

94 Douglass to Smith, August 22, 1854, Smith Papers.
95 Smith to William Goodell, November 1, 1854, Smith Papers, as quoted in Rossbach, *Ambivalent Conspirators*, p. 100; also Friedman, *Gregarious Saints*, p. 120; Harlow, *Gerrit Smith*, pp. 331–2.
96 *FDP*, July 6, 1854; also Smith to Douglass, August 28, 1854, in New York *National Anti-Slavery Standard*, September 16, 1854; *FDP*, September 1, 1854.
97 *FDP*, March 4, September 9, 1853; Pease and Pease, *They Who Would Be Free*, p. 202.
98 ·Smith to Douglass, June 12, 1854, Reel 32, Frame 003, Douglass Papers, Library of Congress; *FDP*, October 13, 1854; Quarles, *Frederick Douglass*, p. 155.
99 Douglass to Smith, August 14, 1855, Smith Papers; *FDP*, July 6, 1855; M. Leon Perkal, "William Goodell: A Life of Reform" (Ph.D. diss.: City University of New York, 1972), 239–50.
100 Douglass to Smith, April 12, 1856, Smith Papers; also *FDP*, December 7, 1855.
101 Douglass to Smith, May 23, 1856, also April 12, 16, 1856, Smith Papers.
102 *FDP*, June 20, 1856.
103 *FDP*, August 15, September 12, 1856; Martin, *Mind of Frederick Douglass*, 34–5; Quarles, *Frederick Douglass*, pp. 160–3; Sewell, *Ballots for Freedom*, pp. 288–9.
104 Douglass to Smith, August 31, 1856, Smith Papers.
105 Sewell, *Ballots for Freedom*, p. 287; Quarles, *Frederick Douglass*, p. 163.
106 Douglass to Smith, December 16, 1856, Smith Papers.
107 Douglass to Smith, October 16, 1858, Smith Papers; *FDP*, October 18, 1857, August 12, October 29, 1858; Douglass to Smith, April 16, 20, 1857, October 16, 1858; Harlow, *Gerrit Smith*, pp. 377–82; Quarles, *Frederick Douglass*, p. 164; Field, *Politics of Race*, p. 96; Rossbach, *Ambivalent Conspirators*, pp. 179–80.
108 Oates, *To Purge This Land with Blood*, pp. 65–7, 85, 90–1, 207, 227, 231: Quarles, *Frederick Douglass*, pp. 169–85; Harlow, *Gerrit Smith*, pp. 395–8.
109 *FDP*, December 16, 1859; John R. McKivigan and Madeleine Leveille, "The 'Black Dream' of Gerrit Smith, New York Abolitionist," *Syracuse University Library Courier*, 20 (Fall 1985), 64–5; Harlow, *Gerrit Smith*, 407–22.
110 Harlow, *Gerrit Smith*, 407–8; Foner, *Life and Writings*, 2:90–2; McKivigan and Leveille, " 'Black Dream' of Gerrit Smith," 74–5.
111 Douglass to Smith, March 22, 1856, Smith Papers; *FDP*, April 6, June 1, 1855; Harlow, *Gerrit Smith*, pp. 338–62; Rossbach, *Ambivalent Conspirators*, pp. 96, 101, 112, 121; Martin, *Mind of Frederick Douglass*, p. 168.
112 *FDP*, May 11, June 8, 1860; *Douglass' Monthly*, 3 (September 1860), 321 (herafter cited as *DM*); Douglass to Smith, July 2, 1860, Smith Papers.
113 *DM*, 3 (June 1860), 276, also 1 (February 1859), 21.
114 Douglass to Smith, July 2, 1860, Smith Papers.
115 Smith to Douglass, July 13, 1860, Printed Circular, Cornell University.

116   *DM*, 3 (August 1860), 306, 308.
117   *DM*, 3 (October 1860), 339; Field, *Politics of Race*, pp. 96, 119–26; Foner, *Frederick Douglass*, pp. 186–7.
118   *DM*, 3 (October 1860), 339–40; Quarles, *Frederick Douglass*, pp. 165–6.
119   *DM*, 3 (November 1860), 353; Douglass, *Life and Times*, pp. 325–8; Quarles, *Frederick Douglass*, p. 166; Harlow, *Gerrit Smith*, pp. 426–8; McKivigan, *War Against Proslavery Religion*, pp. 159–60; Pease and Pease, *They Who Would Be Free*, p. 204; Foner, *Frederick Douglass*, pp. 185–6; Waldo Martin incorrectly states that Douglass supported Lincoln in the election. Martin, *Mind of Frederick Douglass*, pp. 34–5.
120   *DM*, 3 (December 1860), 369; Field, *Politics of Race*, pp. 126–7.
121   Martin, *Mind of Frederick Douglass*, p. 42.

The Shadow of Slavery

Frederick Douglass, the Savage South, and the Next Generation

WAYNE MIXON

"My great and exceeding joy over . . . the abolition of slavery," Frederick Douglass wrote in 1881, describing his emotions at the end of the Civil War, "was slightly tinged with a feeling of sadness. I felt I had reached the end of the noblest and best part of my life."[1] Anything following so glorious an achievement as emancipation would doubtless seem anticlimactic, yet one suspects that Douglass's sadness was anachronistic. The joy had to have been genuine, but the sadness imputed to 1865 rings false.

By 1881, Douglass the fighter for freedom had become Douglass the party placeman, and a second-class one at that, for his "fat office," theretofore filled by whites, had had some of its honors shorn for his occupancy. Although still the preeminent leader of black Americans, Douglass had suffered increasing criticism from other blacks since the heady days of the early Reconstruction years. The failure in 1874 of the Freedmen's Bank, with which he had nothing to do but over which he presided; his endorsement, albeit temporary and in a spirit of trust, of the compromise of 1877, which sealed the doom of Reconstruction; and his opposition to black migration from the South during the Kansas Exodus of 1879 all had brought censure.[2] By the early 1880s he had good reason to feel a tinge of sadness.

After slavery was abolished, Douglass found himself in the anomalous position of being a race leader who didn't think racially. Always a humanist, he had championed the cause of blacks not because they were black but because they were oppressed.[3] Not color but condition, Douglass believed, generated prejudice against blacks. Slavery, rather than an inherent aversion toward blacks among whites, had been responsible for the degradation of African-Americans. If color were all-controlling, how, Douglass had wondered as a slave, did one explain the facts that some blacks were not slaves, that some whites were not slaveholders, and that some people

233

who were nearly white were slaves? What he failed to note was that no one who was considered purely white was enslaved.[4]

Not only was Douglass not a race thinker, he had little in common with the people for whom he served as spokesman. As late as 1890, 90 percent of black Americans lived in the South and 75 percent of those lived on the land.[5] As a slave, Douglass had spent less than two years as a field hand. As a free man, he nurtured to broad learning the literacy he had seized in slavery. His striking physique, natural charm, and good manners, which had been learned from whites and from other blacks while he was a slave, often made him a welcome guest in polite society. Even the likelihood of election to Congress during Reconstruction could not induce him to move to a southern state. Among the many reasons he gave for declining – some of which seem farfetched – one illustrates his perception of the barriers that existed between himself and other black southerners. "I could not," he recalled in 1881, "have readily adapted myself to the peculiar oratory found to be most effective with the newly-enfranchised class. . . . I had acquired a style of speaking which in the South would have been considered tame and spiritless" (*LT*, 485). Three years later, in a letter to a white friend, he observed: "Circumstances have during the last forty years thrown me much more into white society than in that of colored people. . . . My nearest personal friends . . . have been white people."[6]

The distance that Douglass had traveled from his days as a slave can be tellingly measured by examining accounts of his trips back to Maryland after the war. In the late spring of 1877, shortly after his appointment as United States Marshal for the District of Columbia, he returned to his native Eastern Shore for the first time in forty years. Steaming across the Chesapeake from Baltimore, he found himself in the company of 100 or so black excursionists, many of whom were, like himself, heading home for a reunion. For Douglass the crossing seemed endless. All night long, his fellow passengers drank, sang, and stomped to banjo music. The next day Douglass sternly assessed the experience: "The one hundred colored people aboard made as much noise as five hundred whites would have done, and as long as they do these things they are inferior to the whites."[7] On the way to visit his old master, Thomas Auld, Douglass was stopped frequently on the streets of the village of St. Michaels by white men who wanted to shake his hand. The older ones among them told him that "they remembered him as a boy and had always known he would do well." After an emotional twenty-minute interview with the aged, palsied Auld, Douglass delivered a speech to an audience composed of blacks and whites. "I am an Eastern Shoreman, with all that that name implies," he proudly told the crowd. "I love Maryland and the Eastern Shore."[8]

The next year Douglass was back, to deliver a lecture paid for by local Republicans. On the overnight steamer from Baltimore, he was lodged in a stateroom. Upon arrival in Easton he was given a suite in the town's finest hotel, where he received white callers, some of whom had known him as a boy. Among those who extended "a warm and friendly welcome" was the man who, as sheriff over forty years before, had put him in jail for attempting to escape slavery (*LT*, 539). According to the Easton *Gazette*, the audience that heard his lecture contained "quite as many white as colored people." At the conclusion of the speech, "many of the best gentlemen of the county went forward and took Mr. Douglass by the hand."[9]

The trip home that most deeply affected Douglass occurred three years later. This time his destination was the Lloyd estate, which he had last seen fifty-five years before. It had been gratifying to effect a reconciliation with Thomas Auld and to receive the plaudits of Eastern Shore whites. But the visit to the Lloyd estate, the seat of one of the first families of the South, was in Douglass's mind an event of profound significance. "I left there as a slave," he wrote in *Life and Times*,

> and returned as a freeman; I left there unknown to the outside world and returned well known; I left there on a freight boat, and returned on a revenue cutter; I left on a vessel belonging to Col. Edward Lloyd, and returned on one belonging to the United States. (540)

In all of Douglass's autobiographies, few episodes are more poignantly rendered than the extended description of his return to the home plantation. Meeting Edward Lloyd's great-grandson triggered memories of the late patriarch, a man Douglass had "known well":

> He was a gentleman of the olden time, elegant in his apparel, dignified in his deportment, a man of few words and of weighty presence; and I can easily conceive that no Governor of the State of Maryland ever commanded a larger measure of respect than did this great-grandfather of the young gentleman now before me. (541).

"I had seen the elder Lloyd," Douglass continued, "and was now walking around with the youngest member of that name," the little brother of his host, who disclosed "his aristocratic descent in the lineaments of his face, and in all his modest and graceful movements" (541).

A tour of the grounds revealed little change from a half-century before, except that the garden was not kept in as fine condition "as in the days of the elder Lloyd" (544). Nonetheless, Douglass wrote, a "more tranquil and tranquilizing scene I have seldom met in this or any other country"

(544). Upon visiting, at his request, the family cemetery, which included the graves of a Confederate general and a Confederate admiral, Douglass experienced "a feeling of unusual solemnity," the pathos of which was not lost upon the book's illustrator, who penned a drawing of the visitor standing reverently over a Lloyd tombstone, hat off, head bowed, eyes closed (543, 545). A bouquet gathered from the graves "I carefully brought to my home for preservation" (544).

In many ways, Douglass's sentimental yet compelling account of an ex-slave's nostalgia for the old home place might have provoked the envy of a plantation romancer like Thomas Nelson Page. Yet if Douglass proved willing to pay respect to the Lloyds, he also intended that respect be shown to him. And it was. His host gathered the flowers from the graveyard, took him to the veranda of the great house where they sat to enjoy the view, and invited him into the spacious, elegant dining room for wine "of most excellent quality" (544). During his visit a short time later with Colonel Lloyd's daughter, the widow of a Confederate admiral, Douglass was likewise treated with great cordiality:

> She invited me to a seat by her side, introduced me to her grand-children, conversed with me as freely and with as little embarrassment as if I had been an old acquaintance and occupied an equal station with the most aristocratic of the Caucasian race. (547).

In the extended six-page account of his visit with the Lloyds, Douglass devoted only one brief paragraph to the black people on the place, with whom he spent "a little time" (547).

Soon Douglass was back in old slave country, this time at Harper's Ferry, to give the Decoration Day oration. On the platform with him sat Andrew J. Hunter, the prosecuting attorney for Virginia in the trial of John Brown. Hunter greeted Douglass cordially, complimented his speech, invited him to visit his home, and, at parting, wrote Douglass, "gave me a friendly grip, and added that if Robert E. Lee were alive and present, he knew he would give me his hand also" (549–50).

By Douglass's own account, his associations after the war with representatives of the old slavocracy were pleasant and personally satisfying.[10] In virtually everything except color, he had far more in common with privileged whites than with poor blacks. As Peter F. Walker has persuasively argued, Douglass seems to have been haunted throughout his life by the matter of his "whiteness." Less than a year before his death, he journeyed from his home in Washington to Baltimore to seek information about his lost past from a grandson of Thomas Auld. Douglass felt so strongly about this matter that the last entries he made in his diary, though he would live for eleven months more, dealt with this visit. Although he learned some coveted facts, he was not able to solve the mystery of his paternity.[11] He had long known that he had enjoyed special privileges as a slave. Nonetheless, the people who probably comprised his white family failed to acknowledge his kinship. In short, white racism forced Douglass to become "black." As Walker has said, "Douglass spoke more for black Americans than for himself."[12] Therein lies his greatness. Despite the absence of common ground between himself and the vast majority of black Americans, despite the contradictions within himself, late in life he again came forth, in what was perhaps the African-American's greatest hour of need, to lead the fight against white racism. Slavery had cast a giant shadow, and Douglass was still the bearer of light. Contrary to his own assessment in 1881, the "noblest and best" part of his life was not over.

Immediately after Reconstruction, Douglass continued to hold high hopes for racial harmony in the South and for black progress there. He based his opposition to the Kansas Exodus of 1879 upon the conviction that prospects for blacks were brighter in the South than anywhere else in the country. Admitting that the southern white reaction against Reconstruction had brought proscription and violence against blacks, Douglass nonetheless maintained that the "situation at this moment is exceptional and transient." The power of the federal government, he believed, was still on the side of the black man's civil and political rights, which "will revive, survive, and flourish again." The Exodus signaled an abandonment of principle, a retreat from the idea that "the business of this nation is to protect its citizens where they are, not to transport them where they will not need protection." Only in the South, Douglass pointed out, did blacks have "at least the possibility of power," which rested upon the region's dependence upon black labor. The black man's labor had "made him a slave, and his labor can, if he will, make him free, comfortable and independent. . . . It touches the heart of the South through its pocket." Although Douglass appreciated the grim realities facing black southerners, he pointed out that "the way of an oppressed people from bondage to freedom is never smooth." Time, he suggested, would ameliorate the black man's plight, for his condition was the result not of the putative "natural inferiority of the Negro, or the color of his skin" but of the "careless and improvident habits of the South" acquired by blacks and whites alike and "the long exercise of irresponsible power by man over man" that was the legacy of slavery.[13]

Douglass's trips to the Eastern Shore and to Harper's Ferry encouraged him to think that the attitudes of southern whites toward blacks were undergoing significant improvement. "The abolition of slavery," he wrote, "has not merely emancipated the negro, but liberated the whites; taken the lock from their tongues, and the fetters from their press" (LT, 549).

When Edward Lloyd's great-granddaughter presented him with flowers, "with a pleasant smile on her face," he was deeply moved. The gesture

> told me many things, and among them that a new dispensation of justice, kindness, and human brotherhood was dawning not only in the North, but in the South; that the war and the slavery that caused the war were things of the past, and that the rising generation are turning their eyes from the sunset of decayed institutions to the grand possibilities of a glorious future. (*LT*, 547–8)

Within a decade of these remarks, the rising generation of white southerners upon whom Douglass had pinned his hopes was proving to be a tragic disappointment. The wave of lynchings that washed over the South from the late 1880s through the early twentieth century seems to have been a phenomenon initiated by *young* men. As Edward L. Ayers has argued, the lynching crisis developed in part because "a new generation of blacks and whites faced each other across an ever-widening chasm." As segregation tightened its hold on the region, the elite of both races increasingly withdrew into their own communities. Moreover, the racial memory of white and black men under thirty, those people most likely to behave violently, held little besides mistrust and conflict. "These men, white and black," Ayers has aptly observed, "feared each other with the fear of ignorance."[14] This fear bred by ignorance, coupled with the long association of blacks with sexuality in the white southern mind, gave rise to a widespread belief in the ubiquity of the black-beast rapist. Isolated incidents of black-on-white rape, widely reported in the southern press, further fanned the hysteria. White women demanded protection. A southern novelist who described herself as "a woman suffering for women" asserted that there was no such thing as an innocent black, that the "racial attitudes" of blacks merited "racial punishment," and that the virtue of one white woman outweighed "in value the lives of a hundred negro men."[15]

The real separation of young southerners, white from black, and the sexual fear that afflicted the white imagination were exacerbated by hard times. From the mid-1880s through the end of the century, southern agriculture suffered a depression unprecedented in severity. Working hard and producing much, southern farmers, through circumstances largely beyond their control, found themselves sinking deeper into debt. Frustrated as providers, white men, at the urging of their women, compensated as protectors. If they could not keep the price of cotton from falling, they could keep the black man from rising.[16]

The lynching epidemic seems to have caught Douglass by surprise. Nonetheless, he soon rallied. The worst year of the lynching crisis called forth his fire to a degree seldom equaled even during his years as an abolitionist.[17] In an 1892 article, he confronted head-on the primary justification for lynching. The wrath aroused in the South over the reputedly widespread incidence of rape was not the result of the horror generated by "the immorality . . . of the crime itself" but of the races of the rapist and victim. That southern white men had committed this offense against black women for 200 years had, Douglass noted, "excited little attention." Easily charged and only with great difficulty disproved, the crime of rape, Douglass further observed, required opportunity. The Civil War had provided ample opportunity for its frequent commission. Yet, he maintained, "during all that period no instance can be cited of an outrage committed by a negro upon the person of any white woman." Was it likely that, as a class, black men had changed so drastically in only twenty-five years? "The crime," Douglass pointed out, "is a new one for the negro, so new that a doubt may be reasonably entertained that he has learned it to any such extent as his accusers would have us believe."[18]

Not only would Douglass not let apologists of lynching blame the victims, he refused to accept the argument that the "ignorant mob" should bear full responsibility. The actual lynchers, he contended, were simply following "the public sentiment of the South, the sentiment created by wealth and respectability, by the press and the pulpit."[19] The charge was, if anything, understated. As Joel Williamson has shown, radical racists – those who believed that blacks were retrogressing without the benefits of slavery, who looked forward to the ultimate extinction of African-Americans, and who participated in or endorsed lynchings – were often pillars of their communities.[20]

The North was only slightly less culpable, Douglass believed. In an updated version of his *Life and Times* published in 1892, he perceptively observed that black Americans had paid dearly for the reconciliation between white men, North and South, that had been underway for the past fifteen years:

> From the hour that the loyal North began to fraternize with the disloyal and slaveholding South; from the hour that they began to "shake hands over the bloody chasm;" from that hour the cause of justice to the black man began to decline and lose its hold upon the public mind, and it has lost ground ever since.[21]

The "sympathy of the North," he noted elsewhere that same year, had never been "more fully with the Southern [white] people than now."[22]

In a major speech two years later on "the so-called, but mis-called, negro problem," Douglass tried at length to show northerners that such sympathy was woefully misguided. "There is nothing in the history of savages," he told his audience, "to surpass the blood-chilling horrors and fiendish excesses perpetrated against the colored people by the so-called enlightened and Christian people of the South." Most white southerners, he contended, were people "whose ideas, habits and customs are entirely different from those of ordinary men." The "long abuse of irresponsible power" fostered by "a peculiar institution . . . that . . . has stamped them as a peculiar people" had rendered white southerners insensible to the value of human life.[23]

With northern acquiescence, the condition of black southerners had deteriorated so rapidly that Douglass admitted that "the negro is in some respects, and in some localities, in a worse condition today than in the time of slavery." What could be done? Or, as Douglass cast the matter, "How can the peace and tranquility of the South . . . be secured and established?"[24] By framing the question in this fashion, Douglass engaged even the more moderate white southerners on their own ground. Peace and tranquility were the stated goals of many of those white southerners leading the campaigns for statutory segregation and for disfranchisement of blacks. In the highly charged atmosphere of the 1890s, those whites could, with some justice, cloak themselves in the mantle of reform by arguing that by minimizing racial friction they were protecting the persons of black southerners.[25] To Douglass, peace and tranquility did not connote the harmony and stability that would result from a superior-to-inferior relationship in which each party knew his place and was satisfied. Rather, peace and tranquility equally enjoyed by all southerners would come only when there was equal opportunity and equal protection of the law.

Douglass clearly saw that such opportunity and protection had no chance of being realized without protest and agitation. To those black leaders who in despair counseled relocation in Africa, he rejoined that such a proposal, which he labeled "nonsense," was not a solution to the race problem but an evasion that further emboldened rabid white racists and actually deepened despair among blacks. To those black leaders who advocated or acquiesced in the idea of suffrage restriction, he responded that the franchise should be made not "more exclusive, but more inclusive." To those black leaders who advised silence as the prudent reaction to the outrages committed by white southerners, he replied that "a people too spiritless to defend themselves are not worth defending."[26] At the age of seventy-five, Douglass updated his autobiography because he felt morally compelled to argue the case for his "emancipated brothers and sisters who, though free, are yet oppressed and are in as much need of an advocate as before they were set free."[27] Two years later, when he was only a month shy of seventy-seven, the worsening racial crisis summoned him to the podium yet again. Before the audience in Washington's Metropolitan A. M. E. Church, he delivered a long, blistering attack against the forces of injustice, which when subsequently printed made a pamphlet of nearly forty pages.[28] The fire that had sent him to the platform in Nantucket over fifty years before still burned. His constitutional inability to surrender to despair likewise still lived, although he admitted that "the immediate future looks dark and troubled." In light of the enormity of the problem of racism and the reality of his advanced age, Douglass acknowledged that "time and strength are not equal to the task before me."[29] Thirteen months later, he lay dead.

What did Douglass's life mean to the South, the land of his birth and his upbringing, the land he wanted to love?[30] What, specifically, did his life mean to black southerners of the next generation? We can gain some knowledge of that meaning by looking at two biographies of Douglass written by black southerners forty years younger than he.

Although Charles W. Chesnutt left the South at age twenty-five, never to live there again, he could not get the South off his mind. Nor did he want to. When he departed North Carolina in 1883 in search of greater opportunity in the North, he was committed to the task of helping other black southerners secure "recognition and equality" by attacking "the unjust spirit of caste" that enslaved white southerners.[31] Authorship, Chesnutt believed, provided a way to work toward that goal. Virtually all of his best fiction deals with the matter of race in the postbellum South. Leaving the region enabled him to become a southern writer "in the best sense of that term."[32]

Of Chesnutt's six books, only his biography of Douglass is nonfiction. Douglass's life, Chesnutt wrote, appealed to "his imagination and his heart," because he felt "a profound and in some degree a personal sympathy with every step of Douglass's upward career."[33] For Chesnutt, as for Douglass, the commitment to racial justice was a moral imperative and not the result of a sense of community with the southern black masses. The rural, poorly educated blacks into whose company Chesnutt had been thrown as a country schoolteacher seemed to him "the most bigoted, superstitious, hardest-headed people in the world!" Hardly the "romantic" figure that existed in the minds of northerners, the "southern Negro," Chesnutt wrote in 1880, was "commonplace and vulgar." Like Douglass, however, Chesnutt believed that black southerners were inferior not because they were black but because they were southerners. An entry in his journal two years before he left North Carolina recorded his conviction that he was "better than most of the white men I have met in this vale of tears." Like Douglass, Chesnutt harbored a burning desire to improve himself and to associate "with cultivated society," so he, too, headed north and achieved distinction.[34]

Published in 1899, Chesnutt's *Frederick Douglass* appeared in the Beacon Biographies of Eminent Americans, a series of pocket books designed, according to the publisher, for "busy men and women [who] have not the time . . . to acquaint themselves with American biography" (142).

Chesnutt suggested to the publisher that his *Douglass* might also find a market in black schools. Despite many other demands on his time, he met the deadline for *Douglass*, completing the manuscript within ten weeks.[35]

Chesnutt's goal was to "revive among the readers of another generation a tithe of the interest that Douglass created for himself when he led the forlorn hope of his race for freedom and opportunity" (x). Douglass's life, Chesnutt pointed out, should inspire all people of good will, and it should stand especially as an object lesson for black Americans. Douglass's learning to read and write "demonstrated the power of the mind to overleap the bounds that men set for it" (14). His fight with Edward Covey, the slavebreaker, showed that "strength of character, reenforced by strength of muscle , . . . [could win] a victory over brute force" (18). His rise to eminence "by sheer force of character and talents . . . must ever remain as a shining illustration of the essential superiority of manhood to environment" (1). Throughout his life, despite his own signal achievements, Douglass had devoted his efforts to helping his fellow men and women, especially other blacks. Even in bondage, when he might with good reason have thought only of his own misfortune, he had "tried to help others by teaching his fellow-slaves to read the Bible" (19). Clearly, Chesnutt was saying to blacks at the turn of the century: Go and do thou likewise.

Crucial as it was to keep alive Douglass's legacy in the hearts of black Americans, especially those in the South, Chesnutt had additional purposes in mind. Throughout the book, he used Douglass's life as a base from which to launch attacks against the burgeoning racism of the turn-of-the-century South. Chesnutt's assault on the white South commenced at the very outset of his account. With devastating irony, he described the county of Douglass's nativity as "a barren and poverty-stricken district, which possesses in the birth of Douglass its sole title to distinction" (3). Two pages later, after asserting that Douglass's father was white, Chesnutt wrote: "In after years his white father never claimed the honor [of Douglass's paternity], which might have given him a place in history" (5). In this manner, Chesnutt turned the South's racial hierarchy upside down; a black man had brought honor and distinction to the region. Later in the book, Chesnutt again pointedly used Douglass's life to attack white racism in the contemporary South. Discussing the hostility that confronted Douglass in New England early in the 1840s, Chesnutt characterized such sentiment as "but little different from that in the State of Georgia to-day" (35). Many New Englanders of the 1840s, Chesnutt observed, lumped all blacks together, failing to make distinctions on the basis of means, manners, and dress. By the 1890s, Chesnutt implied, New Englanders had learned better. The long-dead practices of New England still existed, however, "in the Southern States to-day" (36).

Such customs, Chesnutt contended, were the result of "Southern instincts," a term he failed clearly to define but by which he seems to have
meant the strong impulses cultivated in whites by centuries of enslaving
blacks (103). In stark contrast to those "Southern instincts" stood the
"essentially affectionate and forgiving character of Douglass and his race"
(126). White southern intransigence rendered improvement virtually impossible. "One cannot refrain from thinking," Chesnutt concluded, "that
a different state of affairs might prevail in the Southern States if other
methods than those at present in vogue were used to regulate the relations
between the two races" (126–7).

Because there was precious little reason to hope for change on the
part of most white southerners, Chesnutt used his account of Douglass's
life to try to alter the attitudes of northerners, to awaken them from their
apathy. Thus he directed his *Douglass* in great measure toward the "average
American of to-day who sees, when his attention is called to it, and
deplores, if he be a thoughtful and just man, the deep undertow of race
prejudice" (7). Apathy unchallenged had helped generate northern abandonment of black southerners. Occasionally, Chesnutt chided those whites
"of little faith" who had given up on the black man "because in [only]
thirty years the emancipated race have not equalled the white man in
achievement" (79). More often, however, Chesnutt reminded white
northerners of evidence of racial enlightenment in the region's past, drawing
generalizations from episodes of Douglass's life. Thus, Rochester, New
York, Douglass's home for a number of years, was "then as now the
centre of a thrifty, liberal, and progressive population" (64). Thus, Massachusetts, which had sponsored black units that Douglass had helped
recruit for the Union army, was "a State foremost in all good works"
(92). Thus, immediately after the Civil War, "the North was favorably
disposed toward colored men" (99), a generalization that Chesnutt should
have known would not bear scrutiny. Post-Reconstruction northern apathy
and ages-old "Southern instincts" were powerful enemies, so Chesnutt
was striving valiantly, in the name of Douglass, to cultivate support for
black southerners however he could.

What is striking is that, given this purpose, Chesnutt chose to slight
Douglass's post-Reconstruction career. By doing so, he missed a prime
opportunity to portray his subject in one of his finest hours as an adversary
of white racism. Given the severe space limits imposed upon the Beacon
Biographies by the publisher – *Frederick Douglass* runs to only 135 pages
of narrative – Chesnutt was certainly right to devote the bulk of his
attention to Douglass's antebellum career. But to give only thirty-seven
pages to the postbellum Douglass and, within that space, to relegate the
post-Reconstruction Douglass to only twelve pages was a serious error
of authorial judgment. It is highly questionable that Douglass's humorously
ironic run-in with white southerners aboard ship in 1845 was worth a

page's treatment, that his 1840s tour of the British Isles merited ten pages, and that his break with the Garrisonians was the subject of twelve pages, whereas his ringing denunciation of the Supreme Court's *Civil Rights* decision, his extended analysis of the "Negro Problem," and his impassioned attack upon lynching received no mention whatsoever.

Not only did Chesnutt virtually ignore the last thirty years of Douglass's life, he interpreted that phase simplistically. For Chesnutt, who was hardly an accommodator of white racism, to say of Douglass that "age had dimmed the recollection of his sufferings and tempered his animosities, . . . [making him] more charitable to his old enemies" can only be attributed to considerable ignorance of the last years of Douglass's life (116). The contention that Douglass was able "to prolong his usefulness a generation after the abolition of slavery" because of a "vein of prudence" could hardly have been made by anyone familiar with even a few of Douglass's most important writings and speeches of the postbellum era (69). Ten weeks of research and writing was simply much too short a time for any writer, even one of Chesnutt's ability, to capture the fullness of Douglass's legacy. Nonetheless, like Douglass, Chesnutt saw the magnitude of slavery's legacy, which had crushed "all semblance of manhood" in blacks and had substituted "passion for judgment [and] caprice for justice" in whites (8–9). Slavery, in short, was "the origin of so many of our civic problems" (9).

Like Douglass, Chesnutt had moved north to opportunity and could view the legacy of slavery from a distance. Unlike either, Booker T. Washington had moved south to prominence and to an environment in which slavery's legacy was immediate and palpable. By the time his biography of Douglass was published in 1906, Washington had been widely recognized for a decade as Douglass's successor. One of twenty-five titles projected for the American Crisis Biographies, a series of full-length studies dealing with the Civil War era, Washington's *Frederick Douglass* was shaped by the Tuskegeean's situation.[36] Refusing to mount the frontal attack on white southerners that Chesnutt had conducted, Washington reversed the strategy, sedulously soothing, whenever he could, the feelings of white southerners as he highlighted northern racism.[37] Unlike Chesnutt's, Washington's account of young Frederick's childhood in Baltimore mentioned his "large circle of [white] friends, who loved him and were loyal to him" (31). Moreover, in that city Frederick was allowed to learn the trade of ship calker and would have had "no trouble in obtaining good employment," although in the North, "even in Massachusetts," of the late 1830s and early 1840s, he was not permitted "to follow his occupation" (153). Whereas Chesnutt omitted the episode, Washington pointedly called attention to the "good-heartedness" shown by Frederick's master in refusing to sell him south after an unsuccessful attempt to escape slavery; Thomas Auld's kindness "was the only thing that preserved our young hero for that larger life which he was to make for himself, and help to make for so many others of his race" (50). Auld's magnanimity reflected the attitudes of countless other white southerners. "Thousands of Southern people," Washington maintained, "felt that slavery was a wrong [and] emancipated their slaves; others were moved to treat them with unusual kindness, and still others held them because they could not help themselves" (91).

The major difference between the two biographies is the central theme of each, or the essence of Douglass's legacy for each writer. To Chesnutt, Douglass was preeminently an advocate of black rights; to Washington, Douglass was, first and foremost, a promoter of black responsibilities. The burden of Washington's biography was to show that the master of Tuskegee was the legitimate legatee of Douglass's mantle. Often quoting extensively from Douglass's speeches and writings on the subject, Washington emphasized throughout the book Douglass' support for industrial education, from his initial advocacy in 1847, "when the passionate controversialist [first] displayed . . . something of the foresight and constructive ability of a statesman," to his role in founding a Virginia industrial school in 1894, "one of his last acts in behalf of his people" (119, 333). Washington was especially proud that Douglass had visited Tuskegee Institute in 1892 to deliver the commencement address. With obvious relish he quoted Douglass's advice to the graduates: "Seek to acquire knowledge and property, and *in time* you may have the honor of going to Congress" (333; emphasis added). Lest any reader miss the message, Washington drove the point home: "Long before Tuskegee Institute was thought of, Frederick Douglass saw the necessity for just such work as many of the industrial schools are doing in the South at the present time" (181).

In Washington's hands, Douglass became the John the Baptist of the Bookerite gospel: Get practical training in agricultural or mechanical science; work hard; make money and save it; stay put; be patient and wait for the rewards of full citizenship that right living would bring. Moreover, echoing his Atlanta Compromise, wherein he tried to assuage the fears of white southerners, Washington argued that Douglass had rejected the idea of social equality. Douglass's acceptance of the office of Marshal of the District of Columbia with some of its perquisites abridged did not involve, said Washington, a "surrender of principle" but instead showed "a fine sense of discrimination as to rights and privileges" (290). Furthermore, according to Washington, Douglass "always declared that political equality was a widely different thing from social equality" (259).

Yet within four months of two of his widely publicized speeches that characterized social equality as a false issue, Douglass did something that seemed to many whites to signify that the possibility of social equality

was all too real, all too imminent.[38] Conversely, to many blacks, his
wedding Helen Pitts constituted a symbolic rejection of his race. Douglass's
marriage to a white woman provided one of the few occasions for criticism
in Washington's biography. "The notion seemed to be quite general,"
Washington said, "that [Douglass] had made the most serious mistake
of his life" (306). He had "failed to take into consideration the offense
his act might give to public feeling," ignoring "how deep-seated was the
sentiment of white and black people alike against amalgamation" (306,
307). The refusal to gauge public opinion, Washington implied, could
leave any leader, and especially a black one, without a following.

A critical tone also informed Washington's assessment of black enfranchisement during Reconstruction, although he refused to berate
Douglass directly for promoting universal manhood suffrage. Unlike
Douglass, who advocated a more inclusive franchise until his death,
Washington thought that the immediate, wholesale enfranchisement of
black men during Reconstruction had been "unwise" (255). Washington
also disagreed with Douglass's stalwart allegiance to the Republican Party
after Reconstruction.[39] "It was unfortunate," he contended, that the
"tendency to political independence on the part of the enlightened colored
men could not have been encouraged" (296). By independence, Washington
did not mean black support for third-party movements such as Populism
but rather a division of black strength between the two major parties.
He concluded that "it is . . . a serious hindrance to the colored man's
political freedom that he must continue to regard the Republican party
as composed wholly of his friends and the Democratic party as composed
wholly of his enemies" (296).

Considering Washington's location deep in the heart of the Democratic
Black Belt, his obeisance to political independence is readily understandable.
What is not so comprehensible is his almost complete lack of attention
to Douglass's fiery denunciations of lynching. Sandwiched between an
account of the accolades Douglass received as Haiti's commissioner at
Chicago's Columbian Exposition and a description of "his restful and
delightful home" where "life went on serenely and happily," only a
portion of one paragraph treats lynching (337). Acknowledging that
"nothing in [Douglass's] lone life of anxiety and struggle for his race so
depressed him as did this new manifestation of contempt for his people,"
Washington nonetheless refused to exploit a beckoning opportunity to
defend *his* people (337). The great conciliator had accommodated dis-
franchisment and segregation, with the rationale that such a policy served
the long-term interests of black southerners. Merely by emphasizing
another man's ringing condemnation of such a flagrant injustice as lynching,
Washington could have done what was morally right and at the same
time could have concealed himself in Douglass's shadow.[40]

In fact, however, Washington, despite all his praise of Douglass, was trying to escape his shadow, to distance himself from the earlier leader. Changed circumstances, he suggested, mandated different leadership. On the very first page of the biography, Washington suggested that whereas Douglass had been a promoter of "revolution and liberation," he, conversely, was an advocate of "construction and readjustment" (5). Three pages from the end of the text, Douglass was described as a leader whose task had been "one of destruction and liberation," whereas Washington's purpose was "construction and reconciliation" (349). Although Washington quite correctly observed that Douglass was "a Southerner in spirit and in his primary attachments" who "loved . . . and believed in the South," the Tuskegeean failed to understand that it was precisely because Douglass loved the South that he could not be satisfied with the Bookerite solution to the southern racial problem (326). To tell black southerners to "endure, and work, and wait" was simply not enough (324). Although circumstances had conspired to prevent Chesnutt from conveying the fullness of Douglass's legacy, the very essence of Douglass's greatness, a moral indignation over injustice courageously proclaimed, received scant expression by the foremost black leader of the next generation.

By 1890, there was little in Douglass's attitude to anticipate the publicly professed faith in the collective goodwill of white southerners that became a cardinal tenet of the Bookerite gospel. Yet, even at the height of the lynching crisis, Douglass acknowledged that the "South is not all a wilderness. There are good men and good women there who will sooner or later make themselves heard and felt."[41] At a time when the "Radical mentality," which envisioned "*no place* for the Negro in the future American society," was fast enslaving the white southern mind, it was virtually impossible for white southerners with dissenting views to speak out on behalf of black southerners.[42] Nonetheless, a few – usually academicians, clergymen, or writers – found the courage to do so.

Seven years after Douglass's death, Andrew Sledd, a professor at Emory College in Georgia, published an essay in the *Atlantic Monthly* that had much in common with Douglass's article on lynching of ten years before. Like Douglass, Sledd would not allow the victims of lynching to be blamed for the crime. "The radical difficulty," he wrote, "is not with the Negro, but with the white man!" White southerners, he continued, "must be *made* to realize, by whatever means, that the black man has rights which they are *bound* to respect." Like Douglass, Sledd rejected the canard that rape was the primary cause of lynching. "It has been repeatedly shown," he wrote, "that only a very small proportion (in some years *one tenth*) of Southern lynchings are due to rape, either actual or suspected." Like Douglass, Sledd minced no words in portraying "the purest savagery" of those who perpetrated or observed "the indescribable and sickening torture and writhing of a fellow human being" and who collected souvenirs from the victim's remains – "knee caps, and finger bones, and bloody ears." The furor created by Sledd's article caused Emory's president eagerly to accept his resignation.[43]

The same year that Sledd's essay appeared, a Baptist minister in Texas published a remarkable volume of nearly 500 pages in which he cataloged black achievements, past and present, in business, politics, and the professions. The Reverend J. J. Pipkin, who praised Douglass as an orator, statesman, philanthropist, and "man of honor," described himself as "a Southern man, born and bred, . . . [who] has been subjected to all the influences that are supposed to breed race prejudice." Yet "as a follower of the Great Master who taught goodwill to all men," Pipkin felt compelled to defend the black man against much of what had recently been written about him, "some of it fanciful, some ill-considered, some malicious, and some utterly fallacious, misleading, and dangerous." With his compilation of black progress, Pipkin sought to protest "against everything that tends to degrade the Negro, and . . . rob him of self-respect" and to "induce more liberal views" of blacks among "fair-minded" whites.[44]

In the turn-of-the-century South, however, fair-minded whites comprised only a hopelessly outnumbered corporal's contingent fighting a rearguard action against the overwhelming forces of radical racism. The situation could well-nigh induce despair. In the aftermath of the 1906 Atlanta Riot, Joel Chandler Harris, who had spent thirty years trying to subvert white racism through fiction – an effort appreciated by William Lloyd Garrison's son – had a white countryman score Atlanta's leaders for letting "a lot of thirty-cent loafers" kill innocent blacks. Unable to find any justification for the violence, Harris's character called it "one of the things you wanter wring your han's over."[45]

People like Sledd, Pipkin, and Harris were the "good men" trying to "make themselves heard" that Douglass had acknowledged in 1892. During the most viciously racist era in the South's history, such whites were nonetheless able, as Joel Williamson has said, "to put themselves in the place of black people and to understand something of the burden that color carried in the South."[46]

Attributing the plight of black southerners to condition, to enslavement, Douglass had underestimated the power of sheer color prejudice in American, and especially southern, society. To his everlasting credit, however, he never lost faith in the ability of human beings to do good. If his legacy was submerged in the racist tide of the turn of the century, it would surface again fifty years later. Like Martin Luther King, Jr., whose advocacy of civil rights was rooted in humanitarianism rather than racialism, Douglass held to the belief, despite repeated rebukes, that white southerners had the capacity to do what was morally right. Whatever progress the South

has made in race relations over the past thirty-five years owes much to
his legacy.

NOTES

I would like to express my appreciation to Mary Horton for acquiring much
material through interlibrary loan; to my colleagues Kay Carr, Carlos Flick, and
Catherine Meeks for critical readings of the manuscript; and to Bessie Killebrew
for typing numerous drafts of the essay.

1 Frederick Douglass, *Life and Times of Frederick Douglass* (Hartford: Park
  Publishing Company, 1881), p. 453. Hereafter, page references to this volume
  will be incorporated parenthetically in the text. When not apparent from
  the context, the citation will be rendered as *LT*.

2 Waldo E. Martin, Jr., *The Mind of Frederick Douglass* (Chapel Hill: University
  of North Carolina Press, 1984), p. 83; Waldo E. Martin, Jr., "Frederick
  Douglass: Humanist as Race Leader," *Black Leaders of the Nineteenth Century*,
  ed. by Leon Litwack and August Meier (Urbana: University of Illinois Press,
  1988) pp. 80–1; Nell Irvin Painter, *Exodusters: Black Migration to Kansas After
  Reconstruction* (New York: Alfred A. Knopf, 1976), pp. 227–8.

3 On the relationship between Douglass's egalitarian humanism and his race
  leadership, see Martin, *Mind of Frederick Douglass*, pp. 92–106.

4 Frederick Douglass, *My Bondage and My Freedom*, ed. by William L. Andrews
  (1855; rpt. Urbana: University of Illinois Press, 1987), p. 60. Examining
  the origins of slavery in the Chesapeake colonies, Winthrop D. Jordan concluded: "Rather than slavery causing 'prejudice,' or vice versa, they seem
  rather to have generated each other." *White Over Black: American Attitudes
  Toward the Negro, 1550–1812* (1968; rpt. Baltimore: Penguin Books, 1969),
  p. 80.

5 Howard N. Rabinowitz, *Race Relations in the Urban South, 1865–1890* (1978;
  rpt. Urbana: University of Illinois Press, 1980), p. xi. Douglass's first visit
  to the rural Deep South, where America's black population was concentrated,
  did not occur until 1888. Nathan Irvin Huggins, *Slave and Citizen: The Life
  of Frederick Douglass* (Boston: Little, Brown, 1980), p. 171.

6 Frederick Douglass to Elizabeth Cady Stanton, May 30, 1884, in *The Life
  and Writings of Frederick Douglass* by Philip S. Foner (New York: International
  Publishers, 1955), IV, 410.

7 Quoted in Dickson J. Preston, *Young Frederick Douglass: The Maryland Years*
  (Baltimore: Johns Hopkins University Press, 1980), p. 182.

8 Ibid., pp. 183–4.

9 Quoted in ibid., pp. 189–90.

10 David W. Blight has recently argued that Douglass's "enduring attitudes
   toward the South" were harsh and vindictive. " 'For Something Beyond the
   Battlefield': Frederick Douglass and the Struggle for the Memory of the
   Civil War," *Journal of American History*, 75 (1989), 1169. Such a generalization
   obscures the complexity of Douglass's relationship to his native region.

11 Peter F. Walker, *Moral Choices: Memory, Desire, and Imagination in Nineteenth-
   Century American Abolition* (Baton Rouge: Louisiana State University Press,
   1978), pp. 210–11, 231. See also Stephen M. Weissman, "Frederick Douglass,

Portrait of a Black Militant: A Study in the Family Romance," *Psychoanalytic Study of the Child*, 30 (1975), 725–51.

12 Walker, *Moral Choices*, p. 223.

13 Frederick Douglass, "The Negro Exodus from the Gulf States" in Foner, *Douglass*, IV, pp. 334, 336, 338, 327, 331, 340.

14 Edward L. Ayers, *Vengeance and Justice: Crime and Punishment in the 19th-Century American South* (New York: Oxford University Press, 1984), p. 241.

15 "Clinton Dangerfield" [Ella Howard Bryan] to Joel Chandler Harris, April 2, 1907, Joel Chandler Harris Collection, Special Collections Department, Robert W. Woodruff Library, Emory University. Bryan's letter reflects a sentiment that had been growing for the previous twenty years. I am grateful to Dr. Linda Matthews of the Woodruff Library's Special Collections Department for permission to quote this material.

16 On the relationship between white sexual anxieties and economic depression in the rise of virulent racism, see, in addition to Ayers, *Vengeance and Justice*, pp. 241–3, Joel Williamson, *The Crucible of Race: Black–White Relations in the American South Since Emancipation* (New York: Oxford University Press, 1984), pp. 301–2.

17 In 1892, the number of blacks lynched in the United States, according to Williamson, *Crucible of Race*, p. 117, reached a peak of 156. The number may have been even higher – 161. See Morton Sosna, *In Search of the Silent South: Southern Liberals and the Race Issue* (New York: Columbia University Press, 1977), p. 35.

18 Frederick Douglass, "Lynch Law in the South," *North American Review*, 155 (1892), 19, 23.

19 Ibid., 23.

20 Williamson, *Crucible of Race*, pp. 111–39, 176–9, 184–5.

21 Frederick Douglass, *Life and Times of Frederick Douglass* (rev. ed.; Boston: DeWolfe, Fiske, 1892), p. 652.

22 Douglass, "Lynch Law," 20.

23 Frederick Douglass, *The Lessons of the Hour* (Baltimore: Thomas and Evans, 1894), pp. 5, 17.

24 Ibid., pp. 28, 33.

25 John W. Cell, *The Highest Stage of White Supremacy: The Origins of Segregation in South Africa and the American South* (Cambridge: Cambridge University Press, 1982), pp. 175–91.

26 Douglass, *Lessons of the Hour*, pp. 26, 21, 8.

27 Douglass, *Life and Times*, rev. ed., p. 620. Although Douglass was actually seventy-four (Preston, *Young Frederick Douglass*, p. 31), he thought he was seventy-five, which for my purpose is what's important. It seems to me that age seventy-five carries a significance that seventy-four lacks.

Douglass did not update the *Life and Times* with rich royalties in view. Over a seven-year period, the original edition had sold only 463 copies. Two years after publication of the revised edition, fewer than 400 copies had been purchased. Benjamin Quarles, *Frederick Douglass* (Washington, D.C.: Associated Publishers, 1948), p. 337.

28 Douglass, *Lessons of the Hour*. Again, I use the age that Douglass believed himself to be.

29 Ibid., pp. 23, 36.
30 Obituaries and editorials in major southern newspapers reveal varied responses
    to Douglass's life. Doubtlessly voicing the hopes of most white southerners,
    the Louisville *Courier-Journal* (February 21, 1895) contended that Douglass
    "did not desire amalgamation, since he believed that the pure, unadulterated
    negro was the best of his race." Conversely, the New Orleans *Daily Picayune*
    (February 21, 1895) maintained that Douglass's "instincts and tendencies
    were all towards the white race" and condemned his marriage to a white
    woman because such evidence of amalgamation showed a "lack of faith in
    the people for whose advancement . . . [he professed] to be solicitous." The
    Atlanta *Constitution* (February 21, 1895) simply called Douglass "an able
    negro."
        When the lower house of the North Carolina legislature, which was
    controlled by Republicans and Populists, voted to adjourn out of respect to
    Douglass's memory after having refused to do so in honor of Robert E.
    Lee's birthday a month earlier, "great indignation" resulted (Baltimore *Morning
    Herald*, February 22, 1895). I am grateful to Ms. Eva Slezak, Afro-American
    Collection, Enoch Pratt Free Library, for furnishing this information.
31 Quoted in Helen M. Chesnutt, *Charles Waddell Chesnutt: Pioneer of the Color
    Line* (Chapel Hill: University of North Carolina Press, 1952), p. 21.
32 Julian D. Mason, Jr., "Charles W. Chesnutt as Southern Author," *Mississippi
    Quarterly*, 20 (1967), 89.
33 Charles W. Chesnutt, *Frederick Douglass* (Boston: Small, Maynard, 1899),
    p. ix. Hereafter, page references to this volume will be cited parenthetically
    in the text.
34 Quoted in William L. Andrews, *The Literary Career of Charles W. Chesnutt*
    (Baton Rouge: Louisiana State University Press, 1980), pp. 6–7.
35 H. Chesnutt, *Chesnutt*, pp. 113, 120.
36 According to the editor, the historian Ellis Paxson Oberholtzer, a member
    of the first generation of Ph.D.s trained in American universities, "the series
    is to be impartial, Southern writers having been assigned to Southern subjects
    and Northern writers to Northern subjects." Booker T. Washington, *Frederick
    Douglass* (Philadelphia: George W. Jacobs, 1906), unpaginated front matter.
    See also Thomas J. Pressly, *Americans Interpret Their Civil War* (New York:
    Free Press, 1962), pp. 182–6.
        Like most of Washington's other works, *Frederick Douglass* was ghostwritten.
    In this case the ghost was Samuel Laing Williams, a Georgia-born Chicago
    attorney who was a personal friend of Washington. Louis R. Harlan, ed.,
    The Booker T. Washington Papers (Urbana: University of Illinois Press, 1974),
    III, 518n. As was the case with virtually all of his other ghostwritten works,
    however, Washington kept a careful eye on ghost and manuscript. Harlan,
    ed., *Washington Papers* (1972), I, xvi; Washington to Williams, June 10, 1905;
    ibid. (1979), VIII, 300–1.
37 Chesnutt's biography is not listed in Washington's bibliography. Washington,
    Frederick Douglass, p. 353; hereafter page references to this volume will be
    incorporated parenthetically in the text.
        Chesnutt and Washington were friends who corresponded frequently. In
    a letter to the Tuskegeean of August 11, 1903, regarding the courses of action

that black spokesmen might pursue toward white southerners, Chesnutt wrote: "Encourage the good ones all you may; I think the rest of us should score the bad ones." Quoted in H. Chesnutt, *Chesnutt*, p. 196.

38   In the latter of those speeches, a denunciation of the Supreme Court's *Civil Rights* decision, which Douglass delivered in Washington in October 1883, he said: "Social equality and civil equality rest upon an entirely different basis, and well enough the American people know it; . . . social equality is a matter between individuals." Foner, *Douglass*, IV, 402.

39   Douglass's loyal, though by no means uncritical, support of the post-Reconstruction Republican Party paralleled the position of most southern blacks. In the South, the Democratic Party was hardly an attractive alternative, and even Populism was badly tainted by racism. Political independentism in the 1880s and 1890s was largely a northern black development. See Bess Beatty, *A Revolution Gone Backward: The Black Response to National Politics, 1876–1896* (Westport, CT: Greenwood Press, 1987), pp. 49–50, 128, 145, 155, and Gerald H. Gaither, *Blacks and the Populist Revolt: Ballots and Bigotry in the "New South"* (Tuscaloosa: University of Alabama Press, 1977), pp. 130–5.

40   Perhaps on no other issue was Washington's dilemma more apparent than in the matter of protecting blacks from mob violence. Hardly an apologist of lynching, Washington was nonetheless acutely aware that his work depended upon the tolerance of white southerners. On the few occasions when he commented publicly on mob violence, he seemed "to condone the lynching of those [blacks] presumed guilty of rape." Louis R. Harlan, *Booker T. Washington: The Making of a Black Leader, 1856–1901* (New York: Oxford University Press, 1972), p. 263.

41   Douglass, "Lynch Law," 21.

42   Williamson, *Crucible of Race*, p. 6; emphasis is in the original.

43   Andrew Sledd, "The Negro: Another View," in *Forgotten Voices: Dissenting Southerners in an Age of Conformity*, ed. by Charles E. Wynes (Baton Rouge: Louisiana State University Press, 1967), pp. 102, 105, 98, 101; emphasis is in the original. On the Sledd affair, see Henry Y. Warnock, "Andrew Sledd, Southern Methodists, and the Negro: A Case History," *Journal of Southern History*, 31 (1965), 65–73, and Ralph E. Reed, Jr., "Emory College and the Sledd Affair of 1902: A Case Study in Southern Honor and Racial Attitudes," *Georgia Historical Quarterly*, 72 (1988), 463–92. Among Sledd's few defenders in the South were a number of black leaders; Washington was not among them. Reed, "Emory College and the Sledd Affair," 482.

44   Rev. J. J. Pipkin, *The Negro in Revelation, in History, and in Citizenship* (St. Louis: N. D. Thompson, 1902), pp. 80, v, vi.

45   Julia Collier Harris, ed., *Joel Chandler Harris: Editor and Essayist* (Chapel Hill: University of North Carolina Press, 1931), p. 216. See also Francis J. Garrison to Joel Chandler Harris, September 27, 1906, Harris Collection, Emory University.

46   Williamson, *Crucible of Race*, p. 488.

Frederick Douglass's
Life and Times

Progressive Rhetoric and the Problem of Constituency

KENNETH W. WARREN

As Frederick Douglass, in his *Life and Times of Frederick Douglass*, accounts for his decision not to move to the South and seek elective office following the Civil War, he recalls having considered three prominent reasons. First, he remembers his sense that a move south would involve a degree of impropriety: "the idea did not square well with my better judgment and sense of propriety. The thought of going to live among a people in order to gain their votes and acquire official honors was repugnant to my self-respect."[1] Second, he claims to have been beset by self-doubt: "I had small faith in my aptitude as a politician, and could not hope to cope with rival aspirants" (398). And third, he refers to his belief that he could be more effective in the politically powerful North: "the loyal North, with its advanced civilization, must dictate the policy and control the destiny of the republic" (399).

It is the second claim, the claim of self-doubt, that chiefly concerns me here, for the vision of Douglass – who had gone toe-to-toe with plantation overseers, Garrisonian abolitionists, and a U.S. president – quailing before potential opposition is not readily credible. Indeed, upon further inquiry, it seems clear that Douglass's self-deprecatory pose is highly ironic. Though he discounts his own ability, he does so in a way that places the burden of blame elsewhere. He explains:

> I could not have readily adapted myself to the peculiar oratory found to be most effective with the newly enfranchised class. In the New England and northern atmosphere I had acquired a style of speaking which in the South would have been considered tame and spiritless, and consequently he who "could tear a passion to tatters and split the ear of groundlings" had far better chance of success with the masses there than one so little boisterous as myself. (398).

Again, Douglass's self-deprecation demands suspicion. "Tame" is hardly the word for Douglass, who was experienced in tailoring his addresses to the needs of his audiences and whose oratory has been characterized as "bold, emphatic, and aggressive."[2] What Douglass seems bent on is not characterizing his own style accurately but in drawing a contrast between his style and that of his rivals.

As Douglass describes the southern political climate, the freedmen, like the groundlings at an Elizabethan theater "who for the most part are capable of nothing but inexplicable dumb shows and noise,"[3] lack the ability to understand and appreciate the oratorical style that Douglass had honed in the "advanced civilization" of the North. As the references to *Hamlet* make plain, Douglass felt that the speakers who could appeal directly to the newly enfranchised class were not merely endowed with different oratorical skills, but with lesser ones of bombast and passion.[4] Yet these lesser skills were no barrier to popularity. In fact, during this period the popularity of what were perceived to be inferior literary styles and forms proved a considerable challenge to those writers or public figures who styled themselves as progressive, democratic spokesmen but employed oratorical and literary styles that often seemed out of sync with popular tastes. It was not that progressive intellectuals were never well received. Many achieved or maintained a great deal of prominence during the 1880s and 1890s, Douglass being arguably one of the three or four most famous Americans of the nineteenth century. His prominence, however, did not exempt him from challenges, and the nature of these challenges prompted him to examine and reexamine the validity of his claim to a democratic idiom.

In the pages that follow, I argue that in *Life and Times*, Douglass, like other social reformers, among whom one can number realist and naturalist novelists, explores the boundary between a democratic style on the one hand and a popular style on the other. Just as the realistic novel staged "a debate . . . with competing modes of representation," chief among which were "the emergent forms of mass media,"[5] so Douglass's autobiography engages a variety of competing forms in seeking to speak on behalf of the true interests of African-Americans. And in recognizing his prospective audience's receptiveness to competing forms, Douglass, like many of his contemporaries, mobilized a democratic apologetic that first located and then spoke on behalf of silenced but sympathetic constituencies. By stressing the strategic nature of this mobilization, I do not mean to suggest that Douglass made these gestures cynically or that there were not disfranchised, silenced communities in need of representation. Rather, I mean to suggest that in having dismissed elective office and pulpit rhetoric as avenues to democratic representation, Douglass, like novelists who downplayed mass market appeal as an indicator of democratic appeal, consistently reinvented means through which popular disregard or disapprobation might be met with implicit democratic assent.

For example, when the southern progressive author George Washington Cable found that his writings on civil justice for black Americans evoked a storm of protest, he endeavored to create and appeal to a "Silent South" – that part of southern society that he saw as constituting "our whole South's better self; that finer part which the world not always sees; unaggressive, but brave, calm, thoughtful, broad-minded, dispassionate, sincere, and in the din of boisterous error round about it, all too mute."[6] This Silent South was not merely fictional. Cable's views had indeed met with some favor during his visits to the South. The term, however, functioned less as a demographic designation than as a rhetorical warrant that Cable, a southerner himself, spoke not as an individual but on behalf of other southerners. Similarly, the editor, novelist, and Christian socialist William Dean Howells often represented himself as speaking for American writers who as a group were estranged from their natural constituency. According to Howells, the writer "is really of the masses, but they do not know it, and what is worse, they do not hear him; as yet the common people do not hear him gladly or hear him at all."[7] In Howells's conception, the novelists' natural constituents responded with hostility if they responded at all, leaving the novelist unable to communicate with those who needed most to hear him. Thus, as editor of *Harper's*, Howells took it upon himself to champion the cause of realistic fiction, both to his fellow writers and to the American public.

For most of his career, of course, Douglass deemed African-Americans, "a people long dumb, not allowed to speak for themselves, yet much misunderstood and deeply wronged" (511), his silent constituency. But he did not play this role without encountering significant difficulty. His various public and personal decisions – from opposing black migration to the North, to staying on as Recorder of Deeds in the District of Columbia following the election of Grover Cleveland, to marrying Helen Pitts, a white woman, some seventeen months after the death of his first wife, to serving as the U.S. Minister Resident and Consul General to the Republic of Haiti – at one time or another enraged his black as well as his white supporters. In the *Life and Times*, Douglass uses these unpopular stands as opportunities to locate other silenced communities – opportunities that would make his unpopular stances if not popular, then, in their own way, democratic.

For example, in responding to his "Afro-American critics" who had chided him when he did not immediately resign his post as Recorder of Deeds for the District of Columbia after the election of Grover Cleveland,

a Democrat, Douglass invokes the anomalous status of the people of the
District of Columbia:

> Then again I saw that there was less reason for resigning because
> of the election of a President of a different party from my own,
> when the political status of the people of the District of Columbia
> was considered. These people are outside of the United States. They
> occupy neutral ground and have no political existence. They have
> neither voice nor vote in all the practical politics of the United
> States. They are hardly to be called citizens of the United States.
> Practically they are aliens – not citizens, but subjects. The District
> of Columbia is the one spot where there is no government for the
> people, of the people, and by the people. Its citizens submit to
> rulers whom they have had no choice in selecting. They obey laws
> which they had no voice in making. They have a plenty of taxation,
> but no representation. In the great question of politics in the country
> they can march with neither army, but are relegated to the position
> of neuters.
>
> I have nothing to say in favor of this anomalous condition of
> the people of the District of Columbia, and hardly think it ought
> to be or will be much longer endured, but while it exists it does
> not appear that the election of a President of the United State should
> make it the duty of a purely local officer, holding an office supported,
> not by the United States, but by the disfranchised people of the
> District of Columbia, to resign such office. (533)

I quote this passage at length to underscore how willfully Douglass echoes
the arguments used in justifying both the American Revolution and the
abolition of slavery. He even employs the exclusion of the disfranchised
from military service (an issue he had pressed before Abraham Lincoln
in the 1860s) as a metaphor. Central for Douglass is the way the real
political needs of a mute constituency with which he is associated can
be mobilized to deflect the criticism that he has placed his private interests
above the interests of party or race.

Although Douglass's brief on behalf of the District of Columbia seems
remarkably significant and prescient in light of the recent efforts of African-
American spokesmen to take up the cause of the inhabitants of our
nation's capital, other issues are more pertinent here. Douglass's dependence
upon mute communities to justify his public stances has a troubling side
to it. Recent studies of American realist and naturalist fiction of this
period have illuminated the way in which the textual strategies of novelists
tended to merge with the managerial and authoritarian aspects of social
reform movements. In her study of the naturalist novel, June Howard
has argued that "it is a very short step . . . from the sympathy of the

naturalist spectator to the altruistic and ultimately authoritarian benevolence of the progressive reformer."[8] The intelligent, articulate spectator, while attempting to reveal the details of these mute, silenced lives, distances himself from those he represents, making them other than himself, and confines them to a realm outside of that inhabitated by the spectator. The condition of representation seems to be alienation.

Waldo E. Martin, Jr., has also observed that on occasion Douglass himself characterized other blacks in ways that "separated himself . . . in an important sense from them," attributing to his fellow blacks qualities he himself did not possess.[9] Martin also places Douglass's sometimes problematic relationships with other African-Americans within the larger sphere of the conflicts of nineteenth-century American reform movements.[10] What I would like to add to Martin's perceptive analysis of Douglass's reformism is a discussion of how many of the problems that surface in *The Life and Times* are constitutive of the problems of realistic representation during the latter part of the century. Though it would take a more lengthy argument to work out fully the mechanics of reading the *Life and Times* as a realist or naturalist fiction, these recent studies offer some tentative help in sorting out Douglass's textual and political strategies.

As an ex-slave and as a black man subject to discrimination following emancipation, Douglass remained intimately tied to the constituency he most consistently represented. And yet, Peter F. Walker has provocatively speculated that Douglass's embrace of the abolitionist cause involved a degree of distancing himself from the race of his mother. Analyzing Douglass's reflections on his speaking debut – "For a time I was made to forget that my skin was dark and my hair crisped" – Walker asserts that during the period before his rupture with the Garrisonians in 1847, Douglass felt himself "divested of his dark skin and crisped hair. He had ceased to be a Negro. The agency, the 'good cause,' was the literal escape from his physical features and from everything that tied him to his black mother."[11] Whether or not Douglass wished to "escape from his physical features," Walker's observations may point to a troubling liability that one may incur when speaking for the silenced: a tendency to underwrite difference in a way that "reinforces the hierarchy between classes" or groups.[12] Significantly, when Douglass speaks out against black migration to the North, he does so in a way that figures his southern constituents as other than himself:

The Negro, as already intimated, is preeminently a southern man. He is so both in constitution and habits, in body as well as mind. He will not only take with him to the North southern modes of labor, but southern modes of life. The careless and improvident habits of the South cannot be set aside in a generation. If they are adhered to in the North, in the fierce winds and snows of Kansas and Nebraska, the migration must be large to keep up their numbers. . . . (438)

In enumerating the impediments to the successful emigration of the freedmen, Douglass seems to forget his own story, his own rise from an "unthrifty district . . . among slaves who, in point of ignorance and indolence, were fully in accord with their surroundings" (27). And in intimating that the inability of blacks to cope with northern climates would prevent them from sustaining their numbers in their new environment, Douglass succumbs to a Social Darwinistic rhetoric that he castigates elsewhere in his story. Despite his commitment to the cause of equality and justice for black Americans, Douglass, throughout his career, but especially in the decades following the Civil War, found himself both empowered by and limited by the rhetoric of reform that was available to him.[13]

One such limitation may have been Douglass's inability to appreciate and to understand fully the voices lifted in answer to his own. Although his autobiographical enterprise had come to be regarded as the work of a "self-made man," Douglass voices from time to time the belief that others would assist in the completion of the "Life" that he had begun. As he neared the end of the 1881 edition, Douglass conjectured that "what may remain of life to me . . . will probably be told by others when I have passed from the busy stage of life" (478). He had not, however, finished writing the story, and as he took up the pen again, there was an air of both pride and pathos in the realization that "the unity and completeness of the work require that it shall be finished by the hand by which it was begun" (514):

> When the first part of this book was written, I was, as before intimated, already looking toward the sunset of human life and thinking that my children would probably finish the recital of my life, or that possibly some other persons outside of family ties to whom I am known might think it worth while to tell what he or she might know of the remainder of my story. I considered, as I have said, that my work was done. (513)

Having angered his children by his marriage to Helen Pitts in 1882, and having suffered criticism from erstwhile supporters for reasons already mentioned, Douglass may have felt, in addition to the potential financial gain to be enjoyed by the publication of another edition of his life's story, that the only voice fully in harmony with the story he had already told was his own. Additionally, Douglass's position on social reform, which inclined him to identify his cause with the values of reason, thrift, self-reliance, and self-control, while identifying the forces of opposition with passion, extravagance, and indolence, confirmed him in his belief that the voice most in evidence among his black constituents was a voice in discord with his own: that of the black preacher.

Douglass's disapproval of black Protestant oratory is well known. As he explains his rhetorical style to his white readers, Douglass claims:

> In my communication with colored people I have endeavored to deliver them from the power of superstition, bigotry, and priestcraft. In theology I have found them strutting about in the old clothes of the masters, just as the masters strut about in the old clothes of the past. The falling power remains among them long since it has ceased to be the religious fashion in our refined and elegant white churches (479–80)

Treating religion as style or fashion, and fashion as being of the utmost importance, Douglass views black and white southern Protestantism as if they were one. And as the possessive pronoun "our" indicates, he locates himself within the fashion of white congregations. The path of progress is clearly marked, with Douglass leading the way; equally well marked is the path leading backward:

> Thus the forces against us are passion and prejudice, which are transient, and those for us are principles, self-acting, self-sustaining, and permanent. My hope for the future of my race is further supported by the rapid decline of an emotional, shouting, and thoughtless religion. Scarcely in any direction can there be found a less favorable field for mind or morals than where such a religion prevails. It abounds in the wildest hopes and fears, and in blind unreasoning faith. Instead of adding to faith virtue, its tendency is to substitute faith for virtue, and is a deadly enemy to our progress. (508)

With religion and progress clearly at odds, Douglass's influence over a people still under the sway of old fashions was questionable. Thus, as he presses his criticism of the black church, Douglass admits to his reader that "My views at this point receive but limited endorsement among my people" (480). And as is evident from his previous remarks, Douglass's only hope lies in his belief that passion is "transient" and that this religion will naturally die out.

Douglass, of course, was not alone among black leaders in decrying the supposed counterproductive role of black religion in the cause of black progress. W. E. B. Du Bois concurred with Douglass's belief in the need to supplant the old-style preacher with enlightened leaders. Writing in "The Talented Tenth," Du Bois argued, "The preacher was, even before the war, the group leader of the Negroes, and the church their greatest social institution. Naturally this preacher was ignorant and often immoral, and the problem of replacing the older type by better educated men has been a difficult one."[14] Just how difficult this task was is made evident in Du Bois's treatment of the issue in the thirteenth chapter of *The Souls of Black Folk*, entitled "Of the Coming of John." In this chapter, Du Bois chronicles the career of John Jones, a "loud and boisterous" young black man who leaves the small southern town of Altamaha to attend a school called the Wells Institute. Although the white people of Altamaha view John's prospective education with foreboding, the black inhabitants invest his departure and eventual return with messianic hopes strong enough to sustain them during what turns out to be a seven-year absence. " 'When John comes,' " the black townsfolk intone, "then what parties were to be, and what speakings in the churches; what new furniture in the front room, – perhaps even a new front room; and there would be a new schoolhouse, with John as teacher; and then perhaps a big wedding; all this and more."[15] The refrain "When John comes" captures the anticipatory anxiety that pervades the early portion of the chapter.

This anticipation, however, is only partly fulfilled. John does return, and the black citizens of Altahama plan great festivities. Their celebration, however, falls flat:

> The meeting of welcome at the Baptist Church was a failure. Rain spoiled the barbecue, and thunder turned the milk in the ice-cream. When the speaking came at night, the house was crowded to overflowing. The three preachers had especially prepared themselves, but somehow John's manner seemed to throw a blanket over everything, – he seemed so cold and preoccupied, and had so strange an air of restraint that the Methodist brother could not warm up to his theme and elicited not a single "Amen"; the Presbyterian prayer was but feebly responded to, and even the Baptist preacher, though he wakened faint enthusiasm, got so mixed up in his favorite sentence that he had to close it by stopping fully fifteen minutes sooner than he meant. (529)

As Du Bois describes it, not only the weather conspires against the success of the welcome; John's "manner" itself blunts the speaking style of the three preachers. They are ineffective and unable to stir the crowd. The usual call and response fails to materialize, and the well-rehearsed sentences become garbled in their delivery. In fact, the traditional oratory is cut short, setting the stage, it would seem, for a new style of address.

Accordingly, John rises and speaks to the congregation (529). The boisterous boy who had left Altahama seven years prior has been transformed into a "tall, grave man" who preaches a gospel of social progress to the townspeople, speaking "of the rise of charity and popular education, and particularly of the spread of wealth and work" (529). He concludes by enjoining them to embrace social, economic, and political progress while eschewing sectarianism, asking, "What difference does it make whether a man be baptized in river or wash-bowl, or not at all? Let's leave all that littleness, and look higher" (530). Predictably, the message fails miserably. He is speaking in a Baptist church to a combined Presbyterian, Methodist, and Baptist congregation that might heed the ecumenical call but would not tolerate out-and-out atheism. John's failure, however, stems not only from his perceived sacrilege but from the inability of the crowd to comprehend him: "Little had they understood of what he said, for he spoke an unknown tongue, save the last word about baptism" (530).

And though the incomprehensibility of John's "unknown tongue" might derive from the words he uses, Du Bois draws equal attention to the style in which John delivers his address. He speaks "slowly and methodically," "reflectively," and "in detail" (527). His manner, which had proved so crippling to the efforts of the three preachers, also disables his own message, and he evokes not assent but "a painful hush" (530).

The hush, however, is only short-lived. After a few moments an outraged man rises from the Amen Corner, raises a Bible, "and then fairly burst into the words, with rude and awful eloquence. He quivered, swayed, and bent; then rose aloft in perfect majesty, till the people moaned and wept, wailed and shouted, and a wild shrieking arose from the corners where all the pent-up feeling of the hour gathered itself and rushed into the air" (530). The physical power of the old man's eloquence contrasts starkly with John's "air of restraint." Freed from the task of honoring John by John's own sacrilege, the old man awakens the assemblage with his rhetoric, and now ironically, it is John who does not fully understand the message. He cannot, however, mistake the implications of the speaker's rhetorical style: "John never knew clearly what the old man said; he only felt himself held up to scorn and scathing denunciation for trampling on the true Religion" (530).

The clash of rhetorical styles in "The Coming of John" seems quite similar to the problem Douglass alluded to in deciding not to seek elective office in the South during Reconstruction: There would be no community between speaker and audience. Similarly, Douglass's denunciation of black religion, which includes no detailed critique of its content, suggests that Douglass, like Du Bois's John, "never knew clearly" what was being said.

Du Bois's story ends tragically. Young John is lynched when he kills his white counterpart of the same name for sexually accosting his sister. Earlier in the story, however, Du Bois has told us that John opens a school for the black residents of Altamaha. Significantly, the only lesson the story narrates is a lesson on style: " 'Now, Mandy,' he [John] said cheerfully, 'that's better; but you musn't chop your words up so: "If – the – man – goes." Why, your little brother even wouldn't tell a story that way, now would he?' " (533). Immediately following this lesson, the school is closed as a result of rumors that John is also teaching about the "French Revolution, equality, and such like" (532). Yet as I have said, the only lesson that the tale narrates is a lesson on speaking and reading. The closing of John's school, John's tragic fate, and the ambivalent note sounded throughout *The Souls of Black Folk* testify to the breadth of the gulf black leaders perceived between them and their intended audiences, both black and white. But John's endeavor to teach a lesson in style, like Douglass's persistence in publishing his story into the 1890s, attests to a continued belief in the missionary potential of the educated voice.

This belief was not specific to the cause of African-American civil rights but pervaded the thinking of many of Douglass's contemporaries in their preoccupation with other social and literary concerns. In fact, this belief in the power of the educated voice was carried to an almost absurd extreme by Henry James in a commencement address he delivered at Bryn Mawr College in Pennsylvania on June 8, 1905. And though James did not have in mind the particular plight of black Americans, his remarks bear reference here, both in terms of seeing how much weight some writers placed on conversational style and in seeing how the conflict in which Douglass's text is embroiled did not lend itself to an easy conclusion.

James's address to the Bryn Mawr graduates is at once a lesson in elocution, a social commentary, and a xenophobic tirade against American ethnic minorities. Proclaiming to his audience that "Of the degree in which a society is civilized the vocal form, the vocal tone, the personal, social accent and sound of its intercourse, have always been held to give a direct reflection,"[16] James not only outlines the threat to American civilization deriving from the lack of a "tone standard," but also describes examples of improper speech and enjoins the young women to embark upon life "sounding the clearer notes of intercourse as only women can, become yourselves models and missionaries, perhaps a little even martyrs, of the good cause."[17]

Attributing the lack of an American tone standard to popular education, mass culture, and American ethnic groups – "to the American common school, to the American newspaper, and to the American Dutchman and Dago, as the voice of the people describes them,"[18] – James defines the threat to American society as a dire one indeed:

> The conservative interest is really as indispensable for the institution
> of speech as for the institution of matrimony. Abate a jot of the

quantity, of the consecration required, and we practically find ourselves emulating the beasts, who prosper as well without a vocabulary
as without a marriage-service. It is easier to overlook any question
of speech than to trouble about it, but then it is also easier to snort
or neigh, to growl or to "meaow," than to articulate and intonate.[19]

James's mingling of mass culture, ethnicity, social dissolution, and a
brutish state signals clearly his almost hysterical reaction to the country
that he found on his return to his homeland in 1904 after an absence of
twenty years. The attack on American vernaculars is unmistakable here,
just as the attack on the black pulpit voice is unmistakable in Douglass's
Life and Times. Douglass, too, shared James's view of mass culture as
vulgar and brutish, lamenting at one point in the *Life and Times*:

> There is, however, enough of the wild beast left in our modern
> human life to modify the pride of our enlightenment and hu-
> manity. . . . In this respect our newspapers tell us a sad story. They
> would not be filled with the details of prize fights, and discussions
> of the brutal perfections of prize fighters, if such things did not
> please the brutal proclivities of a large class of readers. (567)

And yet it would be erroneous to see James's and Douglass's texts solely
in the context of their antagonism toward mass culture and the spoken
vernacular.

For James's attacks, unlike the English-only movements of the present
day, are directed less at the presence of other languages in American
public discourse than at what America itself does with these other languages.
A polyglot, James was quite ready to address American immigrants in
their native tongues. What he discovers, however, as he writes in *The
American Scene*, is that his fluency in Italian is no guarantee of communication
with the Italian laborers he confronts in New York; conversely, the failure
in Italian ensures no necessary success in English. "It was as if contact
were out of the question."[20] James confronts a simple failure to communicate.

Though this qualification does not exempt James from a charge of
ethnic prejudice, one should not ignore the fact that in repeating the
ethnic slur "Dago" and the imprecise term "Dutchman," James attributes
them to "the voice of the people." The popular voice, the vernacular
voice, is identified not merely with the aliens themselves but likewise
with the social intolerance of aliens, as exemplified in ethnic and racial
epithets. Staunchly Anglocentric though James's voice may be, it is a
voice conscious of itself in relation to other voices. As he laments the
absence of an American tone standard, James utters his concern for America's representation "in the international concert of culture," noting that
"the French, the Germans, the Italians, the English perhaps in particular,

and many other people, Occidental and Oriental, I surmise, not excluding the Turks and the Chinese, have for the symbol of education, of civility, a tone standard."[21] The international note struck here provides a gloss on both James's remarks and Douglass's *Life and Times*. Concerned with the vulgarity that they thought they saw destroying the fiber of American public life, both men sought to play the role of social missionary or popular prophet while speaking in tones dignified and reasonable. They sought to have the effect of popular media without employing the styles of these media. And their belief in the success of that mission, whether through the agency of the female voices of the upper-class graduates of Bryn Mawr or the sonorous utterances of Douglass himself, is as poignant as it is unrealistic.

Thus, in assessing Douglass's *Life and Times*, one must keep in mind its attempt to play the prophet without "tearing a passion to tatters." Of the last six chapters of Douglass's life's story, the first two are devoted to the European journey he took in the company of his second wife, the last two are a vindication of his role as Minister Resident and Consul General to the Republic of Haiti, and the other two describe Douglass's role in the election of 1888, which led to his appointment by President Benjamin Harrison as Consul to Haiti.

The first of his European chapters sounds an *ubi sunt* theme. Returning to England some forty years after his first stay there, Douglass expresses a desire to see again "England's great men" whom he had known and seen before: "There were Sir Robert Peel, Daniel O'Connell, Richard Cobden, John Bright, Lord John Russell, Sir James Graham, Benjamin Disreali, Lord Morpeth, and others, but except Mr. Gladstone, not one who was there then is there now" (557). The melancholy litany of absent faces is not meant to distance Douglass from his past. Rather, the chapter serves to distinguish Douglass as one of the few remaining representatives of a heroic age, an age whose speakers spoke in cadences unequaled in the present day. As he describes the abilities of each of these worthies, Douglass rolls out paragraphs of complimentary prose, presenting his reader with a laudatory encyclopedia of the oratorical styles of the great men he had heard years before. And when he reaches the end of the chapter, Douglass need not say, though the point is clear, that his style is a continuing example of that grand oratory of the past.

In the second chapter treating his European travels (Chapter 9 of Part Three), Douglass adopts the more conventional pose of the "American tourist" commenting on the sights and customs in France, Italy, and Egypt: "When once the American tourist has quitted Rome . . . he is generally seized with an ardent desire to wander still farther eastward and southward" (579). This pose for Douglass, however, is fraught with significance. He recalls that on his first trip to England he was refused a passport to visit the continent by George M. Dallas, the Minister to

England, "on the ground that I was not and could not be an American citizen" (587). Contrasting his present privileges to his past restrictions, Douglass exults that "this man [Dallas] is now dead and generally forgotten, as I shall be, but I have lived to see myself everywhere recognized as an American citizen" (587). The trip abroad is an affirmation of his American citizenship – he tours the world as an American.

Douglass, however, mentions another purpose behind his visit:

> an ethnological purpose in the pursuit of which I hope to turn my visit to some account in combating American prejudice against the darker colored races of mankind, and at the same time to raise colored people somewhat in their own estimation and thus stimulate them to higher endeavors. I had a theory for which I wanted the support of facts in the range of my own knowledge. But more of this in another place. (579)

Although Douglass had written and lectured extensively on race and ethnology, that "other place" is not found within the Life and Times but was taken up elsewhere.[22] Douglass does not allude again to this "theory" in his text, but he leaves hints as to what he was about. Remarking earlier in the chapter upon the women he sees carrying burdens on top of their heads, Douglass comments that "I was glad to see, both in Italy and the south of France, that this custom is about as common there as it is among the dusky daughters of the Nile" (563). He continues:

> Even if it was originated by the Negro, it has been well copied by some of the best types of the Caucasian. In any case it may be welcomed as a proof of a common brotherhood.
>
> In other respects I saw in France and Italy evidences of a common identity with the African. In Africa the people congregate at night in their towns and villages, while their living is made by tilling the soil outside. We saw few farmhouses in the south of France. Beautiful fields and vineyards are there, but few farmhouses. The village has taken the place of the farmhouse, and the peasants sometimes go several miles from their villages to work their vineyards. (563)

Having identified this region as the "cradle in which the civilization of Western Europe and our own country was rocked and developed," Douglass proceeds to note the similarities to be found between European and African cultures: communal life, the bearing of burdens, the participation of women in fieldwork, and the carefree attitudes of the inhabitants. Africans need not feel themselves strangers to the civilization of the West; they are indeed a part of it.

In going to Egypt, Douglass perhaps wanted to carry this observation one step further. Egypt was more venerable than Europe, boasting a "civilization which existed when these countries of Europe [France and

Italy] were inhabited by barbarians" (579). And as he chronicles his travels on the Suez Canal and the Nile, Douglass does comment sporadically upon the racial similarities between black Americans and the peoples of the Mideast. The comparisons, however, are limited and amount to very little. Douglass spends a great deal of time musing upon the landscape of biblical history as well as upon the wonders of Egyptian history, but no grand theory materializes. Instead, Douglass recounts his return to Rome, where he meditates on the vanity of human wishes. The chapter then ends with Douglass visiting the tomb of fellow abolitionist Theodore Parker, and with Douglass marveling at the contrast between his former status as a slave and his present state, "when I could and did walk the world unquestioned, a man among men" (590).

What Douglass may have been intending to do before he changed direction was to link black America more securely to Egyptian civilization by finding concrete evidence for his long-held belief "that a strong affinity and a direct relationship may be claimed by the Negro Race to *that grandest of all the nations of antiquity, the builders of the pyramids.*"[23] Additionally, Douglass's scheme may have had a personal note. Peter Walker has commented at length on Douglass's claim that his mother resembled a figure in James Prichard's *Natural History of Man*. Walker notes that the head is supposed to be a likeness of Rameses, and that the likeness, "as far as the picture showed, may have been white." Douglass's fascination with the image suggests for Walker his "continuing conflict" over his racial identity.[24]

As strong as these ethnographic and personal motives may have been, their full articulation in the *Life and Times* seems to have been derailed by the progressive dynamic within realistic representation. Douglass's foreign travels had allowed him to see that religious zeal and emotionalism were not the peculiar property of southern blacks. In Rome he marveled that "fanaticism is encouraged by a church so worldly-wise as that of Rome" (575), and in Cairo he noted:

> If Rome has its unwashed monks, Cairo has its howling and dancing dervishes, and both seem equally deaf to the dictates of reason. The dancing and howling dervishes often spin around in their religious transports till their heads lose control and they fall to the floor sighing, groaning, and foaming at the mouth like madmen, reminding one of the scenes that sometimes occur at our own old-fashioned camp meetings. (587)

Finding in the cradle of civilization evidence of the religious spirit he had derided among the freedmen of the South, Douglass seems to have stumbled upon the keys for striking a harmonious chord with his voice and that of the southern black preacher. In Rome and Cairo were both passion and reason in the form of religious fanaticism and civilized achievement. The peoples responsible for civilization were also responsible for promoting "irrational" practices of faith.

But Douglass cannot long entertain a coexistence of passion and reason other than as a contradiction. In Rome, struck by the aspect of the young seminarians from around the world, Douglass remarks that "On the surface these dear young people . . . are beautiful to look upon, but when you reflect that they are being trained to defend dogmas and superstitions contrary to the progress and enlightenment of the age, the spectacle becomes sad indeed" (575). The outward beauty of the young is belied by the superstitions that they are imbibing through their studies. The apparent harmony is spurious. And though Douglass is willing to admit that in his censures he "may be less wise than the Church" (575), the rest of his travels seem to support his criticism.

It is not that he does not give religion its due. In fact, as he tours the Holy Land, he indulges in lengthy meditations on the significance of these holy places. The settings of these meditations, however, make it clear that the religious spirit is alien to the world of progress. Douglass affirms that humanity is closer to the religious spirit in the lonely wilderness than "in the noise and bustle of the towns and men-crowded cities" (583). Then, while reflecting upon the divine revelations to the apostle Paul and the prophet Mohammed, he finds himself brought up short: "Such speculations were for me ended by the startling whistle of the locomotive and the sound of the rushing train – things which put an end to religious reveries and fix attention upon the things of this busy world" (583–4). The shrill whistle of a train, the note of progress, shakes Douglass from his reveries, reminding him that though the religious world may be beautiful and moving, it is not a world on the move. Even in Rome, "where the longer one stays the longer one wants to stay" and where one desires "to withdraw . . . from the noise and bustle of modern life and fill one's soul with solemn reflections and thrilling sensations" (588), Douglass finds the ruins of a great civilization a scene inimical to human progress, a scene that underscores "the vanity of all things" (588).

The failed reconciliation of reason and passion on Douglass's European tour can be seen as emblematic of the dilemma that American reformers, whether as novelists or as social activists, never resolved. The voice of reason that they adopted seemed necessarily to draw a circle around themselves, separating them from those whose interests they proposed to represent. The Howellsian realistic novelist had to acknowledge that "by far the greatest number of people in the world, even the civilized world, are people of weak and childish imagination, pleased with gross fables, fond of prodigies, heroes, heroines, portents and improbabilities, without self-knowledge, and without the wish for it."[25] And as Minister to Haiti, Douglass found that his unwillingness to represent what he believed were selfish and ignoble interests led to his being rhetorically divested of his American citizenship. Accused by a South Carolinian agent of a New York mercantile firm of being "more a Haitian than an American," Douglass "soon saw myself so characterized in American journals" (616). His critics charged that Douglass's sympathy for the Haitians rendered him unable to represent American interests, and though Douglass maintained otherwise, the voice in which he sought to speak was held to represent nothing in the country from which he derived his citizenship.

Ironically, Douglass saw his rhetorical exile made literal in an unexpected way. He was selected by Haiti to represent that country at the World Columbian Exposition of 1893. And in the final sentence of the *Life and Times*, he mentions that selection and his ministry to Haiti as the "crowning honors to my long career and a fitting and happy close to my whole public life" (620). Given Douglass's account of the difficulties that beset him at Haiti, along with the fact that the organizers of the World Columbian Exposition, which was held in Chicago, barred African-Americans from any substantive participation in the U.S. portion of the celebration, Douglass's crown seemed an uncomfortable one to wear.[26] In Haiti he was charged with representing a nation other than his own; in Chicago he had to represent a nation other than his own in order to walk "among all the civilized nations of the globe" (620). In both cases, although it may be clear to whom Douglass speaks, Douglass's dilemma leaves the reader wondering just whom the writer represents.

NOTES

1   Frederick Douglass, *The Life and Times of Frederick Douglass: Written by Himself* (1892; New York: Collier, 1962), p. 398. Subsequent references will appear parenthetically in the text.

2   John W. Blassingame, Introduction, *The Frederick Douglass Papers, Series One: Speeches, Debates, and Interviews*, ed. John W. Blassingame, vol. 1: 1841–6 (New Haven: Yale U. Press, 1979), p. xxxi.

3   *Hamlet*, act 3, sc. 2, lines 10–12.

4   Donald B. Gibson has argued that *Hamlet* plays a key role in Douglass's 1845 *Narrative*, providing Douglass with a means of objectifying and making public his private experience. Hamlet's inability to "reconcile thought and action" (563) reflects a similar dilemma within Douglass. Gibson's reading is helpful in revealing Douglass's strategies for reconciling "the tension between the social definition that he feels a white audience places on him and his own markedly different, private sense of who he is" (569). Douglass's use of Hamlet here, however, suggests that the tensions between Douglass and his audience did not correspond solely to racial divisions, and that the tensions

between his public and private selves might be more provocatively explored as an interplay between various public selves. See "Reconciling Public and Private in Frederick Douglass' *Narrative*," *American Literature*, 57, 4 (December 1985), pp. 549–69.

5   Amy Kaplan, *The Social Construction of American Realism* (Chicago: U. of Chicago Press, 1988), p. 13.

6   George Washington Cable, "The Silent South," *Century Magazine* (September 1885), rpt. George Washington Cable, *The Negro Question: A Selection of Writings on Civil Rights in the South*, ed. Arlin Turner (New York: Doubleday, 1958), p. 78.

7   William Dean Howells, "The Man of Letters as a Man of Business," in *Literature and Life* (New York: Harper and Brothers, 1902), p. 35.

8   June Howard, *Form and History in American Literary Naturalism* (Chapel Hill: U. of North Carolina Press, 1985), p. 131.

9   Waldo E. Martin, Jr., *The Mind of Frederick Douglass* (Chapel Hill: University of North Carolina Press, 1984), p. 200.

10   Ibid., pp. 136–93.

11   Peter F. Walker, *Moral Choices: Memory, Desire, and Imagination in Nineteenth-Century American Abolition* (Baton Rouge: Louisiana U. Press, 1978), p. 244.

12   Kaplan, *American Realism*, p. 55.

13   Cf. Martin, *Mind of Frederick Douglass*, p. 167.

14   W. E. B. Du Bois, "The Talented Tenth," in *Writings* (New York: Library of America, 1986), p. 852.

15   W. E. B. Du Bois, *The Souls of Black Folk*, in *Writings*, p. 522. Subsequent references will appear parenthetically in the text.

16   Henry James, "The Question of Our Speech," in *The Question of Our Speech/ The Lesson of Balzac: Two Lectures by Henry James* (New York: Houghton Mifflin, 1905), p. 11.

17   Ibid., p. 52.

18   Ibid., p. 41.

19   Ibid., p. 47.

20   Henry James, *The American Scene* (Bloomington: Indiana U. Press, 1968), p. 119.

21   James, "The Question of Our Speech," p. 12.

22   See, for example, Douglass's 1854 lecture, "The Claims of the Negro Ethnologically Considered," in *The Life and Writings of Frederick Douglass*, ed. Philip S. Foner, vol. 2 (New York: International Publishers, 1950–75), pp. 289–309.

23   Ibid., p. 301. See also Martin, *Mind of Frederick Douglass*, pp. 202–13.

24   Walker, *Moral Choices*, pp. 253–4.

25   William Dean Howells, "Novel-Writing and Novel-Reading: An Impersonal Explanation," ed. William M. Gibson, *Bulletin of the New York Public Library*, 62, no. 1 (1958), p. 28.

26   Significantly, Douglass's efforts to speak on behalf of American blacks during the exposition also encountered what I have termed the "problem of constituency." For example, the publication and distribution of *The Reason Why the Colored American Is Not in the World's Columbian Exposition*, a pamphlet

written and compiled by Douglass and Ida B. Wells, was "condemned sca-thingly by many Negro editors" [see Elliot Rudwick and August Meier, "Black Men in the White City: Negroes and the Columbian Exposition, 1893," *Phylon* 26, no. 4 (1965), 356]; similarly, Douglass's support of, and decision to speak at, the "Colored Jubilee Day" occasioned controversy as well [see again Rudwick and Meier, "Black Men in the White City," 357–61, and Robert Rydell, "The World's Columbian Exposition of 1893: Racist Underpinnings of a Utopian Artifact," *Journal of American Culture* 1, no. 2 (1978), 253–75].

Images of Frederick Douglass in the Afro-American Mind

The Recent Black Freedom Struggle

WALDO E. MARTIN, JR.

Frederick Douglass's place in Afro-American consciousness is secure and revealing. Whereas Nat Turner personifies violent insurrection, Harriet Tubman subversive rebelliousness, Booker T. Washington compromise, W. E. B. Du Bois radical intellectual activism, and Martin Luther King, Jr., nonviolent protest, Douglass personifies the imperative of struggle itself. Popular images of the heroic Douglass, like those of most complex historical heroes, tend to emphasize a simplistic treatment. Typically, there is little, if any, room within these images for contradiction or inconsistency. Thus Douglass's rough edges are either smoothed over or ignored. His complexity is often blunted. Even the Douglass of the scholarly realm has often been the victim of conscious and unconscious hero worship.[1]

More important for the present purpose, however, is the content and significance of these images rather than their historical accuracy. My focus is the varied and related images of Douglass among Afro-Americans during the black freedom struggle from the middle 1950s through the early 1970s and the insight these images offer into Afro-American consciousness during the period. A critical analysis of these images provides a window through which we can view not only his central importance as a black hero and symbol, but also the protean nature of complicated historical figures and their cultural significance. Roy P. Basler, who wrote perceptively on the legend of Abraham Lincoln, argued that "when a figure becomes symbolic, [he] . . . is no longer simply historical."[2] Such is truly the case with Douglass. He represents an important cultural as well as historical reference point for all Americans, but especially for black Americans, precisely because of the emblematic character of his life. During the civil rights and black power years, blacks endeavored to fashion an identity that spoke to their pressing political needs. This difficult process of racial discovery, revitalization, and construction is a central element of the Afro-American historical experience. Key figures like Douglass function as authoritative references who simultaneously articulate and legitimize the black quest for self-definition and autonomy.

Scholars have contributed much to our understanding of the recent black liberation insurgency, but essential questions remain. One concerns the meaning of the interpenetration of culture and politics within the movement. In other words, a vital albeit neglected aspect of the movement has been its cultural politics, perhaps most notably the development of an oppositional culture, or culture of resistance. The traditional analytic focus on the movement's political (and civil) thrusts has seriously understated not merely its cultural thrust but also the fundamental connections between them. This essay attempts to illustrate the centrality of black cultural politics generally and its significance specifically for the movement by looking at the role of a pivotal historical icon, Douglass. Such paradigmatic figures represent fascinating prisms through which we can begin to see the symbiotic ties between empowerment and blackness within the resistance culture.

Among twentieth-century Afro-Americans, Douglass's eminence has been widespread and virtually unquestioned. Innumerable black institutions invariably dedicated to racial advancement – businesses, church auxiliaries, schools, clubs, civic groups, and political organizations – have been named after him. For instance, the Frederick Douglass Film Company of Jersey City, New Jersey, founded during World War I, desired to bring "strong black success images" to motion pictures. Similarly, by the 1940s, Toledo, Ohio's, Frederick Douglass Community Association had established a community center for "uplifting, inspiring, training, and guiding Toledo's underprivileged black youth." In November 1939, black leaders in Harlem, New York, from widely disparate political backgrounds, in concert with radical white allies, united to sponsor a Frederick Douglass Historical and Cultural League whose aim was to disseminate Douglass's writings and the truth about the black role in world history. Almost concurrently in Harlem, activists Richard B. Moore and Cyril Y. Briggs, after their expulsion from the U.S. Communist Party, established the Frederick Douglass Bookstore.[3]

Even during Douglass's lifetime, notably the last thirty-five years (1860–95), his contemporaries acknowledged him as the chief black spokesman, the preeminent black of the day, the "Sage of Anacostia." Douglass's apotheosis among blacks was manifest upon his death in countless expressions of overwhelming loss in addition to innumerable tributes to his unparalleled greatness. This commemoration has continued into the present. Black History Month, originally Negro History Week, has traditionally included recognition of Douglass's birthday on February

14.[4] Prior to a heightened concern with black history in the civil rights years, Douglass was a hero with whom many blacks were familiar. This was especially true of those students who attended all-black schools that observed Negro History Week and taught black history. Consequently, even though mainstream American history textbooks as a rule have until recently ignored individual black leaders (with the possible exception of Washington), many blacks have know that Douglass was the most important black leader prior to Washington.[5]

Evidence that Douglass's legacy has persisted in Afro-American memory is overwhelming. In 1916 at its twentieth Annual Meeting, the American Negro Academy (1897–1928) honored the centenary of Douglass's birth with the presentation of five papers on aspects of his life and thought. In 1935, Charles Houston, pioneering black civil rights lawyer and National Association for the Advancement of Colored People (NAACP) special counsel, quoted Douglass on the dangers of a slave mentality as a way to urge greater support for the NAACP's legal fight against educational discrimination. Former Democratic representative and presidential candidate Shirley Chisholm recalled that at Brooklyn College in the early 1940s Douglass, Du Bois, Tubman, and George W. Carver (black botanist and chemist) were leaders she had read about and felt comfortable discussing in the Tubman Society, a black student group.[6] Over time on the black and white left, Douglass had come to assume an increasingly prominent role. After 1936 when the Communist Party in the United States began to emphasize its American roots, Douglass became its major black icon. Revered for his abolitionist commitment as well as his Americanism, he also signified for the party a commitment to working-class or labor unity and interracialism or black–white unity. For instance, these themes are central in the poem "The People to Lincoln, Douglass" by the black party member and leaders of the Southern Negro Youth Congress, Augusta Strong. She refers to Douglass and Abraham Lincoln as quintessential American heroes, "brothers, toilers together," whose memory and common struggle for freedom continued to inspire her generation of freedom fighters in the early 1940s.[7]

Harold Cruse, social critic and historian, has surmised that Douglass as well as Washington, Marcus Garvey, and Du Bois are "well-known to the average Negro as historical personalities." Du Bois and Douglass were the only unanimous choices in a 1972 Ebony poll of black historians – Vincent Harding, Sterling Stuckey, Lorraine Williams, and Benjamin Quarles – asked to name the ten most important black men in American history. Lerone Bennett, a popular black historian, has characterized Douglass as "the noblest of all American Negroes and one of the noblest of all Americans." Douglass has likewise been portrayed as "the most durable of the Negro heroes of American history" and the inevitable choice of "informed black folk" as their greatest leader. Quarles, arguably Douglass's best full-length biographer to date and a Douglass enthusiast, has aptly concluded that "there is about this Negro American the imperishable quality of the truly great."[8]

It is not surprising, therefore, that a handsome portrait of Douglass as a young man graced the November 22, 1968, cover of *Life* because his own life spoke so poignantly to the subject of the cover story: "The Search for a Black Past."[9] Douglass's portrait on the cover of America's major middle-class weekly magazine revealed, on the one hand, his viability as a representative of the growing and increasingly acknowledged quest for a more positive and meaningful black historical identity. On the other, it certified him within the American mainstream as a sterling black example of traditional bourgeois achievement and respectability.

An equally flattering portrait of the mature Douglass had previously appeared on the September 1963 cover of *Ebony*, black America's major middle-class monthly magazine. This cover indicated that he represented the interrelated racial and class struggles of blacks. Furthermore, it strongly suggested that he epitomized both the integrationist and the assimilationist strategies of racial uplift. The focus of that issue of *Ebony* was the centennial celebration of the Emancipation Proclamation. A similar portrait of Douglass also appeared as the frontispiece of the comparable issue of *Freedomways: A Quarterly Review of the Negro Freedom Movement*.[10] In light of his dedication to black freedom in general and to the abolition of slavery in particular, Douglass remains an appropriate symbol of the Emancipation Proclamation.

Douglass's continuing resonance for a people engaged in their liberation struggle became increasingly evident during the recent civil rights movement. Many "freedom schools" and study groups, for example, bore his name. Discussions of the contemporary relevance of his life and ideas grew. In Douglass, blacks possessed a vibrant and multifaceted personality whose lifelong struggle exemplified what Earl E. Thorpe, black intellectual historian, argued is "the central theme of black history": "the quest of Afro-Americans for freedom, equality, and manhood."[11] To the black civil rights movement, Douglass's life struggle came to symbolize "the central theme of black history." This can be seen in the concurrent black images of him as emblematic of the Afro-American search for race pride, full acceptance as American citizens, and manhood.

For many black civil rights partisans, Douglass represented a paragon of black manhood in the sense of a common humanity of blacks, men and women alike. Bennett has maintained that "Douglass was a man, in the deepest and truest sense of that much abused word." Douglass, he has written, exuded the essential qualities of black manhood: self-respect, strong moral character, aggressiveness, and a deep-seated sense of racial pride and responsibility. Most important, Bennett has suggested, was his unswerving commitment to his people's liberation. Another observer noted that as Abraham Lincoln was the Anglo-American idol, Douglass was the Afro-American idol: "the ideal of Negro manhood." In a related vein, those attending the fifth All-Southern Negro Youth Congress urged that "Negro youth of 1942 echo the call of Frederick Douglass in the Civil War, 'men of color to arms.' " Full and untrammeled black male participation in the war effort, they argued, "would immeasurably strengthen the morale and fighting fitness of our fighting men and would insure for them the respect and consideration which is the due of these champions of our nation's security." Echoing a faith championed by Douglass and found in previous and subsequent wars, contrary evidence notwithstanding, they contended that the triumph of black soldiers would earn them respect not simply as soldiers but as men.[12]

Closely aligned with the image of Douglass as the epitome of black manhood was that of him as an archetypal black self-made man. He was extremely and justly proud of his self-made success and saw himself as an example for his people to emulate. He was self-liberated and self-taught as well as an orator, newspaper editor, activist, reformer, politician, and race leader during his lifetime. His achievements were nothing short of astonishing. James McCune Smith, an eminent black contemporary of Douglass's, observed of his friend that

> when a man raises himself from the lowest condition in society to the highest, mankind pays him the tribute of their admiration; when he accomplishes this elevation by native energy, guided by prudence and wisdom, their admiration is increased; but when his course, onward and upward . . . furthermore proves a possible, what had hitherto been regarded as an impossible, reform, then he becomes a burning and a shining light, on which the aged may look with gladness, the young with hope, and the down-trodden, as a representative of what they may themselves become.[13]

Quarles has similarly noted that "Douglass' career is without parallel as a striking example of the American ideal of pulling oneself up by his bootstraps." He personified struggle and achievement.[14] Indeed, his slave origins made his ascent to greatness all the more spectacular. His epic life story of upward mobility – like that of Washington, his immediate successor – constituted a black version of the Horatio Alger vision of American success and respectability. His life validated cultural values central to the Protestant work ethic as well as the American success ethic: hard work, frugality, perseverance, and faith. For the black civil rights generation, the lesson of Douglass's life was clear. They, too, could liberate themselves and initiate a new order of achievement for themselves and their progeny with the proper level of dedication, hard work, and perseverance.

Douglass, as Stuckey characterizes him, undeniably contradicted the notion of white supremacy. For many blacks, as a result, he has functioned as an important symbol of race pride. One commentator observed that Douglass even wore his hair "au naturel." William Branch – black playwright and author of *In Splendid Error*, a play about Douglass's decision not to accompany John Brown on his fateful raid at Harper's Ferry – has stated that he wrote the play largely to promote black pride: "I wanted to write about a black hero. I felt the strong need for black people – and white people as well – to know of the wealth of great and positive images in our heritage, images which somehow rarely showed up in the works by white writers."[15]

Reflecting the growing black concern with race pride and Douglass as a symbol of it, the federal government in 1965 named after him a major bridge connecting the predominantly black Anacostia area in southeast Washington, D.C., with the rest of the city. Grappling with the symbolic significance suggested by the occasion, Quarles explored the simile of Douglass as a bridge builder in a speech delivered at the dedication of the Frederick Douglass Memorial bridge on October 18, 1965. Douglass, Quarles contended, "was a bridge-builder in human relations, a man who made it possible for others to make their way, to cross over. In a three-fold sense Douglass was a bridge-builder – a bridge between slavery and freedom, between Negroes and whites, between struggle and success." Quarles added that Douglass signified a bridge between "humble birth and high purpose."[16]

On the 150th anniversary of Douglass's birth, February 14, 1967, the federal government issued a twenty-five-cent commemorative stamp.[17] Similarly, the federal government's restoration of Douglass's last home, the eight-acre Anacostia estate of Cedar Hill, to its late-nineteenth-century splendor further affirmed and bolstered his significance as a national hero as well as a symbol of black pride. In 1962, the National Park Service had assumed ownership of Cedar Hill as a congressionally designated national monument. It was not until 1969, however, that Congress appropriated the needed money – $413,000 – to renovate the home. The project was completed in time to dedicate the home as a national shrine on February 14, 1972. Cedar Hill represents an inspiration to all Americans, but especially to black Americans.[18] What George Washington's Mount Vernon or Thomas Jefferson's Monticello signifies for white Americans, Cedar Hill signifies for black Americans: a monument to a racial as well as national hero.

The dominant image of Douglass in the black civil rights consciousness was that of patriarch of the movement itself. This particular image encompassed and reinforced those of Douglass as the prototypical black man, self-made man, and race leader. It likewise drew upon the perception of Douglass as a symbol of black pride. Above all else, however, he embodied both militant protest and integrationism. His famous pronouncement in 1857 on reform remains a classic statement of the logic and imperative of struggle, the essence of militant protest. This statement clearly reflected the tactical philosophy basic to the modern civil rights movement and informed its spirit. Douglass asserted:

> The whole history of the progress of human liberty shows that all concessions yet made to her august claims, have been born of earnest struggle. The conflict has been exciting, agitating, all-absorbing, and for the time being, putting all other tumults to silence. It must do this or it does nothing. If there is no struggle there is no progress. Those who profess to favor freedom and yet deprecate agitation, are men who want crops without plowing up the ground, they want rain without thunder and lightning. They want the ocean without the awful roar of its many waters.[19]

Struggle, Douglass argued, meant not only a contest between conflicting wills, but also a contest over the distribution and use of power:

> The struggle may be a moral one, or it may be a physical one, and it may be both moral and physical, but it must be a struggle. Power concedes nothing without a demand. It never did and it never will. Find out just what any people will quietly submit to and you have found out the exact measure of injustice and wrong which will be imposed upon them, and these will continue till they are resisted with either words or blows, or both. The limits of tyrants are prescribed by the endurance of those whom they oppress.[20]

Douglass then applied his analysis to the plight of his people:

> In light of these ideas, Negroes will be hunted at the North, and held and flogged at the South so long as they submit to those devilish outrages, and make no resistance, either moral or physical. Men may not get all they pay for in this world, but they must certainly pay for all they get. If we ever get free from the oppressions and wrongs heaped upon us, we must pay for their removal. We must do this by labor, by suffering, by sacrifice, and if needs be, by our lives and the lives of others.[21]

Although many before and after Douglass have stressed the necessity of resistance to oppression and of dedication to the black liberation struggle, no one has done so more insightfully.

The civil rights and black power generations rallied around the call of Douglass and others for militant protest. In particular, they found Douglass's analysis of the ongoing historical dilemma of black Americans cogent and his call for concerted action to alleviate it inspiring. Student Nonviolent Coordinating Committee (SNCC) activist James Forman argues in *The Making of Black Revolutionaries* that, according to Douglass, "no people deserved their rights if they weren't willing to agitate for them. So we got to make people see that they can fight for their rights." In *Black Power: The Politics of Liberation in America*, Stokely Carmichael and Charles V. Hamilton argue that the frank and passionate language of protest that Douglass espoused was indispensable to interracial understanding and black liberation. They reject the rhetorical masks of civility and moderation. Instead, they demand a truthful and aggressive rhetoric. Invoking Douglass's spirit, they maintain that "anything less than clarity, honesty and forcefulness perpetuates the centuries of sliding over, dressing up, and soothing down the true feelings, hopes and demands of an oppressed black people." Without such communication, they contend, whites are typically misled into believing that interracial relations are fine and improving. The black freedom struggle in the late 1960s, according to them, necessitated a candid and militant language in the rhetorical tradition that Douglass personified.[22]

Douglass thus emerged as the nineteenth-century father of the twentieth-century black liberation insurgency. His own aggressive spirit and fierce personal and political battles deeply influenced the ethos and tactics of the struggle he sired. Cruse has described Douglass as "the first historical prophet of the 'civil rights–radical protest tradition.'" Bennett has referred to him as "the first of the 'freedom riders' and 'sit-inners.'" Moreover, Bennett wrote in 1964 that the August 28, 1963, March on Washington – "the most gigantic civil rights protest rally staged in the history of the U.S. – had its roots in the forceful pronouncements and actions of Frederick Douglass." He pointed out that Douglass had "refused to accept segregation and discrimination; he assumed that every door open to a human being was open to him; and if turned away, he made an issue of it." He vigorously protested Jim Crow restrictions in public accommodations and conveyances. Consequently, Bennett noted, Douglass sometimes had to be removed forcibly from train cars designated for whites only by the conductor and assistants, but not without creating quite a stir.[23]

It is not surprising, therefore, that the image of Douglass as a proponent of nonviolent protest gained increasing currency. John Blassingame, black historian and editor of *The Frederick Douglass Papers*, observes that "Martin Luther King, Jr. could applaud Douglass's nonviolent resistance." In *King: A Biography*, David L. Lewis, another black historian, suggests that Douglass's emphasis on nonviolent militant protest and integration was a vital part of "the unique and creative syncretism achieved by Martin Luther King," unquestionably the foremost American proponent and symbol of nonviolent protest. In his play *In Splendid Error*, Branch uses

Douglass as a symbol of nonviolent protest in contradistinction to John Brown as a symbol of violent protest. Branch explains that "in Douglass' dilemma [whether or not to join Brown in his raid on Harper's Ferry] I saw uncanny parallels between the pre–Civil War racial–political struggles of the 1850s and the post–World War II racial political climate of the 1950s. Thus in subsequent drafts, the play became more and more of a personal statement as to the differing roles people could play in a revolutionary movement."[24]

Yet symbols are characteristically complex and malleable. Branch thus acknowledged in 1974 that in several more recent productions of his play, various directors and producers, "to stress today's relevance, have had Douglass stride off at the end of the play with the musket, rather than the flag." This particular image of Douglass jibed more closely with the growing emphasis on self-defense, violent if necessary, in the black power movement. In other words, self-defense in the cause of black liberation superseded patriotism to an increasingly suspect United States. It was along those lines in the fall of 1970 that activist and scholar Angela Davis – then assistant professor of Philosophy at the University of California at Los Angeles – gave her first lecture on Douglass, viewing him as supportive of violent resistance. His life and thought, she argued, affirmed that "the first condition of freedom is an open act of resistance – physical resistance, violent resistance."[25] Interestingly enough, the notion of violence as justifiable in the struggle for freedom represented a basic American belief, exemplified by the American Revolution, upon which the black liberation struggle plainly drew.

The image of Douglass as favoring violence in the cause of liberty was consistent with perhaps the most dramatic episode of his life recorded in his autobiographies, his battle royal against and the victory over Covey, "the Negro Breaker." Douglass's master had hired him out to the notorious Covey when the slave was only sixteen because of his rebellious spirit. Yet Douglass ultimately prevailed over Covey and was never whipped again. Douglass's victory over Covey, Bennett has argued, signified a "great Moment in Black History," in addition to a major formative experience in Douglass's life. Bennett concludes that Douglass often returned to the "lesson of the Covey fight: 'Men are whipped oftenest who are whipped easiest.' "[26]

Besides the image of Douglass as a militant protestor, both nonviolent and, to a lesser extent, violent, the image of him as an integrationist has also predominated in the Afro-American mind. Douglass, the integrationist, constantly insisted upon the complete assimilation of blacks into the mainstream of American political, economic, and cultural life. Cruse places strong emphasis on Douglass's intergrationism and its historic importance. He has spoken of the "Frederick Douglass integration trend" and of Douglass as the "chief hero of the NAACP integrationists." He has also argued that in terms of the ideology of integrationism "there is almost a direct line of development from him to the NAACP and the modern civil rights movement." Bennett likewise has portrayed Douglass as a "fervent integrationist." Another observer has maintained that Douglass "believed in integration if it did not infringe on [the] rights of blacks."[27] Otherwise stated, integration had to be just and fair.

Douglass's integrationism plainly reflected his deep-seated Americanism. He gloried in his national identity as an American and saw his national and racial identities as inextricably linked. As Quarles observes, "Douglass never thought of the Negro as apart from the mainstream of American life. As he put it, it was better to be a part of the whole than the whole of a part." For black Americans, Douglass personified an unflagging dedication to the best of America's ideals as well as the blacks' intrinsic and unalterable relationship to America. "American to the core," Quarles writes, "he was possessed with a dream of man's equality. The championing of the cause of the downtrodden – this was the task he set for himself. Truth and humanity were his twin goals as he worked zealously to make his America a better land to live in."[28] The integrationist and Americanist thrust of the civil rights struggle, most notably its early phase, found a true hero in Douglass.

In the middle 1960s to early 1970s, the black liberation movement expanded beyond its emphasis on statutory reforms to structural demands. It went beyond a call for civil rights to a demand for black power. With this often anti-integrationist, anti-American, and antiwhite shift in the movement, Douglass's stock as a heroic symbol declined among certain blacks. The issue was not usually the image of Douglass as a militant protestor because, by and large, he continued to be revered for that. Roy Innis of the Congress of Racial Equality (CORE), for example, favored lionizing militant race leaders like Douglass. Yet Malcolm X, the personification of black radicalism for many blacks then and since, suggested that perhaps Douglass had not been radical enough. Although admitting Douglass's greatness, Malcolm X maintained that he himself "would rather have been taught about Toussaint L'Ouverture," the leader of the successful late-eighteenth-century black Haitian Revolution. Afro-Americans, he explained, "need to be taught about people who fought, who bled for freedom and made others bleed." Julius Lester, black activist and polemicist, has complained that "Douglass never firmly resolved in his mind just what tactic should be used against slavery," violence or nonviolence. Such vacillation, Lester has suggested, compromised Douglass's effectiveness as an abolitionist and a race leader.[29]

In general, however, Douglass's critics chided him for his interracialism, integrationism, and Americanism instead of the authenticity of his radicalism, its limitations notwithstanding. Black revolutionaries of various stripes, including Malcolm X, criticized the bourgeois reformism that Douglass had championed. Similarly, for blacks opposed to interracialism, especially interracial marriage, those aware that Helen Pitts Douglass, Frederick's second wife, was white, often interpreted his marriage as a serious, if not unforgiveable, error.[30] In their minds, this fact violated the images of Douglass as an exemplar of race pride, race leadership, and black manhood.

For black power advocates, black nationalists (cultural and otherwise), black separatists, and pan-Africanists, Douglass's integrationism, Americanism, and opposition to African emigration have made him a target for criticism. It has been exceedingly difficult, if not impossible, to exploit him as an unambiguous heroic symbol for their various causes. Nevertheless, according to Cruse, the image of Douglass as an advocate of black power and black nationalism has persisted among many blacks who either ignored or were unaware of conflicting evidence. It is clear, nonetheless, that those past leaders who evinced a more pro-African, race-conscious, and black nationalist spirit than Douglass, such as Delany, Garvey, and Du Bois, have proven to be more viable heroes to the more revolutionary elements of the black liberation movement. Lester, for example, has argued that "Du Bois can be considered the father of radical protest in the twentieth century. His language was in the tradition of Frederick Douglass, but his philosophy went a step further into blackness."[31]

Something of the difficulty Douglass poses for black power advocates can be seen in the curious ambivalence Lester expresses toward him in Look Out, Whitey! Black Power's Gon' Get Your Mama! Although he clearly admires Douglass for his militancy and his independence of mind, he still portrays him essentially as a "good nigger." Blacks like Nat Turner, Garvey, and Malcolm X "resisted White America," whereas those like Douglass more or less accepted white America. Douglass thus represents the assimilationist tradition exemplified in recent decades by, among others, Jackie Robinson, Thurgood Marshall, and Ralph Bunch. According to Lester, whites view assimilationists as "a credit to the race" and resisters in opposite terms. He concludes, moreover, that resisters – not assimilationists – have paved the way for black power. Douglass, Lester suggests, is simply too committed to the individualistic, reformist, and assimilationist ethos of the American dream, "notwithstanding periods of profound doubt and disillusionment," to commit himself to a collectivist, revolutionary, and nationalist concept like black power.[32]

Between the middle 1960s and the early 1970s, black radicals increasingly found Douglass's ardent faith in America less palatable. Harding, for instance, suggests that Douglass embodied the ideology of "Negro History" rather than that of "Black History." The essence of Negro History, he

maintains, "was to stand pat with Frederick Douglass, to confess love
for a land that refused to love, and to believe that the Black Experience
would ultimately be recorded as . . . evidence in favor of America."
Harding and other radical blacks plainly view the "Black Experience" as
evidence critical of America. "Black History," Harding proposes, "is also
another look at Frederick Douglass and an attempt to understand his
deepest dilemmas, unavoidable struggles for all who would be at once
black and honest in America."[33]

The use of Douglass as a key heroic symbol in the recent black freedom
movement signified a search for a positive and meaningful past. It went
beyond mere propaganda or hero worship. In fact, it represented a quest
for historical truth, continuity, and relevance. It revealed the necessity
of a people's being cognizant of and interpreting their heroic antecedents
as a way of understanding and shaping their own history and culture.
Given the centrality of the protest tradition to the Afro-American experience, it stands to reason that the legacy of those like Douglass who
personify that tradition should be invoked during a period of particularly
intense struggle. Besides using Douglass to inspire pride and a positive
self-image, many – especially those who saw him in an analytical, even
critical, light – also used him to explore the complexity of the black
experience. Douglass's life and thought thus represent a reservoir from
which images and symbols reflecting something of the multifaceted reality
of the black liberation struggle can be drawn.

Douglass once remarked that "mine has been the experience of the
colored people, slave and free." He clearly saw himself and wanted to
be seen by others, especially his own people, as a heroic symbol of the
black American experience. To a remarkable degree, he has succeeded.
Nowhere is that success more evident than in the images of Douglass in
the resistance culture of the recent black liberation struggle. Of course,
Douglass's deep-seated Americanism renders him an authentic American
spokesman and hero as well. Playwright Lorraine Hansberry observed
that "vulgarity, blind conformity and mass lethargy need not triumph
in the land of Lincoln and Frederick Douglass and Walt Whitman and
Mark Twain." In this America, she concluded, "we can impose beauty
on our future." This kind of spirited optimism buttresses the most basic
and profound image of Douglass within this black resistance consciousness – Douglass as a humanist in a catholic sense, transcending race,
nationality, politics, and ideology. Indeed, he continues to signify a universal
vision of his people's freedom struggle. Quarles has noted that for Douglass
"the struggle of the Negro was more of a human struggle than one of
race. Paradoxically, it would seem, his belonging to a despised group
had given him a deeper, more inclusive sense of human brotherhood."[34]

To help realize this universal vision of human kinship that Douglass so vividly epitomized constitutes the enduring aim of the black liberation struggle.

NOTES

This essay is a revised version of a paper first delivered at the Ninety-Sixth Annual Meeting of the American Historical Association on December 29, 1981. I would like to acknowledge the following persons for their helpful comments: Catherine Macklin, Raymond Gavins, Robert Cross, Lawrence Levine, Michael Kammen, Audrey Lengel, David Blight, Ishmael Reed, and Robert Hill. Thanks must also go to Daniel Mandell and Nicholas Cullather, my research assistants.

1 Nathan I. Huggins, "Afro-American History: Myths, Heroes, Reality," in Huggins, Martin Kilson, and Daniel M. Fox, eds., *Key Issues in the Afro-American Experience*, Vol. I (2 vols., New York: Harcourt Brace Jovanovich, 1971), 9–16.

2 Roy P. Basler, *The Lincoln Legend: A Study in Changing Conceptions* (1935 rpt., New York: Octagon, 1969), 306. For similar studies of the intertwined cultural and historical importance of pivotal figures in American history, see Marcus Cunliffe, *George Washington: Man and Monument* (Boston: Little, Brown, 1958); Merrill Peterson, *The Jefferson Image in the American Mind* (New York: Oxford University Press, 1960); and Thomas L. Connelly, *The Marble Man: Robert E. Lee and His Image in American Society* (New York: Knopf, 1977).

3 Thomas Cripps, *Slow Fade to Black: The Negro in American Film, 1900–1942* (New York: Oxford University Press, 1977), 173; Program of the 1944 Silver Jubilee, Frederick Douglass Community Association, Toledo, in Frederick Douglass Papers, Box 2, Moorland–Spingarn Collection, Howard University; Mark Naison, *Communists in Harlem During the Depression* (New York: Grove Press, 1984), 299; Robert A. Hill, ed., *The Marcus Garvey and Universal Negro Improvement Association Papers*, Vol. I (1826–August 1919) (Berkeley: University of California Press, 1983), 526.

4 Helen Pitts Douglass, ed., *In Memoriam: Frederick Douglass* (1897 rpt., Freeport, N.Y.: Books for Libraries, 1971); Earl E. Thorpe, *The Central Theme of Black History* (1969 rpt., Westport, Conn.: Greenwood, 1979), 20, 57–8.

5 Frances FitzGerald, *American Revised: History Schoolbooks in the Twentieth Century* (Boston: Little, Brown, 1979), 83–5.

6 Alfred A. Moss, Jr., *The American Negro Academy: Voice of the Talented Tenth* (Baton Rouge: Louisiana State University Press, 1981), 135; Genna Rae McNeil, *Groundwork: Charles Hamilton Houston and the Struggle for Civil Rights* (Philadelphia: University of Pennsylvania Press, 1983), 133; Shirley Chisholm, *Unbought and Unbossed* (Boston: Houghton Mifflin, 1970), 24.

7 I am indebted to historian Robin D. G. Kelley for bringing this point and the following citations to my attention. Harvey Klehr, *The Heyday of American Communism: The Depression Decade* (New York: Basic Books, 1984), 191;

New Masses (July 7, 1936), 9; *Daily Worker* (June 29, 1936); Augusta Strong, "The People to Lincoln, Douglass," in *Cavalcade*, 1:2 (May 1941), 12.

8 Harold Cruse, *The Crisis of the Negro Intellectual* (New York: William Morrow, 1967), 5; "Ten Greats of Black History," *Ebony* XXVII:10 (August 1972), 35–42; Lerone Bennett, "Up-to-Date: Frederick Douglass in His Own Words," *Ebony*, XIX: 8 (June 1964), 70; "Remembering Frederick Douglass," *Crisis*, LXXXIX:5 (May 1972), 148; Benjamin Quarles, "Frederick Douglass, Bridge-Builder in Human Relations," *Negro History Bulletin*, 29:5 (February 1966), 112.

9 *Life*, 64:21 (November 22, 1968).

10 *Ebony*, XVIII:II (September 1963); *Freedomways*, 3:1 (Winter 1963).

11 Benjamin Quarles, ed., *Great Lives Observed: Frederick Douglass* (Englewood Cliffs, N.J.: Prentice-Hall, 1968), 177; Thorpe, *The Central Theme of Black History*, 5, 7.

12 Lerone Bennett, *Pioneers in Protest* (Chicago: Johnson, 1968), 203; Alice Dunbar-Nelson, "Lincoln and Douglass," *Negro History Bulletin*, XXIII:5 (February 1960), 98; Report on Southern Negro Youth Conference, August 13, 1947, FBI File 100-6548-291, p. 27.

13 James McCune Smith, Introduction to Frederick Douglass, *My Bondage and My Freedom* (1855 rpt., New York: Dover, 1969), xvii.

14 Quarles, "Frederick Douglass, Bridge-Builder in Human Relations," 100; Quarles, "Douglass for the Hall of Fame," *Negro History Bulletin*, XXIII:6 (March 1960), 122, 132.

15 Sterling Stuckey, cited in "Ten Greats of Black History," 36; "A Share in the Life of Frederick Douglass," *Ebony*, XXVII:8 (June 1972); 81; William Branch, cited in James Hatch and Ted Shine, eds., *Black Theater, U.S.A.: Forty-Five Plays by Black Americans, 1847–1974* (New York: Free Press, 1974), 587.

16 Quarles, ed., *Douglass*, 177; Quarles, "Frederick Douglass, Bridge-Builder in Human Relations," 99, 100.

17 Dickson J. Preston has shown that Douglass was most likely born in February 1818. See his *Young Frederick Douglass: The Maryland Years* (Baltimore: Johns Hopkins University Press, 1980), 31–40.

18 Quarles, ed., *Douglass*, 177; *Frederick Douglass: A Register and Index of His Papers in the Library of Congress* (Washington, D.C.: Library of Congress, 1976), 4; "A Share in the Life of Frederick Douglass," 77, 76–83; "Frederick Douglass Home Dedicated," *Crisis*, LXXXIX:5 (May 1972), 160–1; "Frederick Douglass' Home Dedicated National Shrine," *Jet*, LXI:25 (March 16, 1972), 72.

19 Frederick Douglass, "West India Emancipation," speech delivered at Canandaigua, New York, August 4, 1857, in Philip S. Foner, ed., *The Life and Writings of Frederick Douglass*, Vol. II (5 vols., New York: International, 1950), 437.

20 Ibid.

21 Ibid.

22 James Forman, *The Making of Black Revolutionaries* (1972 rpt., Washington, D.C.: Open Hand, 1985), 109; Stokely Carmichael and Charles V. Hamilton,

Black Power: The Politics of Liberation in America (New York: Vintage, 1967), ix, x.

23   Harold Cruse, *Rebellion or Revolution* (New York: William Morrow, 1968), 202; Lerone Bennett, "Frederick Douglass: Father of the Protest Movement," *Ebony*, XVIII:11 (September 1963), 5, 56.

24   John Blassingame, *The Clarion Voice: Frederick Douglass* (Washington, D.C.: Division of Publications, National Park Service, 1976), 46; David L. Lewis, *King: A Biography* (Urbana: University of Illinois Press, 1970), 97–8; Branch, cited in Hatch and Shine, eds., *Black Theater*, 587.

25   Branch, cited in Hatch and Shine, eds., *Black Theater*, 587; Howard Moore, Jr., "Angela – Symbol in Resistance," in Angela V. Davis et al., eds., *If They Come in the Morning: Voices of Resistance* (New York: Third Press, 1971), 191–2.

26   Lerone Bennett, "The Coming of Age of Frederick Douglass," *Ebony*, XXX:6 (April 1975), 42.

27   Cruse, *The Crisis of the Negro Intellectual*, 226, 563, 4–6; Bennett, "Frederick Douglass: Father of the Protest Movement," 5; "A Share in the Life of Frederick Douglass," 81.

28   Quarles, "Frederick Douglass, Bridge-Builder in Human Relations," 100; Quarles, "Douglass for the Hall of Fame," 122.

29   Cruse, *The Crisis of the Negro Intellectual*, 429; Betty Shabazz, ed., *Malcolm X on Afro-American History* (New York: Pathfinder, 1970), 68; Julius Lester, *Look Out, Whitey! Black Power's Gon' Get Your Mama!* (New York: Dial, 1968), 47.

30   "An Interview by A. B. Spellman" (New York: March 19, 1964) in George Breitman, ed., *By Any Means Necessary: Speeches, Interviews, and Letter by Malcolm X* (New York: Pathfinder, 1970), 3–14; Huggins, "Afro-American History: Myths, Heroes, Reality," 13.

31   Cruse, *The Crisis of the Negro Intellectual*, 558, 563; Cruse, *Rebellion or Revolution*, 216; Lester, *Look Out Whitey! Black Power's Gon' Get Your Mama*, 74.

32   Lester, *Look Out Whitey! Black Power's Gon' Get Your Mama*, xi, xii, 116–18, 40–8.

33   Vincent Harding, "Beyond Chaos: Black History and the Search for the New Land," in John A. Williams and Charles F. Harris, eds., *Amistad I; Writings on Black History and Culture* (New York: Random House, 1970), 287, 285.

34   Frederick Douglass, "The Present Condition and Future Prospects of the Negro People," speech delivered at the annual meeting of the American and Foreign Anti-Slavery Society, New York, May 1953, in Foner, ed., *The Life and Writings of Douglass*, Vol. II, 245; Waldo E. Martin, Jr., "Self-made Man: Self-Conscious Hero," Chapter Ten in *The Mind of Frederick Douglass* (Chapel Hill: University of North Carolina Press, 1984), 253–78; Lorraine Hansberry to Mr. Chuchvalec, April 4, 1960, cited in Robert Nemiroff, ed., *To Be Young, Gifted and Black: Lorraine Hansberry in Her Own Words* (Englewood Cliffs, N.J.: Prentice-Hall, 1969), 115; Quarles, "Frederick Douglass, Bridge-Builder in Human Relations," 100.

Selected Bibliography

Andrews, William L., ed. *Critical Essays on Frederick Douglass*. Boston: G. K. Hall, 1991.

———. *To Tell a Free Story: The First Century of Afro-American Autobiography, 1760–1865*. Urbana: University of Illinois Press, 1986.

Baker, Houston A., Jr. *Blues, Ideology, and Afro-American Literature: A Vernacular Theory*. Chicago: University of Chicago Press, 1984.

Blassingame, John, et al., eds. *The Frederick Douglass Papers*, 4 vols. to date. New Haven, Conn.: Yale University Press, 1979–.

———. *The Slave Community: Plantation Life in the Antebellum South*. Rev. ed. New York: Oxford University Press, 1979.

Blight, David W. *Frederick Douglass' Civil War*. Baton Rouge: Louisiana State University Press, 1989.

Bloom, Harold, ed. *Modern Critical Interpretations: Frederick Douglass's Narrative of the Life of Frederick Douglass*. New York: Chelsea House, 1988.

Bontemps, Arna. *Free at Last: The Life of Frederick Douglass*. New York: Dodd, Mead, 1971.

Butterfield, Stephen. *Black Autobiography in America*. Amherst: University of Massachusetts Press, 1974.

Cruse, Harold. *The Crisis of the Negro Intellectual*. New York: William Morrow, 1967.

Davis, Allison. *Leadership, Love, and Aggression*. New York: Harcourt Brace Jovanovich, 1983.

Davis, Charles T., and Henry Louis Gates, Jr., eds. *The Slave's Narrative*. New York: Oxford University Press, 1985.

Fisher, Dexter, and Robert B. Stepto, eds. *Afro-American Literature: The Reconstruction of Instruction*. New York: Modern Language Association, 1979.

Foner, Philip S. *Life and Writings of Frederick Douglass*, 5 vols. New York: International Publishers, 1950–75.

Foster, Frances Smith. *Witnessing Slavery: The Development of Antebellum Slave Narratives*. Westport, Conn.: Greenwood Press, 1979.

Fredrickson, George M. *The Black Image in the White Mind: The Debate on Afro-American Character and Destiny, 1817–1914*. New York: Harper and Row, 1971.

Friedman, Lawrence J. *Gregarious Saints: Self and Community in American Abolitionism, 1830–1870.* Cambridge: Cambridge University Press, 1982.

Gates, Henry Louis, Jr. *Figures in Black: Words, Signs, and the "Racial" Self.* New York: Oxford University Press, 1987.

Genovese, Eugene D. *Roll, Jordan, Roll: The World the Slaves Made.* New York: Random House, 1974.

Harding, Vincent. *There Is a River: The Black Struggle for Freedom in America.* New York: Harcourt Brace Jovanovich, 1981.

Huggins, Nathan Irvin. *Slave and Citizen: The Life of Frederick Douglass.* Boston: Little, Brown, 1980.

Kraditor, Aileen S. *Means and Ends in American Abolitionism: Garrison and His Critics on Strategy and Tactics, 1834–1850.* New York: Pantheon, 1969.

Leverenz, David. *Manhood and the American Renaissance.* Ithaca, N.Y.: Cornell University Press, 1989.

Levine, Lawrence W. *Black Culture and Black Consciousness: Afro-American Folk Thought from Slavery to Freedom.* New York: Oxford University Press, 1977.

Martin, Waldo E., Jr. *The Mind of Frederick Douglass.* Chapel Hill: University of North Carolina Press, 1984.

McDowell, Deborah, and Arnold Rampersad, eds. *Slavery and the Literary Imagination.* Baltimore: Johns Hopkins University Press, 1989.

McFeely, William F. *Frederick Douglass.* New York: W. W. Norton, 1990.

Meier, August. *Negro Thought in America, 1880–1915: Racial Ideologies in the Age of Booker T. Washington.* Ann Arbor: University of Michigan Press, 1963.

Moses, Wilson J. *The Golden Age of Black Nationalism, 1850–1925.* Camden, Conn.: Archon Press, 1978.

Nichols, Charles H. *Many Thousands Gone: The Ex-Slaves' Account of Their Bondage and Freedom.* Leiden: Brill, 1963.

Pease, Jane H., and William H. Pease. *They Who Would Be Free: Blacks' Search for Freedom.* New York: Atheneum, 1974.

Preston, Dickson J. *Young Frederick Douglass: The Maryland Years.* Baltimore: Johns Hopkins University Press, 1980.

Quarles, Benjamin. *Frederick Douglass.* Washington: Associated Publishers, 1968.

Raboteau, Albert J. *Slave Religion: The "Invisible Institution" in the Antebellum South.* New York: Oxford University Press, 1978.

Sekora, John, and Darwin T. Turner, eds. *The Art of the Slave Narrative: Original Essays in Criticism and Theory.* Macomb: Western Illinois University Press, 1982.

Smith, Valerie. *Self-Discovery and Authority in Afro-American Narrative.* Cambridge, Mass.: Harvard University Press, 1987.

Stepto, Robert B. *From Behind the Veil: A Study of Afro-American Narrative.* Urbana: University of Illinois Press, 1979.

Stuckey, Sterling. *Slave Culture: Nationalist Theory and the Foundations of Black America.* New York: Oxford University Press, 1987.

Walker, Peter F. *Moral Choices: Memory, Desire, and Imagination in Nineteenth-Century American Abolition.* Baton Rouge: Louisiana University Press, 1978.

Notes on Contributors

Shelley Fisher Fishkin is Associate Professor of American Studies at the University of Texas at Austin. The author of *From Fact to Fiction: Journalism and Imaginative Writing in America* (1988), she has also published on journalism history in *The New York Times Book Review*, *American Journalism*, and *The Columbia Journalism Review*. Her current projects include a book on "race and culture at the nadir" and, with Carla L. Peterson, an anthology of readings from the nineteenth-century Afro-American press.

Jenny Franchot received her Ph.D. from Stanford University and is now Assistant Professor of English at the University of California, Berkeley. She is currently working on a book entitled *Roads to Rome: Catholicism in Antebellum America*.

Henry Louis Gates, Jr., is Professor of English at Duke University. His recent books include *Figures in Black: Words, Signs, and the "Racial" Self* (1987) and *The Signifying Monkey: A Theory of Afro-American Literary Criticism* (1989), as well as several edited collections on Afro-American and African literature. He is the recipient of a MacArthur Foundation Grant, the general editor of the Norton Anthology of Afro-American Literature, and editor of the thirty-volume series *The Schomburg Library of Nineteenth-Century Black Women Writers* (1988).

Donald B. Gibson is Professor of American Literature at Rutgers University. He has published books and articles on Afro-American literature and American literature, among which are *The Politics of Literary Experience: Essays on Major Black Writers* (1981), "Reconciling Public and Private in Frederick Douglass' *Narrative*" (1985), and *The Red Badge of Courage: Redefining the Hero* (1988).

Waldo E. Martin, Jr., received his Ph.D. in United States History in 1980. He has taught Afro-American history at the University of Virginia and is now an Associate Professor at the University of California at Berkeley. The author of *The Mind of Frederick Douglass* (1984), as well as several articles on Douglass and Afro-American culture, he is presently working on a book entitled *"A Change is Gonna Come": Black Cultural Politics and the 1960s*.

John R. McKivigan is editor of the Published Essays and Editorials series of the Frederick Douglass Papers at Yale University and Assistant Professor of History at West Virginia University. He is the author of *The War Against Proslavery Religion: Abolition and the Northern Churches, 1830–1865* (1984) and of articles on nineteenth-century history that have appeared in numerous scholarly journals.

Wayne Mixon is Professor of History at Mercer University in Macon, Georgia. His publications include *Southern Writers and the New South Movement, 1865–1913* (1980), a new edition of *My Young Master*, an 1896 novel by Opie Read (1987), and a number of essays on the cultural and intellectual history of the South. He is currently engaged in a study of Erskine Caldwell.

Wilson J. Moses is Professor of History and English, and Director of Afro-American Studies, at Boston University. His books include *The Golden Age of Black Nationalism* (1978), *Black Messiahs and Uncle Toms* (1982), *Alexander Crummell: A Study in Civilization and Discontent* (1989), and *The Lost World of the New Negro: Essays in Black American History, Religion, and Literature* (1990).

Carla L. Peterson is Associate Professor of English and Comparative Literature at the University of Maryland, College Park. She is the author of *The Determined Reader: Gender and Culture in the Novel from Napoleon to Victoria* (1986). Currently she is at work on a book entitled *Doers of the Word: Afro-American Women Reformers in the Antebellum North*, which examines black women intellectuals from 1830 through the Civil War, and is collaborating with Shelley Fisher Fishkin on an anthology of readings from the nineteenth-century Afro-American press.

Sterling Stuckey is Professor of History at the University of California, Riverside. He has held fellowships from the Center for the Advanced Study in the Behavioral Sciences and the Smithsonian Institution, and is the editor of *The Ideological Origins of Black Nationalism* (1972) and the author of *Slave Culture: Nationalist Theory and the Foundations of Black America* (1987).

Eric J. Sundquist is Professor of English at the University of California, Los Angeles. His books include *Home as Found: Authority and Genealogy in Nineteenth-Century American Literature* (1979) and *Faulkner: The House Divided* (1983), as well as the collections *American Realism: New Essays* (1982) and *New Essays on Uncle Tom's Cabin* (1986). He is completing a study of race in American literature entitled *Alternating Sounds*.

David Van Leer is Associate Professor of English and American Literature at the University of California, Davis. The author of *Emerson's Epistemology: The Argument of the Essays* (1986), he is currently examining the issue of contextualism in a book to be called *The Queening of America*.

Kenneth W. Warren is Assistant Professor of English and African-American Studies at Northwestern University. His writings have appeared in *American Literary Realism*, *American Literary History*, and *Black American Literature Forum*. He is currently at work on a book examining the interrelations of race and literary realism in late-nineteenth-century America.

Richard Yarborough is Associate Professor of English at the University of California, Los Angeles. His essays have appeared in numerous collections and scholarly journals, including *Black American Literary Forum*, *College English*, *Georgia Review*, and *MELUS*. He is currently completing a book on the nineteenth-century Afro-American novel, as well as serving as an editor of the Heath Anthology of American Literature, the Norton Anthology of Afro-American Literature, and the Northeastern Library of Black Literature.

Rafia Zafar received her Ph.D. in the History of American Civilization from Harvard University in 1989 and is presently Assistant Professor of English at the University of Michigan, Ann Arbor. A longer version of her essay will appear in her forthcoming study of early Afro-American writers and mainstream genres, and she is currently coediting her great-great-grandfather's autobiography, *God Made Man, Made Made the Slave*.

Index

Alger, Horatio, 17, 69, 127, 170, 275
Allen, Richard, 32
Anderson, Benedict, 114
Andrews, William L., 48, 180
Anthony, Aaron, 5–7, 73, 107, 143, 146, 148, 150, 156–8
Anthony, Susan B., 152
Auld, Hugh, 6, 9, 13, 74, 104–5, 127, 147, 150, 155, 157–8
Auld, Lucretia, 6, 8, 102, 148, 152
Auld, Sophia, 6, 8, 74, 76–7, 127, 130, 147, 148, 152
Auld, Thomas, 6, 13, 14, 16, 74, 119, 127, 143, 150, 152–3, 156–7, 197, 234, 236, 245
Ayers, Edward, 238

Bailey, Betsey, 5, 7, 24–6, 39–40, 130, 141, 147, 148
Bailey, Esther (Hester), 5, 107, 130–3, 141–8, 156
Bailey, Frederick Augustus Washington (see Douglass, Frederick)
Bailey, Gamaliel, 210, 215
Bailey, Harriet, 5, 130, 148, 158–9
Bailey, Isaac, 5
Baker, Houston A., Jr., 48, 181
Bakhtin, M. M., 204
Baldwin, James, 32–3
Ball, Charles, 3
Ball, Thomas, 16
Bannecker, Benjamin, 113–14, 201
Barnum, P. T., 68
Bennett, Lerone, 273, 275, 279
Bibb, Henry, 84–6, 209
Bingham, Caleb, 190
Birney, James G., 210, 217

Blassingame, John, 3, 60–1
Bledsoe, Albert Taylor, 8
Branch, William, 276, 278–9
Briggs, Cyril Y., 272
Brown, Henry "Box," 67
Brown, John, 15, 149, 150, 194, 222, 236, 276
Brown, William Wells, 13, 50, 70, 72, 169–72, 174–9
Bunche, Ralph, 281

Cable, George Washington, 255
Campbell, John, 168–9
Carver, George W., 273
Chase, Salmon P., 210
Chesnutt, Charles, 241–4
Child, Lydia Maria, 49, 176–9
Chisholm, Shirley, 273
Cinque, Joseph, 172, 181
Clay, Henry, 197, 201
Cleveland, Grover, 255
Covey, Edward, 14, 75, 89–94, 110–11, 118–26, 154, 167, 174, 190, 279
Cox, James M., 100
Cox, Samuel H., 197
Cruse, Harold, 273, 278, 281
Cuagono, Ottobah, 54

Davis, Allison, 73
Davis, Angela, 279
Delany, Martin, 1, 29–31, 40, 50, 281
Dew, Thomas R., 14
Douglass, Anna Murray, 8, 77, 108–9, 216
Douglass, Frederick, principal mention of major writings: "The Heroic Slave" (short fiction), 12, 151, 166–88, 198–

Douglass, Frederick (*cont.*)
  200; *Life and Times of Frederick Douglass*
  (autobiography), 1–11 passim, 16–18,
  23–41 passim, 67–81 passim, 95, 111–
  12, 141–65 passim, 233–41, 253–70;
  My Bondage and My Freedom
  (autobiography), 1–17, 23–41 passim,
  67–81 passim, 141–65; *Narrative of the
  Life of Frederick Douglass, An American
  Slave* (autobiography), 1–11 passim, 23–
  41, 60–3, 67–81, 84–98, 99–117, 118–
  40, 141–65, 166–7, 174, 189–94; *The
  North Star* and *Frederick Douglass' Paper*
  (newspaper), 1, 10, 77, 151, 189–204,
  205–32 passim.
Douglass, H. Ford, 169–70
Douglass, Helen Pitts, 8, 77–8, 258, 281
Du Bois, W. E. B., 1–2, 18, 31–2, 69–
  70, 114, 259–62, 271, 273, 281
Dumas, Alexander, 62, 66

Emerson, Ralph Waldo, 68–9, 130
Equiano, Olaudah (Gustavas Vassa), 54,
  122–3
Everett, Alexander Hill, 53

Fisher, Dexter, 48
Fitzhugh, George, 48
Forman, James, 278
Foucault, Michel, 191
Franklin, Benjamin, 4, 17, 70, 99–117,
  127–8, 132–5
Frederickson, George, 53
Freeland, William, 110, 125
Frémont, John C., 221

Garfield, James, 16
Garnet, Henry Highland, 32, 167, 172,
  217
Garrison, William Lloyd, 4, 6, 9–10, 12,
  49, 50, 53, 62, 120, 132–3, 149, 150,
  176, 189, 197, 205–9, 220–4
Garvey, Marcus, 281
Gates, Henry Louis, Jr., 9, 176
Gibson, Donald, 181
Goodell, William, 217–21, 223
Gordon, Eugene, 17
Grandy, Moses, 3
Gray, Lewis C., 30
Griffiths, Julia, 8, 12, 76–7, 198, 215–16
Gurney, James, 179

Hamilton, Charles V., 278
Hammond, James Henry, 14
Hansberry, Lorraine, 282
Harding, Vincent, 273, 281–2
Harris, Joel Chandler, 248
Harrison, Benjamin, 16, 264
Hawthorne, Nathaniel, 3
Hayes, Rutherford B., 16
Hedin, Raymond, 182
Henson, Josiah, 70
Hernton, Calvin, 168
Hopkins, Pauline, 176–9
Horton, George Moses, 52–6
Houston, Charles, 273
Howard, June, 256
Howells, William Dean, 255, 267

Jacobs, Harriet, 3, 71, 89, 155–6
James, Henry, 262–4
James, William, 87
Jay, William, 217
Jefferson, Thomas, 53, 201, 276
Jenkins, Sandy, 110–11, 126–7

King, Martin Luther, Jr., 248, 271, 278

Lane, Lunsford, 3
Lester, Julius, 280–1
Leverenz, David, 176
Lewis, David L., 278
Lincoln, Abraham, 2, 3, 14, 15–18, 68–9,
  113, 149, 150, 153, 223, 271
Lloyd, Colonel Edward, V, 5, 13, 24, 26,
  28, 235–6
Locke, Alain, 99
Locke, John, 193
Logan, Celia, 144–5
Logan, Rayford, 2
L'Ouverture, Toussaint, 280

Malcolm X, 100, 280–1
Marshall, Thurgood, 281
Martin, Waldo, Jr., 78, 79, 173, 257
McDowell, Deborah, 47
McKim, J. Miller, 189
Melville, Herman, 3, 40
Miller, Kelly, 19
Moore, Richard B., 272
Murray, Anna (*see* Douglass, Anna
  Murray)
Musgrave, Marian, 171

Odell, Margaretta M., 49
Olney, James, 48
O'Meally, Robert, 48

Page, Thomas Nelson, 236
Park, Mungo, 23, 26
Patterson, Orlando, 101
Payne, Daniel Alexander, 91
Peirce, Charles Sanders, 94
Penn, Irvine Garland, 79–80
Phillips, Wendell, 61, 130, 132
Pipkin, J. J., 248
Pitts, Helen (see Douglass, Helen Pitts)
Poe, Edgar Allan, 3
Preston, Dickson, 147

Quarles, Benjamin, 16, 273, 276, 280, 282

Robinson, Jackie, 281
Rogers, J. A., 66
Roper, Moses, 3

Sancho, Ignatius, 54
Scott, Dred, 15
Seelye, John, 90
Shepard, Thomas, 121
Sledd, Andrew, 247–8
Smith, Gerrit, 205–32
Smith, James McCune, 1, 209, 217, 275
Smith, Valerie, 182
Sobel, Mechel, 88
Spooner, Lysander, 217
Stanton, Elizabeth Cady, 78
Stanton, Henry B., 210
Staples, Robert, 168
Stepto, Robert B., 12, 48, 179–80
Stone, Lucy, 152

Stowe, Harriet Beecher, 7, 14, 128, 148,
  170, 180
Stuckey, Sterling, 273, 276

Talbot, P. Amaury, 25
Thatcher, Benjamin B., 49
Thompson, A. C. C., 197
Thompson, Robert F., 30
Thorpe, Earl E., 274
Tubman, Harriet, 271, 273
Turner, Nat, 8, 171, 172, 271
Turner, Victor, 114

Van Buren, Martin, 210–11
Vesey, Denmark, 172

Walker, David, 13, 32, 55, 167
Walker, Peter, 48, 236–7, 257, 266
Walters, Ronald, 175
Ward, Samuel R., 209
Washington, Booker T., 2, 17, 18, 70, 77,
  244–7, 271
Washington, George, 12, 175, 181, 276
Washington, Madison, 12, 172–83, 198–9
Washington, Mary Helen, 71
Washington, Susan, 177–80
Webster, Daniel, 14, 76, 198
Weld, Theodore, 3
Wells-Barnett, Ida B., 18
Wheatley, Phillis, 47–63
Whitman, Albery A., 166
Whitman, Walt, 3
Whittier, John Greenleaf, 57–8
Williams, George Washington, 1
Williams, James, 57–60, 90
Williams, Lorraine, 273
Williamson, Joel, 239, 248
Wittgenstein, Ludwig, 130
Wunderman, Lester, 29

Cambridge Studies in American Literature and Culture

Editor

Albert Gelpi, Stanford University

Charles Altieri, *Painterly Abstraction in Modernist American Poetry: Infinite Incantations of Ourselves*

Douglas Anderson, *A House Undivided: Domesticity and Community in American Literature*

Steven Axelrod and Helen Deese (eds.), *Robert Lowell: Essays on the Poetry*★

Sacvan Bercovitch and Myra Jehlen (eds.), *Ideology and Classic American Literature*★

Mitchell Breitweiser, *Cotton Mather and Benjamin Franklin: The Price of Representative Personality*

Lawrence Buell, *New England Literary Culture: From the Revolution to the Renaissance*★

Ronald Bush (ed.), *T. S. Eliot: The Modernist in History*

Patricia Caldwell, *The Puritan Conversion Narrative: The Beginnings of American Expression*★

Peter Conn, *The Divided Mind: Ideology and Imagination in America, 1898–1917*★

Michael Davidson, *The San Francisco Renaissance: Poetics and Community at Mid-Century*

George Dekker, *The American Historical Romance*★

Stephen Fredman, *Poets' Prose: The Crisis in American Verse, 2nd Edition*

Susan Stanford Friedman, *Penelope's Web: Gender, Modernity, H. D.'s Fiction*

Albert Gelpi (ed.), *Wallace Stevens: The Poetics of Modernism*★

Paul Giles, *Hart Crane: The Contexts of* The Bridge

Richard Godden, *Fictions of Capital: Essays on the American Novel from James to Mailer*

Russell Goodman, *American Philosophy and The Romantic Tradition*

Richard Gray, *Writing the South: Ideas of an American Region*★

Ezra Greenspan, *Walt Whitman and the American Reader*

Alfred Hebegger, *Henry James and the "Woman Business"*

David Halliburton, *The Color of the Sky: A Study of Stephen Crane*

Susan K. Harris, *19th Century American Women's Novels: Interpretive Strategies*

Margaret Holley, *The Poetry of Marianne Moore: A Study in Voice and Value*

Lothar Honnighausen, *William Faulkner: The Art of Stylization*

Lynn Keller, *Re-Making It New: Contemporary American and the Modernist Tradition*

Anne Kibbey, *The Interpretation of Material Shapes in Puritanism: A Study of Rhetoric, Prejudice, and Violence*

Robert Lawson-Peebles, *Landscape and Written Expression in Revolutionary America: The World Turned Upside Down*

Robert S. Levine, *Conspiracy and Romance: Studies in Brockden Brown, Cooper, Hawthorne, and Melville*

John Limon, *The Place of Fiction in the Time of Science: A Disciplinary History of American Writing*

Jerome Loving, *Emily Dickinson: The Poet on the Second Story*

Susan Manning, *The Puritan-Provincial Vision: Scottish and American Literature in the Nineteenth Century*

Elizabeth McKinsey, *Niagara Falls: Icon of the American Sublime*

John McWilliams, *The American Epic: Transformation of a Genre, 1770–1860*

David Miller, *Dark Eden: The Swamp in Nineteenth-Century American Culture*

Warren Motley, *The American Abraham: James Fenimore Cooper and the Frontier Patriarch*

Brenda Murphy, *American Realism and American Drama, 1800–1940*

Michael Oriard, *Sporting with the Gods: The Rhetoric of Play and Game in American Literature*

Marjorie Perloff, *The Dance of the Intellect: Studies in Poetry in the Pound Tradition*★

Tim Redman, *Ezra Pound and Italian Fascism*

Karen Rowe, *Saint and Singer: Edward Taylor's Typology and the Poetics of Mediation*

Barton St. Armand, *Emily Dickinson and Her Culture: The Soul's Society*★

Eric Sigg, *The American T. S. Eliot: A Study of the Early Writings*

Tony Tanner, *Scenes of Nature, Signs of Man: Essays in 19th and 20th Century American Literature*★

Brook Thomas, *Cross Examinations of Law and Literature: Cooper, Hawthorne, Stowe, and Melville*★

Albert von Frank, *The Sacred Game: Provincialism and Frontier Consciousness in American Literature, 1630–1860*

David Wyatt, *The Fall into Eden: Landscape and Imagination in California*★

Lois Zamora, *Writing the Apocalypse: Ends and Endings in Contemporary U.S. and Latin American Fiction*

★ Now available in hardcover and paperback.